PAYING ATTENTION II

God's Extraordinary Movements
in Our Ordinary World

ROLLIE JOHNSON

WESTBOW
PRESS®
A DIVISION OF THOMAS NELSON
& ZONDERVAN

Copyright © 2019 Rollie Johnson.

Interior Image Credit: Tara Swanson (Author's Photo)

All rights reserved. No part of this book may be used or reproduced by any means, graphic, electronic, or mechanical, including photocopying, recording, taping or by any information storage retrieval system without the written permission of the author except in the case of brief quotations embodied in critical articles and reviews.

WestBow Press books may be ordered through booksellers or by contacting:

WestBow Press
A Division of Thomas Nelson & Zondervan
1663 Liberty Drive
Bloomington, IN 47403
www.westbowpress.com
1 (866) 928-1240

Because of the dynamic nature of the Internet, any web addresses or links contained in this book may have changed since publication and may no longer be valid. The views expressed in this work are solely those of the author and do not necessarily reflect the views of the publisher, and the publisher hereby disclaims any responsibility for them.

Any people depicted in stock imagery provided by Getty Images are models, and such images are being used for illustrative purposes only.
Certain stock imagery © Getty Images.

ISBN: 978-1-9736-6750-6 (sc)
ISBN: 978-1-9736-6752-0 (hc)
ISBN: 978-1-9736-6751-3 (e)

Library of Congress Control Number: 2019908749

Print information available on the last page.

WestBow Press rev. date: 7/30/2019

Scripture quotations marked (NIV) are taken from the Holy Bible, New International Version®, NIV®. Copyright © 1973, 1978, 1984, 2011 by Biblica, Inc.™ Used by permission of Zondervan. All rights reserved worldwide. www.zondervan.com The "NIV" and "New International Version" are trademarks registered in the United States Patent and Trademark Office by Biblica, Inc.™

Scripture quotations marked (TLB) are taken from The Living Bible copyright © 1971. Used by permission of Tyndale House Publishers, Inc., Carol Stream, Illinois 60188. All rights reserved.

Scripture quotations marked (GNT) are taken from the Good News Translation (GNT) in Today's English Version- Second Edition Copyright © 1992 by American Bible Society. Used by Permission.

Scripture quotations marked (NLT) are taken from the Holy Bible, New Living Translation, copyright ©1996, 2004, 2015 by Tyndale House Foundation. Used by permission of Tyndale House Publishers, Inc., Carol Stream, Illinois 60188. All rights reserved.

Scripture quotations marked (NRSV) are from New Revised Standard Version Bible, copyright © 1989 National Council of the Churches of Christ in the United States of America. Used by permission. All rights reserved worldwide.

Scripture quotations marked (ESV) taken from The Holy Bible, English Standard Version® (ESV®), Copyright © 2001 by Crossway, a publishing ministry of Good News Publishers. All rights reserved.

Scripture quotations marked (NLV) are taken from the New Life Version, copyright © 1969 and 2003. Used by permission of Barbour Publishing, Inc., Uhrichsville, Ohio 44683. All rights reserved.

Scripture quotations marked (CEV) are taken from the Contemporary English Version®, Copyright © 1995 American Bible Society. All rights reserved.

DEDICATION

To Ady

With deep gratitude and appreciation for your years of sacrifice, love and giving us a wonderful family. Thank you for doing life with me. Te amo.

To my Dad, Fred Johnson, for teaching and showing me faith, strong values, adventure, and the wonders of the outdoor world. I am forever grateful for you.

Introduction

Many people are waiting to find God in some ultimate, dramatic, colossal movement or event. That can be a long wait and you'll miss out on so much of the divine in waiting for something spectacular. I have found that when we can seek out and find God in the simple, everyday and ordinary circumstances, our lives will be so much richer and fuller. Let me help you explore ordinary happenings that reveal incredible movements and blessings of our extraordinary God.

Life is an adventure and meant to be lived to the fullest! Join me while rock climbing Devil's Tower, backpacking the mountains of Wyoming, chasing elk in the Colorado high country, winter camping in the frozen north of the Boundary Waters, or canoeing the rugged and remote upper Missouri River in Montana as I share metaphors of faith from my experiences as an adventurer and explorer. As someone who is in the woods or fields most every day, I am searching, observing and seeking God as He manifests himself in creation and nature. I want to share with you, insights and observations that will help you draw closer to God in your life's journey.

For the past several years, I have written an email devotion (devo) each Tuesday. This is a collection the most recent devos. This book is a sequel and continuation of my first book; Paying Attention: Finding God in the Ordinary.

Twelve Strong

White-wood shavings flew in all directions. Each draw knife coaxing out a thinly sliced curly cue of cream-colored ash or hackberry wood. Brilliant morning sunshine splayed through the young greenery of our yards oak trees adding a cheeriness to the day and warmth to our backsides. It was a good start to our day.

Assembled around a circle in my driveway were twelve men. The bulk of these men sported long beards making me feel as though I were at a ZZ Top convention or part of a *Duck Dynasty* show. The Classic oldies station blared from my ancient garage stereo adding to the relaxed and easy-going atmosphere. The men had come from all over. One had driven eight hours through the night from Iowa, another man awoke early to arrive from Bismarck, others from southern and western Minnesota and even a few local boys added to the mix.

They had all come for one purpose; to learn how to craft a wooden self-bow; a truly Native American Bow carved from one stave of ash or hackberry wood. My good friend and superb instructor, Paul Speral and I were hoping that in eight hours, each man could go home carrying their own hand-crafted and fully lethal bow. Each man sat atop a bow-horse, hand-crafted by four of our church's Helping Hands retired men's group, shaving and shaping sliver by sliver.

But these bow builders were no ordinary men. These men, twelve strong you might say, were Wounded Warriors. They had served our country faithfully in Iraq or Afghanistan and been wounded in combat. And now the Wounded Warrior Project was coordinating various outreach programs and activities for these veterans.

The local WWP coordinator, Dave Colmer, had come to me months before hearing that our church had done some unique and weird ministries that men might enjoy. We had lunch, and in my excitement, I rattled off a dozen ideas ranging from canoe building, to canoe trips, to retreats, to flintknapping, to pig roasts and then we settled on building bows. Within a day of advertising over 20 men had signed up. We chose 12 for our first experience.

So here we gathered in my driveway and yard on a beautiful spring day in May to fellowship via the art of crafting a bow. Each man seemed

Paying Attention II

genuinely delighted and grateful to be here as sweat beaded on foreheads and furrowed brows displayed complete focus of attention to their new task. Paul and I tag-teamed going from man to man, assisting, helping, commenting, cheering on, measuring, testing poundage on the scale and showing them how to properly tiller their bows, making each limb bend symmetrically and equally. A true sense of comradery and fellowship began to grow and flourish.

When guys grew weary of the hard work of carving, we provided our own bows so they could test out and get a sense of flinging arrows from other primitive bows. Noon found us all gathered for a rest and a hearty barbeque on the deck and conversations grew and deepened. One fellow was a tank commander, another rode below the surface of the ocean and piloted a submarine. Some shared of their home lives, some shared of their struggles with civilian life, others shared their hopes and dreams. Some gave details of the tough encounters they experienced at war. A couple of men nodded in agreement that they would go back in a heartbeat. One fellow shared that he struggles big time with anger. For some their physical wounds were obvious, others were hidden. I could only guess at each man's psychological wounds and haunting memories that may lurk beneath the surface.

Late in the afternoon, I shared that our next event would be a canoe ride down the Red that got enthusiastic nods and affirmations from all. The day ended as it began as each man or pair of men headed to their vehicles, most toting a brand-new, home-made bow or at least a partially built one. But before leaving, each man, came to Paul and me with a firm and hearty handshake and a heartfelt word of thanks. *"Thank you, sir. I appreciate you hosting this for us. Thoroughly enjoyed it."* My wimpy words of "Thank You" got stuck below the lump in my throat and barely eked out as I thought of the sacrifices these men have made for me and our country.

I've always loved this quote: *"Your Calling: is where your God-given passions, talents, and gifts intersect with the needs of a hurting world!"*

What are you passionate about? What do you love to do? What talents and abilities has God gifted you with? Have you found a way to use that passion in order to serve someone in need? Love to hunt… then take someone else out and minister to them via the hunt! Love to sew… then sew up a storm and give the garment as a gift! Love to bowl… then take a dad-less kid bowling and minister to them via the activity of bowling! Love to cook… then invite a single mom and her three kids over for one of your fabulous meals and minister to them via your love for cooking. Love to get your hands greasy and fix engines… then hook up with a high school kid who needs a mentor, and minister to them via your love of mechanics! Love to bike… then buy a bike from the fix-it shop for the girl down the street who can't afford it and take her biking with you! Love to go to the lake… then invite a young family who can't afford that option to join you and share your blessing with them!

And you don't have to do ministry in church! In fact, I believe the best ministry actually happens out in the world, on the street, in the real everyday places of life where people work and play. That's what Jesus did! Staves of wood, bow horses, and draw-knives are not exactly on the budget priority list of most ordinary churches! But I believe Jesus and His companion the Holy Spirit were 100% present in the time we spent bow building. You could feel it!

What are you waiting for? Go **now** and serve God by serving

Paying Attention II

someone else with the passions and talents that God first gave to you. Those gifts were not intended to be hoarded by you for your use only. You are blessed to be a blessing to others.

<u>Go Now With God</u> (A Byzantine Blessing)

Go now with God.
Be not tempted
to stay in the safety of known places.
Move from where you are
to where God points.
Go now with God;
be not tempted to go
only in your time,
when it suits when it is sure,
for now is God's time.
Go now with God;
choose not to go alone.
Go in the faith that there is not
wilderness so vast,
that God is not already there
to show you the way.

Our greatest fear as individuals and as a church should not be of failure, but of succeeding at things in life that don't really matter. Tim Kizziar

For we are God's handiwork, created in Christ Jesus to do good works, which God prepared in advance for us to do. Ephesians 2:10 NIV

A Bear in the Trash

To my shock and disbelief, there at the end of my driveway stood a large back bear rummaging through my garbage! I did a double take to confirm what I'd just seen!

Then I laughed as I remembered I'd put the bear out there for Moorhead's annual garbage week! In my early years of hunting, I had attempted all of my own taxidermy work. This was a record book sized bear I had proudly killed with my first homemade longbow many years ago and was my first attempt at a life-sized mount.

I had gotten in way over my head with this project; heavy on desire and enthusiasm, but light on experience and know how I dove in with everything I had. In the end, I could proudly say that it did indeed look more like a bear than a giraffe, and for that I was grateful. But it was not a job well done by anyone's standards and though I did show it off to a few close friends, it never made a public debut or even found a prominent place in our home. He remained hidden in my humble and jumbled man-cave.

For almost twenty years that beast has stood stacked in a corner, moved upstairs for 3 floods, and been shuffled around countless times only to return upside down, or vertically stood in an already crowded room. I was always too proud of it, even with its imperfections, and always in the back of my mind, I thought he'd get his proper due somewhere, somehow. Last week I realized the pointlessness of holding on, and with the streets filling with other people's trash I finally gave in and placed it curbside. It was time to let it go. (I was curious to see if any of the traveling trash scavengers would appreciate my offering to the Garbage Gods. Sure enough a few hours after setting Ol' Blackie on the street, I returned from a grocery store visit, to find Ol' Blackie had escaped! Only now I wish I had had a hidden camera to see *who* had grabbed him and could have watched that scene unfold! One man's trash is another man's treasure for sure!)

It was definitely time to let it go. And letting go had a subtle yet pleasing sense of rightness, relief, and goodness. I had freed up and created new space in my man cave. Throwing away and discarding old stuff was cathartic. I felt a release and liberation.

Throwing away old stuff is good and right. Discarding the jumble and rubbish of our physical lives is certainly necessary and wholesome to do now and again. I need to do it more often that is for sure! (Just ask my wife and kids!)

But I think also on occasion it is good to take inventory and assess the mental and spiritual scrap piles of our lives. To examine the cobwebbed corners of our habitual thought processes and clean out our darkened mental closets.

Have you held on to a negative perception or grudge towards a person for a lot of years? A coworker, a neighbor, a classmate, a friend or an ex? Maybe you can't even remember why you are so filled with hatred or negativity towards them. It's just become habit? Maybe it's time to let it go, forgive and move on. Hopefully, you have grown, the other person has grown and it's time to let it go. After all, the only one you are punishing is *yourself*. And do you know that when you set your issue/anger/hatred out by the curbside it is *you* who will feel lighter, freer and doing so will feel cathartic and liberating? You'll create more space in your mental closet for good and healthy thoughts.

Have you held onto an old negative perception or self-defeating belief about yourself? I'm too fat, I'm too lazy, I'm not very smart, I'm not pretty, I'm so clumsy, I'm a failure, I'm too old, I'm not good enough, I'm so slow, I can't do such and such, I'm too afraid to try such and such, I'm anxious, I'm depressed, I'm ugly, I'm inferior, I can't cook, I can't sing, I hate exercise, nobody likes me, I'll mess up, I'm too shy. Pick your poison. We've all got them and many of us have held on to these belief systems for twenty or more years. We may even shuffle them around mentally from room to room on occasion, but most of the time these negative beliefs have become part of our background, and we don't even see them most of the time.

So maybe it's time to step to the side, do a proper examination of our emotional selves, and prayerfully cast out to the curbside those self-defeating and self-deprecating habitual thoughts that clutter and contaminate our well-being and contentment.

Let us remember that for those of us who love and follow Jesus, healthy and positive self-esteem is a commandment. It's not optional We are far more useful and helpful to a hurting world when we have a positive and healthy positive identity that comes from God.

Hearing that Jesus had silenced the Sadducees, the Pharisees got together. One of them, an expert in the law, tested him with this question: "Teacher, which is the greatest commandment in the Law?"

Jesus replied: "'Love the Lord your God with all your heart and *with all your soul and with all your mind. This is the first and greatest commandment. And the second is like it: 'Love your neighbor **as** yourself.' All the Law and the Prophets hang on these two commandments." Matthew 22: 34-37* NIV That little word "as" carries big weight… tough to love on your neighbor when you think of yourself as scum!

So, what is it that you need to let go of? What emotional trash do you need to lay out curbside for God to take away? What is it that is cluttering up your mental closet that keeps you from acting free and liberated to love and minister to a hurting world?

God is the ultimate liberator and change agent. He takes our old, weary, worn out, and often negative patterns, behaviors, and thoughts and changes them for good. We simply (though not always easy) surrender (throw out) our old and He replaces with it His new. Sometimes we call this confession, sometimes it involves forgiveness, maybe even saying it out loud… to forgive someone else or even ourselves. In the new space freed up by throwing out our old, we replace it with scripture, the good stuff, to create new patterns of Godly thought and belief which lead then to right and good action.

May you have the courage to take an inventory… and discard and let go!

Do not conform to the pattern of this world but be transformed by the renewing of your mind. Then you will be able to test and approve what God's will is—his good, pleasing and perfect will. Romans 12:2 NIV

"A new command I give you: Love one another. As I have loved you, so you must love one another. By this everyone will know that you are my disciples if you love one another." Therefore, if anyone is in Christ, the new creation has come: The old has gone, the new is here! John 13:34-35 NIV

A Driveway Story

The crisp sting of cold winter air stung my nostrils as the garage door opened. The fine, extremely light dusting of overnight snow had left my driveway as a clean slate, as if someone had shaken an Etch A Sketch, and left a perfectly gray-white screen. My driveway had become a flawless canvas and perfect tracking medium. A cottontail rabbit had been the dominant artist and protagonist. His large, oblong hind feet were interspersed with his tiny staggered front feet, indicating a gallop-type, hopping gait. His tracks wove in and out and around and underneath my truck and he seemed particularly drawn to clinging near the tires. Was it that he sensed the safety and overhead protection of the truck from the silent deadly flight of a nocturnal owl? Or had he enjoyed licking the giant black lollipop of the tires most likely salty from winter's road crews? I knew not which.

Enter, our secondary foot artist, or antagonist. Intermingled amongst the plethora of rabbit tracks, were the distinct, careful, and meticulous tracks of a local predator; a house cat. The cat family has crisp, clean tracks as they delicately place each rear paw exactly into the track of the front paw. It appeared to me that the cat had been hunting, following the rabbit tracks, sniffing, searching, and following in search of his next meal; possibly a bit of rabbit jambalaya.

I carefully followed the maze of tracks, half expecting to find a bloodied murder scene in or around the truck or surrounding yard. Finding none, I continued following the cat that had apparently lost interest in the rabbit, as his tracks weaved off down my driveway and into parts unknown.

Ahh, the drama of a driveway still life! No one pays attention to, nor cares about a humble rabbit as it goes about its business of procuring nourishment by searching for seeds, roots, acorns, and legumes. Neither does anyone notice an ordinary house cat that is hunting by night. We may raise an eyebrow if we witnessed the cat in the act of killing a mouse or meadow vole, and we may even gasp in moderate horror if we were to see and hear a cat actually kill and consume a rabbit. After all, rabbits are cute, cuddly, and furry, right? Mean cat!

But truthfully, each creature is simply living out its God-given role or niche within creation. Each creature must intake nourishment and nutrition which gets converted to energy. We humans are no different. Interesting to me is that all of us are created as open systems. Food must come in, waste goes out. All in a never-ending cycle. We weren't created with an installed eternal energy system or everlasting battery.

We continually eat and drink throughout each day taking in energy in various forms. Often times too much!

How intriguing that God created us as this open system that must continually search for and take in nutrients and nourishment in order to survive and prosper in the physical realm. Rabbits, cats, humans are all the same. With one exception; we humans do not only exist in the physical world. We are actually at the heart, at the core, at the center of it all spiritual beings who have been assigned this temporary physical body.

Most of us do quite well at our hunting and gathering of taking in nourishment. The great bulk of us do this to great excess and our physical bodies pay the price. Yet on the flip side, most of us are starving spiritually. Many of us go days, weeks, months or even years without taking in spiritual nourishment. In our go-go world, we strive and strain, we race, and rush, we accumulate and collect, we conquer and achieve… and yet in the hidden spiritual dominion, we are frail, weak, emaciated, and depleted souls.

Just as God hard-wired into our being the need for food and nourishment, I believe he also hardwired into each of us a deep longing and hunger for Himself. It is a hole in our core that can only be filled and fed by Him, and Him alone. We can't fill it with food, or alcohol, or achievements, or trophies, or success, or finances or victories, or porn, or relationships, or children, or hobbies, or sex, or shopping, or fame, or popularity, or toys, or beauty or even creation itself. The hole in our core can only be filled by continually seeking and communing with He who made us.

How many times a day do you seek out and reach for food?
How many times a day do you hunger for and seek out spiritual sustenance? It is only a quiet prayer of conversation away!

But seek first his kingdom and his righteousness, and all these things will be given to you as well. Matthew 6:33 NIV

Do you not know that your bodies are temples of the Holy Spirit, who is in you, whom you have received from God? You are not your own;[20] you were bought at a price. Therefore, honor God with your bodies. 1 Corinthians 6:19-20 NIV

"Come to me, all you who are weary and burdened, and I will give you rest. [29] Take my yoke upon you and learn from me, for I am gentle and humble in heart, and you will find rest for your souls. [30] For my yoke is easy and my burden is light." Matthew 11:28-30 NIV

Jesus is not after your mind, He wants your heart!

All Men Die, Very Few Ever Really Live

The palm trees waved joyously in the early morning breeze, hovering over the park like happy guardians. They danced and waved back-lit by pure-blue Arizona skies. I was out for a morning run through my dad's retirement community in Mesa, and it was a good day to be alive.

I ran easily down clean streets that were packed wall to wall with trailers, some permanent and some of the RV variety. Amazed by how they had crammed so many trailers into tight quarters on such narrow streets, I pondered how you could ever back-in an RV to these narrow lots. Each trailer was neat and tidy, and many still had Christmas decorations up and lights swirling around the palm tree trunks. And although the development was well laid out, organized and spotless, I had the feeling of being cramped and contained. Not my cup of tea to be sure.

Three very long days of driving with dad had landed us here in the Seinfeld equivalent of Boca del Vista. Dad had given me a tour of the park, the pool, the mail room, the café, the party room, shuffleboard courts, tennis courts, horseshoe pits, dance hall, and craft center. He also pointed out who of his friends lived where, and who had quit coming due to poor health, death or dementia. Folks were all friendly and I even attended their worship service on Sunday.

My five days with dad were terrific. The good quality and quantity of time spent with him was priceless. But I was surprised to find that one of the more prevalent feelings that came to me throughout our days was one of sadness. Witnessing the aging process overtake him bit by bit, and viewing this lifestyle first hand caused me to step back and face some blunt realities. As I myself move ever closer to retirement age, which I've normally ignored and pushed to the back of my mind, I was forced to face the undeniable truth that most of us hide from, run from and fear; we **all** age. Then eventually we **all** die.

My time with dad has gotten me to do lots of thinking, reflecting and looking in the mirror. There are no promises, nor guarantees of tomorrow. We are only given today to live. So, **If** I have the privilege of arriving at his age what do I want my life to look like? And as I look back over my life, will I be able to say it was a life well-lived?

Two new men attended our Wednesday night book study last week. They both said basically the same thing. *"I have been saying for years that I'm going to change, going to get involved, do something meaningful in our church… but it never happened. Excuse after excuse. I realized I just need to pull the trigger, step out of the boat and go for it."*

Like so many men and women in the church, the soul-killing word "Someday" had shriveled their soul. Someday I'll sign up, someday I'll go on that mission trip, someday I'll get involved in a service project, someday I'll go on the prayer retreat, someday I'll reach out to my neighbor, someday I'll give financially sacrificially, someday I'll get in shape, someday I'll take that adventure. But someday ***never*** comes. Someday ends in "day" like all the other days of the week but it's not on any calendar.

Ironically, the first week of our study introduced the story of Peter feebly attempting to step out of the boat in faith by walking on the water during the storm to meet Jesus. (Matthew 14:22-33) Peter does the impossible at first and actually does walk on water! Incredible! Yet soon Peter takes his eyes off Jesus and then begins to notice and focus on the storm, the waves, the wind, the issues, the problems, the difficulties and he sinks.

Sadly, Peter usually gets a bum rap. He didn't have enough faith to keep doing the impossible! We criticize him: "Looser! Failure!" Yet, let's look with a new eye or a different perspective.

Who was the **_only one_** to actually believe in what Jesus said? Who was the **only one** to **act** on that belief? Who was the **only one** to trust Jesus and step over the edge and leave the safety and comfort of the boat? Peter of course. He acted with tremendous courage and faith and trust. Not in himself but in Jesus.

The armchair quarterbacks stayed in the boat. The other eleven played it safe. They clung to the comfort of the known. They acted not with courage but with cowardice. They would not move from the comfort and safety of the boat, to where Jesus was calling. The eleven stayed in their church pew. The eleven stayed in their recliners clinging to the remote-control watching TV night after night after night. The eleven chose comfort, safety, and security over following Jesus. They chose routine, boredom, sameness, and apathy over growth, renewal, change, and faith. Jesus was not in the boat. He was on the water and in the storm.

The Tragedy of the Unopened Gift
Author Unknown

To sinful patterns of behavior that never get confronted and changed,
Abilities and gifts that never get cultivated and deployed,
Until weeks become months, And months turn into years
And one day you're looking back to a life of
Deep, intimate, gut-wrenchingly honest conversations you never had;
Great bold prayers you never prayed,
Exhilarating risks you never took,
Sacrificial gifts you never offered,
Lives you never touched,
And you're sitting in a recliner with a shriveled soul,
And forgotten dreams, and you realize there
was a world of desperate need,
And a great God calling you to be part of something bigger than yourself-
You see the person you could have become but did not;
You never followed your calling.
You never got out of the boat.

My time with dad has had me doing lots of thinking. When my final hour has arrived will I look back on a life well-lived? Or will I be filled with remorse or regret? Will my thoughts be full of *"would-haves," "could- haves," "should-haves?"* Will I have lived a life of serving God which is lived out by serving others? Or will it have been just a life lived for self, consuming time, food, experiences and resources? Will I be grateful for all the time I've spent in front of a TV sitting in a recliner? Will I be able to say that I moved in faith past and out of my normal seat on the pew?

Take a moment to reflect on your life. Is it moving in a Godly direction? Are you living life to its fullest?

Are you ready to step out of the boat/pew/recliner when Jesus calls?

"I guess it comes down to a simple choice, really. Get busy living or get busy dying." Andy Dufresne Shawshank Redemption.

"Every man dies. Not every man really lives." – William Wallace, Braveheart

I have come that they may have life, and have it to the full. John 10:10 (NIV)

"It is not the critic who counts; not the man who points out how the strong man stumbles, or where the doer of deeds could have done them better. The credit belongs to the man who is actually in the arena, whose face is marred by dust and sweat and blood; who strives valiantly; who errs, who comes short again and again, because there is no effort without error and shortcoming; but who does actually strive to do the deeds; who knows great enthusiasms, the great devotions; who spends himself in a worthy cause; who at the best knows in the end the triumph of high achievement, and who at the worst, if he fails, at least fails while daring greatly, so that his place shall never be with those cold and timid souls who neither know victory nor defeat."
— *Theodore Roosevelt*

Alone Together

How is your solitude? How is your community?

Arriving early Wednesday morning, I pull into the South Hegman entry point off the Echo Trail. As expected, it is empty, I am the lone visitor. A fitting beginning to a planned five-day solo as my sense of isolation begins immediately. Brilliant sunshine pours through the pines adding a brightness to the day and giving me a buoyed sense of positive expectation.

Temps are moderate for what I'm accustomed to, and I'm grateful for the single digits as I unload my sled, duffle-bag, skis, poles, and snowshoes in the normal pre-trail hyper-active shuffling and organizing of gear, signing permits and shutting down the truck. One last look over everything and I'm off skiing down the 80-rod portage down to the lake.

Trailing behind me like an ever-faithful dog is my sled filled with all the right clothing, gear, equipment and food to provide a safe and comfortable adventure. With the *"Right Stuff,"* the cold becomes a moot point and will not rob me of the serenity, joy and positive sense of expectation.

My intended route is a 20+ mile loop that at this time is still theoretical and hypothetical in nature. The big unknown of my route lies just ahead of me at the end of Holy Lake. I intend to follow a small stream system, and possibly intense 2-3mile bushwhack to get to Boot Lake. The rest of the route should be fairly standard fare of winter route finding connecting Boot, Fairy, Gun, Gull, Home, Angleworm, North Hegman Lakes and the connective tissues of their respective portages.

The crisp, clean, frigid air seems to have an amplifying effect on color and sharpness. The blue sky is deep and rich and intense. The dark spruce-green of pines appears thick and accentuated. The exact border where sky meets jagged saw-toothed tree line is sharp and precise. The cold brings precision and clarity. There is no vagueness or ambiguity, only crystal-clear reality. The cold seems to be bringing this same purification of thought and clarity to my mind and soul. I breathe deeply of the pure, pine-scented air and give thanks for being alive, for fitness enough to be out here, and the solitude of being alone.

I am heeding the call and nudging of the Spirit to come and be alone with my Creator; to listen and learn in the bosom of creation. I know not, the agenda nor the issues, but simply say "yes" to the invitation.

This winter camping solo brings a deep and profound silence. Only the steady whispering and gentle swishing of the wind can be heard through the lofty pines. The only man-made sounds are that of my snow-shoes crunching fresh snow and that of my own heavy breathing from invigorating, life-giving exercise. This silence of the north is essential for the restoration of a soul.

Quiet, solitude, and silence are concepts that are quickly disappearing from our planet as we become more and more entangled in our electronics, technology, computers, and cell phones. We need wilderness and wild spaces and places where we can be still and listen to our own thoughts, feelings, and issues that often get repressed, drowned out, and pushed into the recesses of our consciousness from all the noise, commotion, and hyperactive movement and busyness of our modern citified lives.

Mother Theresa hits it out of the park with this wise and insightful quote: *"We need to find God, and he cannot be found in noise and restlessness. God is the friend of silence. See how nature - trees, flowers, grass- grows in silence; see the stars, the moon, and the sun, how they move in silence... We need silence to be able to touch souls."* Thank you, sister!

All around me, especially on my chosen pathway of lakes, the endless sparkle of shimmering snow crystals glimmers across the landscape. Each lake has been recently dusted with soft powdered snow and it appears as if each has prepared for my arrival by showing off her beauty in the Queen of the Lakes Pageant, and I am the lone judge. Spectacular natural beauty fills my senses at each bend in the trail or slow curve into a new bay. The silence of the North seeps into my being and the discarded waste of stress, anxiety, and busyness lay behind me like an invisible trail of trash. The stressors of talk radio, TV news, immigration, Trump, church life drama and Superbowl hype seem a million miles away. Creation and Creator are having their way with me... by re-creating deep within.

After three nights of solitude and silence, Saturday morning arrives with great anticipation as I tidy up my cozy little campsite, and enlarge the seating ring to allow for my guests. I am giddy with expectation and more than ready for human contact. With no watch to gauge the time and a beautiful gentle snow falling that blocks any sunshine, I can only guess as to their arrival. Having finished my camp chores, I don my skis and head in the direction of the pictographs hoping I will see dogs and humans coming my way.

Sure enough, as I round the bend in the river, through the gray and hazy snowfall I see a group assembled near the cliff of pictographs. I hurry my pace and shout as I approach. My eldest daughter Karina comes running towards me and embraces me with a gripping bear hug followed by her awesome husband Taylor. Their beast of a St. Bernard, Yukon, soon slobbers me with kisses and licks and I am welcomed back into the fold of human and canine companionship.

The rest of the weekend we spend hiking, exploring, swapping stories, feasting on calorie-rich food, and most importantly great conversation, laughter, and real human connection. Being with Karina and Taylor make me so proud, I am thrilled by the gift of my new friends Kate and Max, both superb outdoors people who know their stuff and are equally prepared and at ease in the wilderness. This last day spent in the company of others is rich and thick with community, companionship, friendship, conversation, and fellowship.

As we slowly snowshoed and skied our way out on Sunday morning in the brilliant sunshine, making our way back to the trailhead, I couldn't help but think what a strange and wonderful five days this had been. I had been blessed with abundant solitude and silence; the kind that only nature can provide that cleanses, renews and refreshes. Solitude; where God can wiggle into the cracks of my racing thoughts and hyperactive life movements and actually find space and room to speak. And, I had been so richly blessed by real community and friendship and of a kind so rarely experienced in the everyday rat-race of life.

*Dietrich Bonhoeffer in <u>Life Together</u> titled one of his chapters; **"The Day Together,"** and the following chapter; **"The Day Alone."** Both are essential for spiritual success. He writes; "Let him who cannot be alone beware of community... Let him who is not in community beware of being alone... Each by itself has profound pitfalls and perils. One who wants fellowship without solitude plunges into the void of words and feelings, and one who seeks solitude without fellowship perishes in the abyss of vanity, self-infatuation, and despair."*

<u>The Lonely Place</u>
by Henri Nouwen

Without Silence... Words lose their meaning.
Without Listening...speaking makes no sense.
Without Distance...Closeness cannot be.
Without Separation...There can be no reunion.
Without Aloneness...There can be no togetherness.
Without Disconnecting...There can be no community.
Without Withdrawal...There can be no involvement.

God designed us to specifically be in communion with Him. This is at the heart of being in relationship with Jesus. The great bulk of our faith life is a one-on-one relationship with Him. We must foster this relationship by spending time alone with Him throughout our days and at times we are called to withdrawal or retreat away from the crowd to be with Him for extended periods of time. We cannot stay in solitude, for then we would be of no earthly good in carrying out our main task of serving others and doing good in this world. God also designed us to live in community with others; family, marriage, friendships and a faith community. We are made to be in relationship with others.

May you continue to develop the Godly balance of being alone - together. May you live freely and joyously out of solitude and community!

Very early in the morning, while it was still dark, Jesus got up, left the house and went off to a solitary place, where he prayed. Mark 1:35 NIV

Immediately Jesus made his disciples get into the boat and go on ahead of him to Bethsaida, while he dismissed the crowd. ⁴⁶ After leaving them, he went up on a mountainside to pray. Mark 6:45-46 NIV

Jesus replied: "'Love the Lord your God with all your heart and with all your soul and with all your mind.'[a] ³⁸ This is the first and greatest commandment. ³⁹ And the second is like it: 'Love your neighbor as yourself.'[b] ⁴⁰ All the Law and the Prophets hang on these two commandments." Matthew 22:37-40 NIV

"Be still, and know that I am God..." Psalm 46:10

An Angel, in the Shape of My Mom

World famous Ed Sheeran takes time out to pray at First Lutheran Church Fargo, ND. Yes, you heard that right! Wednesday evening on Oct. 17th, Ed Sheeran performed before a packed house of 20,000 + screaming fans at the Fargodome. I hear it was a fabulous concert from those who were lucky enough to attend.

At some time that afternoon, Ed asked his Fargo Dome hostess if she could take him to a church as he wanted to pray. The hostess happened to be a woman from our church who sings in our choir and so she suggested nearby First Lutheran Church. He agreed. One of the most famous pop stars in the world came and prayed somewhere in FLC. Possibly he prayed in our spacious and quiet sanctuary, or maybe our new gorgeous and cozy chapel.

I can only imagine the potential sense of loneliness he may feel, even though surrounded by thousands of adoring fans, and an entourage of "yes" men and women who want to suckle at the teat of fame and fortune. It must be exceeding difficult to find and maintain normal friendships. Maybe that was part of his reasoning for seeking some quiet prayer in a house of worship.

I myself must have missed this intersection of time and space by just minutes. Having left the church parking lot at 4 pm, with eleven other adventures, we were traveling westward down I 94 headed for our Maah Daah Hey hiking trip. Never ever would I have imagined that the crazy world of fame and stardom would have intersected with FLC.

I entered the kitchen that was bathed in warm afternoon sun shining through our south-facing windows. Flushed with warmth and gratitude for having had a vigorous game of football catch with Shane in the leaf covered back yard, I was in high spirits. As I entered the kitchen, Ady, my wife, was scurrying about pulling drawers and cupboards in what I sensed was an agitated spirit. When I cautiously inquired about what was going on, she half shouted back to me; *"I can't find my mom's recipes… and they are probably the only remaining hand-writing of my mom!"*

As she turned towards me, the true nature of the situation revealed itself. Tears were streaming down her face as she slumped into my arms in a full-blown weeping of deep-felt grief. Her mother Yolanda Margarita Pinto Rodriguez had recently succumbed to the ravages of dementia just a few short months ago. Ady's love and affection for her mother run deep, and her mother's death has left a huge, empty hole that now filled with loss, pain, and loneliness. And as usual, grief had shown up in the most unexpected time and place.

We don't get to choose the when and where of our grieving. A scent in the kitchen, a whisper on a breeze, a song on the radio, a location in our lives, a certain activity, a dream, a song at church, the sound of rain on a window, a movie scene, a perfume, a sunset or ticking of a clock can all trigger memories that bring on the flood of emotions and tears.

Grief demands its day in court. It will be heard and felt whether we like it or not. Many of us for fear of showing weakness or experiencing true intimacy tend to keep grief at arm's length. Most of us do this by immersing ourselves in frantic activity or work. We over schedule ourselves and run from one distraction to the other in a frenzy of activity. We subconsciously rationalize; "If I can just stay busy enough all the time… I won't have to face my sorrow and loss." But like it or not… we can't outrun grief. And if you keep on running fast enough and long enough it will most definitely appear. But when it manifests, it will most likely masquerade itself as depression, or maybe anxiety, or possibly anger, or an ulcer, or sleepless nights, or maybe excessive weight gain.

Grief really just wants to meet face to face, head-on and be recognized. It simply craves acknowledgment. Often when we courage-up and face it in the mirror, its power diminishes and over time after many encounters it no longer has dominion over us.

In recent weeks I have been listening to lots of Ed Sheeran. I have wanted to understand what would cause a most famous pop star to pause and pray in a church prior to his concert. In his songs, I have found a young man of honesty and depth, who writes of life, and love, and heartbreak, and sin, and brokenness and a sense of home. God frequently shows up in his songs.

Listening to him on a recent long drive I happened upon his song; **Supermarket Flowers**, that tugged at my heart at first listen and had me hit the repeat button a dozen times. Tears came each time as I thought of my wife's grieving process and many thoughts of my own mother Beverly who left this world so prematurely almost 16 years ago. Moms are so important in our lives and their departure from this world always invites the unwanted guest of grief.

Take a listen. Maybe Ed's music and words will help you to face your grief head-on and thereby help you to move through grief into its twin sister healing.

Supermarket Flowers: https://www.youtube.com/watch?v=bIB8EWqCPrQ

Jesus Promises: *Blessed are those who mourn, for they will be comforted Matthew 5:4 NIV* He also gives us the strength to face our grief head-on. May you surrender to God's healing power of tears and grieving.

The LORD is close to the brokenhearted and saves those who are crushed in spirit. Psalm 34:18 NIV

He will wipe every tear from their eyes. There will be no more death' or mourning or crying or pain, for the old order of things has passed away." Revelation 21:4 NIV

Resistance solidifies grief. We can allow our grief to dissolve through releasing them to the healing rain of tears. All change carries gain as well as loss. As I release situations which have troubled me, I release, too, my identity as troubled. Embraced and surrendered to, grief creates transformation. Today

I do not deny my feelings of loss. I allow myself to move through them to new growth. Julia Cameron

"I am the bread of life. Whoever comes to me will never be hungry, and whoever believes in me will never be thirsty. But I said to you that you have seen me and yet do not believe." John 6: 35-36 NIV

Jesus said to her, "I am the resurrection and the life. The one who believes in me will live, even though they die; and whoever lives by believing in me will never die. Do you believe this?" John 11: 25-26 NIV

"I am the way, and the truth, and the life. No one comes to the Father except through me." John 14:6 NIV

Arrowhead

The strong, warm, summer's breeze felt good on my skin. The sun beat down and coated the landscape with its life-giving warmth and energy. I breathed deeply of the sweet-smelling aroma of nearby mown hay fields and took a few extra deep breaths to savor its hidden fragrant gift.

High above a lofty bald eagle silently rode the thermals hovering over the rust-colored Red River that lazily meandered northward to Canada. He barely flapped a wing beat as he subtly moved and swung to take advantage of every invisible updraft. I don't think that he was on the clock, he wasn't working for food or sustenance. He like me I believe, was simply enjoying the free grace of one more day, and celebrating his gift for flight. I rose my right hand and sent off a salute, out of both respect and envy.

My agenda was open, light, and loose. My hope was to comb this newly planted field in hopes of finding some interesting Indian artifacts. This tight bend in the Red had proven to be a gold mine of treasures over recent years and on this my first foray into this field, my hopes were high. This location must have been a long-term campsite used over and over for many centuries as evidenced by the many unique items I've found here.

Frequently I let my mind wander and try to imagine what it might have looked like so very long ago. Painted buffalo skin tepees decorated in earth-tone colors of ochre and crimson scattered about with smoke gently spiraling upward from a blackened opening. Children at play scurrying about, dogs barking searching for scraps. And horses picketed

Paying Attention II

about the encampment, resting and readying for the joy of the hunt or for the intensity of war. I knew not the name of this tribe or tribes for that matter, nor how long ago they had camped here. Just the cold hard fact that they had indeed been here.

It had been a slow season of finds so far. Mother earth had been slow to cough up and reveal her secrets so far. After many such journeys into the fields, I'd been quite disappointed. Without a good spring flood to scour the landscapes, it was difficult to spot artifacts. Oh, I'd found several dozen pottery sherds, and dozens of flint sherds indicating I was in the right places, but the real treasures remained shrouded from view.

On this fine day as I ambled along the bright white of two buffalo teeth stood out against the darkened earth. Buffalo teeth are found with great frequency and I'm always amazed that they have endured all these centuries to shine so brightly today! Buffalo teeth always help to assure that I'm on track, and in the zone.

Being drawn to the teeth I slowly sauntered in their direction hoping they would bring good luck. And good luck indeed they brought, for there, just beneath a young soybean plant, lay a magnificent, intact, creamy-white arrowhead! I did a little dance for joy, shouted out a few "Thank Yous!" heavenward and reached to grab hold of history itself. It was beautiful! And in prime condition to boot! I massaged my fingers over the arrowhead, like a blind man reading brail to know and feel its shape and texture. Wetting my fingers with my tongue I cleaned it, to visually inspect its minute details and skilled craftsmanship. This arrowhead had been worth the entire season of searching!

Paying Attention II

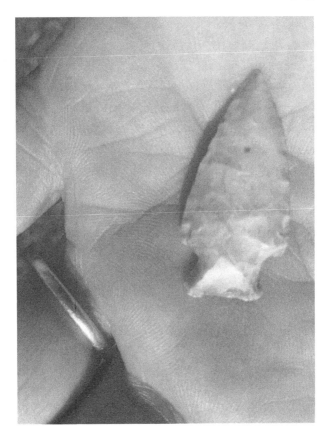

Question: ***Do you know who finds the most arrowheads?*** This is not a trick question by the way. Answer: **The ones that find the most arrowheads are those who go and seek.** You cannot find arrowheads from your couch, nor in your car, nor from your office, nor your back yard.

Question: ***Do you know who finds the most of God?*** His peace, His healing, His purpose, His Grace, His forgiveness, His joy, His contentment, His strength? Answer: **The ones that find the most of God and all he offers are those who actually seek Him.**

God smiles when we actively seek him, when we look for his presence in our world and when we seek His will in every corner and facet of our lives. When we call out the name of Jesus and invite him into our lives. The great thing is we don't have to travel to a forgotten lonely field to find him. He is a simple conversation and an invitation from us.

> "Ask, and it will be given to you; seek, and you will find; knock, and it will be opened to you. For everyone who asks receives, and the one who seeks finds, and to the one who knocks it will be opened. Or which one of you, if his son asks him for bread, will give him a stone? Or if he asks for a fish, will give him a serpent? Matthew 7:7-10 NIV

Let us remember that sometimes God reveals himself to us or answers our prayers instantaneously. We can feel his presence or peace or strength or insight immediately. Many times, though, it is a process, an ongoing progression of God growing us, healing us, renewing us, or encouraging us bit by bit over time. Be patient when you don't find an arrowhead every time you look at the dirt! Keep searching and seeking!

> *If any of you lacks wisdom, you should ask God, who gives generously to all without finding fault, and it will be given to you. James 1:5 NIV*

> *Trust in the LORD with all your heart and lean not on your own understanding; in all your ways submit to him, and he will make your paths straight. Proverbs 3:5-6 NIV*

> *Seek ye **first** the kingdom of God, and all things will be added unto you! Matt. 6:23 NIV*

The best solutions rarely come to pass swiftly. Time, as well as distance, may be necessary to the proper unfolding of events. Choosing to honor the longer view, I surrender my sense of urgency and frustration. I allow my life to unfurl as a gentle wave. I do not push for instant satisfaction. Mine is a patient heart. Faced with delays and apparent reversals, I remind myself that my greater good often comes from adversity. Choosing to honor the tidal nature of life, I do not push for artificial solutions born of haste and indiscretion. I allow God to unfold my life with ***his*** divine timing. Julia Cameron

Audience of One

Brilliant sunshine poured generously over the landscape. Its warmth and positive cheer were a welcome relief from the many afternoons of heavy grey, moody clouds, and frequent hail storms. The sunshine brought cobalt blue skies that met with precision, intersecting the jagged knife edges of the surrounding mountains. Nearby lakes reflected the mood of the sky and offered back deep aqua-marine emeralds that sparkled at the caressing of the wind.

My eldest daughter Karina and I were attempting a 100-mile hike along and near the Continental Divide in western Wyoming's Wind River Mountain Range. Most of our route was taking us above timberline, cross-country, and off-trail. We were weaving our way with map and compass through the fascinating high alpine world not seen by most. Crossing steep snowfields, chaotic and unstable boulder fields, intense 11,000' passes, wide open tundra and dozens of icy stream crossings had tested our mettle and resolve.

Our journey had also blessed us with beauty, grandeur and a sense of awe beyond compare. With each new step, magnificent vistas and picturesque panoramas opened before us. We were privileged to be passing through the mysterious terrain where earth meets sky. We felt honored to be walking through this holy and sacred ground. I could not help myself... I gave thanks and gratitude for where I was, and what I was experiencing continually throughout each day.

Along our journey, we were frequently blessed by pleasing fields of wildflowers of all shapes and colors. On a mountain journey, it so easy to pay attention to and marvel at the big picture, the magnificent panoramas, the majestic mountains, the scenic lakes and vistas, and neglect or forget about the smaller miracles that lay at our feet continually. The macro was so easy to appreciate, but Karina has an eye and appreciation for the micro, the delicate touches, and the subtle blessings that lay before us. She would often pause to kneel and take a photo of these delicate yet hearty wildflowers.

Our favorite shown here in the photo is the beautiful Indian Paint Brush flower. Its red flames dotted the landscape adding brilliant color to an often dull and gray landscape. Throughout our journey, I thought frequently about these vivid wildflowers. It would be my guess, that along the route we chose, most likely less than a handful of human visitors would ever pass by these flowers in a summer season.

These beautiful flowers awake each morning of their short lives and display their beauty to the world. They radiate beauty in the sunshine, in the rain, through the hail storms, and raging wind. By simply being who they are, they bless the world, and they do so regardless of whom if anyone is watching. They live out and enrich the world and most days do so to an audience of one; their Creator. These same flowers are still up there at 10,000' praising and worshiping and most likely there is no one there to pay attention, to affirm them or give them an "Atta boy." They live for an audience of One.

How about you? Can you **"Be who you are, who God created you to be"** for the world? Do you praise and worship when no one is watching, when it's not organized for you? Can you sing praise and or give thanks when it's not Sunday? Do you shine what God gave you back to and into the world? Can you be the best you can be when no one is looking? Can you and I live more for an audience of One?

**For those who wish to experience our recent journey in more detail, click on the link below and enjoy some fantastic scenery and music in our short video.

https://www.youtube.com/watch?v=0Yyussk-wLA

"Be careful not to practice your righteousness in front of others to be seen by them. If you do, you will have no reward from your Father in heaven. "So when you give to the needy, do not announce it with trumpets, as the hypocrites do in the synagogues and on the streets, to be honored by others. Truly I tell you, they have received their reward in full. But when you give to the needy, do not let your left hand know what your right hand is doing, so that your giving may be in secret. Then your Father, who sees what is done in secret, will reward you. Matthew 6: 1-4 NIV

Whatever you do, work at it with all your heart, as working for the Lord, not men. Colossians 3:23 NIV

"And when you pray, do not be like the hypocrites, for they love to pray standing in the synagogues and on the street corners to be seen by others. Truly I tell you, they have received their reward in full. But when you pray, go into your room, close the door and pray to your Father, who is unseen. Then your Father, who sees what is done in secret, will reward you. And when you pray, do not keep on babbling like pagans, for they think they will be heard because of their many words. Do not be like them, for your Father knows what you need before you ask him. Matthew 6:5-8 NIV

Autumn Run

My run on a winding path through Lindenwood Park was peaceful. Ash trees were slowly transitioning to autumnal colors of ochre, amber, and rust. Stoic oak trees were more hesitant and non-committal. They were waiting for their unknown cue before reluctantly changing color. Previous history reveals that when they do, they will be less flamboyant, less fervent, and less boisterous than their colorful cousins: the maples. Like good Lutherans at worship, oaks will only show moderate and subdued enthusiasm- maybe turning a shade of mauve, auburn, or a hint of burgundy. For now, though they held tightly to their rich tradition of long-lasting greenery.

A beautiful September breeze lapped at my sweaty body, keeping me cool for a relaxed five-mile run. As I rounded a bend for my return, I was met by the flood of light from the late afternoon descending sun that warmed my face. The warmth of the sun penetrated my whole being adding life and vitality to my run and my day. I gave a little prayer of thanks, knowing that these warmer days would soon become scarce, as we all prepare for a long winter ahead.

Ahh the sun, what a gift! I am one who spends a great deal of time in the sun. Gone are the days of just sitting underneath the sun for the sake of "catching rays." Wrinkly, aging skin and cancer have pretty well killed that sport. But I will often hear someone at church make a comment like; "Boy, looks like you've been out in the sun!" or "You must have spent some time in the sun…Looks good, looks healthy!"

I'll respond by saying: "Well thanks! You're right. I have been. Just last week I was rock climbing up north, or in the Boundary Waters canoeing or just got back from backpacking in the mountains of Colorado elk hunting or in the fields yesterday looking for arrowheads all day." The point is that I spend a great deal of time outside and the funny, crazy, ironic thing is… that's where the sun tends to hang out! AND… funny thing is, the crazy thing is, the ironic thing is… that when you spend a great deal of time in the sun… it affects you! It changes your appearance. It changes your demeanor. It changes how others perceive and experience you.

So, let me ask you a very difficult and personal question. How is your Son tan? No, maybe you didn't catch that, as I'm not talking about a bronzed body or a Copper-toned super-model. I want to know how is your SON tan? You see for those of us who spend significant amounts of time in, and around, and with the SON, it should affect us. It ought to change our appearance or our demeanor and how others perceive and experience us. If we log significant hours being in the presence of the Son of God, in a personal relationship with Jesus, we ought to have a bit of a glow of warmth, friendliness, joy, and peace about us. It ought to be visible, tangible, and real.

Yet for so many churchgoers, they appear pasty, white, anemic, pale, frowning, cold, frigid, grumpy, judging, and certainly unappealing to both fellow churchgoers and outsiders alike. Maybe it's because too many who fill our pews these days spend plenty of time in and around church, but very, very little time in the presence of the SON, Jesus. But nothing in scripture says: Go to church, and you'll be saved. Nothing biblical says the church will forgive your sins or give you purpose, meaning, or direction. And church attendance never healed a broken marriage, or a broken heart, or a wounded soul. Only Jesus does any of these. And Jesus doesn't need a church to do any of the above.

In fact, I think Jesus does his best work while we do life with him and alongside him in our day-to-day existence. Backpacking, canoeing, rock climbing, gardening, doing laundry, cleaning the house, going for a walk, working, schooling, playing, working out, cooking, sharing a meal, hunting pheasants, sitting in a tree-stand, conversing over coffee with a friend, washing dishes, mowing the lawn, serving in the soup line, reading to your grandkids, playing soccer or hockey, or baking cookies. Simply pause, and invite him into your day. He never turns down an honest and sincere invitation to be present in your moments. And by the way… you can also; pray, read scripture, read a good faith-based devotion or scripture inspired book too. He **will** meet you in those spaces and places as well. Oh, I forgot to mention… you can also invite him to meet you at and in your church worship. He does His best work on Sundays when you actually take the time to invite him to meet you in and through worship.

So, get out there! Get working on that Son Tan!

If God loves you, has accepted you, has forgiven you, has plans and a purpose for you…
THEN PLEASE!!! NOTIFY YOUR FACE!!!

When Moses came down from Mount Sinai with the two tablets of the covenant law in his hands, he was not aware that his face was radiant because he had spoken with the LORD. Exodus 34:29 NIV

The Son is the radiance of God's glory and the exact representation of his being, sustaining all things by his powerful word. Hebrews 1:3 NIV

*the Lord make his **face shine** on you and be gracious to you;* Numbers 6:25 NIV

*Restore us, God Almighty; make your **face shine** on us, that we may be saved.* Psalm 80:7 NIV

*For God, who said, "Let light **shine** out of darkness," made his light **shine** in our hearts to give us the light of the knowledge of God's glory displayed in the **face** of Christ.* 2 Corinthians 4:6 NIV

Beavers, Bones and Boundary Waters

The air was still and cool. Soft, quiet sunlight filtered through the thick canopy of forest, dappling the woods with random acts of light and shadow. The subtle, pleasing scent of wet leaves filled our lungs with clean, pure, and fresh oxygen. Our trail snaked out before us as we instinctively followed the path, never seeing more than a hundred yards in front of us, through various forest biomes. Stately, towering red and white pines dominated the granite ridgetops like proper kings and queens of the Canadian Shield, leaving a carpeted, cozy, floor of rust-colored needles and spongy mosses. Black ash and alder thickets dominated the lowlands, along with the dark ambiance of the thick cedar groves where daylight dared not enter. Hillsides of dense poplar soon gave way to intermittent stands of jack-pine, spruce, and balsams. Tamaracks were the only remaining autumn show-offs, flaunting their flaming yellow and orange needles, giving one final color burst to the fall woods before falling to the forest floor. Our journey was a never-ending smorgasbord of visual stimuli.

Our group of eight, had to have been divinely assembled, for one would be hard pressed to find a more eclectic party of hikers. Ages 18-55, all size and shapes, some terrified, some delighted, some fit, some not so much, but all called by a spirit of adventure and challenge to hike the 32-mile Sioux Hustler Trail deep in the heart of the Boundary Waters Canoe Area Wilderness. Four days without cellphones, Facebook and thumb- talking. Four days to hike and camp. Four days away from kids, spouses, boyfriends, and coworkers. Four days to converse, pray, listen, and be still. Four days to be challenged by the rugged terrain and ever-changing weather. Four days to confront oneself, one's issues, limitations, weaknesses, and hidden strengths.

Our journey held many obstacles; steep hills, long miles, stream crossings, and some cold, steady all-day rains that dampened both bodies and spirits. Beaver ponds that flooded the trail, proved to be one of the trickiest. Slick, mud covered sticks made even greasier by the rain, had us doing a tight rope walk across these wilderness Hoover Dams. We teetered and tottered, balancing our way across the water-soaked ridges, attempting to avoid the six-foot fall to one side or the plunge into icy cold water on the other. In the end, these precarious obstructions became a trip favorite for many, as overcoming the challenges became a fun and unpredictable adventure. Many of us paused to ponder and wonder at the magnificent engineering marvels created by a mere rodent that could so dramatically change and alter the landscape.

On two occasions, we stumbled upon the remains of the dominant north woods undulate. At first glance, I thought I had spied a broken canoe paddle, only to find the large flat scapula of a cow moose. Wondering further downhill, I scanned the woods and soon came upon the more complete set of bleached, creamy-white bones. The bones were picked clean, and tell-tale green tinges of moss told of at least a year's passing since the time of death. Vertebrae, ribs, femurs, tibias, fibulas, hip bone, skull and jaw bones were all strewn about a twenty-foot circle.

As I reconnected the large, rounded femur ball to the socket of the hip, I pondered for a long time what this death must have looked like. Old age can rarely be blamed in the deep north woods, for the apex predators can sniff out the weakness of age or illness. No, this large female was most likely the victim of a well-coordinated, highly evolved, brutal, and completely lethal wolf attack. I mused; had she been the quarry of a surprise sneak attack that took her quickly in her bed? Or had she been pursed through miles of deep snow, her heart pounding with fear and heavy labored, steamy breathing? How long did she suffer?

Was it four or six or ten wolves that had converged on her? What must it be like to die at the hands of such savage tooth and claw?

Not made for a Disney movie you say? Nor could this be a warm and fuzzy devo? And I don't mean to further malign the all too often villainized wolf. But this **IS** the reality of our natural world of God's creation. It happens daily in our backyards and suburbs, although most often the scenes are hidden from view. Coyotes kill and eat deer, the fox slays the hare, the owl swoops to consume a gray squirrel, a mink devours a trout, a raccoon ravages a frog, a robin slurps down a nightcrawler, a bat at dusk gulps down mosquitos, a frog slurps up a fly and our cats, thankfully, kill and dine on our house mice. Is one life more or less valuable than the other? Is the wolf more malevolent because of the size and beauty of the creature he kills?

Let's take it one step further. Is the wolf more villainous than we who will sit at the Thanksgiving table and dine on delicious turkey? Or dunk a tasty chicken McNugget in barbeque sauce? Or carve up a nice prime rib at Sunday's brunch? Or sit on luxurious leather seats in our SUVs, or carry our designer Coach or Gucci leather handbags? I think not. Let's be honest. We, humans, have simply hired ***others*** down a long, multi-layered, and well-hidden chain to do the dirty work. The wolf is just more honest.

Anyone who knows me knows that I am a lover of nature and creation. And I am most at home and most at peace when I am immersed in the natural world. But never, ever do I worship or revere creation as the ultimate be all, end all. Creation is flawed, just as is our own humanity. Floods, hurricanes, earthquakes, blizzards, fires, tornados, avalanches, and tsunamis all do their share of horrific damage that ends in tragedy and heartache for our human race.

Let us remember that our help does not come from the hills, or the sunsets, or the flowers, or the trees, or the lakes, or the mountains, or the furry creatures of creation. Our help, our hope, our salvation, our sustenance comes from the Lord, who made heaven and earth.

Rollie Johnson

I lift up my eyes to the hills— from where will my help come?
My help comes from the LORD, who made heaven and earth. Psalm 121:1-2 NIV

When I consider your heavens,
the work of your fingers,
the moon, and the stars,
which you have set in place,
[4] what is mankind that you are mindful of them,
human beings that you care for them?[a]
[5] You have made them[b] a little lower than the angels[c]
and crowned them[d] with glory and honor.
[6] You made them rulers over the works of your hands;
you put everything under their[e] feet:
[7] all flocks and herds,
and the animals of the wild,
[8] the birds in the sky,
and the fish in the sea,
all that swim the paths of the seas.
[9] Lord, our Lord,
how majestic is your name in all the earth!
Psalm 8:2-9 NIV

Blindfold Drum Stalk

The darkness in the deep of night was overwhelming for most. One felt as if the inky blackness of night might swallow them whole. The night sounds of the great north woods were subtle but immediately amplified by adding a blindfold to each participant. When one shuts down our overused sense of sight, our hearing and listening instincts seem to come to full alert. The fear and anxiety were palpable, as I led the group who were silently holding hands, down the long, twisting trail deeper into the shadowy blackness of the forest.

At metered distances along the trail, I stopped to release a person from the line and instructed them to remain in place until the signal to begin was heard. I could physically hear the deep breaths taken in, and felt the tensing of their bodies as they now realized they were completely alone and blindfolded in a remote location of the expansive 2,000-acre woods of Camp Wilderness.

After spacing each of the twenty participants out along a quarter mile of trail, I radioed to the endpoint team, to begin with the drumming. Located 500 yards away was one of our leaders who would pound out a steady beat every 5 seconds or so, on a wooden drum. The task of the participants was to simply listen for, and walk towards the sound of the drum beat. In between the drummer and blindfolded walkers were dense saplings, large pines, blowdowns, underbrush, and meadows. They were to use the Native American stalking skills they'd learned previously in the week to gently feel their way through the thick vegetation and around and through the various obstacles with the soles of their feet. My gentle but firm mantra repeated over and over was. "Be quiet, listen, go slow, and follow the steady, quiet voice of the drum."

This unique activity is called the Blindfold Drum Stalk, one of many teaching tools from our SOLO Trip. For most that chose to go on this trip, it's one of many activities designed to take them well beyond their normal comfort zones to experience new personal breakthroughs, gain insights, and deepen their trust and faith in God. For the majority of those tossed into this scenario, the anxiety and fear level was through the roof. All landmarks and bearings are ripped away due to the black of night and blindfolds, so now they are forced to rely on other senses of touch, awareness and especially listening. "Be quiet, listen, go slow and follow the steady, quiet voice of the drum."

For many who have taken on this challenge, the fear and anxiety soon begin to melt away, as they come to listen for, and trust in, and move towards the quiet, gentle beat of the drum. Many describe being able to hear their own heartbeat. Many report a heightened awareness and sharpened sensory perception as they begin to flow into a peaceful rhythm of movement and trust. And for many who arrive safely at the drum after an hour or more of slow, steady stalk walking, they report a beautiful sense of being guided, cared for and comforted during the darkness of their long sightless journey.

The analogies, metaphors, life and faith comparisons fairly jump off the page shouting to be heard and I grow giddy with excitement for helping people to make those connections. Walk by faith not by sight! Listen! Listen more... talk less! Be still, be quiet. Wait upon the Lord. Listen and then obey. Fear not I am with you! Walk in the direction of Gods still small voice. Slow down! Life can be dark and scary... so keep listening to and following the voice of God. You will never, ever walk alone. I am with you. I will watch over you. I will protect you. Even though you do not see the way... I will guide you on the right paths. In life, you will encounter many obstacles and difficulties, but you will not meet them alone. I am with you.

I urge you to set aside your sense of sight that most rely on for 99.9% of our perception of life. Instead, learn more and more to; "Be

Still, listen and wait upon the Lord." He and he alone will guide you and watch over you.

I will lead the blind by ways they have not known,
Along unfamiliar paths I will guide them; I will turn the darkness into light before them and make the rough places smooth. Isaiah 42:16 NIV
We live by faith, not by sight! 2 Corinthians 5:7 NIV

I waited patiently for the Lord; he turned and heard my cry. He lifted me up out of the slimy pit of despair, out of the mud and mire. He set my feet upon a rock and made my footsteps firm…
*Many will see and fear, and **put their trust in the Lord**. Psalm 40:1-3 NIV*

Camo Moth

Strolling north along Broadway, I ambled along in no hurry heading back to church from my afternoon coffee run to Sandy's Donuts. With my caffeine jump starter in hand to clear away my post-lunch brain fog and a gorgeous sunny day at hand, I felt ready to finish out the day. Rounding the corner on 6th street I noticed something out of place on the long black security fence recently erected for our construction site. The thirty- yard-long pure black fence screen was taut and clean except for one spot that begged for my investigation. Whatever it was stuck out like the proverbial sore thumb.

Looking both ways, I crossed the street curious about the blemish on the clean dark slate of the fence. As I drew closer, an "Ah Ha" moment of recognition came as I realized it was a large moth. Closing the distance and getting up close and personal, I could observe the beauty of its natural coloring. The triangular shaped moth showed beautiful pallets of earth tones; tan, blacks, greys, browns, and opaque cream. An unknown artist must have studied their color charts putting together these gorgeous complimentary colors.

Being a bow-hunter and woodsman at heart, I realized this moth was covered in a beautiful camouflage. The major bummer for this moth, was his chosen background and landing spot. He had chosen to rest on the homogenous backdrop of the black construction cloth which made him stand out and be noticed from a hundred plus yards away! Had he landed on a nearby stoic oak tree, or sturdy hackberry tree trunk, he would have been virtually invisible and completely unnoticed. Upon the grayed bark background of a tree trunk, he would have simply blended in.

I have often pondered the art of camouflage. And I ask the question; as a Christian should we be camouflaged and blend into our world and the culture around us? Or as followers of Jesus should we stand out, be different, and in contrast to the world like this moth so distinctly set himself apart on the black fence?

Are we called to blend into the world and its culture and be indistinguishable from everyone else? Are we to become invisible, so as to infiltrate the world like a spy or secret agent for Jesus, blending in through the norms and dictates of society around us to impact those around us for God?

Should our coworker or neighbor be able to know that we are a follower of Jesus based on our lifestyle? How we speak? The language we use? What we buy? How we act? What we drive? What we do with our free time? Who we hang out with? What we do with our time and money?

Does your life represent a mirror to the world's culture, a reflection of everything it says we should do and be? Or does your life look in contrast to what the world offers, does it stand out, stick out and is it visibly different to others from a distance? Is your life a lighthouse calling others to safety and life? Or when others pass by you, have you become invisible by blending into the cultural background?

Are we called to be quiet, minding our own business, unnoticed like a moth on a tree trunk? Or are we to be noticeable, unique, separate, and obvious? Are we called to be "dorks for Jesus," "fools for Christ sake?"

Would someone else *"know you are Christian by our love, by our love?"* Or do you love like the world loves, when it's convenient, when it's practical, when it's reciprocal, and when others are loveable?

Are you the same person and do you act the same at Walmart, McDonald's, work, on the golf course, in school, on the basketball court or in your home as you are in church?

Jesus was often times counter-cultural, going in opposite directions from cultural norms. The world says claw your way to the top, do whatever it takes to make it. Yet Jesus always walked in downward directions seeking out the lepers, the lost and the lonely.

Most of us seek out and love to rub elbows with the wealthy, influential and powerful. Jesus sought out the sinners, the broken, those who had failed and messed up. The world says be #1, Be all you can Be, buy more, Be more. Jesus simply says; *"Whoever finds their life will lose it, and whoever loses their life for my sake will find it."* Matthew 10:39 NIV

Most of us by nature look out for me, myself, and I. Jesus points in another direction; Mark 8:34-37

Most of us want to be great, to be recognized, to be honored, and lifted upwards. Jesus moves us in the opposite direction; *"Whoever wants to be my disciple must deny themselves and take up their cross and follow me. ³⁵ For whoever wants to save their life[a] will lose it, but whoever loses their life for me and for the gospel will save it.³⁶ What good is it for someone to gain the whole world, yet forfeit their soul? Mark 8:34-37 NIV*

Not so with you. Instead, whoever wants to become great among you must be your servant, ²⁷ and whoever wants to be first must be your slave— ²⁸ just as the Son of Man did not come to be served, but to serve, and to give his life as a ransom for many." Matthew 20-26-28 NIV

I don't have a nice tight, neat and tidy, simple answer for you. I wrestle with the same questions daily. The world places so much pressure on all of us to act, do and be a certain way. Jesus most often reminds us that we are not to blindly follow the siren calling and the seductive beckoning of the world. He has walked in and through our world. He knows what it is like. He offers us alternatives that better serve those around us, and bring each of us more peace, contentment, and real purpose and meaning.

May you choose to land in a dark word to offer a contrast to those around you with the hope and light and life given by Jesus.

Would you rather stand with Jesus, and be judged by the world?
Or Stand with the world, and be judged by Jesus?

"You are the salt of the earth. But if the salt loses its saltiness, how can it be made salty again? It is no longer good for anything, except to be thrown out and trampled underfoot. "You are the light of the world. A town built on a hill cannot be hidden. ¹⁵ Neither do people light a lamp and put it under a bowl. Instead, they put it on its stand, and it gives light to everyone in the house. ¹⁶ In the same way, let your light shine before others, that they may see your good deeds and glorify your Father in heaven. Matthew 5:13-16 NIV

> *What good is it, my brothers and sisters, if someone claims to have faith but has no deeds (good works)? Can such faith save them? Suppose a brother or a sister is without clothes and daily food. If one of you says to them, "Go in peace; keep warm and well fed," but does nothing about their physical needs, what good is it? In the same way, faith by itself, if it is not accompanied by action, is dead. But someone will say, "You have faith; I have deeds." Show me your faith without deeds, and I will show you my faith by my deeds (good works). James 2: 14-18 NIV*

Candle Light Campfire

The lights of the gym were dimmed. A hundred plus Carl Ben Eielson 7th graders sat on the floor in a circle, gathered 'round our little home-made campfire. Several dozen tea lights sat atop a blue Rubbermaid container, giving off a gentle, quiet, inviting, soft light. Twenty-some leaders from South High stood stoically around the multi-layered ring of 7th graders like guardians of the sacred circle. Soft piano music played in the background to set the contemplative mood. Silence was the price of admission, and only those who dared the courage to enter the circle, could light a candle and earn the right to speak their truth into the microphone.

This Sacred Circle was the culmination of our Day of Compassion Retreat. The previous five hours had been filled with loud, fun music, mixers, games, teambuilding exercises, singing, dancing, and small group discussions. Humor and laughter had been our entry point of the day as we worked hard to break down walls of communications, cliques, negative expectations, and apathy. Woven throughout all this frenzy of activity were meaningful vignettes and object lessons speaking to the kids about compassion, kindness, and respect. My retreat partner, Erik Hatch, had done a magical job of using his humor and love of people to quickly earn the trust of these kids, and so by the time he spoke on a more serious nature, the kids were attentive and ready to listen. We simply show kids real-life lessons of the right way to treat people and then ask them to look at how they treat one another. Can you move beyond thinking simply about yourself? Or can you act with Compassion, attempting to walk in another's person's shoes for a moment, an hour or a day?

This was our second day at CBE, with the second half of the 7th-grade class, and both days had been fabulous with over the top enthusiasm and participation by all kids, leaders, and staff. This was our 20th retreat this school year in a wide variety of elementary, middle and high schools. And though this cannot be a "faith" based retreat that never prevents me from walking the empty gym in the early morning to pray over this sacred space and invite the Holy Spirit to move in the hearts of kids, leaders, and staff, or offer up silent prayers throughout our day.

Our campfire was moving along beautifully. Kids could choose to come forward, light a candle and then speak a word of gratitude or thanks to a friend, mentor or teacher. It was also a time to offer up words of apology to anyone they have injured through words, actions or neglect. As with many of these campfires, the day's lessons and comradery began to sink in and for many students and staff alike, it can be a tearful time as classmates pour out their hearts in honest gratitude or regret for wrong done.

As we neared the end of our campfire time, a young South High leader arose and entered the circle. She knelt and lit a tea light with hands that lightly trembled for nervousness. She quietly arose and took the microphone. Even in the soft glow of candles, I could see her red-rimmed and moist eyes. She stammered briefly, and then quietly spoke her truth. *"I have had a tough life. My family situation has never been good. In fact, when I was your guy's age, the worst part of my day..."* and she choked on her words, *"was hearing that final bell signaling the end of the school day...knowing I had to go home."*

My heart broke. The lump in my throat refused to be swallowed. Silence hung over the darkened gym like a heavy blanket. Heads nodded in agreement, tears flowed, arms reached out to hold the person next to them. By honestly sharing the yuk and the muck of her heart, she gave permission for others to do the same, and what followed was an outpouring of compassion, understanding, acceptance, and empathy.

What I witness on so many of these retreats, is echoed in the quiet space of my office as folks come to visit, or heartfelt conversations across the table in a coffee shop. We live in a world filled with a great deal of hurt, pain, disharmony, sadness, and struggle. It matters not whether you're in a crowded school hallway or sitting in a church pew or a busy office. Simply toss a pencil just a few feet and within that short radius, you'll find a hurting person. And don't be fooled by the smiles and laughter that present on the surface in front of you, for many a wounded soul lies hidden beneath our well-constructed façades and smiling faces.

It's funny what happens when one person, in the security of a safe environment, takes the risk of vulnerability, by sharing their own weakness, failure or fragility. It is contagious, liberating and leads to healing and connectedness.

You and I as followers of Christ are now called on more and more, to be the hands, and ears and voice of Christ to a hurting world. It is through your listening ear, your gentle invitational question of; "How are you doing these days?" That healing can begin and Christian community and connection can grow. We are rarely called to climb great mountains or hit a home run, just simply be present to those who are hurting and lonely. Jesus brought "presence" to those he encountered. His presence brought healing and hope to hurting people.

Today may you have eyes to perceive, who God is calling you to share His presence.

Therefore encourage one another and build each other up, just as in fact you are doing! 1 Thessalonians. 5:11 NIV

CANOE

Her time had come. She was old and broken down, and she had outgrown her usefulness. She had lost the beauty, elegance, and grace of her youth. Her skin once smooth and glossy now looked dulled and lifeless. No longer was there a beautiful glow about her, only wrinkles and scraggly patches that covered her skin like a diseased leper. It was time to put her down.

The dumpster sat in the driveway silently awaiting her corpse. I quietly gassed and oiled my chainsaw. It was time to cut her up into pieces. I solemnly clicked up the start button, grabbed the pull handle and stood over her lifeless body. My mind screamed with practicality and shouted: "time to let her go!" But my heart pleaded and mourned and grieved me to stop. I could not do it. I could not destroy what I had created. Maybe there was another way.

This was the very first canoe that I had built with my own two hands in the early '80s in my parent's basement. It was a pure labor of love and adventure into the unknown. I had blindly plowed my way into the project following the directions from a book. After months of hard work, love, sweat, and tears, I had birthed a brand-new canoe into existence! And she was a wonder of creation. The honey and auburn colored virtually glowed in the sunshine. And though she had dozens of mistakes and flaws she was my pride and joy and I loved to show her off from the roof of my car, or on a nearby lake or river.

She had proved faithful and safely seen me through dozens of

Boundary Waters Wilderness trips, ran with me on my trap lines, hauled out my record book bear from a north-woods lake and carried out nice bucks along the Red. She was a seaworthy, wilderness savvy, hearty voyageur.

But alas she had sat in our back woods for the past 10-12 years unprotected from the elements. Sunshine and wind and snow had broken down her fiberglass, rotted her oaken gunwales, thwart, and seats. Neglect had grown a grotesque exterior of black and green mold and mildew. She was now a sorry sight.

On a gut level hunch, I exchanged chainsaw for a power washer. Spraying with the powerful force of water, I was stunned to see the mold and mildew peel away with each sweep of the washer. Underneath the grime and dirt, I could see the original cedar! Maybe… just maybe I could clean up my canoe by power washing then spend the summer sanding the original fiberglass to restore and possibly repaint the canoe. It was final, the dumpster would not receive her soul.

Paying Attention II

I spent the better part of this past spring and summer working on this canoe. Tearing and peeling off the entire exterior of the old fiberglass, I got down to the original cedar wood. Hour and hours of sanding made the wood smooth. By re-fiberglassing the entire exterior, the cedar came back to life in all of its vibrant, beautiful natural colors. New deck plates, new gunwales, new seats, new thwarts, and a new yoke were all created that now await to be installed.

This canoe, my original creation, into which I had placed so much time, energy, work, and love is now being reborn. It is undergoing a rebirth, a re-creation, a renewal, a restoration. It is being repurposed, renovated, repaired and revitalized. What was old, weary, worn, broken, un-appealing, and un-useful is once again a new creation. I will soon finish her and present her as a gift to my oldest daughter Karina and her husband Taylor.

I have had lots of time to think during a project like this. The parallels to the life of faith are unmistakable. All of the cleaning and restoration of the canoe was done by me... the Creator. Not a single improvement or clean up or restoration has been done by the canoe itself. It simply needed to **BE STILL**... and wait...before its maker. The renewal is the job of the **Creator**, not the creation. Will power, New Year's Eve resolutions, goal setting, self-discipline, self-improvement, working harder, reading self-help books or doing more did nothing for the canoe. The work of restoration, cleaning, and repair is that of the Maker.

How about you? Feeling old, weary, worn, broken, flawed, un-useful, put out on a shelf, forgotten, failed or flawed? Got some bad habits, negative moldy attitudes, or some ugly addictions that you can't lick yourself?

I know of a meticulous and gifted repairman. He is the healer of souls. His name: Jesus. He is in the business of restoring wounded, broken, worn out, burned out, addicted souls. Lay yourself before him.

Be Still... before the Lord.

Do not conform to the pattern of this world, but be transformed by the renewing of your mind. Then you will be able to test and approve what God's will is—his good, pleasing and perfect will. Romans 12:2 NIV

Therefore, if anyone is in Christ, the new creation has come: The old has gone, the new is here! 2 Corinthians 5:17 NIV

but those who hope in the Lord will renew their strength. They will soar on wings like eagles; they will run and not grow weary, they will walk and not be faint. Isaiah 40:31 NIV

*...Be **still**, And know that I am God. ..Psalm 46:10 NIV*

*Be **still** before the Lord, And wait patiently for Him… Psalm 37:7 NIV*

he leads me beside quiet waters, he refreshes my soul. Psalm 23:2-3 NIV

Paying Attention II

Can't Take It With You

"Maah Daah Hey" comes from the Mandan language meaning *"Area that has been around for a long time."* Our group of 12, an eclectic and random mix of souls was meandering slowly through this rugged and spectacular landscape for a four-day hike. Several petrified tree stumps and the multi-layered and multi-colored stratified layers of badlands soils testified as to the truth of its name. We were walking through layers of history millions of years old. We were journeying through the land that time forgot.

Paying Attention II

We had been truly blessed by magnificent, pure sapphire skies, brilliant sunshine, cool breezes and incredible sights and vistas that changed with every bend in the trail. Eye candy for the soul you might say. Blazing warm campfires and frosty, star-filled nights were accented by the howling, yipping, and barking of the local Coyote Union 404. This lonely, rugged landscape brought about feelings of solitude and isolation.

After trekking 8-9 miles into the heart of the Achenbach Hills of the Teddy Roosevelt National Park on day one, our bodies were worn and weary. The toil and strain were rewarded by a campsite with stunning and breathtaking views in all directions. Each change of light particularly during sunrises and sunsets cast a magnificent display of colors, textures, and shadows across the landscape. Our morning coffee times became holy and sacred as we sat and watched a new day being birthed over the Little Missouri and its bottomlands. Small bands of bison could be seen below as eagles floated on the updrafts off the ridgelines.

Day two found us on casual a day-hike as we dove down into the convoluted bottoms. At times we hiked through easy meadows and grassy hillsides. Other times we wrestled through brush-choked coulees and crowded stands of juniper. Having no particular destination, we certainly weren't lost, but rather followed the Spirit's leading with the one intention of hoping to sneak up closer to a herd of buffalo.

We grappled our way through one more tangle of brush and limbs and as fate would have it, or more likely just another one of God's thousand-plus blessings, we stumbled upon a large bison skull complete with full black horns! It was huge! I was ecstatic and thrilled beyond belief! I hoisted it proudly in the air for all to see and soon the entire group was handling it and collecting the rest of the massive bones that lay strew about the bramble of the thicket. It was an incredible find and in all this vast and hidden terrain, we had stumbled upon it! What an awesome surprise and miraculous unexpected gift!

We spent time assembling and fondling some of the bones and connecting the ball of the femur to the socket of the hip bone. We pondered that in his prime he must have been king of this basin. We speculated as to the reason for its death. Most likely this had to have been an old herd bull, and the likely cause of death without any natural predators was old age. It looked as if it would be a perfect fit for a Native American Tipi. How privileged I felt to have found it here in this vast tangle of wilderness.

My mind raced as to how to transport this heavy and awkwardly large object back home. I look like a kid in a candy store when I find an elk antler shed in the mountains, or a neat rock on the river bed, or a skull or nest in the woods and my joy in finding this was through the roof. But then I was sadly reminded, that it is illegal to take something like this skull from a National Park. And so, the sad truth sunk in, that I could not take it with me.

How strange that this skull found hidden in some unnamed coulee in middle of nowhere North Dakota could remind me about a hard truth of real life. We can't take it with us.

Like this once majestic and powerful herd bull, we too will all pass away. Doesn't matter who we are or how powerful and important we are in this life… we will all, one day weaken and fade away to die. And when we leave this earth, we will go as we came, naked and alone. We don't get to bring all our "stuff" with us. We don't get suitcases, or backpacks or storage units, or pockets. Our stuff has to stay. We can't take it with us.

We all cling to our "stuff" so tightly. We hoard and we collect. We build bigger houses, and more garages and extra storages units to hold all our "stuff." We covet and envy the "stuff" of others and crave even more "stuff." But alas… the rules are quite clear, ashes to ashes, dust to dust, we can't take it with us. All of our important titles and prestigious careers, outstanding accomplishments, our trophies, ribbons, and medals; we can't take them with us. Our 401 K's, our savings, our diversified portfolios, and our wise investments… they all stay. Our large homes, our SUV's, our shiny toys, our lake cabin, and our favorite pets, they too do not get to make the journey. Nor does your attractive girlfriend, your faithful husband, your esteemed parents or your dearly beloved children. Unfortunately, the rules are quite clear, ashes to ashes, dust to dust, we can't take it with us.

Jesus teaches: *"Do not lay up for yourselves treasures on earth, where moth and rust destroy and where thieves break in and steal, but lay up for yourselves treasures in heaven, where neither moth nor rust destroys and where thieves do not break in and steal. For where your treasure is, there your heart will be also. Matthew 6: 19-2*

Maybe this old herd bull can teach us that we need not spend so much time collecting and clinging to "piles of old bones." But rather focus on our relationship with our Maker and Creator. When we seek first the kingdom of God, all other things fall into place. When we get our relationship with Jesus right, all "the stuff" is a bonus. When we focus on strengthening our walk with Jesus, we then learn to give to and serve others as our main purpose here on planet earth. There is only one thing we take with us to the afterlife, the real life, the next life and that is our soul. And our soul cannot grow, or live on, or be fed by "stuff." All that "stuff"… we can't take it with us.

May you lean into your walk with Jesus this day!

Very truly I tell you, whoever hears my word and believes him who sent me has eternal life and will not be judged but has crossed over from death to life. John 5:24 NIV

"I am the resurrection and the life. Those who believe in me, even though they die, will live, and everyone who lives and believes in me will never die." John 11: 17-27 NIV

"I am the way, and the truth, and the life. No one comes to the Father except through me." John 14:6 NIV

Carson & Rory

The two lives intersected in a chance encounter at a local gym. One, a regular, who works out faithfully three times a week but makes very little visible progress, the other a celebrity guest who happened to be in the neighborhood, and needed a place for a solid workout and is at the pinnacle of athletic prowess. One is fighting for day to day survival; the other is crescendoing towards peak physical performance. One is in his mid-fifties, the other in his early twenties. One will work out in silence with no one to applaud but his trainer and aid. The other will be watched and cheered by literally millions.

One demonstrates incredible fortitude and courage by facing what he has lost, with a positive attitude and showing gratitude for what he still has, displaying determined grit and unequaled perseverance. One displays tremendous fortitude and courage by living gracefully under the tremendous pressure and strain of the public eye, and the enormous weight of responsibility.

One shot his first buck this past fall with a bow, one tried but did not. One will watch the Superbowl silently from his quiet living room perched in his wheelchair. One will most likely someday play in a Superbowl or three in a crowded stadium filled with hundreds of thousands of screaming fans watched by millions of people worldwide. One will run like an Olympian, the other will not.

One can only speak via the aid of a computer and one will rarely ever speak without a microphone in front of his face.

Paying Attention II

None of us know the fates that this life will bring neither the triumphs nor the tragedies and life is certainly filled with both. Life is not so much about what happens to us, but rather how we react and respond to it. Our attitude and outlook are really at the heart of what we can actually control. Thank God that he can and does work through all events and happenings in our lives, good or bad. Romans 8: 28 declares: *"And we know that in all things God works for the good of those who love him, who have been called according to his purpose."*

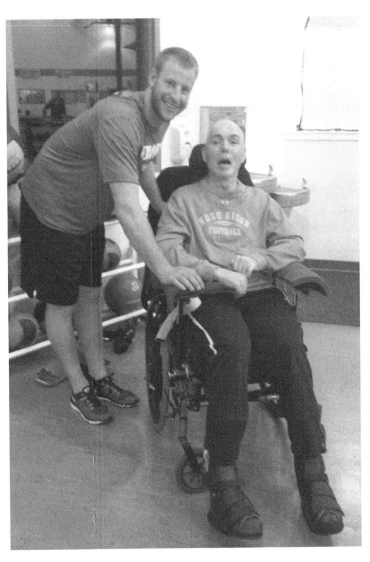

Both men I have called friend. Both men have taught me of life and faith. Both men honor their Creator and Maker. Both are trying to make the best of what life has dealt them. Both men have my deepest respect and strongest admiration. Both men are being used by God to change the world for the better. Both men are my teachers. I have much to learn from each about grace, gratitude, humility, perseverance, attitude, and fortitude,

May God bless both these men of courage and faith; Carson Wentz and Rory Eidsness.

The greatest of human freedoms is the ability to choose one's own attitude. Victor Frankl

..Whatever is true, whatever is noble, whatever is right, whatever is pure, whatever is lovely, whatever is admirable- if anything is excellent or praiseworthy- Think about such things! Philippians 4:8 NIV

"If God wants it to, my life will be useful through my word and witness. If he wants it to, my life will bear fruit through my prayers and sacrifices. But the usefulness of my life is His concern, not mine. It would be indecent of me to worry about that." Brother Dominque Voillaume

Rejoice always, pray continually, give thanks in all circumstances, for this is God's will for you in Christ Jesus.
1Thes 5:16-18 NIV

The remarkable thing is we have a choice every day regarding the attitude we will embrace for that day. We cannot change our past… we cannot change the fact that people will act in a certain way. We cannot change the inevitable. The only thing we can do is play on the one string we have, and that is our attitude. I am convinced that life is 10% what happens to me and 90% of how I react to it. And so it is with you… You are in charge of your attitudes. Charles Swindoll

Chalice and the Bow

Sitting alone in our basement TV room late the other night, I felt a great sense of contentment and peace. The stillness and quiet had calmed both my busy mind and restless soul. In one hand I held an intriguing and alluring Spanish Novel; "Las Navajas" which continued to draw me back each evening into the fascinating medieval world of the re-conquest of Spain.

In my other hand, I held a beautiful wooden chalice which ironically happened to be filled with a delicious Spanish red wine. The chalice was a hand-made wedding gift given to us years ago by a pair of students who had been in a former youth group of mine. Their grandfather Frank was a gifted woodworker who turned these magnificent and unique goblets on his lathe. The goblet's mate, a smaller more petite version, remained alone on the dining room shelf.

As I journeyed through the captivating world of fifteenth-century Spain with swords, chain-mail, and bloody battles, I paused looking up from my book and happened to notice my longbow leaning against the wall a few feet away. The longbow was the most recent of the many hand-made creations that I had been working over and tuning up for the spring. I had birthed this bow a year ago and it had been chosen from a plethora of other teammates hanging in my man-cave to be readied for the spring turkey season.

What suddenly caught my eye was the striking similarity of woods used in the chalice and the bow. It was remarkable! It was almost as if they had been crafted as compliments to one another, yet by separate craftsmen and made years apart.

I knew the make-up of my bow as only a creator knows his creation. I had laminated exotic hardwoods together to compliment and contrast one another in color and texture. I could see the similar woods contained in the chalice as well. The beautiful dark contrasting grain lines of zebra wood mated perfectly with the deep mahogany of purple-heart. Light accents of blond maple stood juxtaposed in perfect balance.

The beauty and grace of these woods added character, warmth, and attractiveness. The gentle, soft, sexy curves of the chalice invited holding and caressing. The handle of the bow did the same, and where palm met grip there became a most natural union.

I am a lover of all things wood. Wood is good. Wood has a warmth, a beauty, a unique quality and character of its own. It is natural, birthed from the earth and I can trace its origin back to creation and the Creator. Metal seems to me cold, distant, and heartless. And plastic… well, that just reeks of all things man-made that have placed our earth and climate where it is today.

As I sat in silence pondering these two dissimilar yet connected objects, I began to wonder. The chalice is a thing of beauty to behold for sure. It looks attractive whether sitting on a table or held in my hands. But the real gift of the chalice is the empty space contained within. It is meant to hold, carry and deliver good beverages! An aromatic savory red wine, or refreshing water or ice-cold milk ready to receive a few delicious dunkings of Oreos. The goblet has purpose and meaning beyond its exterior beauty.

Paying Attention II

My bow is similar. It has a beauty and elegance of its own and looks good adorning my wall. Yet the real purpose lies in the unseen and hidden energy stored within the fiberglass and wood of the curved and tensed limbs. The bow serves no purpose on its own. Yet when paired with a straight and well-fletched arrow it can propel and launch that projectile hundreds of yards! That bow, when used in partnership with an arrow and hunter, can put meat on the kitchen table or provide a child with the thrill of a target well hit.

I believe you and I are so similar. We are beautiful, wonder-filled, exotic, and lovely creations. We are unique, one of a kind, hand-made projects of our Creator. Though similar; we are all made of flesh and blood, i.e. the same materials, we each were handcrafted with a purpose, task, and mission uniquely our own.

Like the chalice, we can choose what we carry in our life cup. We can be filled with self: self-criticism, selfishness, self-indulgence or self-pity. We can be filled with anger, negativity, resentment, bitterness, and jealousy. And ironically then, this is all we have to offer the world and those we encounter at work, school or in our neighborhood or home. We can conversely begin each day, by asking God to fill us, to acknowledge the presence of the Holy Spirit already implanted within us. When we begin our days with this invitation, our cup can be filled with peace, purpose, wisdom, patience, and strength beyond ourselves. These are delightful, Godly gifts that you can then pour out on others.

Like my bow, we do not operate in this world in a vacuum or on our own. We are meant to live in relationship with others. We were handcrafted to work with others to impact our world in Jesus name. Who is it that you could help propel via your strength, your energy, your kind words, your note of affirmation, your encouragement, and your passion? God needs you today to help serve and launch others into our world of need.

Remember you have intrinsic value and beauty just as you are. You are a magnificent work of the creator. But Please! Don't just sit on a shelf of life and try to look good. You are meant to engage in the world and make a difference with your purpose and gifts! Get out there and serve!

Psalm 139:1-18, 23-24 NIV

You have searched me, Lord and you know me.
² You know when I sit and when I rise; you
perceive my thoughts from afar.
³ You discern my going out and my lying down;
you are familiar with all my ways.
⁴ Before a word is on my tongue you, Lord, know it completely.
⁵ You hem me in behind and before, and you lay your hand upon me.
⁶ Such knowledge is too wonderful for me, too lofty for me to attain.
⁷ Where can I go from your Spirit? Where can I flee from your presence?
⁸ If I go up to the heavens, you are there;
if I make my bed in the depths, you are there.
⁹ If I rise on the wings of the dawn, if I settle on the far side of the sea,
¹⁰ even there your hand will guide me, your right hand will hold me fast.

Paying Attention II

¹¹ *If I say, "Surely the darkness will hide me and*
the light become night around me,"
¹² *even the darkness will not be dark to you;*
the night will shine like the day,
for darkness is as light to you.
¹³ *For you created my inmost being, you knit*
me together in my mother's womb.
¹⁴ *I praise you because I am fearfully and wonderfully made;*
your works are wonderful, I know that full well.
¹⁵ *My frame was not hidden from you when*
I was made in the secret place
when I was woven together in the depths of the earth.
¹⁶ *Your eyes saw my unformed body;*
all the days ordained for me were written in your
book, before one of them came to be.
¹⁷ *How precious to me are your thoughts,[a]*
God! How vast is the sum of them!
¹⁸ *Were I to count them, they would outnumber the grains of sand—*
when I awake, I am still with you.
²³ *Search me, God, and know my heart; test*
me and know my anxious thoughts.
²⁴ *See if there is any offensive way in me and*
lead me in the way everlasting.

Christmas Eve Gospel

The soft, amber lights of the Christmas trees twinkled gently in the low light of Celebration Hall. 'Twas the night before Christmas, as I sat down in my corner nook next to the pillar, and a poignant video played on the screen above. The hall was packed to the brim with folks from all walks of life, and overflowing with extra chairs placed along the sides, and deep into the hallway. The energy of Christmas Eve was electric with dozens of our regular faithful worshipers, their relatives and friends, kids returning home from far away, and the reinforcements of Christmas and Easter types who come out of tradition, sentimentality or family pressure. Bottom line; the "why" of their presence was inconsequential, they were there, and that is all that mattered.

From my hidden sideline nook, I often watch and observe the crowd, to gage and understand better what connects with people in the pews and what doesn't. Part way through the beautiful song and video, from my tangential observatory, I witnessed a most beautiful happening. The Gospel was being enfleshed, right there before my eyes!

A middle-aged First Lutheran couple sat a few rows away but clearly visible from my perch. These two people are wonderful, down to earth, real, honest, hard-working, devout, faith-filled, fun-loving, giving, affirming, servant types whom I am proud to call friends. They have already raised four children of their own into young adulthood, and each of their children is unique, positive, wonderful young men and women.

In recent years, this couple has taken upon themselves as part of their life, calling, and ministry to be foster parents. I am always amazed by the love, and selflessness shown by this family, as they have taken in several young people over the years that have been abandoned, neglected or abused. Within this family, these lost kids have found stability, safety, love and a place to belong.

Sitting next to the mother, this Christmas Eve, sat a young boy, maybe ten or elevenish we shall call Daniel. This was a second time around for Daniel and this foster family. Daniel had spent several months with this foster family awhile back until the great news had arrived, that he and his four siblings were to be adopted permanently by his "forever family". A "forever family" is the ultimate goal for any foster child, who coming out dysfunction, neglect, abuse or trauma crave a home, a place of safety, a loving set of parents, proper boundaries, and place to belong. He had gone off to his "forever family" to be reunited with his four siblings into one home. That is until the sixth month trial period had ended, and Daniel was once again rejected due to a variety of behavioral issues. His four siblings had adjusted well and now were permanently embedded into this "forever family". Daniel though, returned into the foster care system, once again rejected and defeated. I can only imagine the negative self-talk and low self-esteem that must pour through Daniel's thought process.

So now, once again, Daniel had been invited into this church family as a foster child. These two compassionate, faith-filled parents were now of late, pondering, mulling over, contemplating, and most importantly praying about a very, very difficult decision; should they, now in their mid-50's adopt this young boy, who has been rejected by all others. I cannot even imagine all that must be considered in the weight of this heavy decision.

And so, it came to pass this Christmas Eve that Daniel, sat alongside his foster mother, twiddling and fidgeting with a Lego toy he had recently assembled. On the screen of Celebration Hall played a touching video of Mary, that so realistically portrayed her fear, struggle, anxiety, and confusion of understanding God's will in bringing a child into the world through her own womb, named Jesus. The beautiful song being played and sang was titled *"Be Born in Me"*, and having viewed it a dozen times before, it still choked me up. In the end, Mary simply surrenders to God's will, even without full comprehension of what it meant. She offers these words; *"I am not brave, I'll never be. The only thing my heart can offer is a vacancy, I'm just a girl, nothing more, I am willing, I am yours."*

And as the words of this chorus echoed over the packed room, the foster mother quietly and slowly lifted her arm and gently placed it over and around the small shoulders of Daniel drawing him softly into her loving grasp.

Here ends… or maybe begins, the Gospel of the foster mom.

Then he said to them, "Whoever welcomes this little child in my name welcomes me, and whoever welcomes me welcomes the one who sent me. For it is the one who is least among you all who is the greatest."
Luke 9:48 NIV

Climbing Blind

The room was a beehive of activity. Noise and commotion ruled. Vertical ropes tout with weight swayed to and fro. Shouts of support and encouragement rose from ground level upwards and echoed off the 30' high walls. Just another typical Sunday night for our *"In Search of Faith and Footholds"* confirmation class.

Twenty-some students and adult leaders were crammed into the tiny floor space of the Y-West climbing wall room to learn the basic skills of rock climbing and follow-up bible study. I've always had a personal beef that we as a church miss the boat when it comes to kids and learning about God. We take kids who have sat in a classroom for the better part of 8 hours a day and been "spoken at," then repeat that process on a Wednesday night by "speaking at" them in a 20-minute lecture (sermon,) then spend another hour "speaking at" them in another class. Seems to me… there's got to be a better way to share, show and reveal who God is to young people. Thus, my attempt through this class!

This evening would be our fourth and final class. All participants had made fantastic progress throughout our weeks in learning to trust in the rock-climbing process. They had learned to trust in the mechanics of an immovable solid anchor, a sturdy and reliable rope, and a trustworthy and competent belayer. All of us had had to face our fear of heights, fear of falling, fear of even starting, fear of looking foolish and most of all our fear of failure. We had learned in a visceral sense (i.e. real life, full-body, whole person-physical-mental, and spiritual sense,) not from a book or a lecture, that when we place our faith and trust in a worthy strong/sturdy anchor, we can then take risks, we can go for it, we can try for the next move and not worry about failing or falling, and we know that if we do fall... it's not ultimate failure because we are held safely and securely by our anchor, rope and caring competent belayer.

In our Bible studies, we had talked extensively about God as our rock-solid anchor and that our rope could be the strong connecting link of prayer between climber and anchor. We had digested the differences between imagined/ anxious fear and real fears. We had processed the gap between our perceived self-limits and what we are actually capable of when we have complete trust in a loving forgiving God. We conversed extensively about when we know that we are held safely by God, we are freer to take risks and step beyond our comfort zones.

But this our final night of climbing would be different. Tonight, we would climb blindfolded.

The nervousness and anxiety in the room were palpable. I could hear the silent doubts and uncertainties reverberate throughout the room. *"How can he expect us to climb without our sight?"*

Michael, one of our young middle-schoolers approached me with apprehension as I tied him into his belay line. He placed his blindfold over his eyes and let out a big sigh. We quietly issued our back and forth safety commands and then he began his slow ascent. Floundering and flailing at first, he soon gained his first hand and footholds. He methodically felt his way slowly up the wall, searching left and right with one hand first, then a foot, then the other hand. Sometimes he would backtrack or back down to a more secure stance or handhold, but he maintained strong perseverance. Quietly and steadily he took his climb one foothold and one hand hold at a time. No need to look ahead and see the whole difficult route, for the blindfold took away that future worrying. Live in the now, focus on the next step.

I was very proud of Michael, for in previous sessions he had been timid about going higher. He had been shy about taking risks and was slow to push himself. Yet here he was taking on a tough climb and pushing through his own fears and insecurities. He was changing before my very eyes.

He climbed slow and steady and seemed to gain confidence the further up the wall he went. He seemed to relax into the climb. He appeared as though he had complete trust and confidence in his belayer and anchor, and so falling or failing became a moot point. He was simply free to climb and achieve great heights. Within a few short minutes, I shouted out *"Congratulations Michael! You made it!! You're already at the top! Well done! Way to go Michael! You did it!"* The look of surprise and joy on his face lit up the room as I gently lowered him back to mother earth. After removing his blindfold, we high fived, and I told him how proud I was of him. He had done well.

In real life, we rarely get to see the clear path laid out before us. We don't get a roadmap or private instructions for what will happen next. To be sure, there will be many difficulties, hardships, struggles, backtracking, and wrong turns. Moments of confusion, chaos, and uncertainty. There will be times when we don't think we're going to make it and feel our strength has completely run out.

I really think God made life this way on purpose. After all, if we could see exactly where we are headed, knew exactly how to get there, and we knew the guaranteed outcome… we would have no need for faith!

Brennan Manning in his book, <u>Ruthless Trust,</u> really nails it. *"Craving clarity, we attempt to eliminate the risk of trusting God. Fear of the unknown path stretching ahead of us destroys childlike trust in the Father's active goodness and unrestricted love. Our trust does not always bring final clarity on this earth. It does not still the chaos or dull the pain or provide a crutch. When all else is unclear, the heart of trust says, as Jesus did on the cross, "into your hands I commit my spirit". The way of trust is a movement into obscurity, into the undefined, into ambiguity, not into some predetermined, clearly delineated plan for the future. The next step discloses itself only out of a discernment of God acting in the desert of the present moment. The reality of naked trust is the life of a pilgrim who leaves what is nailed down, obvious and secure and walks into the unknown without any rational explanation to justify the decision or guarantee the future.*

Why? Because God has signaled the movement and offered it his presence and his promise."

Climbing blindfolded has much to teach us about our own life and faith journey. Sometimes we need to slow down, feel our way prayerfully through our current situation, and trust that God will see us through and provide us with the exact very next hand or foothold that we need in life, just one step at a time. When we know that we are held securely, safely, and strongly by a loving compassionate God, we can live in the now without having to know or see the entire journey laid out before us. And then… our life becomes a constant journey of intimacy, trust, and faith with our Maker.

May you know that your Creator loves you, and holds you safely in his strong, dependable arms. You can trust Him. You do not need to know the way. Simply trust and climb!

The most persistent choice you face; is whether to trust Me or to worry. You will never run out of things to worry about, but you can choose to trust Me no matter what. Jesus Calling, Sarah Young

> *My grace is sufficient for you, for my power is made perfect in your weakness. 2 Corinthians 12:9 NIV*

For I know the plans I have for you declares the Lord, plans to prosper you and not to harm you, plans to give you hope and a future. Jeremiah 29:11 NIV

> *For we live by faith, not by sight. 2 Corinthians 5:7 NIV*

> *The righteous will live by faith." Galatians 3:11 NIV*

Coming of the Dawn

The twin sisters; silence and solitude were the uninvited yet requisite guests of my morning. They had quietly accompanied me since leaving my car parked along the desolate and forgotten backroad south of Kindred. I now sat perched in my tree-stand in complete blackened darkness awaiting the birth of a new morning. The thermometer had read six below zero, yet being properly dressed from head to toe in wool and down, with bulky boots and poofy mittens, and being warmed by my internal furnace from the half-mile walk in, I was perfectly cozy, warm and content.

I embrace and cherish these early morning sits. The darkness shuts down all normal visual stimuli, and without TVs, or radios, or cell phones beeping or blaring the noise of the world is drowned out by the deafening silence leaving none of the usual amusements or distractions that divert us from our true selves and communing with our Maker. Without the external noises, one is forced to pay attention to what's going on in one's own head and heart. Issues come to the surface that need to be addressed, yesterday can be reviewed and thanks given for the many blessings or Godly encounters. There is also time to look forward to what may lie ahead in the day and seek out Godly wisdom for that which we cannot see. The silence and solitude and darkness are actually blessings for beginning a new day.

But the best part of a hunting morning is that the darkness is only temporary, and I know with a certainty beyond most any knowing in my life, that soon, the light will eventually pierce the sky and flood the landscape and world around me. And with the coming of this marvelous light comes also warmth and color, life and vitality. The coming of the dawn is a pure gift. And many days this marvelous gift comes wrapped in magnificent colors and textures that are pleasing to the eyes and soul.

Miraculously, this coming of the dawn gift has transpired each and every day for the 58 short years of my own life. By rough calculation, that's at least 21,170 sunrises in my own life, some of which I have acknowledged and given thanks for, and yet the great bulk of these "coming of the dawns" I have taken for granted, overlooked, ignored, or never noticed. What a shame and tragedy this is. One of the greatest gifts that God has given to us; the dawning of one more day to live, most of us barely acknowledge or notice.

God is beyond generous. He gives this gift to **all** peoples regardless of their beliefs, creeds, color, politics, nationality, or finances. He graces the entire planet with this gift each and every day since the dawn of time and long, long before we humans ever walked the planet. This gift is given to all regardless of circumstances, habits, career, finances or personality. And miraculously He gives to **all** of us regardless of who acknowledges the gift or the giver.

With the coming of the dawn today, God will shed his light on **all** people. Some will plod through work or school groaning and moaning the whole way, others will give thanks for the gift of work and a meaningful career. Some with give birth to new life, others will breathe their last breath. Some will be anxious, afraid and worried, others will find peace and contentment from knowing God. Some will argue or fight or give the silent treatment, others will embrace in the tangle of passionate lovemaking. Some will live for themselves seeking only selfish gain, others will seek to serve and lift up. Some will use their tongues to curse and swear and berate, others will praise and affirm in order to bless others by building them up. Some will stumble, fall and fail, others will find success and achieve great victories. Some will destroy and damage, others will create and build. Some will lament what they lack, others will simply give thanks for what has been given.

What is for certain, is that God sheds his light generously upon **all** of us. What will you do with the incredible gift that you have been given today; the gift of one more coming of the dawn?

And God said, "Let there be light," and there was light. And God saw that the light was good. And God separated the light from the darkness. God called the light Day, and the darkness he called Night. And there was evening and there was morning, the first day. ... Genesis 1:3-5 NIV

As long as the earth remains, there will be springtime and harvest, cold and heat, winter and summer, day and night." Genesis 8:22 TLB

that you may be children of your Father in heaven. He causes his sun to rise on the evil and the good and sends rain on the righteous and the unrighteous. Matthew 5:45 NIV

*The people walking in darkness have seen a great light;
on those living in the land of deep darkness, a light has
dawned. Isaiah 9:2 NIV*

*he is like the light of morning at sunrise
on a cloudless morning,
like the brightness after rain
that brings grass from the earth.' 2 Samuel 23:4 NIV*

Comparison

I sat in the comfortable receiving room awaiting a visit with my good friend. There were several nicely-done glass cabinets that held a myriad of plaques, awards, commendations, and trophies. All well-deserved by my dear friend who had become highly successful in the business world. I thought back to my own office. I don't have a single plaque, award, commendation or trophy hanging in mine. I could feel the ugly head of the **critic within** beginning the assault of attack-oriented questions; *"Why don't you have any of awards hanging in your office? What's wrong with you? How come you haven't achieved excellence or recognition or acclaim in your world?"* I had already placed one foot on the dangerous slide of comparison. The slippery descent had begun.

I was soon greeted with a big bear hug, warm smile and ushered into my friend's office. We go back a long way so it was good to catch up on life, family, and work. It felt good to be with my friend. As we did so he rattled off a list of recent accomplishments, new sales records, new purchases, entrepreneurial undertakings, speaking engagements, and impressive investments. And he had rightfully earned all of those by being bold, daring, wise and taking good risks. I had to admit I was quite impressed. But soon that ugly voice inside my head, the **critic within,** began taunting me again; *"What have you done lately of any note? Where are your investments and significant purchases? You're still in the same old job you've been at for 23 years! How come you haven't achieved* *any acclaim or fame or wealth?"* The pit in my stomach betrayed that I had already begun slipping into the ugly pit of comparison.

I had wrongly compared apples to oranges. I had fallen for one of the oldest and most reliable tricks in the devil's toolbox: "comparing." Comparing ourselves to others has only two outcomes and neither is helpful or beneficial. When I compare myself to another and come out on top so to speak, I can be filled with a sense of pride, ego, and superiority. That may feel good on the inside, but it gives off a nasty stench of arrogance and narcissism to others. On the flip side, as I had experienced in my friend's office, when I feel like I don't measure up, I experience a downward spiral into envy, jealousy, lowered self-esteem and self-pity. Both are ugly and ungodly ways to experience life. And if we leave our thought life unchecked, we can live in those dark spaces for long periods of our lives. Comparing ourselves to others never ends well!

Thank God that he provides proper mental feeding and correct thought process training via the compass bearings of scripture! All the better reason to make sure that quiet times of prayer and scripture reading are a vital part of your daily routine. These excellent habits get us back on track with good mental health and help us douse the fires of the devil's taunting and the negative and belittling voice of the critic within.

May you listen to the one true voice that counts!

Make a careful exploration of who you are and the work you have been given, and then sink yourself into that. Don't be impressed with yourself. Don't compare yourself with others. Each of you must take responsibility for doing the creative best you can with your own life. Galatians 6:4-5 MSG

Do not conform to the pattern of this world but be transformed by the renewing of your mind. Then you will be able to test and approve what God's will is—his good, pleasing and perfect will. Romans 12:2 NIV

> *You shall not covet your neighbor's house. You shall not covet your neighbor's wife, or his male or female servant, his ox or donkey, or anything that belongs to your neighbor." Exodus 20:17 NIV*

Do you not realize that Christ Jesus is in you?
2 Corinthians 13:5 NIV

being confident of this, that he who began a good work in you will carry it on to completion until the day of Christ Jesus. Philippians 1:6 NIV

But he said to me, "My grace is sufficient for you, for my power is made perfect in weakness." Therefore I will boast all the more gladly about my weaknesses, so that Christ's power may rest on me.
2 Corinthians 12:9 NIV

CONDUIT

Shane sat on the stairs of our entry landing putting on his shoes ready to go outside. I had just returned from church and I stood hovering directly in front of him. Pulling out a white envelope from my coat pocket, I carefully tore open one end of it, a slight smile growing across my face. Licking my fingertip, I carefully began peeling off one bill at a time placing each one in his hands. With each bill, his eyes grew larger. After counting off 25 clean, crisp, brand-new $100 bills, he looked up at me with expectant and hopeful eyes; "For me?" I laughed out loud and quietly replied; "Sorry dude! Nice try! Not!" His look of disappointment was palpable and laughable.

Following one of our Celebration worship services earlier in the day, a couple had pulled me aside and handed me the envelope. The husband winked, the wife smiled and said; "You know what to do." The transfer had been made. I had now become temporary owner... no, maybe more like a temporary custodian of $2,500 cold, hard cash. The instructions were simple enough, just give it to those I deem in need. I had been entrusted, empowered and now had become the steward of this cash. What a phenomenal opportunity and privilege. What an enormous responsibility.

This scenario was not new to me. The past five or six years this couple has done the same thing. They trusted that I, through my position at church, would know of folks who could use a special Christmas surprise gift. No parameters were given; not how many people, nor any limit per person. Just a pure faith that I could be trusted with what had been given.

I smiled at the opportunity and the power given to me to impact others in a positive financial way. I also felt a tinge of anxiety as I felt the enormous responsibility for which I had been entrusted. How would I know if I got it right? How would I know if I gave to people truly in need? To alleviate my anxiety, I did what I've always done… I started praying. "Lord, grant me a Godly, Holy Spirit wisdom, to know in my gut… when, and who, and how much." The days to come would bring a continual dialogue of seeking, asking and discerning.

First to ring my *"God in the Gut"* instinct bell was a gentleman from our men's group. He had just been laid off. Lots of medical bills, house payments, and thoughts of an empty Christmas and was staring Him in the face. Lunch at the Fryingpan Restaurant and a blank envelope filled with cash was handed across the table. I told him; *"This is not my money, I am simply the conduit, the channel, the agent who brings this gift on behalf of another. May God bless you through this gift."* He said very little, but I know the money had to be a blessing. I left the encounter with a big smile and warm feeling inside.

Second stop was a bar. I left an envelope filled with money for a young 19, year-old woman who grew up in our church. Two separate major tragedies had robbed her of the love and life of both her mother and father. The bar owners knew how to contact her and promised to deliver the gift to her personally. She had cut off all contact and connections with me long ago, maybe from pain, maybe from anger toward God. I knew not the specifics of the reasons or rational but knew in my gut the right thing was to bless her. Along with the cash, I left this note in the envelope. *"This is not my money, I am simply the conduit, the channel, the agent who brings this gift on behalf of another. May God bless you through this gift."* I left the encounter with a big smile and warm feeling inside.

Days later, I stopped at a local school. A young woman works there who had been widowed a few years back when her husband lost a hard-fought battle with cancer. She had since been raising her four young daughters alone. I can only imagine the trials and struggles of parenting alone, let alone the financial struggles from one meager income. I gave her a big bear hug and told her what an awesome mother she was to those four girls. I thanked her for her loving and compassionate work with all the kids of this school. I then reminded her: *"This is not my money, I am simply the conduit, the channel, the agent who brings this gift on behalf of another. May God bless you through this gift."* Tears wet her eyes and a look of deep gratitude and relief filled her face. I left the encounter with a big smile and warm feeling inside.

Earlier in the fall, I had led a retreat at one of our local high schools. Near the end of this retreat in the darkness of our candlelight campfire, a young lady opened up to her classmates about what a struggle her life had been of late. Through tears and a stammering, cracked voice, she shared that she and her mom had been homeless for a period of time. This scene had stuck with me all fall. The tug in my gut moved me to query via kids I knew from church about her name. Two days later I showed up in the office of this school with an envelope filled with cash, and the girl's name written on the outside. I told the secretary to make sure that this was delivered to the student, with strict and firm directions that this is anonymous. Inside the envelope were these same words; *"This is not my money, I am simply the conduit, the channel, the agent who brings this gift on behalf of another. May God bless you through this gift."* I left the encounter with a big smile and warm feeling inside.

What an incredible blessing it had been to be the one who "gets to be" the giver and the visible face of such beautiful gifts. I was so richly blessed and uplifted by being the giver of someone else's money. But as I moved through this season, I was reminded that what I had been experiencing is exactly what real stewardship is all about. Using what God has given to us, to then use to bless others. We often forget, that whatever money we have in our wallet, bank account or portfolio, is actually **God's money** on loan to us temporarily, to steward, to take care of and use for Godly good in the world. This goes for our possessions, our time, our gift packages, our talents, and our skill sets as well. We can use what we have been given to selfishly hoard and fulfill just our wants and desires, or we can learn to bless others by what we have been given.

We are each a channel or conduit if you will, of God's blessings. Much as an extension cord is used to take power to a light or appliance, we called to do the same. There is no power in an extension cord. It is simply a connector or carrier that passes on the power and electricity given to it by the power source. Without being "plugged in" to a source of power, we have nothing to give.

The reality of being a conduit of God is that we are called to pass on so much more than cash. Godly men and women, we are called to pass on what has first been given to us; forgiveness, compassion, second chances, grace, and love. And the beauty and wonder of giving these blessings away are that we get blessed in the process! We may leave an encounter with a smile on our face and a warm feeling inside.

During this season, I pray that you and I would realize how richly we have been blessed. If this is true, I challenge you to give away blessings that were first given to you to bless others.

Give, and it will be given to you. A good measure, pressed down, shaken together and running over, will be poured into your lap. For with the measure you use, it will be measured to you." Luke 6:38 NIV

Each of you should give what you have decided in your heart to give, not reluctantly or under compulsion, for God loves a cheerful giver. 2 Corinthians 9:7 NIV

A generous person will prosper; whoever refreshes others will be refreshed. Proverbs 11:25 NIV

You will be enriched in every way so that you can be generous on every occasion, and through us your generosity will result in thanksgiving to God. 2 Corinthians 9:11 NIV

Contrasts

Shane and I stepped off the Green Line Metro. The excitement and anticipation were palpable for each of us. People of all sizes and shapes scurried to and fro. The cold December air brought a chill to our faces and steamed our breath. Shane's eyes grew large and his smile broadened as he looked skyward toward the pinnacle of the pointed roof... and there before us, in all its glory stood the brand-new US Bank Stadium. Our long pilgrimage from Fargo had finally brought us to Mecca, and we were beyond pumped to cheer on our beloved Vikings.

We entered the colossal structure in awe of its grandeur and magnificence. Truly a marvel to behold.

Taking our seats, we soon joined 66,000 others in screaming and cheering for The Defenders of the North. Purple and gold were everywhere and we joined in as the SKOL chant accelerated with each beat of the deafening drum. Loud music blared between downs, the ginormous screens brought controversial replays, patriotic vignettes, and Pride of the North interviews from Hall of Fame Vikings players. Scantily clad cheerleaders danced to fast-paced hip-hop music tossing their hair back and forth continuously and smiled for the cameras. Each defensive down, the noise level rose to deafening levels as we the fans took our *12th man* role seriously raising the roof with an uproar and din that made it hard to even think. Shane and I were thrilled to be a part of it all and got caught up in the emotion, production, and hype of it all.

The following afternoon, I was quietly ushered into my tiny

hermitage or cabin at Pacem In Terris(Peace on Earth). Stepping inside the simple one-room hermitage, felt like coming home, or putting on a warm, familiar, and cozy blanket. This was my seventh 7th such journey into the silence and solitude of Pacem, and I couldn't wait to slide into the stillness and quiet rhythm of this peaceful setting.

The weekend is restful and cleansing, and solitude and silence are the tools God uses to calm one's soul, quiet the noise and incessant chatter of our fast-paced, ever moving world. Time is spent staring out the large picture window, thinking, contemplating, reading scripture, conversing with our maker, rocking in the rocking chair and simply being still and silent; something most of us avoid at all costs. Occasional walks via the many trails and woods bring healthy, gentle, exercise and fresh air to lungs and brain alike. Nature can have a marvelous healing and calming effect on body and soul. Many Pacem partakers report napping and sleeping like never before. A common post-Pacem report is; "I never knew how tired I was until I stepped into that Hermitage!" A Godly rest, is what the Pacem workers call it.

What a contrast it was for me to move from the colossal stadium filled with constant and deafening noise to the absolute silence of my Pacem hermitage. What a contrast it was to sit amongst 66,000 screaming Vikings fans to sitting alone in a rocking chair in pure solitude. What a contrast it was to pass through all the hype, the show, the extravaganza, the constant stimulus and the show of the Vikings spectacle, to sitting still in a tiny one-room cabin. What a contrast moving from what the world lifts up as super important, essential and central to waiting on the Lord for the real-life critical and crucial. What a contrast moving from the frivolous, trivial, shallow and superficial, to the heart of the matter in God's eyes. What a contrast moving from a "game," to the depth of human existence and relevance both here and now, and for our future with God.

Pacem is a journey all too often shunned, pushed aside or neglected by the masses. It is a journey that must be done alone. It is the journey feared by most that we all must take; the journey inward to face ourselves. Most of us live our lives like a Vikings game, filled with constant motion, hype, movement, and filled with the unimportant, in order to avoid facing ourselves. In the silence and solitude, we discover our true selves in the presence of our Maker, Counselor, God, and Friend. We end up facing our fears, sins, insecurities, shortcomings, anxieties, and inadequacies. But more importantly, we meet face to face with Jesus and His unconditional love, forgiveness, acceptance, rest, comfort, purpose, direction and meaning. Most of us come away from this solitude feeling cleansed, rested, renewed, re-created, and refreshed.

*He said to them, "**Come with me by yourselves** to a quiet place and get some rest." Mark 6:31* NIV

*"**Come to me, all** you **who are weary** and burdened, and I will give you rest. Take my yoke upon you and learn from **me**, for I am gentle and humble in heart, and you will find rest for your souls. For my yoke is easy and my burden is light." Matthew 11:28-30* NIV

I give thanks for the joy and fun of the Vikings. I will forever be a fanatical and passionate purple and gold super fan. I am grateful for the fun, distraction and spectacles of a Vikings game. But more importantly, I give great thanks that we have the privilege of spending significant time with our Creator and Maker one-on-one in solitude and silence. You do not need to go to Pacem In Terris to experience this marvelous solitude. Simply find a quiet space and spend some time one on one with God.

Dancing With Buffalos

The blazing heat had beat down upon us all day long. The eighty plus degrees a rare gift for late October had left us parched on the dusty and dry Maah Daah Hey trail. The spectacular sights and scenic vistas had not disappointed as every bend and twist in the rugged trail had left us in awe. Golden cottonwoods flashed brightly against the deep dark green of juniper choked hillsides and the multi-colored horizontal striations of greys, purples, pinks, and ochers reminded us we were in classic badlands. We quietly passed alongside strangely shaped formations of wind and water sculpted clay, that could have passed for alien fortresses on a faraway planet. Our ten-mile hike had taken its toll, making us bone weary and anxious to find a source of fresh water to fill our empty water bottles and quench our yearning thirst.

The sun's rays were making the peaceful long shadows of late afternoon as we finally found a small system of beaver ponds in the normally bone-dry sand-filled creek bed. We were relieved to set up a cozy campsite alongside the creek and filter-up clean, fresh, cool water. It felt good to be in such a beautiful wide valley with a good source of water and a protected camp.

As we ate our supper, we could hear grunting, snorting, and hoofbeats and much to our surprise and delight rounding the bend of a nearby hillside appeared a herd of buffalo! Unaware of our presence they were headed directly to our same water source! At sixty some yards, they paused briefly, pondering the strange sights and most likely smells of these humanoid creatures. After a tense standoff, they wisely chose a parallel trail that detoured around our campsite and they headed back up into the hills!

Brilliant warm sunshine greeted our next morning. Being our layover day, following a hearty breakfast, we headed up into the Achenbach Hills to see if we could locate the herd. After climbing for a couple of hours and gaining the high grassy plateau we finally crested the final ridge. A stiff warm breeze whipped our clothing and hair and a magnificent 360-degree view of the Little Missouri was our reward. And there below us, to the north, stood a small herd of buffalo! We had found them.

The small herd began moving up and to our right and appeared as though they would cross our very ridgeline. We began to follow along the crest hoping to intercept and get closer to this small band of bison. We ran along the ridge and headed up a small knoll that marked the apex. Unbeknownst to us, as we topped the crestline, there before us lay the entire herd of buffalo just 50 yards away!

We stood in awe and wonder as each of the forty plus bison ran over the ridgeline just a stone's throw away and headed for the grassy bowl we had just come through. We were seated ringside, center aisle, to a magnificent display of power, grace and natural wonder. A rare treat that few on this planet are privileged to witness. I could do nothing but smile and give thanks and gratitude for being able to witness such a spectacular phenomenon.

We had come to hike the Maah Daah Hey for a variety of reasons. Some had come to test their mettle, to find out what they're made of. Some had come to explore, some had come to step away from their routines, to break away from their cell phones and experience nature on her own terms. Some of us had come to walk and talk with our Creator, to immerse ourselves in the solitude and quiet of nature. Some just came for the pure fun and adventure of it all. But none of us had expected or hoped to run and dance alongside the buffalo!

I often find that when I say "yes" to one of God's invitations to step out of my comfort zone, to get outside of my normal routines or step outside my box of habitual ways, He gifts me with additional blessings and bonus surprises! When He finally gets us to say "yes," he pours out his blessings and treasures in great abundance! And often in ways or forms that we had never anticipated or expected.

On this particular hiking trip, we received the many blessings of the trip itself; healthy physical exercise, fresh clean air, mind-boggling scenery, tremendous comradery and deepened friendships, solitude, stillness and serenity for quiet time and reflection, fantastic scenery, a sense of accomplishment and "I did it!" Many of us experienced a deepening of our relationship with Jesus. But I believe God threw in many bonuses, icing on the cake so to speak.

God is the greatest giver of gifts. He is generous beyond anything we can humanly comprehend. When we say "yes" to His invitation, I believe he smiles, and then he pours out blessing after blessing.

May you say "Yes!" to a Godly invitation to grow!

I have come that they may have life and have it to the full. John 10:10 NIV

The Lord is my shepherd, I lack nothing. He makes me lie down in green pastures,
he leads me beside quiet waters, he refreshes my soul.
He guides me along the right paths for his name's sake.
Even though I walk through the darkest valley I will fear no evil, for you are with me;
your rod and your staff, they comfort me.
You prepare a table before me in the presence of my enemies.
You anoint my head with oil; my cup overflows.
Surely your goodness and love will follow me all the days of my life,
and I will dwell in the house of the Lord forever. Psalm 23 NIV
Out of his fullness, we have all received grace in place of grace already given. John 1:16 NIV

Every good and perfect gift is from above, coming down from the Father of the heavenly lights, who does not change like shifting shadows. James 1:17 NIV

Dave and Rory

I drove down our street, returning home from an early morning errand. The sun was bright and the skies showed blue. A gem of a spring day was blessing all who would experience it. On the big curve in our street where it bends north, I could see him walking. I frequently see him walking with his dog throughout our neighborhood enjoying the life-giving exercise of a good walk and a new day. I slowed my big truck from my normal hurried pace and pressed the small lever to lower my passenger side window as I carefully pulled up alongside him to have a little chat.

He seemed pleased that someone would stop to visit, by the smile on his face as he eased both himself and his dog closer to my window. "Hi, Dave! Rollie Johnson here," I began, and he bellowed back a "Good morning," as his hands felt for the truck window. He is always very friendly, and seems eager to chat, always upbeat, positive and I enjoy hearing what he has been up to, where he's been or his take on today's events. Today he was not wearing his sunglasses. His eyelids were closed and appeared a bit sunken, but in spite of being completely blind, he maintained a very positive outlook.

In spite of having no sight, his viewpoint is always upbeat and full of gratitude. In spite of having no vision, his insight, observations, and awareness are keen and optimistic. I thought of my own moodiness throughout the Easter weekend from relationships, finances, aches, and pains, weather, work, etc., and humbly remembered ... ***"Sometimes it takes a blind man to teach us how to see."***

I stood in the expansive commons and cafeteria of the new Davies High School waiting. I watched smiling, as his attendant pushed with all her might as they fought through the hurricane force gusts of the long wind tunnel to get to the doors. Once again, I was impressed... as always, right on time! My good friend and age-mate Rory had arrived, and we were due down the hall shortly to speak to the girl's track team. I greeted both of them with my usual joking and teasing and he responded right back with his wide open-mouthed smile and laughter. It always feels good to be in his presence. We switched drivers and I got behind the wheelchair and pushed him down the long hall and then prepared the room for our little spiel.

Soon the room was filled with beautiful, athletic, young ladies and their coaches. The audience was expectant and attentive as they always are when Rory speaks. And how ironic, that all the audiences that we speak to, are so tuned in to Rory, who has long ago lost his ability to speak due to his tragic stroke?

The head coach asked his pre-numbered questions to Rory, who had stored his pre-typed answers in his computer which is mounted to his wheel chair. Rory now used his eyes to manipulate the screen which reads his irises, and he then clicks on letters or answers by blinking his eyes. He methodically and carefully scanned his screen and then blinked on # 3, then blinked on the command button; "Speak" and his computer voice spit out the following response:

"Before my stroke eight-plus years ago, I was like most folks, worrying about stuff that really doesn't matter, but I thought it did. I was running, and life was passing me by. What I have learned is this; don't wish your life away. It is all the little things that I miss the most. And remember to live every day like it's a gift... because it is." Rory Eidsness

70 sets of eyes were glued on Rory and every ear absorbed the wisdom pouring forth from Rory via his computer voice. Sometimes we need to hear the voice of a man who has had so much taken away from him, to realized and appreciate and recognize and give thanks for the 10,000 blessings we experience each day but fail to acknowledge.

May you take time today, to stop, smell the roses and give thanks to your Maker for the infinite blessings and gifts that have been poured out upon you.

And Whatever you do, whether in word or deed,
do it all in the name of the Lord Jesus,
giving thanks to God the Father through him. Colossians 3:17 NIV

…Whatever is true, whatever is noble, whatever is right, whatever is pure, whatever is lovely, whatever is admirable- if anything is excellent or praiseworthy- Think about such things! Philippians 4:8 NIV

Be joyful always, pray at all times, be thankful in all circumstances. This is what God wants from you in your life in union with Christ Jesus.1 Thessalonians 5: 16-18 GNT

There is nothing wrong with happiness. It's wonderful. The only problem is that it's based on circumstances, and circumstances tend to shift. Joy is not a feeling. Joy is a choice. It is not based on circumstances; it is based upon attitude.
Pain is inevitable but misery is optional. We cannot avoid, pain, but we can avoid joy. God has given us such immense freedom that he will allow us to be as miserable as we want to be.
Joy is simple (not to be confused with easy) At any moment in life we have at least two options, and one of them is to choose an attitude of gratitude, a posture of grace, a commitment to Joy.
Tim Hansel- You Gotta Keep Dancing

The Constitution only gives people the right to pursue happiness. You have to catch it yourself. ~ Ben Franklin

Do not conform to the pattern of this world but be transformed by the renewing of your mind. Then you will be able to test and approve what God's will is—his good, pleasing and perfect will. Romans 12:2 NIV

DECK

The sweet inviting scent of freshly cut clover drifted over from the dike where a farmer had recently cut his first crop of hay. A deep breath of that fragrant air brought life and vitality to my tired and sore body. The morning's cool breeze was invigorating as I readied for the day's task at hand. Soon the aroma of freshly cut pine brought a smile to my face as the miter saw spit out thousands of bits of sawdust that coated my face, hair, and arms with a fine pale dusting.

The rhythmic "klink," "klink" of my tool belt gave a steady beat as I carried heavy board after heavy board of green treated lumber from the driveway to my back yard. The quiet cooing of mourning doves echoed from the canopy of my heavily wooded yard, which I interpreted as helpful encouragement from these self-appointed avian supervisors. Warming sunlight filtered in from the eastern sky through my oak and ash trees making for a joyful and optimistic start to the morning.

The task at hand; rebuild our deck. Heretofore never having attempted a project of this nature before, I hesitantly dove in. Thank God for instructional books and YouTube Videos! To say I was intimidated and skeptical would be an understatement. But economics and the complete deterioration of the original deck made back in the '80s demanded action and immediacy. There would be no turning back!

The previous week had involved destruction and demolition of the old deck which had been rotting, and failing for years. Even the underlying support beams, posts, and joists would need to be removed for a complete restart and rebuild from the ground up. My 11-year-old son Shane and I soon developed a smooth synchronicity of teamwork using pry bars and hammers to remove plank after plank from the deck boards. For stubborn and rebellious boards, I introduced Shane to the *"Persuader,"* a six-pound sledgehammer and his younger brother the *"Intimidator,"* a three-pound hammer that were both highly successful at helping uncooperative and stubborn resistors. Shane seemed to relish and delight in coaxing rebellious boards with the power of the *Persuader* and *Intimidator*.

As we tore off plank after plank, occasionally a board would split in two. I was shocked to realize that beneath the surface of the gray, rotten, blackened, and weathered surface of many boards lay a solid, beautiful, sturdy heart of redwood. In fact, I soon began to realize that most of the boards had only superficial surface and end rot and that the great bulk of most boards held healthy, firm lumber deep inside. We began to slow down and use more caution as we soon realized that within many of these outwardly appearing old boards lay a hidden treasure of useful, practical and quite valuable redwood.

My mind has since been bubbling over with creative ideas of how I might repurpose and use this precious and prized resource. I had originally intended all of the old deck for firewood and kindling, but now I have realized that removing the old, and building my deck a new, has also brought the added and surprise gift of this free and spectacular resource of cherished redwood.

Many of us are so slow and resistant to letting go of the old. It's familiar, it's comfortable, it's less work, it's habitual, it's known, and it's much easier. It takes a lot of effort and energy to tear down, throw away, clean out and remove the old, to make room for something new; a new outlook, a new attitude, a new approach, a new project, a new ministry, a new career, or a new relationship. But I have been surprised by this deck project. Tearing out the old and cleaning up to make room for a new deck has been energizing and invigorating. I have found new life and vitality and creativity as I birth a new deck from foundations of footings and posts, joists and beams, brackets and deck boards. Square, plumb, and level have brought satisfaction and fulfillment. Purposeful action and visible progress and have brought contentment and pride for a job well done. And to top it all off, the outwardly ugly, unattractive and unappealing previous wood I had condemned to the funeral pyre, has now become a beautiful and treasured gift for repurposing.

God has a knack for taking old and worn-out objects, ideas, ministries, and people and making them new, useful and purposeful. He specializes in taking our weary and worn, to show us the beauty, integrity and purposeful use of what lies below the often neglected known and familiar exteriors.

Jesus especially excelled in seeing the worth and value of people below the surface. He saw beneath the abrasive and edgy surface of Zacchaeus. After the encounter, Zacchaeus left with a new outlook, attitude, and purpose. When Jesus knelt alongside the woman who had been caught in adultery, He did not see the well-used body and weary demeanor that all other men had seen each day. He instead looked to the beauty and goodness within her, treating her with dignity, forgiveness, and love. She left that Jesus encounter, a new woman, with a new perspective, new outlook and new self-identity.

Richard Foster gets it right in his book Prayer;

"Frequently we hold on so tightly to the good that we do know, that we cannot receive the greater good that we do not know. God has to help us let go of our tiny vision in order to release the greater good he has in store for us. In time we begin to enter into a grace-filled releasing of our will and flowing into the will of the father. It is the prayer of relinquishment or surrender that moves us from the struggling to the releasing. *Not my will but yours be done.*" We are to trust in the wisdom of God and ask for the grace to rest in his peace. When we surrender, we know that we are only falling into the strong and gentle arms of Jesus, fully satisfied, fully at rest."

We **all** go through ages and stages of feeling worn out, weary and broken. Or we may simply feel a vague sense of emptiness, meaningless, boredom or dull routine. In my twenty-one years of ministry in this church, I've been through many bouts or seasons if you will, of this general malaise. Through all of these times, God has repeatedly proven to be completely trustworthy and faithful in renewing and repurposing my life, ministry, and attitude. Sometimes he has completely torn out the old that no longer worked, to simply make room for something brand new. And many times, He has taken something that appeared old or broken, or weary and worn, to repurpose it with a new life, fresh vitality and recharged meaning.

May you surrender your life to the one who brings change, purpose, renewal, and meaning!

"Forget the former things; do not dwell on the past.
See, I am doing a new thing! Now it springs up; do you not perceive it?
Isaiah 43:18-19 NIV

Distracted

On a recent trip to the North Dakota Badlands, my son Shane and I happened upon a very large prairie dog town. There were hundreds of little dirt mounds in a very expansive field with grass mowed immaculately short by the resident rodents. Prairie dogs scurried to and fro to the safety of their underground bunkers and occasionally they stood at full attention scanning the horizons barking and chirping to sound the community alarm that foreign invaders were present. Our arrival had created quite a stir amidst the neighborhood.

Our dog Bruno had never witnessed such a scene before. The smells, sights, and sounds of the barking prairie dogs had put him in a frenzy as his hunting instincts came to full alert. He would chase one prairie dog as it popped it's head up from a hole only to disappear, and another would pop up on the near horizon and Bruno would chase after that one. A distant chirping would call him to pursue another direction and so he zigged and zagged, on and on in an endless game of "Whack-A-Mole." After thirty minutes of pure frustration and failures, he returned to us exhausted, spent, weary and worn. The look on his face spoke of humiliation and vexation.

Shane and I laughed at the whole situation as all of his attempts at success were thwarted. It was quite comical. But as I watched, I couldn't help but think that Bruno was mirroring for me a look at our own modern-day lives. I had laughed at him and his ridiculous pursuit of prairie dogs, yet he had shown me a fairly clear view of everyday life for most of us.

Paying Attention II

Most of us are overly distracted. We chase one thing after another and gain very little real success, peace or contentment. A new phone pops up over there with more bells and whistles so we run and chase after that newest, latest phone. We race from work mound to soccer mound, to hockey mound, to orchestra mound, to choir practice mound to church mound. Our work chirps at us for more and more so we pursue that at the expense of marriage and family. And even our church offers up fabulous new program/book/bible study that we need to grow so we chase after that. Dinner out at the local wings bar has seventy T.V.'s that chirp and bark for our attention so that our visual focus goes from game to game and rarely lands on the eyes of those with whom we are dining. Our IPad, iPods, Kindles, laptops and smartphones beep, bark, chirp, and ring constantly, begging to be answered instantly and call us in a dozen different directions.

Suddenly Bruno doesn't look so much the fool, but rather **we** that pursue the worldly game of "Whack-A-Mole." We race from mound to mound in the fruitless and endless game of busyness pursing all that glitters or chirps. We end up feeling exhausted, spent, weary and worn.

105

There is an antidote to the "Whack-A-Mole" lifestyle. It has nothing to do with pursuit, chasing or speed. It has everything to do with allowing yourself to be pursued and loved by your Maker. *"Be Still… and know that I am God."* (And we are not!) Psalm 46

"Come to me, all you that are weary and are carrying heavy burdens and I will give you rest. Take my yoke upon you, and learn from me; for I am gentle and humble in heart, and you will find rest for your souls. For my yoke is easy, and my burden is light." Matthew 11:28-30

It's pretty simple, yet not so easy. Carve out 7 minutes today, shut the door, go outside maybe, turn off all the chirping devices and Be Still before the Lord. He will then exchange your exhaustion, weary and worn for peace, purpose, passion, and contentment.

he leads me beside quiet waters, he refreshes my soul. Psalm 23:2-3 NIV

Be still before the Lord, And wait patiently for Him. Psalm 36:77 NIV

I waited patiently for the Lord; He turned to me and heard my cry. He lifted me up out of the slimy pit, Out of the muck and mire. He set my feet upon a rock And gave me a firm place to stand. He put a new song in my mouth, A hymn of praise to our God. Many will see and fear And put their trust in the Lord. (Psalm 40: 1-3) NIV

Dogbane

Glancing briefly at my weekly calendar I smiled. My own handwriting, that looks far more like chicken scratching than discernable penmanship, simply read "Collect Dogbane." Who am I to disobey my own orders that were written there earlier in mid-July? So off I went northward in the direction of Trollwood Park that lies alongside the Red River of the North. I was venturing forth on a treasure hunt of sorts and the positive expectations of potential discovery quickened my pace.

Months earlier in the heat of the summer, my friend Victor, son Shane and I were off on a bike ride. We had cruised the winding bike trails of Trollwood and stopped for a rest break where the trail met the bank of the Red River. The high humidity, fierce heat, and vigorous exercise had us sweating profusely and overheated. Shane blurted out; "Dad… we should just jump in and go swimming in the Red." The thought sounded like a great idea, and in a heartbeat, I replied; "Let's go for it!"

Within seconds we had discarded sweat soaked t-shirts, socks, and tennies and slithered down the sloped and muddied embankment into the cool and refreshing waters of the Red River. Ahhhh! What a relief it was! The chilled waters rejuvenated our spirits and bodies as we dove and swam against the current. What a gift this Red River was on a steamy summer's afternoon.

As I finished with my impromptu dip, I ascended the bank part way to dry myself in the sun. I happened to look down and notice a particular plant. The shape of its leaves and alternating leaf structure jogged something loose in my memory. I knelt down, and sure enough, its main stem was colored red. I grabbed a lobed shaped leaf and bent it in two. Sure enough, it oozed a milky-colored sticky sap. I did the same to the stem and the results were the same. My excitement grew. Had I finally found Dogbane, after all these years? I almost danced for joy! In looking around me I saw dozens of similar plants. Making a strong note of it to myself, I promised to write it in my calendar and come back and verify in October after the first frost.

As I walked the tarred bike path in the grey of a dreary fall day, my anticipation grew to the point of being giddy. Would I be able to find them again? Was I correct in identification? Was my timing for harvest correct? I crested the bank and descended to where I thought I remembered we had swum previously. Trying to match locations from the green and lush summer memories, to the now brown and tans of lifeless plants caused me to second guess my landmarks. I grabbed at a couple of plants in the cornucopia that grew everywhere around me. My samples just didn't look right. And then, there was the verification I had needed… hanging from a three- foot high red stemmed stalk … hung a couple of the narrow, three inches long "V" shaped seed pods! I was right! I cracked open the seed pod and sure enough, there were the downy parachute-like seeds waiting to launch!

Looking around me I soon discovered dozens of more plants as I began dancing, shouting out thank you prayers and collecting as many stalks as I could! After so many years of not knowing, I was now becoming familiar with Dog Bane, sometimes called Indian Hemp. Dogbane was one of the premier plants used by Native Americans for making cordage; i.e. rope, netting, snares, bowstrings, and harnesses. It is one of the strongest natural fibers and makes strong, durable and excellent cordage.

As I traversed the surrounding banks searching for more, I soon realized that in this one stretch of the Red River were also abundant shoots of both Milkweed and Stinging Nettles or as some call it "itch weed." Stinging Nettle is discernable by its squared stem when you roll it in your fingers, and common Milkweed by its large opened seed

Paying Attention II

pods. Stinging Nettle and Milkweed have long been my friends as I have collected them for years to teach cordage making.

I sat down to ponder and give thanks. Here I sat in a forgotten bend in of the Red River of the North.

Surrounding me on all sides were three of the most useful and talented plants that have gifted man for generations upon generations. I was sitting in natures very own hardware store. For twelve thousand plus years these three plants had been given as gifts from the Creator. And these gifts had been given in such outlandish abundance. In this tiny stretch of river bottom, there were perhaps hundreds or even thousands of stalks. And what about the other side of the river, and the hundreds of miles of this river? Not to mention the acres upon acres of fields and forest that surround us.

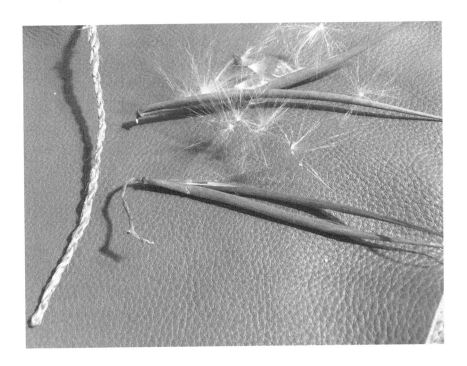

And yet to the common man or woman of our generation, we walk by, overlook and pass by without notice. We're in a hurry to get to the next appointment, meeting or practice. We race to buy the newest gizmo that rings, buzzes, and beeps. Yet in the process of hurry and consuming we miss the blessings that already surround us. Our appetites and frantic pace place us far from the blessings found in Creation that were specifically placed there for our use, pleasure, and enjoyment by our loving Creator.

Jesus speaks clearly and bluntly to his disciples: *"Because the knowledge of the secrets of the kingdom of heaven has been given to you, but not to them. Whoever has will be given more, and they will have an abundance. Whoever does not have, even what they have will be taken from them. This is why I speak to them in parables: Though seeing, they do not see; though hearing, they do not hear or understand.*

In them is fulfilled the prophecy of Isaiah

"'You will be ever hearing but never understanding you will be ever seeing but never perceiving. For this people's heart has become calloused; they hardly hear with their ears and they have closed their eyes. Otherwise, they might see with their eyes, hear with their ears understand with their hearts and turn, and I would heal them.' But blessed are your eyes because they see, and your ears because they hear. Matthew 13: 14-16 NIV

Could it be that during this Christmas season, what your soul craves, needs, and desires cannot be purchased or found in frenetic activity? Maybe what you need most from God is actually right here all around you for the taking. Peace, patience, joy, gratitude, acceptance, forgiveness, and purpose are given in abundance to those who seek and take time to sit and be still in the presence of our Creator. May you have eyes to see and ears to hear the many rich blessings of God that lay abundantly all around us.

And my God will meet all your needs according to the riches of his glory in Christ Jesus. Philippians 4:19 NIV

Every good and perfect gift is from above, coming down from the Father of the heavenly lights, who does not change like shifting shadows. James 1:17 NIV

And God is able to bless you abundantly, so that in all things at all times, having all that you need, you will abound in every good work. 2 Corinthians 9:8

From his abundance, we have all received one gracious blessing after another. John 1:16 NIV

I pray that the eyes of your heart may be enlightened so that you will know what is the hope of His calling, what are the riches of the glory of His inheritance in the saints, Ephesians 1:18 NIV

How blessed is the man who finds wisdom And the man who gains understanding. For her profit is better than the profit of silver And her gain better than fine gold. She is more precious than jewels; And nothing you desire compares with her. Proverbs 3:13-15 NIV

Eduardo

Footsteps could be heard descending our stairway. Immersed in the excitement of my latest sewing project; a new wind jacket for my daughter Karina, I raised my eyes to find my wife, Ady, standing before me with a look of great concern on her face late Sunday evening. She shared that she was receiving a series of texts indicating that no one from her Concordia Spanish Department, had heard from Eduardo, a fellow professor, over the entire weekend. He had missed a dinner out and not returned anyone's phone calls or texts. Eduardo is from Peru and is a beloved and loveable colleague for students and faculty alike. He lives alone in an apartment, and with no family here, great concern over his wellbeing was manifesting in those closest to him. Mary, the department chair, wisely and courageously took action to initiate a wellness check by the Fargo Police.

Fear, worry, and anxiety showed in Ady's face as I tried to ease her concerns, and comfort her that there must be a rational reason for his silence, that would soon be cleared up. I returned to my sewing, and Ady retreated back upstairs. She would hopefully here from Mary soon via text or phone call.

I eased back into the concentrated focus of interpreting directions, pattern pieces, seam allowances, zippers, and zig-zag stitching. The TV program *"Naked and Afraid"* played quietly in the background occasionally drawing my attention away from the fabric and stitching.

Time passed. Sleeves got added to the back, a hood got connected to the neckline, a kangaroo pocket and zipper joined the front.

Daylight savings and a glaring full-moon had left me wide awake at a very late hour when suddenly stumbling footsteps came running down the stairs. This time, Ady came weeping and sobbing as she eked out the difficult words; "They found him dead. He is gone." Tears and sadness flooded the basement as the awkward silence of heavy grief and the hard truth of reality began to slowly sink in. Eduardo was no longer present with us in this world.

Eduardo was a loveable character. He was Ady's closest friend, confidant, and coworker at Concordia. He carried an infectious smile, laughed easily and possessed a quick wit and keen sense of humor. Throughout the years he became my friend as well. I enjoyed knocking on his door, being invited into this office and sitting for lengthy periods of time conversing. He was always gracious and forgiving with my mangled attempts at conversing in Spanish. He showed me great patience and affection and my mistakes in Spanish were safe within the bounds of our friendship.

And so, what had been a routine, normal, flat-line, quiet, and ordinary Sunday afternoon, had now been transformed into a crawl through the valley of the shadow of death. From the relative comfort of monotony and sameness, we had been body-slammed into the hard-truth reality of death, loss, and grieving. There had been no forewarnings, no prelude, no preparations, no illness, nor signs. Here yesterday, gone today. At 57 years of age, "He most likely died of natural causes, he simply died in his sleep," stated the police.

That for which we've grown so accustomed to, and for whom we take for granted, had been wrenched from our lives with no rhyme or reason, no rational, and no formula to answer our many questions of "why?" The harsh reality of death, loss, and grief had landed in our home without invitation, warning or solicitation.

I think back over many years of friendship and I would occasionally suggest, "Hey I miss Eduardo and your Spanish gang. Why don't we invite them over for a glass of wine or barbeque?" Our excuses were typical: "This house is too messy! … Wait till we redo the kitchen… Not till we get rid of this ugly furniture! We can't have anyone over with this crumbling deck!" Our vain and timid excuses ruled, and no gatherings or parties took place. And now it is too late. The opportunity to fellowship, dine and share with Eduardo has passed, never to return again.

And so, with death and grief, I am reminded again that life, and relationships and fellowship are precious and to be treasured. We often forget or ignore the fact that important relationships in our lives are temporary and fleeting when considering the bigger picture of life.

Mothers and fathers, sons and daughters, sisters and brothers, husbands and wives, mentors and muses, teachers and students, coaches and players, friends and coworkers are not forever, at least in this earthly life. They are on temporary loan to us. They are simply a gift given in this day only. There is no guarantee or promise of tomorrow, nor the relationships contained within that tomorrow.

So do not put off for tomorrow, what must be done today. Call your mom or dad to tell them of love and appreciation, speak the truth of love and affection to your children, forgive as you wish to be forgiven, send the card of gratitude and affirmation that you've been meaning to write, walk away from this screen to give thanks or blessing to a coworker down the hall, type out an email of appreciation for your brother or sister, plan a gathering, a meal, a party in spite of a messy house, enter the kitchen tonight and hug your spouse for a long time. The possibilities are endless… but our lives on this earth are not.

What I have learned is this; don't wish your life away.
It is all the little things that I miss the most.
And remember to live every day like it's a gift… because it is."
Rory Eidsness

I shall but pass this way but once; any good, therefore, that I can do or any kindness that I can show to any human being, let me do it now. Let me not defer nor neglect it, for I shall not pass this way again. William Penn

*"Blessed are those who mourn, for they shall
be comforted." Matthew 5:4 NIV*

*God has given us eternal life, and this <u>life is in
his Son</u>. Whoever has the Son <u>has life</u>;
whoever does not have the Son of God <u>does not have life</u>.
1 John 5:11-12 NIV*

Rollie Johnson

But seek first his kingdom and his righteousness, and all these things will be given to you as well.
Matthew 6:33 NIV

"So do not worry about tomorrow, for tomorrow will bring worries of its own. Today's trouble is enough for today. Matthew 6:25 NLT

Grieving Dad(whose young daughter was killed in a tragic car accident): "I want to trust God. But, I don't understand what he's doing."
Pastor: "God doesn't promise an explanation, but he does promise to walk with us through the pain."
Pastor: "The hard choice for you is; whether or not you will be angry for the *time you didn't have* with her, or *grateful for the time you did have.*"
A scene from the movie Courageous.

Eyes to See

The freezing cold of our never-ending winter bit at my face as I walked northward from church over narrowed, snow-covered sidewalks. The bright and blinding sunshine lifted my spirits but did little to alleviate the chill. Turning left I amble down the sloping sidewalk to enter under the parking awning.

Welcome to Roger Maris. Not home runs. Not crew-cuts. Not golf tournaments. Not the big leagues. Just the hustling and bustling Roger Maris Cancer Center. A place of paradox. It's not a place you just visit on a whim or go to by choice. If you're here, life has taken a very difficult turn. And yet If your life is in a difficult way, there is not a better place you'd rather be. Most of us are oblivious to this place, and all that takes place here.

First to greet me at the door was my good friend Chuck. Chuck works for Roger Maris part-time parking cars each morning. Fully retired from the Air Guard, he wanted to have part-time work that had purpose and meaning. He greets everyone with a cheerful smile, and a hearty "good morning!" as he assists them out of their cars, opening doors and then carefully parks their vehicles in the ramp. He is the first face you see as you enter, and last to bid you farewell as you leave. His honest cheerfulness and warmth make a difference in those lives he encounters. He is grateful for his work, knowing he can make a positive difference in simple ways by assisting those who are fighting for their lives. He loves his work and has eyes to see that he is blessed to be a blessing to those in deep need. His work driven by faith gives him perspective.

As I pass through the waiting room and busy corridors, I'm immediately shocked by how many people are wrestling and fighting with cancer. It seems epidemic. I shake my head in disbelief, knowing I am passing through these halls only briefly and am amazed by how many are here to be treated.

I continue down a maze of hallways and corridors following signs and happen upon Allison and Julie, both dedicated nurses who have chosen to work here on the front lines of the battle. I've known each of these awesome young ladies for years and know that they are here by choice. They have chosen to be at the crux, to work with and be present for people in the most difficult spaces and places of their lives. They each walk with a bounce in their step, a bright smile on their faces, and a tangible love in their hearts for the people they encounter each day. They know that their work, and more importantly "how" they do their work… matters. Julie and Allison both have eyes to see that they are blessed to be a blessing. Their work driven by faith gives them perspective.

I finally arrive at infusion room nine and knocking on the wall, I receive a curious "Come on in!" Parting the sliding curtain, I am greeted by a warm and beautiful smiling Jamie. A fleece cap tops her now balding head, and she is seated cozily with a blanket and a good book. Her IV drip is hung above and to her side, quietly going about the invisible and unseen business of entering her body.

Jamie seemed genuinely grateful to see me and smiled throughout our conversation. From the get-go, her optimism, positivity and mega-sized faith filled the spaces of the tiny room. She shared of her battle with breast cancer, her recent surgery and now her treatment plan of chemotherapy. She spoke of her gratitude for being able to continue her work at the bank from home.

As we conversed, I realized that once again, the roles have been reversed. I had come with the intention of ministering to Jaimie, and she had unknowingly turned the tables on me. She gave witness and testimony over and over again of her trust in God. God had been faithful and trustworthy in so many other difficulties and trials in her life previously... why would he not continue to do so now? God had proved faithful over and over again. Why doubt him now? Jamie's heartfelt smile added conviction and certainty to her living testimony. Before departing I asked if I could hold her hand as I prayed for God's blessing up her and her healing.

Leaving the room, I knew in my heart that it was *I* who had been blessed by the encounter. I said a quiet prayer of thanks that my spirit had received an infusion of real, practical and living faith from Jamie. Jamie had loaned me her eyes to see that we are a blessed to be a blessing in all circumstances good or bad. Jamie, driven by faith, had given me perspective.

In my role as a worship leader and preacher, I get the privilege of interacting with hundreds of people each Sunday and Wednesday. Most often conversations and encounters tend to stay on the surface, as most of us put on a Sunday morning church smile and robotically spew forth the standard issue "How are you?" "Fine." But from my lofty perch on stage, I can often perceive those who are hurting, who are struggling, who are wrestling with difficult situations. Maybe a tired, weary and worn face, tears wiped away during a song, or possibly the long gaze of someone lost in troubled thoughts.

Normally, it's not until you sit face-to-face with someone over coffee when you get to see and hear of the real struggles and difficulties that people carry on their shoulders. Whether it's a coffee chat, our Wednesday night men's group, a retreat, or honest dialogue in my office, I am always amazed, by how much pain, hurt, hardship, and challenge people face daily. If only we take the time to ask, or questioningly poke below the surface, do we realize how much tough stuff is out there. And when we do, we realize we are not alone in our struggles. Life is hard.

Sit in church, or in your office, or in your classroom, toss a pencil, and within that radius, you'll find someone who is hurting. Someone who needs you, who needs your listening ear, your attention, your faith, your shared struggle, your acceptance and your testimony to God's faithfulness.

Life is hard. And yet, You and I have been blessed to be a blessing.

Pray that God will give us eyes to see beyond the surface, to know that each and every person we encounter has a back story. Pray that God will give us each his perspective of faith, hope, and love.

Here is a fabulous little video, about seeing peoples lives below the surface. If We could see inside other people's hearts-lives:

https://www.youtube.com/watch?v=bPsiLi89PQ4

"I have told you these things, so that in me you may have peace. In this world, you will have trouble. But take heart! I have overcome the world." John 16:33 NIV

And now these three remain faith, hope, and love. But the greatest of these is love. 1 Corinthians 13:13 NIV

Therefore encourage one another and build each other up, just as in fact you are doing. 1 Thessalonians 5:11 NIV

…I have come that they may have life, and have it to the full. John 10:10 NIV

Come to me, all you who are weary and burdened, and I will give you rest. ^{29} Take my yoke upon you and learn from me, for I am gentle and humble in heart, and you will find rest for your souls. ^{30} For my yoke is easy and my burden is light." Matthew 11:28-30 NIV

Expectations

I've recently come to a fairly significant revelation about myself. It has taken me by surprise and caught me off guard. I'm not really proud about it either. In fact, I'm a little perturbed with myself. Maybe even disappointed. I have come to the realization that... I have a giving problem.

Well maybe giving is not the right word, as normally I'm a fairly good giver. I try to be a generous giver of affirmations, thank-yous, blessings, gifts, hand-made crafts, kindness and my time. My problem it seems may lie in my **expectations**. Meaning that If I give a significant gift to someone... I **expect** that gift to be acknowledged in the form of returned gratitude or a thank you, either expressed verbally or written.

My mother Beverly was a stickler for thank yous. We kids were required to frequently sit down and write them to anyone who had given us a gift or done something significant for us in any way. I remember as a young 10-year-old our old-school station wagon blew out a tire and a kindly young man stopped on the freeway and took time to help us change the tire. My mother took his number and address, went home and baked him a hand-made apple pie, and delivered the pie the very next day. A true token of gratitude, a gift from the heart and hand. That has always stuck with me. To this day I do my best to extend thanks, verbal gratitude and hand-written heartfelt notes to those who have gifted me in some way.

I recently delivered a significant gift to dearly loved friend. It was a gift that I had invested a great deal of time, money, sweat, pride and love into. It was a hand-made, home-made, beautiful creation. I had vividly imagined how the receiver would react to my gift and I smiled each time I imagined the encounter and the giving of the gift. I had crafted this gift specifically for this person and thought of them all through the creation process.

When I handed over my present, the receiver barely acknowledged the gift. Hardly a glance was given. And there was no acknowledgment or appreciation of craftsmanship, beauty or time spent.

I returned home disappointed, disheartened and frankly a little saddened. I had **expected** so much more in the encounter. The exchange had certainly not gone the way I had envisioned or **expected.** And therein lies the problem that is mine and mine alone; I gave with an **expectation** that I would receive thanks, gratitude, and praise.

In recent days I've done some good soul searching and realized that I've had many such disappointments similar to this in recent years from a wide variety of people and situations. Always with as me the giver of some kind of gift of time, effort, service rendered or craftsmanship and a receiver that showed minimal or no thanks, gratitude or appreciation. Similar results ensued with me feeling saddened, disappointed or frustrated by the lack of gratitude or thanks on the part of the receiver. Sometimes it was family, sometimes friends, sometimes a co-worker, and sometimes a complete stranger.

I believe I might be rounding the corner on some self-knowledge here. The real problem has not been with the gift recipients, nor their lack of responsiveness, enthusiasm or gratitude. The heart of the matter is that **I gave with the expectation** that I would be affirmed, thanked, liked, or loved back because of my gift. This is not true gift giving. I gave with strings attached! Invisible strings maybe, but strings none the less. My giving has lacked the God-like quality of giving without expectation, giving because it's right to give, and giving because it's good for the giver. To give without expectations of gratitude.

The fact that sometimes I haven't received love, thanks, acknowledgment or gratitude in return for a gift does not negate the original Godly prompting within me to create or give to someone. The giving is still good!

Jesus is the great giver. He generously gives life, freedom, forgiveness, purpose, passion, direction, strength, guidance, wisdom, solace, comfort, acceptance, and direction. These gifts are poured out on each of us every day, whether we acknowledge, accept or give thanks. Many of us walk through life oblivious, blind and ungrateful. We barely pay attention to the food on our plate, the clean crisp water that pours from our faucet, the fresh air that we breathe, that we can hear melodious music, or speak words that a friend can hear and interpret. But God just keeps on giving anyway. He is the great giver.

But imagine my friends, on how He must smile… on the person who pauses throughout their day to give thanks for the many blessings laid at their feet!

Today May you give without expectation. May you give because it is good, and Godly and right! May you also pause to give gratitude and thanks for the many gifts and beauty that surround you!

Each of you should give what you have decided in your heart to give, not reluctantly or under compulsion, for God loves a cheerful giver. 2 Corinthians 9:7 NIV

"If you love those who love you, what credit is that to you? Even sinners love those who love them. ³³ And if you do good to those who are good to you, what credit is that to you? Even sinners do that. ³⁴ And if you lend to those from whom you expect repayment, what credit is that to you? Even sinners lend to sinners, expecting to be repaid in full. ³⁵ But love your enemies, do good to them, and lend to them without expecting to get anything back. Then your reward will be great, and you will be children of the Most High, because he is kind to the ungrateful and wicked. ³⁶ Be merciful, just as your Father is merciful. Luke 6:32-36 NIV

Evanescent Yellow

The warm afternoon sun felt comforting on my face as I ran along the bike path between Dike East and Lindenwood Park. Twice a week while Shane is at soccer practice, I run this five-mile loop taking in quiet suburban neighborhoods and this lovely park. A crisp, cool fall breeze at my back added to the beauty of the day as the scent of fallen leaves filled my lungs with fresh invigorating air. The paved trail gently curved and undulated like a serpent tightly paralleling the river course. It felt good to be alive and I silently offered up many thank you prayers for life, vitality, health and the beauty around me.

Rounding a bend, I came beneath a cluster of mighty and majestic cottonwood trees. The girth of their trunks demanded attention, as did their impressive height. They stood stoically, stout, proud and attentive as if they were the sentinels of this entire river bottom. Their presence, strength, and size spoke to the wisdom of their years. I had run this trail many times throughout the spring, summer and fall and each time I had nodded my head to them in homage to their presence, splendor, and beauty. But today they were even more impressive with their autumnal leaves of gold as if they gave off light and color to this bend in the river.

As I drive home each afternoon, I take one final curve or bend in our road before reaching our short dead-end street. This bend in the road is lined with poplar or aspen trees. These humble, gentle trees bend slightly over the roadway and for the past few weeks have all been aflame with bright yellow foliage. Poplars are the first trees to shake and rustle with even the slightest breeze. Many days I both begin both my morning and end my day being waved at by the quiet rustling and shimmering of these bright, cheerful yellow dappled trees.

Many evenings and mornings of late find me in a tree stand waiting and watching the natural world unfold as I await the presence of a monster buck. Most times out in the forest or field edge I cannot help but smile. The woods of late have a common theme here in the Fargo/Moorhead area as most of our local ash, elm and basswood trees have turned in unison and this year's dress code theme is simply evanescent yellow. Yellow is on my brain and I am reminded daily that this is our color of the season. But it alas is not a permanent color… it is only evanescent.

Evanescent. What a great word. I like saying it, hearing it, and reading it. But truth be told, even though I'd heard it many times before… I have to admit, I had to look it up. Evanescent; fleeting, passing, brief, momentary, short-lived, ephemeral are all synonyms. And this word describes perfectly the yellow that fills my senses daily of late. The majestic cottonwoods, the gentle poplars, and the ash and basswoods are all only aflame for a brief, fleeting and transitory time. It is a beautiful but short-lived finite time of yellow.

These next few weeks will be filled with pumpkins of all shapes and sizes. Pumpkins really have but two choices. Some, being fearful or fear-filled, choose to stay in the pumpkin patch, after all, it's the only life they've know. It safe, quiet and nothing is demanded of them but to sit and stay in the same place. Play it safe, don't step outside the box, don't take risks, go for security and comfort. Never look beyond the patch. Those pumpkins will in short order die on the vine, never having moved more than an inch from where they were born, safe and secure. They will die, having never impacted anyone for fear, laziness or comfort.

Other pumpkins will submit to movement, to the unknown, to the great adventure of what's out there, to the thrill of taking a risk. They will soon come under the hands of a creative teenager or babbling four-year-old, or an artsy-fartsy grown up. They will pick up triangle eyes, and pointy teeth and a jagged smile. Some will look rough and awkward, others a work of art. But each of these risk-taking pumpkins will soon shine a light from within to adorn a doorstep or deck, or window. The beautiful, glowing yellow light will not be from themselves, but rather a gentle light that was planted within them, and that light will shine forth and bring light, and beauty, warmth and smiles to all who encounter them. This too will be an evanescent yellow light. It will be brief, fleeting passing yellow light.

You and I are all evanescent. Realistically, in the big picture of life, we are all here for but a brief, very temporary, and short period of time. Our lives are transitory and fleeting. As I age, I come to know and feel the reality of this truth more deeply. People come and go in our lives. Accidents, illnesses, cancers, dementia, wars, floods, hurricanes, fires, and tragedies rob us of loved ones, friends and family. This IS the reality of our lives on earth.

So, I ask you… are you allowing the beautiful light and love of God to shine in and through you to the world around you? Like the mighty cottonwoods, ash and poplars are you sharing the beauty of God's love, forgiveness and grace through your life? Are you allowing the gentle candle of Jesus to shine through your being to illuminate God's light into a dark, hurting and difficult world? Have you surrendered your life into the hands of a magnificent Creator and said, *"Have your way with and in me? Do with me as you please! Create in me something useful for the world."* Or have you just settled for the same ol', same ol' life in the pumpkin patch?

Some of us will live to only 17, some to 38, some to 53, others maybe even make it to 100. But in the big scope of life here on planet earth, we are all only evanescent yellow.

So how will you live your fleeting life? For whom will you live your brief life? Will you just live for you? Or will you surrender to God and allow Him to burn his beautiful yellow light into this world?

Why you do not even know what will happen tomorrow. What is your life? You are a mist that appears for a little while and then vanishes. James 4:14 NIV

Teach us to number our days, that we may gain a heart of wisdom. Psalm 90:12 NIV

for he knows how we are formed he remembers that we are dust. The life of mortals is like grass, they flourish like a flower of the field; Psalm 103:14-15 NIV

FAILURE

Daylight had not yet arrived on this particular side of the planet. I hurriedly wolfed down a bagel and some steaming coffee to shock my lethargic brain into action. I hurried out the door into the darkness of predawn doing my best to be quiet so as not to awaken dog or family. Filled with positive expectations, the joy of anticipation, and amped-up on caffeine, I was more than psyched for the day that lay before me. The cool air of this spring morning filled my lungs bringing life and vitality to my sleepy body.

I scrambled up the dike behind our home, under the low wattage of morning stars that were beginning to fade. A light grey began to pierce the eastern horizon foretelling the arrival of a new sunrise. I stood still in the hush of the pristine morning, quietly listening and sensing. Several gray shadows of deer ran from the dike seeking cover in the nearby woods with only the white of tails visible waving goodbye.

Though the morning was silent from the absence of the sounds of man, the water filled coulee was blaring with the clamor of a virtual orchestra. The Leopard, Spring Peeper, and Chorus frogs were performing a full concert and doing so with great gusto and vigor. Passing tourists; the Mallard Ducks and Canadian Geese were squawking and honking up a storm as they prepared to leave Motel 6 Oakport and head northward.

I listened carefully amidst the clamor of nature's predawn warm-up symphony, trying to discern the solo voice of a gobble. Hearing none,

I let loose a loud series of hen clucks. The response was instantaneous and boisterous from the woodlot to the north a mere 300 yards to the north. Bingo!! My personal fun-meter just hit the RED ZONE! Wild Turkey had just been placed on the menu and I was anxious to invite young Tom to dinner!

I scurried quickly through the darkness and found a perfect place to make my stand, just out of sight, but close enough to be heard. With adrenaline pouring through my arteries, I hurriedly popped open my blind, pulled a Jake and two hen thespians from my pack and placed them four yards out and slid into my humble abode. I sat in a folding chair, put on my black gloves and face mask, and readied my bow and arrow. Let the gobbler games begin!

After an hour of intimate back and forth conversation with Tom and no visible sighting, I had begun to lose hope that he would show. Full daylight had now arrived and with it the birth of a gorgeous spring morning. And then... there he was! A bright red head 150 yards away at full strut, working his way around the dike, and slowly down the tree-line towards my three bird Cirque du Solei. Would he come all the way? Or would he "chicken out" and hang up at 40 yards as they are so famous for doing. Males, in general, are so pathetic at commitment!

Soon my dozen little silent prayers were answered as he made a slow and steady bee-line towards my Jake. My heart pounded in my throat and breathing accelerated to Mach One. As he passed by the corner of my blind at four yards I drew and released my arrow which skidded harmlessly into the grass. A complete miss and failure to hit the mark! Tom simply side-stepped and continued on his determined path strutting his stuff like an avian John Wayne. I fumbled for another arrow, nocked, drew and released again with the same results! A complete miss! A complete failure! Twice from only four yards! Having only had two arrows in my quiver, my opportunities for any chance at success had just ended! What an epic fail!

Tom was one tough hombre as he knocked my Jake off the stick and pummeled him several times with his spurs. I felt his devious mocking as he flaunted and strutted outside my hut for the next ten minutes never more than 4-5 yards away. He fanned his backside to me several times flaunting and tormenting me as he gloated in his victory and laughed at the poor unseen failure inside the blind. He ended our time together by scratching the dirt with his toes as if biblically shaking the dust off his feet.

I sat heartbroken in my blind, silently chastising myself for blowing it. I couldn't have asked for a better shot, and to get two opportunities was a double strike! In bowhunting turkey, close-up opportunities do not come with regularity! The entire previous season I had never even drawn my bow back! The inner dialogue of self-chastisement, disparaging remarks, and demeaning self-talk were brutal.

Failure... what an ugly word, and I could feel the full weight it in my gut. At least my failures had taken place in private and not in the middle of a football stadium filled with thousands of fans and replayed on the Jumbotron or on ESPN highlights film over and over. Nor had I harmed anyone with my failure as is often the case when we fall short. And in the big scope of life, my mistake will not count or matter for anything. I simply missed an easy opportunity for success.

For many folks, the fear of public speaking, or spiders, or heights is # one. For many of us though, including me, fear of failure is top of the list. Especially fear of failing in front of others or in public. It is often the driving force behind so many people's striving, over-achieving, hard-charging nature.

A baseball strike-out, a failed field goal attempt in football, or in my case a missed shot is fairly benign in the big picture. But when we fall, trip, or miss-step as a moral failure, the stakes get higher. So many of us base our entire self-esteem and self-image on our successes and failures and follow that same line of thinking when it comes to our relationship with God. If we do well, are successful and productive and don't mess things up... God will love us. If we fail, sin or make some wrong turns... God will turn His back on us.

Thank God that He doesn't think or act like we humans! Take a listen to Sarah Young's *Jesus Calling* (December 26):

Absolutely nothing in heaven or on earth can cause Me to stop loving you. You may feel more loved when you are performing according to your expectations. But My Love for you is perfect; therefore, it is not subject to variation. What does vary is your awareness of My loving Presence. When you are dissatisfied with your behavior, you tend to feel unworthy of My Love. You may unconsciously punish yourself by withdrawing from Me and attributing the distance between us to My displeasure. Instead of returning to Me and receiving My Love, you attempt to earn My approval by trying harder. All the while, I am aching to hold you in My everlasting arms, to enfold you in My Love. When you are feeling unworthy or unloved, come to Me. Then ask for receptivity to My unfailing Love.

I tend to be a people-pleaser, over-achiever, striver, and closet perfectionist at least in behavior and morals (my wife would not agree in regards to home or yard!). And these tendencies have benefited me and the world in many ways. But they do nothing to bring me closer to God. A Failure is a wonderful teacher and a great reminder that life with Jesus is purely and simply about unconditional love, and pure undeserved grace. It's not about my perfection, achievement, success or failures. It's about a God who gives second chances over and over.

May you learn to relax into the arms of God's grace, forgiveness, love, and mercy.
P.S.: Redemption came a few days later. Tom eventually agreed to come home for dinner!

Faith Flight

The throttle pushed forward creating a great noise and vibration that I could feel throughout my being. As we accelerated forward, G-forces pulled me back into my seat as we overcame inertia. As the noise, speed, and vibration accelerated, so too did my heart rate and blood pressure! We gained momentum rapidly and within seconds we were released from the bonds of mother earth in that magical moment when driving turns to flight. We were airborne.

We were on our way to Springfield Missouri to a men's conference, flying in a private, six-seater TBM, single-engine airplane. I the lone passenger, got to sit "right seat" for the entire two-hour flight and I must admit to both excitement and anxiety. I've always had a bit of a love-hate relationship with flying. Sometimes I am at peace, tranquil and relaxed and at other times, even on commercial flights, I can get uptight and anxious. I have never been able to pinpoint the source or trigger of this nervousness.

John, my astute and skilled pilot had twenty five years of flying experience and it showed in his demeanor and skill. He was relaxed, cool, calm and at home in the cockpit. The sense that John loved his job was evident in both his words and actions. The fact that we were both men of faith made for delightful conversation the entire flight.

After making a wide turn south out of Fargo, we began a slow and steady ascent to 25,000 feet. We soon entered a hazy cloud structure that lasted the entire flight. I wanted to pop out of the cloud, to get above so I could see where we were going. I'm one who likes to have visual references to know how far we've come and how far we've got to go. I want landmarks. I want to see the route and the weather. I want to see the obstacles and know the way. None of that clarity came to me the entire flight.

As I observed John, for most of the flight, his hands remained calmly in his lap. From early on, he had given control of the plane to the autopilot. He was still in charge of the plane but had relinquished the minute details and guidance and destination to the autopilot. In addition to answering my thousand annoying questions about flight and piloting, he would occasionally tap several buttons on the various screens and dials, but only rarely did he grab the wheel. Instead, he constantly listened to, responded to and obeyed the commands and communications from the radio.

His complete and absolute trust in his instruments and auto-pilot allowed him to relax into the now and present of a beautiful flight. What a contrast this was between John and his complete faith, in spite of the absence of visual references, and me who was uptight and craving knowing and seeing. Ironically, we both arrived safe and sound at the Springfield airport at the same time.

Yesterday before worship, I read from my daily devotional "Jesus Calling" by Sarah Young: *"If you learn to trust me- really trust me with your whole being, then nothing can separate you from* **My Peace**. *Everything you endure can be put to good use by allowing it to train you in trusting me. This is how you foil the works of evil, growing in grace through the very adversity that was meant to harm you... Do not fear what this day or any day may bring your way. Concentrate on* **trust in Me** *and doing what needs to be done.* **Relax in My sovereignty,** *remembering that I go before you, as well as with you, into each day. Fear no evil, for I can bring good out of every situation you will ever encounter.*

Jesus often equates **trust** in Him, with peace. For many of us, we falsely equate control or sight or knowing with peace. It rarely ever works that way. We whisper to ourselves; *"If only I could see how this situation/struggle/illness/obstacle/problem turns out? Then I will have peace!"* **Not!** God promises ***His*** peace anywhere, anytime, any situation no matter how scary, confusing or terrifying and it has nothing to do with control, knowing, seeing or understanding! It simply has to do with trust: **Faith** in the auto-pilot of God. The details, guidance, and destination are His when you are surrendered. And surrender and trust are always a choice… a choice that you make of your own free will.

May you and I choose trust in God, over worry, fear and anxiety!

"Peace I leave with you, My peace I give to you; not as the world gives do I give to you. Let not your heart be troubled, neither let it be afraid." John 14:27 NIV

"These things I have spoken to you, that in Me you may have peace. In the world, you will have tribulation, but be of good cheer, I have overcome the world." John 16:33 NIV

Do not be anxious about anything, but in every situation, by prayer and petition, with thanksgiving, present your requests to God And the peace of God, which transcends all understanding, will guard your hearts and your minds in Christ Jesus. Philippians 4:6-7 NIV

Family

Celebration Hall was empty and still. Soft, warm light filled the room from sunlight streaming from the high windows. Scurrying about, I busied myself with various tasks in preparation for Wednesday night worship. The quiet and stillness were a welcome change from the movement, motion, and commotion of Sunday's worship.

There soon appeared a middle-aged father with two kids in tow, who upon entering Celebration Hall, looked around with an initial scan of the room, then headed for the kitchen. The two young children followed the dad dutifully, with a youthful bounce in their steps and a constant wave of chatter. This trio entered the kitchen, and then soon reappeared with dad appearing as though he were searching for something or someone.

Strolling over near them, I queried to see if I could help them find someone or something. The dad stammered a bit and then it clicked! Pastor Corey had mentioned at staff meeting, that a young homeless family had been to our outdoor worship Sunday and may be back to get some food. "Oh," I said aloud, "Pastor Corey mentioned you all might be coming, so let me get you some good eats!"

Immediately, I went into host mode, shook the dad's hand, introduced myself to the two little ones and set about raiding the walk-in-cooler for leftovers from Sunday's delectable barbecue. The kids grinned from ear to ear, and the articulate and well-groomed dad seemed to be delighted by the prospect of a good meal.

Sitting them down at the table, I filled their plates with piles of scrumptious barbecued chicken, baked beans, bread rolls, and coleslaw. When I handed each a fork, they dove into the heaping stack of food like a hungry pack of wolves. The eyes of the kids grew as wide as the mouths that were trying to keep up with the constant flow of incoming food.

It was more than obvious, that it had been a long time since their last meal. Seconds, then thirds were piled on to the now empty plates and slowly a look of satisfaction and relief replaced the previous faces of want and hunger. After downing a few chocolate kisses they all seemed to be satisfied and satiated.

As we chitchatted, following the feast, I tried to engage the children in conversation to explore their interests and passions. They were polite and well-mannered and seemed delighted to share their little world with me. The young boy was seven and the young lady was nine. When I probed further to ask where they went to school, the young gal responded enthusiastically, "I'll be a fourth grader at Ellen Hopkins."

Upon hearing those words, my heart skipped a beat followed by a rising lump in my throat. My own son, Shane, attends this very same school and will soon be a fifth grader. This little family could no longer be anonymous; they could no longer be from somewhere—from some unknown place. Homelessness now had a face and a name and they had landed smack dab in the middle of my little sphere. How many times over the years had I walked by this young family in the halls of that school or on the playground when picking up Shane? How many others were like them who live right on the razor-thin line between making it—and homelessness?

It is easy to become cynical, jaded, and detached in a place like First Lutheran, a large downtown church that has a steady flow of needy folks that walk through our doors daily. Many are people with chronic, long-term, life-long problems of substance abuse and mental illness. Many folks hop from institution to institution to use and abuse the system. But, it's hard to ignore the faces of these two children; the homeless face of Jesus.

In Celebration Worship, we sometimes sing the song, *Jesus My Lord* with these words*: "Have you seen Jesus my Lord, He's here in plain view."* Oh, how true! He is right here, in plain view. Keep your eyes open!

Love the Lord your God with all your heart and with all your soul and with all your mind and with all your strength.' The second is this: 'Love your neighbor as yourself.' There is no commandment greater than these."
Mark 12:30-31 NIV

> *He called a little child to him and placed the child among them. And he said: "Truly I tell you, unless you change and become like little children, you will never enter the kingdom of heaven. Therefore, whoever takes the lowly position of this child is the greatest in the kingdom of heaven. And whoever welcomes one such child in my name welcomes me. Matthew 18: 2-3 NIV*

> *…'Truly I tell you, whatever you did for one of the least of these brothers and sisters of mine, you did for me.'*
> *Matt 25:40 NIV*

Not so with you. Instead, **whoever wants to be***come great among you must* **be** *your servant.*
Matthew 20:26 NIV

FLUFF

Goosebumps grew upon my skin. Chills ran up my spine. Electricity and energy filled the air. Awe and reverence filled my thoughts. The sheer massiveness and grandness of space that lay before me filled me with amazement. At my side was my fourteen-year-old son Shane. He too seemed to be wide-eyed and filled with wonder, an unpretentious smile crossing his face. We had journeyed far on our pilgrimage. We had arrived at Mecca and surrounding us was a sea of purple. We had come to raise our voices, to scream, to shout, to cheer and to lose ourselves in the battle.

Our voices added to the 66,000 other faithful clad in purple and gold to raise our voices in victory chants as our Vikings, Defenders of the North, went on to defeat the Evil Empire of the Greenbay Packers. The energy of the "Force" and the spine-tingling SKOL chant helped us to overthrow the dark-side powers of the green and gold. Even with the commanding presence of the Darth Vadaresque Aaron Rodgers, the Pack could not overcome the united front of the Viking Hoard both on the field and in the stands.

Call me sappy. Call me a sucker for sentimentality. Call me delusional. Call me naïve. Maybe it's my Norske heritage but truth be told I am a Minnesota Vikings fan through and through. The magnificence of our new US Bank Stadium, the Gjallarhorn horn blaring out is low and menacing tone, the incredible pump-you-up videos of pride and history on the giant screens, jamming music beats, and the incredible unifying togetherness of the SKOL chant all had my spirits soaring as I became lost in the celebration.

Noise, volume, commotion, loudness, masses of people, distractions galore, over-stimulation, and crowds are a Vikings Game. And as much as I love the Vikings, and being present at a rowdy game, the reality of a professional football game is that it is really just "fluff." For many of us, our entire lives are filled with nothing but "fluff."

This Friday morning, I leave for Pacem In Terris, a Catholic Retreat Center in Isanti, MN. I'll be taking with me only two other souls. Out of thousands invited, only two have responded to the calling of God to come and be quiet and still with Him for 48 hours. Having been at Pacem several times, I will slide into the cozy one-room cabin called a hermitage, like slipping into a familiar and comfortable pair of jeans. A single bed, a propane light, a one burner stove for heating coffee water are the simple comforts provided. A rocking chair faces out through a full-walled picture window overlooking a picturesque-woods of oak and birch

My task for the weekend will be simple, yet not always easy… especially for a normally hyperactive, ADHD type character like me; to be still and know that He is God… and I am not. Silence and solitude are the requisite twin sisters assigned as my guardians and guides for this experience. All computers, cell phones, and other electronic gizmos and forms of distractions will be left at home. God is a jealous God… and he wants our undivided attention.

We will each be given a small basket of modest food for our weekend; a couple of oranges and apples, a banana, a home-baked muffin, two freshly baked loaves of bread, and a chunk of cheddar cheese will be our table fare. The food is both symbolic and practical. It echoes the simplicity of the weekend; to discard from our lives all the fluff and excess of noise, over-consumption, hyperactivity, and busyness that fill our lives.

Quiet, stillness, solitude, emptying, alone, and surrender are all words and concepts most of us avoid. And most of us avoid these for the deep-down fear of having to face ourselves…our true selves in the mirror. Our deeper anxieties, our darker fears, our ugliest selves, our hidden sins of the heart and head, our inadequacies, our broken dreams, our pain, grief, and loss can almost always be pushed down and away by drowning out in the noise and busyness of crowds and frenzy of activity of fluff.

Pacem, or other experiences like it where we immerse ourselves in quiet and solitude to pray, have a way of stripping us of the "fluff" and chaff of life. Alone times with God bring us back to center. Prayer and daily quiet times restore a Godly eye for our world. Quiet times calm the inner turmoil and agitated waters of our souls. Silence and solitude are the antidotes to a world that mostly offers us the glitter and dazzle of "Fluff."

Ponder for a moment if you will, your own death. Imagine that you are hovering over your own funeral. Consider these difficult questions:

Who will come to my funeral? Will they come out of duty, or love and sadness for my passing? What will be told of the trail of my life? Will they speak of golf or hunting or work as my priorities or that faith permeated all? Will a gaudy and expensive casket hide a man whose priorities and passions in life were futile or aimless or vain? Will they say here lies a woman who lived from the center of faith, and all things flowed from that center? Or will they talk about trivia and the fluff of a woman who craved the "things" that glitter and dazzle? Will they say that my life made a positive difference in their life's journey? Or will they say that he loved success, or achievement, or notoriety, or recognition or business or money? Will they say that I loved and lived a life for Jesus?

I give thanks for great entertainment like a Vikings Game. I'm grateful to occasionally get lost in the grandeur of those kinds of celebrations. And thank God that we are free to enjoy many forms of fun, distractions, and enjoyable pass-times, hobbies, and diversions. These are some of the great freedoms and blessings of being a follower of Jesus.

But let us not become lost and immersed in following the "fluff." Know that life at its core, at its center, is meant to flow from being in relationship one-on-one with our creator. And the relationship must flow from time alone with Jesus. Neglect this core relationship and all you have left is fluff.

May you have the courage to enter into some quiet and solitude with your Maker. He is waiting to listen, forgive, guide, direct and embrace you.

An old orthodox proverb states: "If the Devil can't make you bad, he'll simply make you busy."

...Be still, and know that I am God.
Psalm 46:10 NIV

*Be **still** before the Lord, And wait patiently for Him... Psalm 37:7 NIV*

he leads me beside quiet waters, he refreshes my soul... Psalm 23:2-3 NIV

Be silent before the Sovereign Lord, for the day of the Lord is near. Zephaniah 1:7 NIV

Forged In Fire

"Ping!" "Ping!" "Ping!" "Ping!" "Bang!" "Bang!" "Bang!" "Bang!" Incessant, continuous, non-stop and uninterrupted. The sound of hammers meeting metal resonated continually throughout our days. Beginning at daybreak until late in the afternoon, these humble, hardworking men of our host village of Mexil, hammered away in their simple homemade forges.

Small electric fans channeled fast-moving air into tubes that breathed life and flame into the small pile of carbon (homemade wooden charcoal) at the base of the fire. Sparks and yellow flames danced above the heated metal. Within minutes the steel took on the temperature and hue of its host and became a glowing and mesmerizing brilliant orange. The intense temperature of the forge had converted the steel making it malleable. The powerful combination of hammer and anvil beat the metal into usable tools of ax heads, knives, and machetes. All this under the direction of the master craftsman whose sweat-covered brow and muscular forearms betrayed the intensity of both the work and heat of the forge.

Visiting the forge each day, I was fascinated by their work and wanted to learn more of this lost art. Their efficiency in converting scrap metal, mostly abandoned leaf-springs from old cars and trucks, was remarkable. I was completely impressed by their work ethic; hammering away for over eight hours each day under the intense and stifling heat of the Yucatan sun compounded and amplified by the five separate fires of the forge! The hodge-podge roof of tar-paper and tin seemed to hold in the heat of the forges creating an oven for both metal and men.

How interesting that intense heat, fire, and a severe pounding are the vehicles that take a lump of useless metal and shape it into something of purpose and usefulness for our world. The extreme temperatures of the forge make the steel malleable or moldable. Under the watchful hands of the blacksmith, a creation of function and purpose is revealed.

We recently celebrated Holy Week with Good Friday and Easter Sunday taking top billing. Not much gets said about the Saturday in between. No sermons, no celebration or even remembrance, doesn't even have a name. Maybe because as quiet church goers we don't want to talk about or say the word "Hell." You know… fire, brimstone, oppressive heat, suffering, unending thirst, and flames. How about this: *"I believe in God, the Father Almighty, creator of heaven and earth. I believe in Jesus Christ, his only Son, our Lord, who was conceived by the Holy Spirit, born of the Virgin Mary, suffered under Pontius Pilate, was crucified, died, and was buried; he descended into* **Hell**." There… we said it. Pheeew!

I wonder if it wasn't this forge of Hell that changed Jesus. I believe it was this forge of hellish suffering; the beatings, the crown of thorns, the humiliation, the flogging and the agony of the cross that molded and shaped and more importantly changed Jesus. It was this forge of hell that converted Jesus from the son of Mary…into the Savior of Mary… and the Savior of you and me. After all, our biggest need in this life is that of a Savior. A Savior who has been to hell and beyond, knows what it is like to experience pain, agony, and suffering and then to overcome, defeat, and conquer the devil and his # 1 tool that we all secretly fear: Death. Jesus came out of the grave Easter morning completely changed. He had been transformed by the heat and forge of hell.

How about you? Have you come away from Easter transformed or changed? Do you sense that you have an even greater need of something, someone stronger, wiser, more powerful than you… a Savior who has overcome death and the grave? Easter is meant to transform people.

And if you are currently in the throw of suffering, difficulties, problems, and storms that seem insurmountable… remember that Jesus has overcome the world. Sometimes our sufferings and difficulties come as the result of our own poor or selfish choices and we are caught in the consequence of those decisions. Sometimes life just throws the heat and hard hammering of illness, accidents, job loss, heartache, broken relationships, or loss of a loved one at us out of the blue. But in either circumstance, God will use these sufferings, trials, and difficulties in your life to forge, change and reshape you into a more Christlike person. You will come through the forge a stronger, wiser, more compassionate and more purpose-filled man or woman of faith.

The fire and forge produce men and women of strong character and deep faith.

Not only so, but we also glory in our sufferings, because we know that suffering produces perseverance; perseverance, character; and character, hope. And hope does not put us to shame, because God's love has been poured out into our hearts through the Holy Spirit, who has been given to us. Romans 5: 3-5 NIV

"I have told you these things, so that in me you may have peace. In this world, you will have trouble. (life is hard, tough and not fair) But take heart! I have overcome the world." John 16:33 NIV

so that the genuineness of your faith—being more precious than gold that, though perishable, is tested by fire—may be found to result in praise and glory and honor when Jesus Christ is revealed. 1 Peter 1: 7 NRSV

Gift Giver

The phone call came late Saturday afternoon. I had been giddy, with anticipation, awaiting this call for three days. I smiled throughout each of those days, patiently waiting, as I envisioned the reaction. I had hoped to speed up the process, but there is no hurrying the U.S. Postal Service. Packages take time and having shipped the red, white, and blue Priority Flat Rate box Wednesday afternoon, I had figured the earliest was Friday, maybe, but more likely Saturday. I was like a kid on Christmas ... I just couldn't wait for the presents waiting under the Christmas tree!

My cell phone rang, and I glanced at the number and name. It was Karina, my eldest, living in Duluth. I tapped the glass and grinned from ear to ear. Her hyperactive speech and rapid-fire, high-pitched adrenaline- filled talking betrayed outright enthusiasm and deep gratitude. She barely took a breath in her first several sentences. I paraphrase; *"Dad I just love my new jacket! It's so cool and I just love it! And it fits perfectly! And I can wear a couple of layers underneath it and I just love it! The colors are perfect and it's just so totally unique and cool, and I even just wore it for a long run with my friends, and they said; 'Hey that's so cool, your new jacket, where'd you buy that?' and I told them my dad made it for me and they just thought that was so cool and said 'Jeez, I wish my dad would make me a cool custom-made jacket!' and so I took it on my run and it worked great and fit great and I just love it! I just love it and it's just awesome and I love you, dad!"* Breathe Karina, Breathe!

The smile on my face was undeniable. The deep, deep satisfaction of a job well done and good gift given, was extremely rewarding. I had just made my daughter happy and pleased with a one of a kind, tailor fit, custom-made, hand-crafted gift. I had purchased a special pattern, with her in mind. I had picked out fabric and color with her in mind. I cut the fabric pieces to her specific size. For two weeks I sat each night in front of the T.V., with my sewing machine humming, as I cut pattern pieces, pinned sleeves to shoulder seams, ripped mistakes with my seam ripper, inlaid zippers and got lost in the tangle of inside-out, backwards instructions all the while thinking of Karina, and knowing I was making a gift for her that she would cherish and more importantly use.

Good fathers give good gifts. And we love giving good gifts, especially to our children. And a good gift purchased with thoughtfulness and purpose is a good thing. But a gift that is hand-crafted by the maker is a gift of the heart and soul of the giver. It comes with extra special love, caring, TLC, and targeted thoughtfulness. I am one who loves to make things; create with my hands and mind. The act of creating is divine and comes directly from our Creator and when we birth a gift using hands and heart, we touch the divine.

I believe wholeheartedly that our heavenly Father does the same with each of us. He bestows upon each of us hand-crafted, tailor-made, perfectly-sized, user-specific, one-of-a-kind gifts! And the great thing about these gifts is they are practical and meant to be used! And the gifts we receive are targeted for specific activities! These gifts are meant to be cherished and then used in the real world!

Imagine how I would feel on my next visit to Duluth if I found Karina had neatly hung this new jacket in a darkened closet for fear of dirtying it or ruining the fabric? I created this Anorak specifically for Karina, knowing she is an active climber, runner, backpacker, and adventurer. It's meant to be used in the real world! And the real world is messy and dirty.

I cringe when I see so many people in our church and world that shelve their Godly gifts in the privacy of a darkened closet or even worse locking them up in a trophy case to display what was or has been. Excuses abound. I'm too old, I'm not good enough. How could I ever make a difference? Nobody needs what I have to offer. I've done my time. It's too much effort. People might laugh at me. I'm comfortable where I'm at. Yadda, Yadda Yadda.

And God never stops giving. He gives us the one-time gifts of salvation, eternal life, and faith, yet via the implanting of the Holy Spirit in each of us, his gifts are new and fresh each day. The Holy Spirit is continually renewing our minds, and refreshing our spirits.

Imagine how I will feel next time I see Karina and she is wearing and using the gift I created for her? It will fill me with great joy. Imagine how our Heavenly Father feels when you use the unique gifts, talents, time, resources and skill sets that he has specifically gifted to you? I believe there will be great joy in heaven. So, get out there, and use your gifts! And don't forget to continually look under the tree!... The Holy Spirit continually renews and gives gifts each day for those who are watching and paying attention!

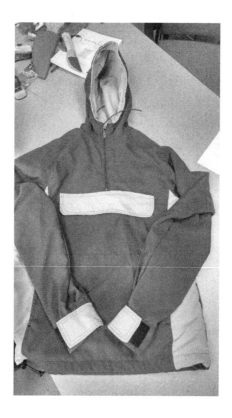

Ask and it will be given to you; seek and you will find; knock and the door will be opened to you. For everyone who asks receives; the one who seeks finds; and to the one who knocks, the door will be opened. "Which of you, if your son asks for bread, will give him a stone? Or if he asks for a fish, will give him a snake? If you, then, though you are evil, know how to give good gifts to your children, how much more will your Father in heaven give good gifts to those who ask him! Matthew 7: 7-11 NIV

So if anyone is in Christ, there is a new creation: everything old has passed away; see, everything has become new! 2 Corinthians 5:17 NRSV

*For this reason, I remind you to fan into flame the gift of God, which is in you, through the laying on of my hands. For God did not give us a Spirit of timidity/fear/anxiety, but a Spirit of power, love, and self-discipline.
2 Timothy 1:6-7 NIV*

But you will receive power when the Holy Spirit comes on you; Acts 1:8 NIV

"I am making everything new!" Then he said, "Write this down, for these words are trustworthy and true." Revelations 21:5 NIV

Giving Up Church for Lent

We pulled into the parking lot, eager and hungry for lunch. I could feel my belly begging for the warm and tasty Potato Ole's! My friend Todd and I were ready to partake of the superb and authentic Mexican cuisine offered up by our friendly, neighborhood Taco Johns. We ordered up and were soon seated in a corner booth, mowing down tacos and delicious, overly-salted Ole's. Mmmn good!

Todd was always humorous and hilarious and kept me laughing most often. Our conversation flowed in all directions and our laughter and nonsensical banter flowed freely about everything and nothing at the same time.

All was well until something happened most strange.

From the booth next to us, seated behind Todd, arose a portly young lady. She stood, and turned towards us and walked a couple of steps to stand next to our table, hovering directly in front of me. I knew not her face nor her name, a complete stranger to be sure. She paused briefly, then uttered these words as she stared directly at me: *"God has been speaking to me just now. He has told me that He wants you to do a three day fast. If you do this, He will give you the ability to speak to young people."* She turned, picked up her tray and garbage, disposed of it on her way out the door, and disappeared.

I sat dumbfounded for I know not how long, completely stunned and frankly quite shaken. Todd and I looked at each other with a mix of wide-eyed awe, trepidation, confusion and ultimately laughter! We guffawed out loud; "What in the world just happened!" Whoaaa! Had we just heard a direct message from God himself on the Bat Phone Direct, or had we just experienced a nut-job having fun messing with our heads! We sat for quite a time attempting to process what had just happened with a mixture of laughter, tension, and anxiety. Who could have known that Taco John's had now become the Oracle?

Returning to my office, I could not focus or concentrate. Frankly, I was quite disturbed. Thinking about the Oracle encounter at Taco Johns upset me. Was it prophetic or lunatic? It appeared that I had two options, one was to blow it off as a crazy person's ranting and do absolutely nothing. That's probably what it was. For sure. Right? But… what if it wasn't? What if this young lady spoke the truth? What if this Close Encounter of the Kooky Kind was for real? All throughout the Bible God spoke to people in strange and unusual ways, right?

In my state of confusion and anxiety, I wandered upstairs and plopped down in the office of my then boss. Pastor Craig Hanson seeking advice and wisdom. After relating my story of the Taco John Prophesy to Craig, he burst out in laughter tossing his head back and grinning from ear to ear! After a time, he settled down, leaned forward, winked an eye and muttered; *"Sounds like you'd better start fasting Rol!"*

This event happened 18+ years ago. I've told very few people in my life about this bizarre incident. I did do the fast. I fasted from food for the next three days taking only water. I did not enjoy fasting. I'm one who looks forward to breakfast the night before. I wake up excited for breakfast. I crave a mid-morning snack around 10-10:30, and then I look forward to lunch. Around 2 pm, I crave a mid-afternoon latte and maybe a donut. By 5-6:00 ish, I'm rearing to go for a big supper. Evening snack of cookies and milk or a big bowl of popcorn round off the day. So, my fast spoke quite strongly to my over-use and addiction to food. I did my best to just suck it up and turn my thoughts towards prayer and leaning into God.

Fasting was not pleasant, but it did teach many strong truths about myself, life and God. I've done several lesser fasts since the Taco John Revelation, and all have proven healthy, worthwhile and insightful. Most of all, I believe fasting shows us quite clearly our flaws and our addictions. We realize what we cling to, and where go to *for "filling our tank"* to receive affirmation, identity, and fulfillment.

We begin the season of Lent tomorrow. For many faith traditions, it is a time of giving up **something** for Lent. We surrender some part of our lives that gets in the way of our relationship with God. Some addiction or crutch or false identity giver that we normally use to attempt to fill the "God Hole" in each of our hearts. For years my standard sarcastic line I've offered up is; ***"I'm giving up church for Lent."*** It usually gets a good laugh.

But this year, I've become aware that I have some addiction issues. I've realized I'm looking for love in all the wrong places. I crave and seek the affirmations and "Atta boys" that come with posting on Facebook. It's very subtle, as most of what I post is for and about God. All good in the end. But I get affirmed and blessed for doing it. Sometimes it's to post about some recent accomplishment of my own, or my kids, but it's a sneaky and understated or hidden way of fishing for compliments plain and simple. Much of it is about ego feeding.

I know I'm not alone. My theory is... the more you use social media, the less secure you are in yourself, plain and simple. Now don't get me wrong. So many good, Godly and wonderful things happen in and through social media. Great ministries and fabulous good for the world take place via these social outlets. It' just that I've come to know in my gut, that for me, it's time for a fast, time to let go, time to surrender my use of my primary social media; Facebook.

Any fasting that takes place most often is temporary, i.e. when you fast from food for a day or week, you always return to eating food. We need to eat food. But I firmly believe that by stepping away from something that has become so integral to our lives, we will receive some great spiritual teachings, some internal Godly wisdom, potential profound insights and possibly some deep unexpected blessings. Most importantly if you fast **from something**, let it lead you into deeper communion with God. Surrender this time and process to Him. Ask for the Holy Spirit to guide and speak to you as you let go. Let Him fill the vacuum created by what you've given up.

I challenge you to join me in fasting this Lenten season. Let the next

40 days have meaning and significance. Do an honest search of your life. What is it that you need to give up, surrender and let go of for 40 days? May you have the courage to **Fast** from something significant in your life.

Then Jesus was led by the Spirit into the wilderness to be tempted by the devil. After fasting forty days and forty nights, he was hungry. The tempter came to him and said, "If you are the Son of God, tell these stones to become bread." Jesus answered, "It is written: 'Man shall not live on bread alone, but on every word that comes from the mouth of God.' Matthew 4:1-4 NIV

Vision comes through fasting and prayer to those who Wait patiently for it.

When Jesus had a problem, he did not seek to solve it only by the power of his own thought; he did not take it to others for human advice; he took it to the lonely place and to God. William Barclay

Why Fast?
God must be the **central focus** of our fast.

1. to grow closer, more intimate, more dependent upon God.
2. to gain Godly wisdom, spiritual guidance, and discernment.
3. to receive vision, purpose, and direction.
4. to gain insight into a problem or situation.
5. to gain understanding and personal insight into personal addictions or inner strife.
6. to purify and release your body of harmful toxins.
7. to become more centered, focused and humble.
8. to become unified and of one mind as a group or church.

Fasting is not pulling a trigger, or flipping a switch to control, manipulate or "bring on" God's power, insight, etc. Fasting is a preparation of the heart and mind, a tilling of the soil to listen and receive God in a deeper and more intimate way. Yet remember, that as in all matters, we can expect God to reward those who diligently and humbly seek Him. We must remember that it is **still** more about the **Blesser**, than the **blessing**.

Good Food

Pulling into my driveway in the late afternoon, the mellow soft glow of low sunset light brought a pleasing end to my day. I halted short, next to our basketball hoop as my normal parking space was obstructed. To my delight and surprise, one of my winter camping pull-sleds had been filled with bright yellow, full cobs of corn. Having received no calls or texts to claim this generosity, I was oblivious as to the donor. Several cobs were scattered across the front lawn most likely due to over-zealous squirrels that had encountered this newly found winter Shangri-La of free food! But seeing as a cob of corn most likely weighs nearly the same as our local squirrel, I'm guessing not many cobs made it up and into the pantry.

Thrilled by the gift, I immediately hauled the sled to the back yard, and dumped the large pile 10 yards from our deck, and strategically placed it within the best sight line from our sliding deck door. My gut hunch told me it would not be long before our first visitors would arrive. We normally feed deer for a few months each winter to help them through the cold and deep snow period, but had not done so yet, so to have this generous gift of free food was an added bonus.

For weeks we have had several deer bedding in the narrow, wooded fringes of our yard. They have looked gaunt and weary with the recent foot of snow that has covered their usual food sources. Night or day I can pick out their darkened shadowed forms bedded in the deep snow; their presence given away by the tell-tale "V" of their ears against the white of snow. Our local deer herd must have signed a detente peace accord with our hyperactive dog Bruno, for when we let him out, he dares not cross the borderline between yard and woods. He must be suppressing his inner-wolf.

After supper, making sure the kitchen was dark so I wouldn't be back-lit, I slowly crept to the dining room to the sliding door, and sure enough, three deer were already feeding contentedly on the corn pile. I sat down and enjoyed the scene in the low light of the half-moon. I was thrilled to be getting better acquainted with our new neighbors.

As per my internal prediction, within two days, the number of visitors grew from three to 16, that I counted in one setting. What a miraculous growth in attendance! Apparently, news had spread via word of mouth and the Oakport animal social media network! Evidently, word on the street must have been; that good, nutritious, healthy and life-giving food was to be found at the Johnson household! And even better... it was free!

It's no surprise how in a tough, hurting, cold winter, deer will flock to good food. I'm guessing that not a single deer used the "Four Spiritual Laws", or a bible to bring other deer in to be fed. I would wager that it was simply about telling their story, and an invitation. I would imagine it went something like this: *"Hey Buck, I know that you've been going through a rough time, that you are hungry and searching. I know that you want to be fed with real food. I know this place, that I go to, where I usually come away feeling like I've been filled, and well fed. Why don't you come and join me?"* So simple, so clean, so real, and so easy to say, yet so many of us never dare neither the story nor the invite.

When was the last time you invited someone, a friend or coworker to worship with you? When was the last time you invited a neighbor to join you in attending a bible study group or fellowship event or mission trip? When was the last time you told your story about where you get fed?

Our world is filled with gaunt and weary folk who are emotionally and spiritually starving. They seek warmth, comfort, and sustenance yet look in all the wrong places and activities to find it. You don't need to have a theology degree or know the bible inside and out. You don't need to be gifted with words or have a dramatic testimony or story to tell. Just tell your story, show someone where you get fed, and invite them to join you!

we cared for you. Because we loved you so much, we were delighted to **share** *with you not only the gospel of God but **our lives as well**. 1 Thessalonians 2:8 NIV*

"Come, follow me," Jesus said, "and I will send you out to fish for people." Matthew 4:19 NIV

> It is no use walking anywhere to preach
> unless our walking is our preaching. St. Francis of Assisi

God's Timing

Of late, with this winter that seems to be clinging to the landscape with all its might, Shane and I have been putting out corn for our local deer herd. Our heart goes out to these scraggly deer who are having a difficult time making ends meet in terms of energy expended compared to energy taken in. We're trying to tip the balance in their favor until spring reluctantly shows its much-anticipated face!

I've noticed lately that much of the human herd looks a bit like these hungry, fatigued, and weary forest dwellers. I hear a lot of; *"I'm sooo tired." "All I want to do is sleep!" "Why is everyone so crabby lately?" "I'm just feeling like I'm in a funk these days."* Now I certainly think our long, drawn-out and extended winter has had a significant impact on all of our psyches. This is just normal for March/April in the northern plains, but my theory is that this has been compounded by the very early occurrence of daylight savings time change in March. It's thrown us all off of our Godly, natural rhythms. It's now still full daylight at 8 pm and we'd normally be playing catch in the yard, but now with continued storms adding snow to the ground, our senses are all off!

Our friendly neighborhood deer herd still shows up for feeding time at the normal sunset hour.

They're operating from a completely natural, and God-given rhythm and cycle. No one told them about daylight savings time and they made no adjustments to fit ***our*** new man-made schedule. I laugh at ourselves and how we humans think that we can manipulate or change God's time. And look what it has gotten us?

This morning upon returning to work, I passed through the Celebration Hall. The sweet and aromatic smells of the Easter Lillie's permeated the air. Their fresh, life-giving air was pleasant and appealing to my senses. I laughed inside for on Easter Sunday just two short days ago, these same lilies, had failed to perform on time. On our timing that is. They had been placed in a prominent position in the front of the worship center, and they were still beautiful and visually appealing, but the flower petals had remained closed, and with this closure, they had also withheld their pleasing perfume. I smiled again being reminded that God and his creation have their own timing and rhythm. Just because we as mankind or a church declare that Sunday, April 1st is Easter, it is not necessarily to be so. Oh, how foolish is man to think that we are in charge!

I too, am often foolish and think that I am in control, that I control the timing of life's happenings and events. Now I don't mean to diminish the proper place of accepting personal responsibility, thoughtful planning, and personal ownership of my decisions and actions. This is all good and right. But, much of this life is under God's rhythm and timing. I can either; deny it, fight it or surrender to it. Fighting or denying usually lead to exhaustion, failure, fatigue, and frustration. Surrender, on the other hand, puts God back in the God spot. I do much better under his guidance and timing!

Would you rather have your prayer answered immediately as you would have it be, or wait to see it unfold according to a Godly timing and a God-given outcome for your life?

> *Trust in the Lord with all your heart and lean not on your own understanding in all your ways submit to him, and he will make your paths straight. Proverbs 3:5-6 NIV*

Are you in a difficulty about your way? Go to God with your question; get direction from the light of his smile or the cloud of his refusal… get alone, where the lights and shadows of earth cannot interfere, where the disturbance of self-will does not intrude, where human opinions fail to reach-... wait there silent and expectant, though all around you insist on immediate decision or action- the will of God will be made clear, and you will have... a new conception of God, and deeper insight into his nature. F. B Meyer

*I will lead the blind by ways they have not known,
Along unfamiliar paths I will guide them; I will turn the darkness into light before them and make the rough places smooth. Isaiah 42:16 NIV*

*I will instruct you and teach you in the way you should go;
I will counsel you with my loving eye on you... Psalm 32:8 NIV*

*in all your ways submit to him,
and he will make your paths straight. Proverbs 3:6 NIV*

*Wait for the Lord; be strong and take heart
and wait for the Lord. Psalm 27:14 NIV*

We don't often consider that sometimes Jesus is our
strength to simply sit still(wait). Our natural tendency
when we have a painful happening in our lives is to go into
action- to do something. Sometimes it is wiser to wait and
just be still. The answers will come. Billy Graham

Good, Bad and Ugly

The phone call came in between church services. I had come to my office briefly to check my emails. It was Karina, our oldest. *"Dad, I just wanted you to know that I just finished my first 20-mile run!"* I responded back; *"Awesome girl! Way to go. I'm sooo proud of you. Well done!"* Karina was in her training build up for her first marathon attempt. Pretty cool I thought to myself. Just getting that long, high mileage run completed is a huge psychological and physical accomplishment.

Returning to my office after church I gathered my stuff to head for home, and the phone rang again. It was Karina. She was in tears, and whimpered; *"I don't feel right, can you come over and be with me please?"* She didn't say what was going on, but I said: *"I'd be there in five."*

Upon entering her apartment, it was clear that she was just plain and simply worn-out physically and emotionally from the long run. Having been sick earlier in the week, her body was flat out depleted and exhausted. The long run had drained her of all energy and sense of well-being. She felt out-of-sorts in every part of her body, mind, and spirit. I sat on the sofa, she laid her head across my lap and for the next hour I gently massaged and rubbed her back.

Karina is a highly independent and successful young woman. Yet what a privilege it was as her father, to be invited into the hurt, confusion, and pain of her day. To be trusted with the yuck and muck of a day where she felt as if she had lost her bearings, honored me as her dad. To be present, to be leaned on for strength, wisdom, and comfort by Karina, now a young adult blessed me as a father.

I said my thank you prayers the entire way home for I am indeed a lucky man. Blessed beyond what I deserve. Two weeks later I had the privilege of watching her cross the finish line and share in the joy, accomplishment, and celebration of her first marathon.

How about you and your heavenly Father? Do you give him access to all parts of your being? Are you able to lay your head across his lap on the days when you are out of sorts, when the physical or emotional pain is so great, when confusion reigns, when nothing makes sense? Can you share with Him the good, the bad, and the ugly?

I believe that God desires this kind of intimacy with His children. We need not shine up our life, put on our best outfit, clean up our attitude, cover over the blemishes, nor stash the undesirable stuff of our lives into the closet. We can come before him hurts, pains, successes, triumphs, and confusion in all of our totality. When we do, it honors Him, as it did me as a father.

May you come before God today with complete honesty and transparency. Bring Him; the good, the bad, and the ugly of your life.

"Come to me, all you who are weary and burdened, and I will give you rest. ^{29} Take my yoke upon you and learn from me, for I am gentle and humble in heart, and you will find rest for your souls. ^{30} For my yoke is easy and my burden is light." Matthew 11:28-30 NIV

And he said: "Truly I tell you, unless you change and become like little children, you will never enter the kingdom of heaven. ^{4} Therefore, whoever takes the lowly position of this child is the greatest in the kingdom of heaven. Matthew 18:3-4 NIV

GRANT

The lunchroom was a buzz of noise and movement. The hum of conversations and plastic trays meeting silverware created a white noise that was both deafening and numbing. Playing out before me was the daily social experiment called school lunch, which is mimicked in thousands of high schools across America. This is a make or break territory, where fitting in, popularity, and friendships are defined, and the fleeting outcomes of self-acceptance, self-esteem, and loneliness are at stake.

Sitting alone at the end of a long lunch table sat a young ninth grade girl. This the third week of a brand-new school year, in a large suburban high school, was also her third week of sitting alone. Today she sat, elbows on the table with her face in her hands. Tears flowed freely from her reddened eyes and her shoulders shook with each sob. She was diminutive in stature, due to some form of physical handicap that also caused her to limp. One can only imagine the loneliness of isolation and not fitting in, compounded by the laughter, smiles, and conversations that surrounded her. The proverbial gut-wrenching loneliness in the midst of a crowd of hundreds.

Sitting not three tables away was a group of boisterous young guys, mostly jocks and dudes doing their guy thing. Ninth graders are by nature conformists seeking to stay within the strict boundaries of cool and acceptable high school norms, not wanting to be noticed or exceptional to avoid any negative teasing, ribbing or loss of stature. Yet from within this mix of testosterone-filled adolescent males, rose our protagonist, Grant.

I've known Grant since childhood. A quiet, polite, kid who always greets with a smile and a firm handshake. He's an athletic, highly intelligent, good-looking guy, who has excelled at his passion of hockey for years. He is modest and humble to the nth degree and I've witnessed him sitting on the same side of church week after week for years. I'm assuming that within his school he is well-liked and respected by many.

Grant was a keen observer, and over the first few weeks of school, he had noticed this young lady sitting each day all alone. Yet today, witnessing her tears and trembling, the scales tipped from intention to action and he quietly stood, grabbing his lunch tray and slowly headed in her direction. The table of guys watched with queried faces and occasional out loud jibes as they perceived his intended destination.

Ignoring his buds, Grant approached the table from opposite the young lady, stood awkwardly before her and politely asked if he could sit with her. She looked up through tear-soaked hair, and apprehensively nodded a silent "yes." Grant introduced himself and began a conversation. Tears were soon wiped away, and by the end of the 20-minute lunch period, laughter could be heard coming from the end of the table. At the sound of the bell, Grant stood offering a gentleman's handshake and said; "This has been very nice, how about each Friday we meet like this and have lunch together?" She smiled shyly looking down, and nodded a grateful "yes."

I believe that two lives were changed on that fateful day. All because one courageous young ninth grade boy had the courage to step beyond teenage norms, and act upon the compassion planted in his heart by the Holy Spirit. He chose to see through the eyes of Christ, rather than by the exclusive laws of high school popularity, beauty, and approval. And this courageous act was so simple, yet profoundly impactful. He didn't have to be a missionary in Africa, or raise a million dollars for charity, or climb a mountain in the name of God. He simply listened and then acted upon Godly promptings within to extend the hand of friendship, kindness, compassion, and belonging to a hurting and lonely fellow student.

This preceding story that happened four years earlier, came full circle this past week. This young lady was chosen by, then escorted by Grant to a fun-filled evening of Prom, proving that class, character, and compassion are not one-time events, but rather are integrated into the whole of a person of integrity and faith.

May you become more and more cross-eyed. May you act with Godly compassion and courage.

May you see with the eyes of Christ.

<u>Cross-Eyed:</u> a. the ability to see below the surface, to see the beauty, dignity, and God-given qualities inherent in people.
b. to see Christ in others
c. to know, acknowledge and embrace Christ within yourself.

Can it be that grace takes us by surprise in the midst of the ordinary and the repeated? Why shouldn't this be so, because grace is from outside us, not within? It is God's interruption, his wonderful invitation.

For most of us, God's command doesn't take us away from what we are presently doing. It fills our lives with new significance by reordering our priorities and requiring us to submit our activities and plans to the test of Christian concern and love. Gerhard Frost

It is not our task to judge the worthiness of our path; it is our task to walk our path with worthiness. We have been blinded by the light of heroes and saints. We must learn to trust the small light we are given, and to value the light that we can shed into the lives of those around us." Kent Nerburn *"<u>Small Graces</u>*

GRATITUDE

Reaching the staff work-room from a late arrival to work, I reached up and peaked into my mailbox. It mostly sits empty, so I was surprised to see two envelopes patiently waiting for me. One was generic junk mail, but the other was handwritten and even came with an old-school return name and address. Hmmm... I pondered to myself. Handwritten letters are usually of only two varieties; the proverbial *Nasty Gram* from a disgruntled and angry church member wanting to vent about something this or something that. Thankfully those are quite rare... but boy do I have a memory for them! The other kind of hand-written letters are of the opposite flavor and contain words of appreciation, gratitude, thankfulness and often times help to affirm and recognize one's gifts, talents and positive impact on the world. I wondered: which would this be?

Holy Week often has a heavy, oppressive weight to it. Fuzzy pink bunnies, chocolate eggs, and Easter Break are foreign to us that work in the church. We are hustling to organize music, plan meaningful services that are fresh and new, write multiple sermons, practice, and organize, all with the anticipation and expectation that Easter will be our biggest day of the year.

So, as I entered my office, I felt a bit of melancholy with the heavy workload of the week and my own normally way-to-high expectations of myself. The cool dreary day outside matched my mood on the inside. And then, in a heart-beat everything changed!

I had opened the letter and found a full-page hand-written letter from a gentleman whom I did not know. He outlined that he had recently received my new book, Paying Attention: Finding God in the Ordinary, as a gift from a very good mutual friend. His letter was filled with compliments, gratitude, and deep appreciation for the contents and meaning found in the book! His words of affirmation struck a strong chord in my heart as my face filled with tears of my own gratitude for his appreciation. I quietly said my own thank you prayer for this gentleman and his kind words. It was just the encouragement I had needed.

In previous weeks I had been frustrated with progress, the unknown, and not knowing if, who, when, where the book was being purchased or enjoyed or appreciated. I had even spent a significant amount of prayer time wrestling with God on this issue. This gentleman's kind note was a beautiful answered prayer that uplifted my spirit, renewed my drive, and restored my outlook for the upcoming week. Those words of gratitude put a bounce back in my step and filled my energy tank with love fuel.

Each year I receive dozens of solicitations to sponsor someone on a mission trip or to write a recommendation for them. The ones that come as a simple form letter are tough to act on. The ones that come with a hand-written note are much easier to support. Last week I received a solicitation from a young man at church asking for an Eagle Scout recommendation. In addition to the form letter, he had hand-written a long note of respect, gratitude, and appreciation for me. I perked up at the blessing and proceeded to write him a long and heartfelt, highly positive, glowing recommendation! It is simply amazing what honest words of gratitude and affirmation can do!

I am often disappointed in students who do not write personal thank you notes when I gift them with a financial sponsorship or special favor or "extra mile" worth of effort on their behalf. Maybe it's their parent's fault, as we breed more and more indulged kids and entitled parents. I sometimes think it is an attribute of millennials. But then again, one simply needs to read scripture to realize it has nothing to do with age or generations. Even Jesus encountered people who were ungrateful, or silent in words of gratitude and appreciation.

Now on his way to Jerusalem, Jesus traveled along the border between Samaria and Galilee. As he was going into a village, ten men who had leprosy[a] met him. They stood at a distance and called out in a loud voice, "Jesus, Master, have pity on us!"
When he saw them, he said, "Go, show yourselves to the priests." And as they went, they were cleansed.
One of them, when he saw he was healed, came back, praising God in a loud voice. He threw himself at Jesus' feet and thanked him—and he was a Samaritan.
Jesus asked, "Were not all ten cleansed? Where are the other nine? Has no one returned to give praise to God except this foreigner?"[19] Then he said to him, "Rise and go; your faith has made you well."
Luke 17:11-19 NIV

Jesus received just one for ten. And Jesus completely changed their entire lives for the better by healing them of the hideous and gruesome disease of leprosy. Wow! Shocking! Hard to believe that only one in ten would instantly run back to the source and give gratitude and thanksgiving! I'd say not much has changed in this day and age!

It is intriguing to me that in his last sentence Jesus ties **"Gratitude"** with **"Faith."** I believe with all my heart that the most grateful people are also the most faith-filled people. And the most faithful people are also those that show and give and demonstrate and speak gratitude, appreciation, blessing, and affirmation.

If an undercover stranger were to watch your life for a week… would they observe you to be: "THE one?" or simply one of the nine?

Therefore encourage one another and build each other up, just as in fact you are doing.
1 Thessalonians 5:11 NIV

> Flatter me, and I may not believe you. Criticize me, and I may not like you.

Ignore me, and I may not forgive you. *Encourage me, and I will not forget you.* William Ward

Too often we underestimate the power of a touch, a smile, a kind word, a listening ear, an honest compliment, or the smallest act of caring, all of which have the potential to turn a life around.   Leo Buscaglia

> The biggest secret of dealing with people:
> *Give honest and sincere appreciation.* Dale Carnegie

HABITAT

The invitation came from Terry, our administrator. His passion and love for this ministry were catchy and admirable, his enthusiasm contagious. My ten-year-old son, Shane, and I could spare a few hours, so I signed on the dotted line and committed to a morning's worth of labor. Helping someone else by using our hands and getting dirty would be good for both of us, and possibly provide some teachable moments with Shane. For someone like me who continually invites, prods, pokes, and cajoles others into service and volunteering, I figured I'd better put my sweat where my mouth is and do some volunteering of my own.

We arrived at the Habitat for Humanity build site under the warmth of gorgeous morning sunshine. Several of First Lutheran's faithful, always-ready, volunteer yeomen greeted us with smiles and handshakes. Their ongoing example of steadfast servanthood, shown as a quiet reminder to me, of what faithful mission work is all about.

Shane and I were quickly given a task for the morning. At first, I was excited, as it was a very simple assignment, and seemed like a good matchup for our skill sets. The house was nearing completion so most of the larger, more construction-like tasks were already complete. Our job was to take colored putty, and simply fill all the nail holes on all the finish trim work of the house. Easy enough, I thought to myself, and we can't really screw that up, and Shane and I would have plenty of time to chit chat. All good.

So off we went to the basement and in the shadowy low-light of

Paying Attention II

no electricity, we began filling tiny holes of the baseboard, windows, closets, and door trim. The work was not difficult, nor taxing, but certainly tedious, monotonous and boring. And Shane was quick to point this out! I too kept looking at my watch, and saying to myself, "Man there are lots of holes and so much trim, we're only on the first of many rooms!"

Though the task was uninteresting and wearisome, it provided good father-son conversations and banter throughout the morning. Topics of conversation included: The Vikes, The Bison, Adrian Peterson, man is this boring, Teddy Bridgewater, are we done yet? Carson Wentz, soccer games, Messi, Rooney, how much more is left? Girls, deer hunting, do we have to do the whole house? Naked and Afraid, can we be done yet? New soccer shoes, this is really not very fun! And what's for lunch?

By 11:30 we had finished the whole house. My right index finger was sore and had turned a funky shade of tan-brown. We bid our adieus to our fellow workers and site supervisors, grateful to be done and onto the next day's events.

As we journeyed home, I thought of what Shane might have learned this day. Our task was simple, uncomplicated, easy, yet extremely tedious and boring. No one who entered this new home would ever notice, pay attention to, or thank us for our time and work. It was certainly not glamorous or exciting work, nothing to write home about. No one would pat us on the back and say "Good job" or "Atta boy." Nor would we reap any great internal reward, or experience a sense of great accomplishment. It was pure and simply unnoticed, unexciting, background, grunt-work, but work that needed to be done, by someone.

As followers of Jesus, we are all called to a life of service. Service and mission are not optional! Take a listen to Rick Warren's excellent words; "Great opportunities often disguise themselves in small tasks. The little things in life determine the big things. Don't look for great tasks to do for God. Just do the not-so-great stuff, and God will assign you whatever he wants you to do. There will always be more people willing to do "great" things for God than there are people willing to do the little things. The race, to be a leader is crowded, but the field is wide open for those willing to be servants."

Rollie Johnson

Our day with the fellas working for Habitat was a good reminder to me, that servanthood and Christ-like mission in our world is often unglamorous, tedious, and boring. May we all be reminded that there is work to be done!

> Life's most urgent question:
> "What are you doing for others?"
> Martin Luther King

And let us consider how we may spur one another on toward love and good deeds, ²⁵ not giving up meeting together, as some are in the habit of doing, but encouraging one another—and all the more as you see the Day approaching. Hebrews 10:24-25 NIV

And whatever you do, whether in word or deed, do it all in the name of the Lord Jesus, giving thanks to God the Father through him. Colossians 3:17 NIV

HARE

Making my way through the darkened empty streets of downtown in the predawn hours, I drove slowly headed to the Frying Pan restaurant for an early morning breakfast. The streets were damp from the overnight rain and the glare of stoplights and streetlamps reflected in puddles and wet pavement. The city had slept and now only a few stirrings could be witnessed on quiet sidewalks and empty roadways. The morning felt like evening still, a sodden and soggy beginning to a day that still lay ahead.

As I came to the first set of railroad tracks, I noticed a tiny figure working its way across the street. The giveaway was its movement as it passed from the shadows through the light of the reflections on the street. My instincts called for cat, yet within a few seconds, I could see from the rocking-horse gait that it was a small hare or rabbit slowly making its way across the moist avenue.

From where he had come, and where he was headed? I did not know. I could discern no noticeable cover or natural refuge nearby. A flicker of a smile came across my face as I nodded in approval of this normal dweller of field and forest that had made a home in the midst of railroad ties, concrete, pavement, and steel. What a strange thing I thought to myself as my mind filled with questions. Why would this rabbit choose a home in the inner city? Had anyone else ever witnessed this urban bunny? Did he ever show his face in the light of day or was this some sort of lagomorph superhero who roamed the city streets and shadows by night in search of justice and truth? Could he have been the Dirty "Hare"-ry of Fargo? *"Go ahead punk…make my day!"* With so much natural park space nearby, and a city surrounded by fields and river bottoms… why had he chosen to live downtown? How could he survive in such a landscape that appeared to be devoid of life and nourishment? Only questions remained.

In a quiet corner of the mostly empty restaurant, I stared at the headlines. **"59 dead - 500+ Wounded in Vegas By A Lone Gunman."** I shook my head in disbelief and my gut clenched as I sullenly repeated: *"What is our world coming to?"* We, supposedly the greatest nation in the world, kill one another in our schools, malls, theatres, streets, and churches with such regularity that most of us, including me, have grown callous and numb to these appalling tragedies that appear almost weekly on our televisions and newspapers. How and when and where did we as a society learn that if we're upset or emotionally wounded, we gun down innocent people and children?

I have no answers or solutions to such complex and tragic issues. Only sadness, disbelief and questions remain.

My predawn rabbit encounter reminds me of a simple truth though. A long time ago when God wanted to get serious about interacting with his creations, he did a strange and wonder-filled thing. He sent himself in the form of a human being and inserted himself in the midst of an inhospitable, messed-up place called earth. He walked amongst us and was present in the midst of human suffering and tragedy. He wept with the weeping, he celebrated and danced with the wedding party, he stood up for the weak and defenseless, he suffered alongside those who were suffering and he spent much of his life and time lurking in the shadowy spaces where lepers, blind, sinful, lonely and broken people dwelled.

God is present still today and often goes unseen and unnoticed in the form of the Holy Spirit. He is present today for those who are at the epicenter of suffering and loss from this recent tragedy, and he is with each of us suffering quietly at the outer ripples of the pond, who knew no one personally but cry out in disbelief, fear, and sadness.

And let us not forget another simply Godly truth: **You** are the hands, face, and words of Jesus in this inhospitable and often difficult world. It will be your kindness, your compassion, your comforting word, your gentle hand on a shoulder, your quiet prayer, your warm smile, and your random act of kindness that will change the world around you for the better in Jesus name.

May God bless you on your journey today as you minister to our hurting world.

Dear friends, let us love one another, for love comes from God. Everyone who loves has been born of God and knows God. [8] Whoever does not love does not know God, because God is love. [9] This is how God showed his love among us: He sent his one and only Son into the world that we might live through him. [10] This is love: not that we loved God, but that he loved us and sent his Son as an atoning sacrifice for our sins. [11] Dear friends, since God so loved us, we also ought to love one another. [12] No one has ever seen God; but if we love one another, God lives in us and his love is made complete in us. 1 John 4: 7-12 NIV

Therefore, as God's chosen people, holy and dearly loved, clothe yourselves with compassion, kindness, humility, gentleness, and patience. Bear one another's burdens and forgive one another as I have forgiven you. Colossians 3:12 NIV

If anyone acknowledges that Jesus is the Son of God, God lives in him and he in God. And so we know and rely on the love God has for us. God is love. Whoever lives in love, lives in God and God in him. 1 John 4:15-16 NIV

Hold Loosely

The bow drill squeaked and creaked as Chris drew the bow forward and backward in a rapid sawing motion along his body. Kneeling on one knee, with his chest powerfully planted over his front raised knee, he held the socket in his left hand firmly against his left knee. With his right hand holding the bow, he drew a steady rhythm forward and backward and soon produced a light smoke rising up from the bottom where the rotating spindle met with the fire board. Picking up speed and intensity, smoke thickened and billowed up in thick dark clouds. The pleasing scent of burning cedar filled our nostrils. After 40 seconds of bowing, a dark cone of dust had collected beneath the notch cut in the fire board. Chris carefully ceased drilling and raised his back upright to breathe fresh air and catch his breath.

We all waited in rapt anticipation to see if the pyramid of dust had actually produced an ember. After the major smoke had cleared, we could all clearly see a small wisp of smoke spiraling upward from a tiny dark spot growing in the dust pile. He had an ember! Goal number one accomplished!

After catching his breath, Chris carefully coaxed the ember away from the fireboard with his knife and lifted the birds-nest made of collected plant fibers, grasses, and shredded bark closely to his face and delicately squeezed the bird's nest around the glowing ember. He began to blow, softly at first, rotating the nest around and round, and then increased the intensity and volume of air. As he did, so too did the

Paying Attention II

volume and intensity of smoke. With each breath, the smoke thickened and grew stronger. He had to keep a fine balance of squeezing the nest firmly enough to keep feeding the internal ember with new material and being careful not to squeeze too hard and extinguish the coal. As the smoke grew thicker and thicker and our anticipation rose to a frenzy, the birds next spontaneously burst into flames! Cheers and applause erupted from all of us. The smile on Chris's face for birthing fire from scratch was priceless!

This was the scene from our recent SOLO trip at Camp Wilderness. It was a fantastic week of learning Native American/ primitive living skills; friction fire, natural cordage, flint-knapping, a sweat lodge, the high ropes course and all capped off with a 36-hour solo in the wilderness; a fantastic week of faith, learning and personal growth.

As a kid do you remember holding a young bird that had prematurely fallen from its nest gently in your hands? It was a delicate balance of holding tightly enough to not allow it to escape and fly away, and not holding too tightly so as to crush or suffocate the bird. Firm yet tender, enough grasp to keep it contained, yet enough delicateness to allow freedom, air, and slight movement. Grasp too tightly and you'd have a dead collection of feathers, grab too loosely and the bird was gone.

I believe with all my being that the Holy Spirit is in the business of planting dreams, visions, creative ideas and goals in each of our hearts. Dreams that match our skill set, talent package, and passions. Most of us though are too busy to listen or pay attention. But for those who take their spiritual lives seriously and spend significant amounts of time listening in prayer and solitude, the Holy Spirit can breathe life into these dreams and make them into reality to bless and benefit others in our world. A dream or vision is something that must be held firmly yet gently, like the bird's nest in the bow drill fire method, or a young bird that has fallen from the nest. Hold too loosely and the goal will disappear in the wind. Grasp too tightly at your dream and you may kill it.

In the formative stages we have to ask ourselves; *"Is this dream or goal of God or is it simply my selfish ego wanting attention?"* We need to surrender the dream to God and lay it at His throne. If it is of God and has its origins in the Holy Spirit, it will be given back to us. He will bless it and gently blow it into flame and provide the resources and connections to birth it into reality.

I have witnessed this process over and over again in my own life and ministry. I have also witnessed many beautiful, meaning-filled and powerful ministries of friends and coworkers fanned into life by the Holy Spirit. They dreamed big, visualized a dream, prayed fervently, listened, sought council of the wise, surrendered and then waited patiently before the Lord. When you are given a vision or dream or goal, hold it firmly, yet gently. Continue talking to God about it and surrender it to Him. And if it *is* of God… He we gently blow the wind of the Holy Spirit upon it and birth it into existence to bless the world around you!

For this reason I remind you to fan into flame the gift of God, which is in you through the laying on of my hands. ⁷ For the Spirit God gave us does not make us timid, but gives us power, love and self-discipline.
2 Timothy 1:6-7 NIV

For many people, God doesn't give insight into their callings all at once. He often quietly plants dreams in their hearts. The dreams lie there, under the surface, growing and maturing, not necessarily coming to the surface in a spectacular, flash of light moment. Your mission is a lifetime endeavor, not a one-year deal. God calls us to what we really want to do and what we were designed to do. And when you engage in your purpose, it brings a deep sense of satisfaction and significance.
A mission is really a dream planted in us by God. John Maxwell

When you are confident that it's of God, stand firm, even against other people's doubts. Be strong and resolute. That's a part of **walking by faith**. There are times when other people will say, "there's no way in the world God could be in this"; yet you know absolutely in your heart that He is. At times like this simply stand firm. You won't be able to convince them, but that's all right. God is still doing unusual things.
Charles Swindoll, <u>Flying Closer to the Flame</u>

Holy Now

A tiny rivulet of moisture trickles down from the snowfield somewhere above 12,000' high on the continental divide of northern Colorado. The rugged grey of mountain mass meets with crystal clear azure skies. The jagged knife-edged mountain separates earth from sky. In a basin like this begins several small creeks that have silently agreed to meet downhill to form one stream. They join forces to increase speed and volume as their zig-zagging downward journey continues.

Descending the ridge top, I seek the stream in the bottom of the bowl and kneel to partake of this life-giving water. The high mountain dry air and heavy exertions have left me dry and parched. The ice-cold water refreshed both my body and spirit as I drank until satiated. Cupping my hands, I scoop water over my head and neck, and then washed dust and sweat from my face. I smile, shaking my hair being cooled and renewed by the clean water and fresh mountain air. I have been revived inside and out. I am born again, baptized in Holy Water. Have we, that have continual and unlimited access to water forgotten that water is indeed Holy?

Leaving these sacred mountains elk-less, and bidding farewell to my two good hunting buds Duncan and John, I begin my long and lonely 14-hour drive home. I cherish this journey and treasure the solitude and time for reflection. Most of this passage is over and through the wide-open spaces of the plains of eastern Wyoming and the Western Dakotas. The vast undulating spaces and long vistas seem to expand my thoughts and perceptions. This time is Holy now.

Moving northward I look west through hazy sunshine I witness the shadows of the distant Laramie Mountains. Each successive layer of ridges grows lighter in the background. They are my last "Adieu" to the mountain west. A tinge of melancholy washes over me, wondering when I will next return. These many mountains have blessed me an enriched my soul. They are Holy now.

Continuing northward through the Dakotas the deserted highway seems to curve and bend connecting the dots of the many buttes that thrust skyward from the prairie. Doggie Butte, Chimney Butte, Crow Butte, South and North Cave Hills, White Butte, and Rainy Buttes to name a few. I ponder what strange forces of wind and water and time had formed them into such attention-getting features of the landscape. I could imagine bands of Native Americans: the Sioux, the Cheyenne, The Arikara, the Lakota navigating from butte to butte. And what about their more primitive ancestors that most likely roamed the landscape 12-14,000 years ago? This landscape must be Holy now.

Scattered across the expansive rolling prairie were golden fields of wheat. With the wind blowing they appeared to move and flow like the hair on the back of a golden lab. Where fields had been cut, the yellow was bright and blinding. These fields would soon provide flour, bread, Wheaties, pizza dough and pasta. Tall patches of sunflowers paid homage to their namesake raising their heads to the sun. Soon we will spit their husks at a ball game, or cook with their oil. The fields with amber waves of grain and brilliant yellow must be Holy now.

Massive squares of landscape filled with soybeans and tall stalks of corn. These plants appeared to be torn between their adolescent fullness of summer greenery and their maturation into the tans and browns of their fullness of the fall. Like me, they seemed to be resisting the aging process, not quite ready to surrender and give in to nature's eventual and unavoidable processes. These fields of grain will soon become dozens of products in my home that I take for granted. These corn and soybeans must be Holy Now.

Dotting the prairie were scores of black and brown cattle peacefully grazing and doing what cows do. I assume that they will soon become my next steak or Big Mac, or maybe a wallet or Gucci purse, or 9West pair of dress shoes Neiman Marcus Wing Tips, or belt that holds up my pants. Have we forgotten or taken for granted that these creatures are indeed Holy?

Standing just ten feet from the highway I passed a young white, tan and black mother antelope. Attending to her side, was a young calf who, neck and head extended upward, pushed and prodded sucking at her mother's teat receiving life and nourishment from her mother, who had received her life and nourishment from this prairie. The calf would have been birthed earlier in the spring and conceived about this time of year by a rutting buck who mated with a doe last fall. And from this amorous union came this incredible miracle of a calf. This cycle of rut and birth, and life and death has continued for untold millennia over this terrain. It is mimicked in our human race as well. This must be Holy Now.

Interspersed along my journey were countless old abandoned farmsteads in various states of disrepair. Most were darkened gray and leaned over slightly. I pondered as to the who and when of their inhabitants and their stories. Occasional tiny cemeteries flowed over hill-sides and I wondered over their histories and lives and deaths. I wondered where will my final resting place be? Certainly, this life we've been given must be Holy?

Take a listen to this superb song by Twin Cities folk artist, Peter Mayer: "Holy Now."

https://www.youtube.com/watch?v=KiypaURysz4

Most of us are waiting for God to work a dramatic miracle in our lives. We want lightning flashes, dramatic changes, skywriting, a booming voice from heaven, a pillar of fire, or hand-written letter from Jesus with specific instructions for our lives. We get caught in the mundane, the routine, the everyday boringness of our lives and think that miracles only happened long ago.

Peter sings:

"And I remember feeling sad, that miracles don't happen still, But now I can't keep track, Cause everything's a miracle… So the challenging thing becomes, Not to look for miracles, But finding where there isn't one."

My journey took me to Colorado to try and take an elk. Having failed in that quest, I had a long journey, and my goal was to simply just get home. The "in-between" of Colorado and home usually doesn't count for much. Thank God He showed me differently.

Maybe you will be racing towards your next appointment, meeting, destination, activity, conquest or goal today. Maybe you could ask God to show you **His Holy** along the way.

> I believe in God like I believe in the sunrise, not because I can see it, but because I can see everything it touches. C.S. Lewis

Open my eyes that I may see, wonderful things in your law. Psalm 119:18 NIV

But blessed are your eyes because they see, and your ears because they hear. For truly I tell you, many prophets and righteous people longed to see what you see but did not see it, and to hear what you hear but did not hear it. Matthew 13:16-17 NIV

At that time Jesus said, "I praise you, Father, Lord of heaven and earth, because you have hidden these things from the wise and learned, and revealed them to little children. Matthew 11:25 NIV

"Seeking the face of God in everything, everyone, all the time, and his hand in every happening; This is what it means to be contemplative in the heart of the world. Seeing and adoring the presence of Jesus, especially in the lowly appearance of bread, and in the distressing disguise of the poor." Mother Theresa

Homeless Meets Homeless

Slowing down for the crosswalk beneath the Sanford Hospital overpass, I continued slowly south on Broadway, then flicked my turn signal and entered the left lane to make my way to work Tuesday morning. Kiddy corner across the intersection I could see our Homeless Jesus statue. Today was different though. For upon the bench where the blanket-covered Jesus lay, sat an actual homeless man. He too was covered in a tattered and torn blanket. The blanket he had wrapped tightly around his head, and I could easily see puffs of steam rising upwards from his breathing in the frosty, chilled morning air. At his feet lay a camouflage day-pack and another satchel that looked like an old laundry bag. What a strange juxtaposition I thought to myself; a homeless man, sitting on the Homeless Jesus bench.

It was obvious he was engaged in deep verbose conversation with someone, although I knew not who. It might have been the bronze Jesus at whose feet he sat. It may have been to passersby across the street, or simply to himself, or some imagined audience somewhere in his foggy thoughts. It appeared to be quite a boisterous and spirited conversation!

As I gradually turned the corner, I could see his face more clearly and recognized him as one of the regulars from the couple years we had served lunch each Monday at the Salvation Army. I could not retrieve his name from my dulled memory banks but remembered him as always being friendly, grateful and a man who spoke freely of faith, the bible and God.

My mind teetered back and forth as I made my way to the parking lot; "Should I go out and engage with him? Or take the easier route and head in to start my day." Neither He nor anyone else would ever know no matter which path I chose. Fortunately, I chose the path of courage and made my way around the sidewalks and corners of the church.

As I approached, I greeted him with a friendly; "Good Morning! How's it going?" A bit startled from his lack of vision behind his blanket, he seemed pleased by the encounter and he gave it right back to me with an enthusiastic; "Good morning to you!" Extending my hand, I told him my name and that I remembered him from my days at the Salvation Army. He returned the favor with a toothless smile and stuck out his hand from beneath the worn blanket. A cold handshake ensued. "I am Anthony" was his quick reply.

He had been writing in a spiral-bound notebook, in what appeared to be lines and lines of neat and tidy scripture verses. His penmanship and writing were well-ordered, precise and methodical. I thought, "How odd that such clear and concise writing, came from a man whose life appeared to be anything but well-ordered or clear! I politely asked if he'd be interested in a hot cup of coffee inside, to which he showed great enthusiasm. I threw his laundry bag over my shoulder like a premature Santa, Anthony grabbed his backpack and we headed inside.

We sat in the gathering space and conversed freely. He devoured his hot coffee and scrambled eggs I'd heated up for him. He shared bits of his story freely with me. Said he hadn't had a puff of crystal-meth for over a week and was feeling pretty good. He proudly showed me his Bible, then rambled on about the unfairness of certain homeless shelters, quoted a variety of scripture verses and shared his thoughts on churches and his life. And then he hit me with a question that is still resonating in my brain as I write these thoughts.

He slowly leaned in towards me and nodded his head westward and quietly whispered; *"Do you think the Bishop and those priests over across the street ever serve at the Salvation Army?"* I hemmed and hawed and pleaded ignorant in that I didn't know much about St. Mary's... but the bombshell had already exploded in my gut.

In my mind I thought; never mind about my neighbors to the

Paying Attention II

west, how can I point out a splinter in their eyes when there is a log is in my own. Internally I reversed the question and said to myself: "Do we as pastors, staff, and parishioners serve freely and faithfully at the Salvation Army? We that have placed a Homeless Jesus statue in front of our church. We that are about to spend $13 million on a shiny new building? We who have sound minds, untold wealth, strong physical health, and in numbers sufficient to serve… <u>*are we serving*</u> to the best of our abilities?

I had begun the day in hopes of ministering to Anthony. He had unknowingly turned the tables and spoken prophetic words of truth and challenge to me. A chance encounter, or maybe not …God had used a humble crystal meth-addicted homeless man to speak words of caution and counsel to me, and maybe even our larger church.

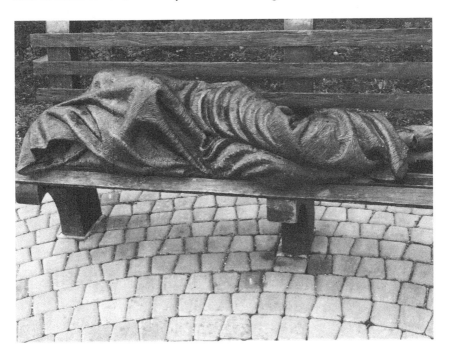

May we, who are in the midst of constructing a vision and building that will serve generations to come, for whom we cannot even yet see, be reminded that we must serve those placed at our doorstep in the here and now. Let us not have our eyes set so far out on the generations that will come... that we forget about the Anthony's who are in our midst this day.

What good is it for someone to gain the whole world, yet forfeit their soul? Mark 8:36 NIV

Sheep & Goats
"Then he will say to those on his left, 'Depart from me, you who are cursed, into the eternal fire prepared for the devil and his angels. For I was hungry and you gave me nothing to eat, I was thirsty and you gave me nothing to drink, [43] I was a stranger and you did not invite me in, I needed clothes and you did not clothe me, I was sick and in prison and you did not look after me.'
"They also will answer, 'Lord, when did we see you hungry or thirsty or a stranger or needing clothes or sick or in prison, and did not help you?'

"He will reply, 'Truly I tell you, whatever you did not do for one of the least of these, you did not do for me.' Matthew 25: 41- 45 NIV

Homeless Man

We strolled along the sidewalk marveling at all that surrounded us; magnificent brick buildings, mirrored, steel skyscrapers soaring into the gray overcast sky. Christmas lights blinked from tall apartment windows and empty water fountains now stood silent in the cold of winter. Storefront windows displayed all the latest and best, along with fluffy fake snow, sparkling tinsel and the red and green of candy canes and Christmas trees. People of all makes, sizes, and ages hustled and bustled along the festive avenue.

Downtown Minneapolis, Nicolette Mall to be precise, is where my daughter Marissa, my son Shane and I were ambling along on our way to the Metro, to catch a ride to the Vikings game. The three of us were enjoying the unique sounds and sights of the big city and soaking up every minute of it. The look of pure delight and wonder on Shane's face as he gazed skyward, neck craning, made the whole trip worthwhile for me. We're not in Kansas/Fargo anymore Dorothy!

The three of us looked completely out of place in this metro shopper's paradise. We were dressed from head to toe in our warmest winter fleeces, down jackets, snow pants, and big boots. I felt like the Michelin Man or Stay Puff Marshmallow boy lost in the concrete jungle. We each sported brand new purple and gold Vikings stocking caps to honor and show loyalty to our beloved team. A gigantic purple and gold plastic necklace hung from Shane's neck, and I dubbed him the new Flavor-Flav of Vikings country.

We stopped for a rest and sat down upon a concrete bench just below the magnificent blue mirrored IDS tower. Just a few yards away sat a disheveled older man, with an untidy, scraggly beard. His long, unkempt, gray hair, dirty, worn out jeans, and grubby tattered white and purple Vikings jacket, and torn up boots, made him the picture of homelessness. He held a cardboard sign, and at his feet were two small tins propped open, upon the cement sidewalk.

We'd witnesses several others like him on our walk, and as I sat there, I went through the mental games of *"Should I, or Shouldn't I"*, that we all must play when faced with such realities. Do a good deed, do the right thing, be charitable, be a blessing vs will he use it to buy booze or drugs? Is he a full-time lazy scammer? And I mentally balanced my billfold of available cash on hand vs. expected costs for metro tickets, treats, gas home, etc.

I handed Shane a couple of bills and directed him to go and place these into the tins as I nodded in the man's direction. Shane's eyes locked on to mine for a few brief seconds as he realized what I was asking, as he searched for a way out. I knew this was taking him way beyond his comfort zone, but he soon dutifully obeyed and was on his way. I whispered, *"Make sure to wish him a Merry Christmas!"*

Shane carried out his unwanted mission without protest and was met with a warm, genuine smile from the disheveled man. *"God bless you son and have a Merry Christmas!"*

Shane returned to our post, none the worse, and we stood up to continue on our journey. As we passed the man he broke into a big smile and shouted out, *"Have a great time at the game folks! I hope they win. This could be our year! God bless and have a Merry Christmas!"* We scurried onward to the Metro.

The Vikes Game was a marvelous experience for us all. A magnificent stadium, filled with enthusiastic, passionate, and fervent fans of all shapes and sizes. Zealous followers dressed in hilarious attire entertained throughout each section. Delicious, unhealthy ballpark food filled our gullets, and a rare, fully dominant performance by our Vikings capped the day as we put, "Daaa Bearsss," to rest.

Post-game, we retraced our footsteps through the sardine-packed

Metro, and then back down Nicolette Mall towards our hotel. And there to my surprise and wonder, four hours later, sat the same homeless man. Upon recognizing us, he perked up, and began asking about the game, playoffs, AP, and how did Teddy do? We briefly clued him in, and continue on our way, bidding him a "Merry Christmas!"

The long drive home gave me plenty of time to ponder. I wonder what Christmas will be like for him? Is this truly the *Hap, Happiest time of the year* for him?" I contemplated; *"Is it beginning to feel a lot like Christmas* in *his* world? Will there be; *"Chestnuts roasting on an open fire, or Jack Frost nipping at his nose?* I ponder how much peace, joy, and good will toward men he will encounter. Will he be home for Christmas?

Tough to say. Only conjecture on my part. My cynical side offered up only words of condemnation and judgment. My compassionate voice called for love and empathy. If only the ghost of Christmas past could walk me down his back trail a ways. I'll bet I would find in his *his-story*, plenty of reason to act with kindheartedness and benevolence.

But maybe, just maybe, the judgment is actually upon us, those to whom much has been given. Maybe his use of the money was irrelevant and inconsequential. Maybe God is using these situations to judge the heart of the giver, of we; "The Haves." I cannot control how someone, anyone, uses a gift I give, whether a friend, a family member or a stranger. What I can control is my attitude and intention in giving. May we *"The Haves,"* practice cheerful giving this Christmas season.

…From everyone who has been given much, much will be demanded; and from the one who has been entrusted with much, much more will be asked. Luke 12:48

The Widow's Offering

Jesus sat down opposite the place where the offerings were put and watched the crowd putting their money into the temple treasury. Many rich people threw in large amounts. But a poor widow came and put in two very small copper coins, worth only a few cents. Calling his disciples to him, Jesus said, "Truly I tell you, this poor widow has put more into the treasury than all the others. They all gave out of their wealth; but she, out of her poverty, put in everything—all she had to live on." Mark 12:41-44 NIV

Each of you should give what you have decided in your heart to give, not reluctantly or under compulsion, for God loves a cheerful giver. 2 Corinthians 9:7 NIV

If I Should Die Tonight

'Tis the season! But this never-ending snow cover and endless winter are like a long, overstayed mother-in-law. They just won't leave! Normally by this time in April, I'm spending every free moment walking the nearby fields in search of arrowheads and other sundry artifacts that have worked their way to the surface from the natural freeze-thaw process, or the possible assistance of the farmers plow from last fall. But not yet! This winter will not end!

Sitting last evening in my chaotic yet highly organized man-cave I thumbed through some of my drawers of found treasures. I smiled as I fondly remembered each artifact, as I recalled what field it came from and the absolute joy I had felt upon its discovery. Being a highly tactile being, I massaged each item, and quietly entered the spiraling time tunnel of questions that took me back to the how, where, who, and when of long-ago history. These amazing artifacts help me reach out over the expanse of time and space to connect with a people and animal kingdom long forgotten.

Each of these hand-crafted artifacts is linked to a person. A human being, a man or woman of native heritage, and these artifacts are a part of their legacy. Their faces, names, and language a blur to me as I see through the dim and foggy window of time. Yet these items have outlived their lives by possibly 300-1,500 years. And today I touch them via their legacy.

Rollie Johnson

(Clockwise from left to right: White black-bear canine tooth, Purple pipestone with bird track carving Arrowhead of Knife River Flint (author's making), Arrowhead of Knife River Flint, Deer antler tip used for flint-knapping, Two Celts or axe-heads, Three Knife River Flint turtleback thumb scrapers, Bone awl, Three elk ivories, Three grey pottery sherds)

On each of the many adventure and mission trips I lead, I give each participant a devo book filled with scripture verses, interesting quotes, and journaling questions. Participants use these devo books for their quiet times and small group discussions. In most of these booklets you'll find a journaling page like this:

If I Should Die Tonight

What if you were to die tonight?
What is your greatest regret?
What would you like to do over?

Whom do you need to forgive?
To whom do you need to say "I'm sorry?"
With whom do you have words left unsaid?
What will your closest friends say about you at your funeral?
What will your family members remember about you?
How will you be remembered by your children?
What will you leave behind?
What will your legacy be?
What will you be remembered for?
What will God say to you upon your departure from this world?
What will you ask God?
Are you living your life today in a manner that will help you prepare for this meeting with God?

Caressing these Native American artifacts has me thinking long-term. Both of the past, but now personalizing it, I ponder my own life:

What will I leave behind? Money, wealth, stuff or a positive impact on others?

What will be my legacy? Things, toys, buildings or lives that have been influenced in Godly ways?

> How will my children speak of me? He loved to bow hunt, golf, drink _____ he was selfish, or that he loved us?
> What will my wife speak of as she says my name? He loved his hobbies…_____ more than me? He was in our house, but He was never there. Or he helped make me a better person? Or He just loved me.
> Will I hold grudges and anger that accompany me to my grave? Or will I release others and free myself through the power of God's forgiveness?
> Will I have lived my life wasting time on striving for what the world tells me I need, or will I have listened to the One True Voice and lived my life with passion, purpose, joy, and gratitude?

> When I meet with my Maker, what will He have to say about how I used my time, my life, my possessions, and my wealth in service to Him and our world?

Sometimes it's good to contemplate the past. Sometimes it's good to meditate on hi***story*** in order to reset, refocus, and reshape our story. And the best way to make your story count is to connect your story to **His** story.

"Our greatest fear is not that we are inadequate, but that we are powerful beyond measure. It is our light, not our darkness that frightens us. We ask ourselves, "Who am I to be brilliant, gorgeous, handsome, talented and fabulous?" Actually, who are you not to be? *You are a child of God*, your playing small does not serve the world. There is nothing enlightened about shrinking so that other people won't feel insecure around you. *We were born to manifest the glory of God within us.* It is not just in some, *it is in everyone.* And, as we let our light shine, we consciously give other people permission to do the same. *As we are liberated from our fear, our presence automatically liberates others.*" Nelson Mandela, Inaugural Speech

> *For we are God's handiwork,*
> *created in Christ Jesus to do good works,*
> *which God prepared in advance for us to do.*
> *Ephesians 2:10 NIV*

Each of you should use whatever gift you have received to serve others, as faithful stewards of God's grace in its various forms. 1 Peter 4:10 NIV

"*The King will reply, 'Truly I tell you, whatever you did for one of the least of these brothers and sisters of mine, you did for me.*" Matt 25:40

INCOGNITO

The darkened eye-liner traced already existing crow's feet to make them more visible from afar. Rubbing my index finger back and forth in the deep blue and grey of the make-up kit, I wiped obscure shadows above and below my eyes making my sockets appear hollow, weary and tired. The pungent and displeasing scent of spirit gum offended my senses as I brushed it generously over my face, chin, and neck. Its stickiness and stench made me question my current course of action.

Cutting sections of the braided theatre grey crepe hair, I began creating a full beard starting fist with the mustache and working my way around my face until soon I had the rough and unkempt full beard I was looking for. The sticky spirit gum and tickling hairs made me want to claw my face off. I topped off my head with a full grey wig complete with a braided ponytail. A dirty old brown bandana added a nice drab look, and an old pair of horned-rim glasses, complete with touches of athletic tape, finished off the look of my face.

Earlier in the week, a quick trip to the thrift store had given me a sack full of over-sized clothing. The quality and cleanliness were too great, so I spent an evening in the garage giving the clothes a more lived-in look. The bench sander proved useful in wearing holes in the knees and elbows and helped to create fringy seams and hemlines. Oil, sawdust, and dirt helped give some realistic looking stains.

Dressing in these worn, weary and dreary clothes I then removed my wedding ring and watch. Adding a few touches of brown and red make-up around my neck, hands and bare ankles the look was complete. I looked dirty, weary, and downtrodden. Completely street worthy. And all that remained was the "piece de resistance;" I doused my beard, face, and clothing with a generous supply of brandy, followed by the generous sprinkling of my clothing with fox urine.

Today I would become incognito homeless.

Sneaking quietly out a seldom-used door of the church, I began limping and slowly staggering down the sidewalk like a drunken sailor. My first stop was the *Homeless Jesus* statue bench that sits right at the entry of our church sanctuary. I posed as a slouching, sleeping drunk leaning on Jesus. Bright, clean fall sunshine streamed down as well- dressed churchgoers paraded past me climbing the stairs for the nine o'clock service. The overly cool breeze made me crave warmth and heavier clothing. To their credit and much to my surprise, several churchgoers bravely offered a polite "good morning!" Others nervously walked by in silence. Some chose an alternative route to avoid passing by me.

Gaining my feet, I continued staggering down Broadway and made my way around the corner to the main parking lot. Taking a seat on the curb a few feet away from an entrance I slumped on the sidewalk. I could see curious stares and uneasy glances as worshipers entered the building. Many friends passed over me sidestepping my extended legs. Some offered a greeting, others passed in silence at a quickened and uneasy pace.

Curiously, it was the small children who offered the most solace. A beautiful young, blond girl of maybe four or five years of age, stopped and looked me in the eyes and innocently asked; *"What are you doing?"* Her mother held her hand and quickly led her away. It was most interesting to observe the Sunday morning church world through the eyes of a downtrodden homeless man.

Waiting until seven minutes after the start of the service, I stumbled my way up the stairs and headed for the main sanctuary. I wanted the service to be past the first song so that all would be seated. Grabbing a bulletin from a wary usher, I walked into the packed service in full and plain view of the several hundred worshipers. Pausing briefly in front of all I wavered and then stumbled into a crowded pew creating a minor scene. The tension and discomfort were palpable. There was definitely an "elephant" in the room, and It was he!

We soon arrived at the reading of the gospel. As the reading finished and the crowd sat, there was a long, awkward pause and waiting for the preacher. After counting to ten, I slowly stood and walked toward the pulpit. Any sleepiness or daydreaming had left the building and the words awkward, uptight, tension, anxiety, and curiosity had taken their place. I grabbed the microphone and proceeded to give my sermon.

The disguise, for the most part, had worked its magic. The great majority of folks were completely unaware of my true identity. That includes close friends, coworkers and many parishioners whom I know well. The dupe had worked for those who had seen me at a glance from afar, and for those who walked by me face to face in the hallway. I had entered the church incognito.

We who are Christians often hear something like; *"Be kind to the stranger. Maybe that person you are kind to might actually be Jesus."* Maybe the homeless man or the woman pushing the shopping cart might be *Jesus in Disguise.*

Good reminders to us all for sure. Take it one step further and anyone; your wife, your husband your neighbor, your teammate, your coach, your teacher, your coworker, friend, your enemy… anyone could be Jesus. So how do you treat them? Especially outside of church. Or maybe, more importantly, how do you treat the awkward, unusual, or unpleasant *IN* your church?

My journey into a typical Sunday morning church world as an incognito homeless man was quite thrilling and revealing to be sure. Peering out through fake glasses, behind a scrubby and scruffy beard wreaking of urine and brandy I so desperately wanted to simply shout out; *"Hey! It's just me! It's me… Rollie."*

I wonder how many times I have walked past the downtrodden, the lonely, the desperate, the defeated, the loser, the forgotten, the outcast and the unlovely and I missed hearing; *"Hey! It's just me! It's me… Jesus!"*

You will never look into the eyes of someone… That God does not already love.

[41] "Then he will say to those on his left, 'Depart from me, you who are cursed, into the eternal fire prepared for the devil and his angels. [42] For I was hungry and you gave me nothing to eat, I was thirsty and you gave me nothing to drink, [43] I was a stranger and you did not invite me in, I needed clothes and you did not clothe me, I was sick and in prison and you did not look after me.'
[44] "They also will answer, 'Lord, when did we see you hungry or thirsty or a stranger or needing clothes or sick or in prison, and did not help you?'
[45] "He will reply, 'Truly I tell you, whatever you did not do for one of the least of these, you did not do for me.'"
Matthew 25:41-45 NIV

Invisible Force

The late afternoon sun cast a warm soft light over the marsh. A gentle breeze from the west created a slight rippling to the surface of the pond that added texture and movement to the landscape. And even though the marsh was still dressed in its fall and winter browns, tans, and greys, it was bursting with the vibrant life of motion and sound. Spring was being birthed, and I sat center stage, front row to creation in full concert.

I sat comfortably rocking in the deck chair at the end of a long boardwalk that extended from the shoreline snaking out through the floating bog of cattails, alders and marsh grasses. I gave thanks for the warmth of the sun on my back that was rejuvenating and life-giving after the long cold winter. Our three- day silent retreat at Pacem in Terris, north of the Twin Cities was restoring my soul.

Twenty yards out from the dock end, there appeared two small, one inch, triangles that appeared to be out of place. Sure enough, the triangles disappeared below the surface, and my hunch was correct; a pair of young painted turtles. Ice out must have only been a few days past so I wondered was this their first journey to the surface? Had I witnessed their first draft of fresh clean air? What must it be like to be buried beneath bottom mud of the pond for 6 months? How can a turtle hibernate for so long without fresh air, and what signals its journey to the surface? What invisible force guides and directs the life of these turtles?

Through my binos, I could clearly see a gaggle of geese on the far side of the marsh. Their continuous and boisterous honking was hard to not notice as if it were a Kardashian family reunion and all were shouting "look at me!" In an instant, the cacophony of honking, wing flaps, and water splashing grew louder as the flock of ten erupted simultaneously into flight. The flock made a low ascending circle round the lake below tree line and as I followed their flight through the binoculars it appeared as if they would crash headlong into the trees as they headed east. The field of view distorted by my binos had deceived my perception as they disappeared through some unseen hole in the canopy headed for parts unknown. What had signaled their departure? Had they made a group decision? Was there a leader? Had they filed a flight plan? How could they know where north was? Would they return to an exact same lake somewhere in Canada? In their nickel-sized brain did they have a built-in GPS? And what signals their migration each fall and spring? What invisible force guides and directs these geese?

A bit later, I heard squawking above and looked skyward and noticed a flock of five Sand Hill Cranes silhouetted against the light blue sky. Their herky-jerky flight was less graceful than that of the geese or nearby eagles. With long legs and even longer wings flapping to and fro they made a more awkward and less efficient flight. Were they too headed north? I understand they mate for life. What can we humans learn from them about marriage and relationships? What invisible force guides and directs these long-legged cranes?

Just before sunset, a pair of punk-rock Pileated woodpeckers landed on a nearby set of barren tamarack trunks. Their brightly plumed red mohawks shone brilliantly in the sun. I had heard the jungle-like bird calls from across the pond, and now they pecked and poked like the proverbial Woody the Wood Pecker just thirty feet away. Could they hear bugs beneath the surface of the hard exterior? Could they smell the insects crawling under the bark? Were they too, grateful for the return of warm sunshine and the onset of spring? What invisible force guides and directs these crimson topped bug hunters?

Near final light, as the sunlight slowly climbed the trees on the eastern shore, and the wind abated to bring mirror calm to the water's surface, I noticed the tell-tale "V" of rippled water heading my way along the shore of the marsh grasses. The large head of a beaver was patrolling above the surface to begin his night shift of work. On a previous walk through the woods, I had noticed one of his dams and had stopped to ponder this north-woods wonder. How is it that this plump, beautifully furred rodent could have a master's degree in civil engineering? How, when and where did he learn to alter the landscape with mud and sticks? Was he taught by his parents? I know that I myself could never build such a structure that is as solid, watertight and structurally sound as he. What invisible force guides and directs this chunky, buck-toothed beast?

On the quiet and slow walk back to my hermitage, I couldn't help but ponder what I had just been privileged to witness on the marsh. There was an invisible rhythm and orchestration to all that I had witnessed; a steady heartbeat and pulsing energy connecting all of the marsh life that remained hidden from most of us fast-paced, modern city dwellers. It was as if there was an intangible connective web or labyrinth of life force moving over the pond.

Native Americans speak of *"the spirit that moves through all things."* I pray to one called the Holy Spirit. I believe that this is the one and same invisible force that formed the entire universe, continues to create and renew, and can now guide and direct our lives when we tune in and invite Him to lead and direct our lives!

May you tap into, listen to, and be guided by the invisible force, power, and creativity of the Holy Spirit!

> *"But when He, the Spirit of truth, comes, He will guide you into all the truth; for He will not speak on His own initiative, but whatever He hears, He will speak; and He will disclose to you what is to come. John 16:13 NIV*

> *In the same way, the Spirit helps us in our weakness. We do not know what we ought to pray for, but the Spirit himself intercedes for us through wordless groans And he who searches our hearts knows the mind of the Spirit, because*

the Spirit intercedes for God's people in accordance with the will of God. Romans 8:26-27 NIV

In the beginning God created the heavens and the earth. ² Now the earth was formless and empty, darkness was over the surface of the deep, and the Spirit of God was hovering over the waters. Genesis 1:1–2 NIV

In the beginning was the Word, and the Word was with God, and the Word was God. He was in the beginning with God. All things were made through Him, and without Him nothing was made that was made.
John 1: 1-3 NIV

Flesh gives birth to flesh, but the Spirit gives birth to spirit. You should not be surprised at my saying, 'You must be born again.' The wind blows wherever it pleases. You hear its sound, but you cannot tell where it comes from or where it is going. So it is with everyone born of the Spirit. John 3:6-8 NIV

Invisible Tracks

The freezing wind-chill cut at our faces making them ruddy and raw as we walked the CRP and cattails directly into the strong north wind. Three friends, a couple of labs and I walked the fields in hopes of flushing the red-headed rooster pheasants. Not having my ND license, I had been converted to retriever, two-legged flusher, and gun bearer. Our morning was a great time of good healthy exercise, laughter, and conversations of work and life. The Sand Hills seemed alive as the wind rustled the prairie grasses like the soft hairs on the back of a red fox.

We descended into one of many coulees that had been at one time an active beaver pond. The wind was silenced with the protection of the terrain and trees, and we felt relief from its biting cold. Cautiously testing the ice, we were relieved to find a solid 12" thick, so we enjoyed a leisurely jaunt down the pond exploring its many nooks and crannies.

I'm one who is always searching and watching for *sign*; tracks, droppings, feathers, marks, rubs, anything that will give a clue as to an animal or bird having passed. I soon found the almost invisible tell-tale tracks of a large raccoon that had walked up the coulee on the ice. There was no snow, just ice, as smooth as glass so the tracks were not obvious to the untrained eye. When attempting to show the tracks to my friends they bent and muttered; "where… where?" The raccoon's warm feet had simply melted the microscopic thin layer of frost on the surface, and when one knelt down and "side headed," the tracks fairly jumped off the surface and screamed to be noticed. Now kneeling low, they could be seen, plain as day looking like a **baby's feet** and hands had neatly walked down the ice creating a rhythmic pattern of cookie-cutter prints.

It seems that in our fast-paced, modern commercialized version of Christmas, the reason for the season has become almost invisible. Most folks, including many good church-going faithful, can no longer see the "what" and "why" of Christmas. Traditions of house lights, Christmas trees, decorations, goodies, cards, gifts, bonuses, church programs, concerts, music, Santas, candles, and cookies have numbed and blinded us so we can no longer perceive what is at the heart of Christmas.

Funny, when you remove **Christ** from **Christmas**, all you have is "mas," or in Spanish; more. More stress, more strain, more running, more exhaustion, more money spent, more debt, more junk, more garbage, more to do, more tiredness, more sadness and melancholy, more hectic, more emptiness and more "is this all there is?"

Maybe we too need to take a few moments of silence and solitude to kneel and observe. I believe that when we humbly kneel with an expectant and searching heart, we may then be able to see the almost invisible footprints of a baby. A baby that weaves its way through our wild world, but is unseen by most. And I believe that we do not celebrate a simple moment in history like we would remember Pearl Harbor or our day of independence. No, we celebrate because those tracks lead to a living, breathing God that is still moving and active in our world.

I challenge you to take a time out today. Find a quiet space to be alone. Kneel. Ask God to show and reveal himself in the world around you and especially in your own life. It's incredibly exciting... when you can finally see the tracks and then realize... **He** is near!

For to us a child is born, to us a son is given and the government will be on his shoulders.
And he will be called Wonderful Counselor, Mighty God, Everlasting Father, Prince of Peace.
Of the greatness of his government and peace there will be no end.
He will reign on David's throne and over his kingdom, establishing and upholding it with justice and righteousness from that time on and forever. The zeal of the Lord Almighty will accomplish this. Isaiah 9:6-7 NIV

Come, let us worship and bow down, Let us kneel before the LORD our Maker. Psalm 95:6 NIV

For since the creation of the world God's invisible qualities—his eternal power and divine nature—have been clearly seen, being understood from what has been made, so that people are without excuse. Romans 1:20 NIV

The Son is the image of the invisible God, the firstborn over all creation. Colossians 1:15 NIV

Joy In The Rain

Shane and I entered the darkened woods behind our house and over the dike. These woods have been our playground, sanctuary and sanity maker for so many years now. The sky was dark and dreary with a stiff, cool, swirling breeze that hinted strongly at rain and storm. The favorable smells of sweet grass and mown clover filled our lungs with pleasing scents. We entered the forest in search of supplies for our upcoming SOLO trip in August. Tops on our list were last fall's milkweed stalks for teaching cordage, and bows for practicing primitive fire. Shane carried his stout folding knife for trimming, and I held the tree saw for cutting the arched three-foot longbows from overhanging curved branches.

Shane was his usual chatty self and I felt a deep sense of contentment and satisfaction for the privilege of walking and talking in the woods with my son. We wandered easily through the woodlot eyeballing branches looking for the right curve and thickness. Upon finding a prime candidate I would saw off the branch and Shane would then shave off nubbins and pokey twigs all the while conversing about soccer, middle school, and movies.

As our stockpile of rough-hewn bows grew, the wind increased dramatically as limbs and leaves danced above us with greater vigor. Thunder could be heard in the distance as the forest became darker and darker as if someone had hit a dimmer switch. Shane felt the first drops, nodded towards home and declared; *"Maybe we should head back!"*

As we collected our bows the rain began in earnest as we quickly scampered towards home. Lightly at first, but as we exited the woods and gained the opening of the grassy dike the tempest had arrived in full force. Tremendous winds blew in all directions as trees bent and swayed in dramatic, un-choreographed movements and rain-soaked us from all sides. As we crested the dike, Shane slowed his pace, looked up, smiled through the downpour and declared; *"This is pretty awesome dad! We should just stay out and play in it!"*

Our normal, modern- day, common-sense, city-dweller instincts move us to do the opposite. Run quickly, avoid getting wet or uncomfortable at all costs, seek safety, shelter, warmth, and protection immediately! Yet, from the mouth of my twelve-year-old son, came the beckoning voice to play, to feel, to sense, and to immerse ourselves in the beauty of a summer rainstorm.

What could I do? I stifled the stern, caution-filled voice of the adult inside, and instead leaned into and followed the playful calling of the child. We threw the bows in the shed, headed for our garage, peeled off shirts and shoes and ran for the rain! The middle of our small street was dancing with raindrops and large puddles that begged to be stomped in. Salt stung my eyes washed off from an earlier run in the day. The coolness was accentuated by the wetness and stiff breeze that tightened our skin and brought our senses to full life and vitality. There was great joy in being full-body immersed in the storm. Laughter, joy, and smiles bounced back between Shane and me.

Upon entering the house, a dry fluffy towel felt comforting on cold skin, warm soft cotton socks felt better than ever, and a cozy sweat-hood and jeans returned warmth to our chilled bodies. I felt invigorated, fresh, clean and alive!

Sometimes in life, we need to say *"No"* to the cautious, stifling, reasonable, prudent and habitual voice of the adult. Sometimes the Godly child within calls and beckons us to experience life and nature on its terms and in its fullness. Comfort, security, safety, ease, and surety are often placed as the ultimate goal, yet we miss out on so much of the joy of life when we neglect spontaneity, curiosity, joy, and play.

Jesus is fairly blunt and direct, and scripture quite specific about not losing our child-like joy in life.
This week may you loosen your stiff, adult-like, caution-filled collar. There are life, vitality, and joy waiting when you do!

He called a little child to him, and placed the child among them. ³ And he said: "Truly I tell you, unless you change and become like little children, you will never enter the kingdom of heaven. ⁴ Therefore, whoever takes the lowly position of this child is the greatest in the kingdom of heaven. ⁵ And whoever welcomes one such child in my name welcomes me. Matthew 18:2-5 NIV

Rejoice always, pray without ceasing, give thanks in all circumstances; for this is the will of God in Christ Jesus for you. 1 Thessalonians 5:16-18 NIV

Then people brought little children to Jesus for him to place his hands on them and pray for them. But the disciples rebuked them. Jesus said, "Let the little children come to me, and do not hinder them, for the kingdom of heaven belongs to such as these." Matthew 19:13-14 NIV

People were also bringing babies to Jesus for him to place his hands on them. When the disciples saw this, they rebuked them. But Jesus called the children to him and said, "Let the little children come to me, and do not hinder them, for the kingdom of God belongs to such as these. Truly I tell you, anyone who will not receive the kingdom of God like a little child will never enter it." Luke 18:15-17 NIV

June Berry

The cool evening held the flavor and feel of fall more than mid-summer. The fresh clean air hinted sweetly of prairie grasses and unknown flowering plants. Leaving our car, we crossed the parking lot and headed across the street. Clear blue skies and a brilliant late afternoon light flooded out faces as the sun began sinking into Red Hawks stadium. Our timing had been perfect... an hour and a half after game start time, put us after the fifth inning when the entrance is free. Call me cheap, call me frugal, or just speak my truth that three to four innings of slow baseball are plenty!

As we crossed the street and gained the sidewalk, I happened to notice some newly planted saplings. Out of the corner of my eye, as I passed, I noticed it had several dozen small fruits dangling from its branches. My first thought was crab apples, but my instincts caused me to stop, reverse my tracks and examine further. Sure enough, my gut hunch was correct! The little crown on the berries revealed indeed its true identity. Unbelievable to me it was a June Berry bush! And it was filled with delightful ripened berries!

June Berries are the lesser known and taller cousin of the infamous blueberries that lie low to the ground. I normally find and gorge on both of these delectable fruits on summer forays into the Boundary Waters of northern Minnesota. Juneberries are a bit larger, more of a purple than the blue of the blueberry, and to my palette even sweeter. I shouted to Shane, and his buddies; Henry and Victor, to come and try.

Smiles and nods of approval went all around as we filled a couple of handfuls into our mouths and savored the delicious sweet juices. As I looked around, I saw that every third tree was a June Berry bush! How crazy is this! Fantastic and free berries outside of Newman Outdoor Stadium! I pondered how many hundreds of people had just walked by this treasure and never paid it notice or second glance.

The gorgeous evening did not help the Hawks as they tanked, but the fireworks more than made up for their failures. We left the stadium in the darkness of the night and filed out like a heard of slow-moving cattle. My gang had to stop at the bushes for a quick refill of June Berries. The many people rushing by us must have had many strange looks and quiet comments as the four of us picked and plucked in the darkness like giraffes grazing in trees of the savannah.

Upon arriving home, we built a bonfire in the back yard, toasted SMORES and then crawled in the sleeping bags on the trampoline for a back-yard campout under the stars. What a great evening it had been. As we nodded off to sleep, I suggested; *"How about berry pancakes for breakfast?"* Groggy *"Yeses"* came back in unison.

Sometime after daybreak, I awoke Victor and we headed back to the stadium. Within five minutes we had each picked full containers of delicious June Berries and devoured several handfuls for good measure. We left some bushes still full for the birds and other observant passersby. Upon return home, I made a fantastic sausage and Juneberry pancake breakfast, compliments of our fine NDSU foresters!

I wonder how many rich Godly blessings you and I walk by each and every day. Most of us are goal- oriented i.e. each movement and decision are moving us towards a task, destination or activity. Our goal that Friday night was to go sit in a stadium and watch a ball game. Yet God had planted a delicious and unexpected treasure right in our pat if only we could enjoy the journey, go slow enough to observe and be open enough to alter our schedule.

Maybe you are headed to the lake cabin and that is your weekend destination and activity...yet might there be a delicious sunset along the way or a spectacular farmland scene filled with a thousand shades of summer greenery that begs you to pull over and savor? Maybe there will be a lemonade stand or garage sale along your path to work tomorrow... might that be a Godly invitation to pull over and see what blessing lies within? Maybe you're headed to Yellowstone National Park with the family to see the wonders of that strange and exotic land... and you miss the beauty, serenity, and vastness of the magnificent Great Plains... or the quiet conversations and family chatter along the way?

WE INTERRUPT THIS DEVO FOR THE FOLLOWING: As I sit on my deck writing this devo (my intended destination/activity,) several deer have just invaded my yard. Two spotted fawns are racing and prancing playfully in and out of my woods. One stops to be caressed by her mother as she gently licks her fawn with reassurance and tenderness. The momma doe flicks her tail back and forth after scanning the area; all is well. Songbirds flicker and dive at our bird feeders and a gray squirrel a mere ten feet away is circling the oak pondering a run for the bird food. Blessings along the way? I think so!

Maybe you'll head to church this week expecting/wanting to hear God in a sermon, that is good and right…But what if God places himself outside the church in the scent of aromatic blossoms in the air, or in the sunrise, or a gentle rainfall on your car roof, or someone you encounter along the way? Will you pause and acknowledge and appreciate and give thanks… or merely stumble on your routine way.

May you pay attention; God is hidden in the Ordinary of our lives! He has blessings abundantly strewn across your pathway.

"But ask the animals, and they will teach you, or the birds in the sky, and they will tell you; or speak to the earth, and it will teach you, or let the fish in the sea inform you. Which of all these does not know that the hand of the LORD has done this? In his hand is the life of every creature and the breath of all mankind. Job 12:7-10 NIV

"Earth is crammed with heaven. And every bush aflame with God. But only those who see take off their shoes." Elizabeth Barrett Browning, poet

"The whole earth is a living icon of the face of God. … I do not worship matter. I worship the Creator of matter who became matter for my sake, who willed to take His abode in matter, who worked out my salvation through matter. Never will I cease honoring the matter which wrought my salvation! I honor it, but not as God. Because of this I salute all remaining matter with reverence, because God has filled it with his grace and power. Through it my salvation has come to me."— St. John of Damascus (675-749)

> *"We have seen that the Son of God created the world for this very end, to communicate Himself in an image of His own excellency. … When we behold the light and brightness of the sun, the golden edges of an evening cloud, or the beauteous (rain)bow, we behold the adumbrations of His glory and goodness; and in the blue sky, of his mildness and gentleness."— Jonathan Edwards (1703-1758), preacher and Pastor*

LAUGHTER

Upon entering the large building, it became clear that I was not the only one in need of healing. I had come to receive therapy. It appeared as though others had come for similar reasons but I knew not the specifics of their journey nor was I aware of their personal issues. I sensed though that we had all come with high expectations of being uplifted, and relieved of our individual burdens... least for an hour or so.

We had all heard of this healer, and others like me had laid down good money for this extra-ordinary and unusual treatment. I was so optimistic about what could happen to me as a result of this hour spent with this famed therapist, I had even brought my 13-year old son Shane, wife Ady, daughter Marissa and her boyfriend, Garrett. Deep in my heart, I knew that we could all benefit from this therapeutic experience. I was anxious for us all to experience this healing together.

Before entering the therapy room, we got in line and made our way through the full-body scanners. Highly unusual I thought to myself. Never before had I needed to have a full-body scan before receiving treatment. We followed the growing crowd and soon entered the larger room. I was impressed to see so many other gathered and in need of healing. I could only guess as to those present, but my best guestimate would put us in the 7-8,000 people total.

Soon the lights dimmed, and a booming voice could be heard over the intercom; "Welcome Ladies and Gentlemen, the Fargo Dome presents Jim Gaffigan!" From behind the darkened curtain, our therapist appeared. And for the next hour and a half, we laughed non-stop until we cried, or couldn't breathe. As I looked around me during the performance, I saw pure smiles, shoulders shaking and others rocking back and forth with gut-level laughter. My son sitting next me had a look of delight and joy that was priceless. My wife continued to wipe away tears and a few pointed elbows to my ribs here and there reminded me this comedian was "right on" with "real life stuff." Marissa and Garrett kept looking my way with huge smiles of pleasure and enjoyment. I offered up several thank you prayers in gratitude for Jim and his incredible gift of comedy.

As we filed out of the dome, I felt purged, relieved, exhausted (in a good way,) and that burdens had been lifted. My money spent on therapy had been well spent. I had exchanged the melancholy of a long, dreary winter for joy and laughter. I was the better man for having visited this incredible therapist. I went home and slept like a babe.

Laughter is so healing. I believe it is one of God's two primary emotional gifts for getting through tough stuff; crying and laughter. Both are a physiological release of energy; a gut level, visceral way to release tension, sadness, anxiety, and stress. And for most of us, we do too little of both and are the worse for it. Men, in particular, are poor at best for good crying, hiding behind a machismo and bravado that refuses to step out from behind the manly mask to be real.

One of my own pet peeves for both my church and "the" church, is that the church (and that is us) takes itself waaaay too seriously. Most church services are solemn, pious, somber, serious and to be frank, quite boring. Is there any wonder why youth so quickly walk away from churches never to return? Who would want to be a part of a church where a bunch of stern-faced, frumpy-grumpies sist staring out from the pews?

Rules and regulations, dos and don'ts, shoulds and should nots. Clean-up and polish the outside, hide the angry, pious, jealous, judgmental and condemning inside. These are the ways of the Pharisees, folks who lived by the law, the rules and proper protocol.

Jesus had very little time for these churchgoers. In fact, the only time Jesus got confrontational, "in-your-face'" and conflictual was with… Pharisees.

Jesus was certainly a serious s man who lived his life with great passion, purpose, devotion and resolve. But Jesus was a whole and complete man. He was the greatest example of wholeness we've ever seen. He frequented parties and weddings and continually hung out with and dined with the "wrong people." In fact, the very first miracle he performed after coming out of 40 days in the wilderness was turning water into wine. John 2:1-11 tells us Jesus commanded the servants to use six stone jars that contained 20-30 gallons of water each. My friends… that is no small amount of wine! Somewhere between 120 and 180 **<u>GALLONS</u>** of wine! Not bottles! The story says nothing about getting drunk or out of control, but it does tell us that Jesus was about life, goodness, food, fellowship, laughter, merriment, and family!

On our local Christian station KFNW (97.9,) they air little two to three-minute bits by national Christian comedian Ken Davis. His stories and humorous vignettes are always entertaining and when I hear the intro, I turn up my radio. I'm usually blessed by laughing out loud or at least a smile cracks my faces. He ends his segment with; **"Lighten up… and Live!"** Ken is right on the money. God has given us the incredible gift of laughter. Let's use it! Lighten up overly serious Christians! And Live!

> *A cheerful heart is good medicine, but a broken spirit saps a person's strength. Proverbs 17:22 NLT*

Our mouths were filled with laughter, our tongues with songs of joy. Then it was said among the nations, "The LORD has done great things for them. Psalm 126:2-3 NIV

There is a time for everything, and a season for every activity under the heavens:
a time to be born and a time to die, a time to plant and a time to uproot,
a time to kill and a time to heal, a time to tear down and a time to build,

a time to weep and a time to laugh, a time to mourn and a time to dance, Ecclesiastes 3:2-4 NIV

Woe to you, scribes and Pharisees, hypocrites! For you are like whitewashed tombs which indeed appear beautiful outwardly, but inside are full of dead men's bones and all uncleanness. Even so you also outwardly appear righteous to men, but inside you are full of hypocrisy and lawlessness. Matt 23:27-29

Woe to you, teachers of the law and Pharisees, you hypocrites! You clean the outside of the cup and dish, but inside they are full of greed and self-indulgence. Blind Pharisee! First clean the inside of the cup and dish, and then the outside also will be clean. Matthew 23:25-26 NIV

Lessons from a Long Hike- Part I

The brilliant azure sky served as a backdrop curtain to the featured performers of the rugged, wild- west landscape; endless valleys and canyons dappled with the intermittent, stubby darkened green junipers, and striated, multi-colored bandings of ochre, pinks, purples, and greys in this forgotten and lonely badlands. The moody sisters of silence and solitude were my uninvited, yet required companions on this long and lonesome journey through the desolate wilderness of western North Dakota badlands.

I was here to hike the 97-mile *Maah Daah Hey* Trail that connects the north and south units of Theodore Roosevelt National Park. The trail is a dragon's spine of endless ups and down. You walk your way up one scenic drainage, cross a ridgeline or tabletop prairie with endless vistas that reach towards eternity, and then descend another rugged, wild, remote canyon only to repeat this pattern over and over again all day long. For those who have difficulty with numbers, 97 miles is like starting in downtown Fargo and walking straight west to six miles past Jamestown.

I had come to the *Maah Daah Hey* for a pilgrimage. I desired a solitary journey in which I could lose all distractions, peel off the layers of my comfortable suburban lifestyle and disrobe from the many pretenses and postures that I unconsciously wear in a churchy work world. Most of all, I craved being alone with my Creator and wanted to be bathed clean from the inside-out through and by His Creation.

The vast, weathered, forsaken badlands terrain swallowed me

wholly into its silence and solitude. The entire six days of my pilgrimage I encountered not a single hiker. This left only 24 hours a day for conversation with myself and my Maker. The badlands generously poured out its blessings with magnificent vista after vista, endless painted panoramas, and secret views revealed at each new bend of the trail. Bison, elk, whitetail and mule deer, wild turkeys, coyotes, hawks and eagles all accompanied me for brief periods of time along my trek.

The name *Maah Daah Hey* comes from the Mandan Indians and means *"an area that has been or will be around for a long time."* The trail is easy to follow in the sense that 4" x 6" posts are placed the entire length of the trail intended to be placed so that you can see the next post from the previous post. Each signpost is branded with the Native American turtle symbol which appropriately symbolizes; patience, perseverance, determination, and steadfastness.

I found great meaning and metaphor with this symbol as my pilgrimage would have to be a slow, steady and patient journey. No sprint here, just methodical and continuous progress down the trail. I often found myself reaching out and tapping the symbols with my hands, maybe to receive some karma or strength for the long and difficult journey. Those who know me understand that I do neither patient, nor slow, so this *Maah Daah Hey* trail would now become my teacher, my mentor, my muse.

These simple turtle branded signposts came to have great significance for me. The map I was carrying was of such small scale that you could not interpret terrain or topography features, so I humbly *surrendered to not knowing* and gave in to simply *following* the posts. Each bend or turn of the trail or crest of a hill would be revealed in its own good timing. I would not have to know what lay ahead. I was being called to simply participate in, appreciate, enjoy, celebrate and be present in what lay before me in the immediacy of now. Anytime my mind would habitually wonder back to problems, issues, or struggles back home or at work, a new turtle branded signpost would quietly call me back to observe and be aware of the plethora of blessings laid-out before me.

Paying Attention II

    This signpost mentality continually pointed as a metaphor, the way back to God. We are all called to daily walk hand-in-hand with God. His ultimate desire has *all to do with relationship*, and not much to do with accomplishment. He simply desires our ongoing, continual presence by seeking Him in each step of our journey throughout our day. We have been given the incredible free will to use our thoughts to go backward; to replay pointless regret, disappointment, and remorse of our past, or skip ahead in worry, fear, anxiety and negative anticipation of what *may* lie down our life trail. *Or* as the signpost beckons; just walk hand-in-hand with Jesus in the here and now, realizing, that we are indeed walking on Holy and Sacred ground that lays all around us at our feet, if we but have eyes to see.

    The solitude, aloneness, and silences that I had purposely sought out, I found in generous abundance in these wild-west spaces of the badlands. These deserted lonely **bad**lands of the Maah Daah Hey had proven to be oohh so **good.**

Rollie Johnson

> *"Stand at the crossroads and look;*
> *ask for the ancient paths,*
> *ask where the good way is, and walk in it,*
> *and you will find rest for your souls.*
> *But you said, 'We will not walk in it.' Jeremiah 6:16 NIV*

Trust in the Lord with all your heart and lean not on your own understanding in all your ways submit to him,
and he will make your paths straight. Proverbs 3:5-6 NIV

> *If you knew Who walks beside you on the way that you have chosen,*
> *worry and fear would be impossible.*

Then Jesus said: Therefore I tell you, do not worry about your life, what you will eat; or about your body, what you will wear. Life is more than food and the body more than clothes… Who of you by worrying can add a single hour to his life? Luke 12:22, 25 NiV

Do not be anxious about anything, but in every situation, by prayer and petition, with thanksgiving, present your requests to God. And the peace of God, which transcends all understanding, will guard your hearts and your minds in Christ Jesus .Philippians 4:6-7 NIV

Lessons from a Long Hike II

The cool waters of the muddy Little Missouri River were a soothing balm of relief for my burning and blistered feet. The previous 18 miles of sun-baked badlands from this day's journey had worn out my body and the cooling waters of this river were like an oasis for my weary body and soul. I was deeply relieved to have arrived at this psychological landmark signifying the halfway point of my journey and receiving the respite for soothing my aching feet. I slowly shuffled my way through the shin-deep waters, leaning on my walking staff pausing occasionally to bask in the refreshing relief of these rejuvenating waters. Upon gaining the western shore I released my back from the sweaty captivity of my pack and then set about the task of filling my water pouches through my filter and then drank heavily of the life-giving cool water.

I next set about finding a decent camping spot to hang my hammock for the evening along the river bottoms. I continued down the trail growing more and more frustrated having found no acceptable camping spots in the first ½ mile of walking. The trail then took a tight turn and began the steep ascent up the river bluff. Being bone weary and tired, the last thing I wanted to do was head uphill. I hesitated briefly, then said a prayer, gritted my teeth and headed up.

Within 500 yards I topped out on the rim and to my enormous relief was rewarded with fantastic spectacular views in all directions of the Little Missouri River and its bottomlands. I soon located a little crow's nest of rocks and juniper trees that made a cozy, protected, and comfortable campsite. After stringing my hammock, and releasing my feet from the confines of my hiking boots, I set about cooking a delicious supper which I devoured in minutes.

With the sun beginning its slow descent behind me to the west, I gained a small rocky outcropping a few yards from my campsite to savor the final moments of the day and engage in some quiet time and thanksgiving. Beautiful, soft, afternoon sunlight flooded the Little Missouri River bottoms and surrounding badlands and cliffs with breathtaking colors and shadows. The spectacular panorama had swallowed me into its grandeur, beauty and lonely solitude.

What soon captured my attention though was a small group of hawks, who were soaring above the cliff edges drafting upwards in lofty circles on the late afternoon thermals. One hawk, in particular, grabbed my awareness as he was the picture of calm, serenity and flowing grace. Rather than circling on the updrafts as the others were doing, this particular hawk seemed to have a different goal. It appeared to me that he was attempting to achieve motionlessness, that is, he seemed to be trying to fly, without movement of wings or body to remain in the same place without wingbeat, fore or aft, nor side to side movement.

I was completely mesmerized by this flying sage. A subtle shift of a wings edge, an imperceptible tilt in yaw, or angle of wing fold or tilt of tail feather. I never saw him take wing flap for minutes at a time. If a thermal or updraft caused him to move backward or sideways, he simply and unconsciously adjusted to again flow into a state of non-movement. It was a thing of beauty to behold. I felt as if I was watching a Shaolin 10th degree master practicing his avian Kung Fu.

This master of flight caused me to muse. My life is most often one of constant motion and movement. And ironically, even this journey I was undertaking was filled with forward movement, action, a sense of gaining, accomplishing, or achieving. All good, and worthy in the right context and balance. Yet I wonder if this flying predatory mentor wasn't calling me to something different; non-movement, non-action, and stillness. And I ponder… had this hawk, during those times of silence and stillness… felt the presence of or seen the face of his Maker?

I am a restless person by nature. I don't think that is good or bad, it just is. But modern man and American society are taking restlessness to whole new epidemic and hyperactive proportions!

In her book _Poustinia_, Catherine deHueck Doherty- writes; *"Restlessness is a running away from self… a turning from the journey inward that all men must undertake to meet God dwelling within the depth of their souls."*

> Today is God calling you:
> To Action or Stillness?
> To Movement or Waiting?
> To Now or Later?
> To Speak or Listen?
> To Do or Be?

There is nothing wrong with movement, action, achieving, and accomplishing. In fact, that's how most of God's work and mission in our hurting world takes place. Praise God for all of this! But if your life is missing the key ingredients of silence, stillness, non-movement, non-action…then you will rarely experience the presence of, nor see the face of your Lord and Maker.

May you find balance in your daily walk with Jesus.

> The mark of solitude is silence, as speech is the mark of community. Silence and speech have the same inner correspondence and difference as do solitude and community. One does not exist without the other. Right speech comes out of silence, and right silence comes out of speech."
> Dietrich Bonhoeffer

Lessons from a Long Hike III

My recent six-day hike through the North Dakota badlands walking the Maah Daah Hey trail gave me 144 hours of silence and solitude. Precisely what I was looking for; Time to sort out, time to think, time to not think, time to contemplate purpose, direction, meaning and evaluate my back trail and consider what might lay ahead of me on this next bend of the journey called life. Lots of time to immerse myself in the rugged beauty of the badlands landscape, and let the terrain wash over my soul to cleanse it from undesirable baggage of worry, doubt, anxiety, and fear.

The desolate ravines, cedar choked coulees, and high open grassy traverses seemed to open my soul like a can opener to release the toxins of fast-paced modern-day life, which left room for God to plant new seeds of growth, purpose, thoughts, and directions. The constant effects of varied weather from brilliant blue skies, to frigid cold mornings, to baking hot sunshine, to cool, misty windy rain all added flavor, texture, and mood to my solo journey.

When you walk alone like this for extended periods of time you have only two conversation options; yourself and your Creator. And I laugh because, by day four, I frequently found myself talking out loud! Ample opportunities each day to give thanks for what was; the incredible scenery, the weather, the gift of health, the gift of freedom, the gift of food and nourishment, the gift of clean water, the gift of the open trail and adventure, the gift of a coyote howling or an eagle circling or the bounding flight of a mule deer. I like to think of it as a very long prayer walk, or *"Walking with Jesus"*, a pilgrimage if you will. Good for body, mind, and spirit!

On this long journey, I found a new favorite piece of equipment; my walking staff pictured above. Over 3 decades of lengthy backpacking trips in the high mountains, and dozens of elk and bear hunts backpacking the mountains of the west, I had never used a walking staff. I had considered it a useless or excess piece of equipment. But from the entry gate at the starting trailhead to my final steps into Medora, I came to love my walking staff as the MVP of my pilgrimage.

I was amazed by the stability it gave me on uneven and difficult terrain. On the dozens of difficult uphill climbs, I was astonished by the extra power it gave me to surge onward and upward. On steep and slippery descents on the greasy gumbo badlands clay, my staff offered a third limb of steadiness and on more than a couple occasions my walking staff prevented me from a hurtful tumble or fall. Many times, I found myself leaning on it for rest to catch my breath. It became my silent, steady and faithful companion on this unknown and sometimes difficult journey.

From the first day of my walk, these words came to me over and over again throughout each day; "You are with me; your rod and *your staff*— they comfort me." Truer words were never spoken.

Holding this walking staff throughout my journey made me realize we are never alone unless we choose to ignore the support and presence of our silent companion. Holding fast to the hand of our Savior brings comfort, stability, strength beyond ourselves and steadiness during the difficulties, struggles, and trials of this life's journey. Of course, we are given the freedom to choose to do any journey without holding onto His support. But as for me, both here in everyday life, and out on-trail, I'll be holding tightly to the Hand of my Savior.

The LORD is my shepherd, I shall not want.
He makes me lie down in green pastures;
he leads me beside still waters; he restores my soul.
He leads me in right paths for his name's sake. Even though I walk through the darkest valley,
I fear no evil; for you are with me; your rod and your staff—they comfort me. Psalm 23:1-4 ESV

Trust in the LORD with all your heart, and do not lean on your own understanding. In all your ways acknowledge him, and he will make straight your paths. Proverbs 3:5-6 ESV

I will lead the blind by ways they have not known, Along unfamiliar paths I will guide them; I will turn the darkness into light before them and make the rough places smooth. Isaiah 42:16 NIV

This is what the Lord says: "Stand at the crossroads and look;
ask for the ancient paths, ask where the good way is, and walk in it,
and you will find rest for your souls. Jeremiah 6:16 NIV

Rollie Johnson

Whether you turn to the right of to the left, you ears will hear a voice behind you, saying "This is the way; Walk in it!" Isaiah 30:21 NIV

When I am afraid, I put my trust in you. In God, whose word I praise, In God I trust; I will not be afraid.
Psalms 56:3 NIV

Light and Dark

Moving ever so slowly, I felt my way through the darkened forest. With only a slivered moon, the stars proved insufficient to illuminate my path. More than once, an occasional invisible branch slapped me in the face reminding me to slow my eager pace. Wide-angle, peripheral vision was my only guidance, for looking ahead in a focused manner caused the darkness to only thicken and details dissolve. I eventually sensed my way to the base of my tree-stand, climbed the steps, strapped on my safety harness, hung my pack, and nocked an arrow to my longbow, which I hung from the tree in front of me. Then out came a deep breath of relief for having arrived, and then the waiting began.

Pure, inky black darkness now owned the land. Though suspended twenty feet in the air, depth and spatial perception were absent, and I felt swallowed whole by the night. With my visual sense shut down, my sense of hearing became enhanced. Two owls were bantering back and forth with vigorous conversation, possibly bidding farewell after working the night shift. The rustling of leaves nearby on the forest floor meant either a meadow vole or possibly a snowshoe hare were also returning home. In the distance, the sound of a car door slamming, and a beet truck rumbling down the highway could be heard as the human world began to awaken long before dawn.

But today my intention brought me to darkness and light. Though I completely relish and delight in my 45 minutes of silence and waiting in the murkiness of the waning night, it is the daylight of the forthcoming sunrise my mind and spirit crave and desire. It's as if the whole of creation including my whole being, is waiting in anticipation for the coming of the light.

Yet, light does not enter the landscape in one instantaneous flick of the light switch.

Light comes ever so slowly, gently, quietly, unobtrusively in imperceptible milliseconds and micro-movements. Blurred, ghostly, ambiguous outlines refine themselves as details and edges slowly return. Scary shadows soon lose their façades and give way to friendly tree stumps and bushes. At some unknown time, gray and black are pushed away as color bleeds back into the surroundings. All of these subtle changes occur long before sunrise. Full vision and perception are completely restored by a full half an hour before the sun ever breaks the horizon.

A friend once shared with me there are many different ways to come to Faith. For some, coming to faith in Jesus is like being in a dark room, and then the light switch gets turned on instantly. You go from pure darkness to light in a millisecond. You can point back to a date and time and place; a dramatic evangelical crusade, an emotion-packed night at bible camp or a tear-filled conversation with a pastor or spiritual mentor. For many others like me, coming to faith is much more like the slow birthing of light in the woods as described above. Slow, steady, non-dramatic, almost imperceptible progressions of greater depth, clarity, and understanding of God my Maker and Creator. An ever-progressive growing relationship with Jesus.

When did light return to the forest? Tough to say. At what moment did God enter my life? Tough to say. Maybe, multiple hundreds of times in subtle, quiet, often imperceptible ways. Maybe you're one who was blessed with a dramatic conversion experience. Hurray! Thank God. Maybe you're one who was blessed by a slow, steady, quiet, sunrise-type of coming to faith. Hurray! Thank God.

Thanks be to God, that He is not limited to one way of drawing his creation back unto Himself.

through whom we have gained access by faith into this grace in which we now stand. And we boast in the hope of the glory of God. Romans 5:2 NIV

know that a person is not justified by the works of the law, but by faith in Jesus Christ. So we, too, have put our faith in Christ Jesus that we may be justified by faith in Christ and not by the works of the law because by the works of the law no one will be justified. Galatians 2:16 NIV

LISTENING

The darkness in the deep of night was overwhelming for most. One felt as if the inky blackness of night might swallow them whole. The night sounds of the great north woods were subtle but immediately amplified by adding a blindfold to each participant. When one shuts down our overused sense of sight, our hearing and listening instincts seem to come to full alert. The fear and anxiety were palpable, as I lead the group who were silently holding hands, down the long, twisting trail deeper into the shadowy blackness of the forest.

At metered distances along the trail, I stopped to release a person from the line and instructed them to remain in place until the signal to begin was heard. I could physically hear the deep breaths taken in and a tensing of their bodies as they now realized they were completely alone and blindfolded in a remote location of the expansive 2,000-acre woods of Camp Wilderness.

After spacing each of the twenty participants out along a quarter mile of trail, I radioed to the endpoint team, to begin with the drumming. Located 500 yards away was one of our leaders who would pound out a steady beat every five seconds or so, on a wooden drum. The task of the participants was to simply listen for, and walk towards the sound of the drum beat. In between the drummer and blindfolded walkers were dense saplings, large pines, blowdowns, underbrush and meadows. They were to use the Native American stalking skills they'd learned previously in the week to gently feel their way through the thick vegetation and around and through the various obstacles with the souls of their feet. My gentle but firm mantra repeated over and over was. *"Be quiet, listen, go slow and follow the steady, quiet voice of the drum."*

This unique activity is called the Blindfold Drum Stalk, one of many teaching tools from our SOLO Trip. For most that chose to go on this trip, it's one of many activities designed to take them well beyond their normal comfort zones to experience new personal breakthroughs, gain insights and deepen their trust and faith in God. For the majority of those tossed into this scenario, the anxiety and fear level is through the roof. All landmarks and bearings are ripped away due to the black of night and the blindfolds, and so now they are forced to rely on other senses of touch, awareness and especially listening. *"Be quiet, listen, go slow and follow the steady, quiet voice of the drum."*

For many who have taken on this challenge, the fear and anxiety soon begin to melt away, as they then come to listen for, and trust in, and move towards the quiet, gentle beat of the drum. Many describe being able to hear their own heart-beat. Many, report a heightened awareness and sharpened sensory perception as they begin to flow into a peaceful rhythm of movement and trust. And for many who arrive safely at the drum after an hour or more of slow, steady stalk-walking, they report a beautiful sense of being guided, cared for and comforted during the darkness of their long sightless journey.

The analogies, metaphors, life and faith comparisons fairly jump off the page shouting to be heard and I grow giddy with excitement for helping people to make those connections. Walk by faith not by sight! Listen! Listen more... talk less! Be still, be quiet. Wait upon the Lord. Listen and then obey. Fear not I am with you! Walk in the direction of Gods still small voice. Slow down! Life can be dark and scary... so keep listening to and following the voice of God. You will never, ever walk alone. I am with you. I will watch over you. I will protect you. Even though you do not see the way... I will guide you on the right paths. In life you will encounter many obstacles and difficulties, but you will not meet them alone. I am with you.

I urge you to set aside your sense of sight that most of us rely on for 99.9% of our perception of life. Instead learn more and more to; "Be

Still, listen and wait upon the Lord." He and he alone will guide you and watch over you.

Whether you turn to the right or to the left, your ears will hear a voice behind you, saying "this is the way; walk in it." Isaiah 30: 21 NIV

My sheep listen to my voice; I know them, and they follow me. John 10:27 NIV

Whoever listens to me will live in safety and be at ease, without fear of harm." Proverbs 1:33 NIV

Listen to my instruction and be wise; do not disregard it. Proverbs 8:33 NIV

Do not merely listen to the word, and so deceive yourselves. Do what it says. James 1:22

In quietness and trust is your strength. Isaiah 30: 15

The LORD said, "Go out and stand on the mountain in the presence of the LORD, for the LORD is about to pass by." Then a great and powerful wind tore the mountains apart and shattered the rocks before the LORD, but the LORD was not in the wind. After the wind, there was an earthquake, but the LORD was not in the earthquake. [12] After the earthquake came to a fire, but the LORD was not in the fire. And after the fire came to a gentle whisper, a (still small voice) 1 Kings 19: 11-12 NIV

Maah Daah Hey

Soft, baby-blue skies, moderate temps in the 60's and magnificent scenery as far as the eye could see, made for ideal hiking conditions. The clean, fresh, sage-scented air seemed to purify body, mind, and spirit with each labored breath. It felt with each step we took, there was a positive energy exchange. With each footfall, we deposited our stress long carried on stooped shoulders from work, school or family. The strain, anxieties, and tensions of fast-paced city life seeped from our bodies and leeched into the arid soil of the Badlands trail. Unknowingly we were being renewed, refreshed and restored from the inside out via the forgotten teachers of hard physical labor, close human companionship and the awe-inspiring surroundings of creation. This Maah Daah Hey trail in the Badlands was proving oooh so good!

Midway through our first day's hike, we descended from a grassy table top, snaking our way down into a deep juniper choked coulee. A narrow meandering stream had cut its way through the bottomland forming a 15' deep gorge that we descended to cross the shallow intermittent stream. The amber colored water was barely trickling and we scampered over the muddy high spots traversing through the gorge for a brief period to regain the trail. I paused for a moment to ponder the effects of the long-term erosion that had been the sculptor of so much of these badlands, and there emerging from the camouflaged clayed bank was the back end of an ancient bison skull and horn base!

Rollie Johnson

We were in awe of how well the mud and clay had preserved this skull. We could only hypothesize as to how long this skull had been here. Was it hundreds of years? Could it possibly have been thousands? Maybe even tens of thousands of years? The only thing we knew for sure was that we were passing through a landscape that held clues to a very, very long history.

The following day we awoke well before dawn to begin our trek out of a long valley. As we ascended through the classic badlands multi-layered, multi-colored strata we soon came upon several giant petrified tree stumps. We paused for a break to caress and touch these millions of year-old trees. Scientists theorize that these were massive Cyprus trees that were part of an enormous area of tropical swamp. It was hard to believe that these dry, arid, desolate badlands had at one time been a thick, humid, richly foliated swamp.

Questions began bubbling forth like coffee in a percolator. Had these massive trees likely witnessed a variety of dinosaurs scurrying about beneath their canopies? How could a tree turn to stone? What brought about the dramatic change in climate? The only thing we knew for sure was that we were passing through a landscape that held clues to a very, very long history.

Under a clear dusk sky, with the evening's first stars appearing, we gathered 'round a roaring fire for our devos and group time. Brisk fall temps had us each bundled in stocking hats and cozy clothing. 360 degrees of magnificent scenery surrounded us. Tired bodies and sore limbs felt relieved and grateful for the evening's rest from the long day of strenuous hiking over the dragon's spine trail.

As we debriefed our long weekend together, one of the questions from our Devo book drew numerous responses. "Where or how have you witnessed God this weekend?" Many heartfelt and beautiful responses came forth; *"I witnessed God in the creation all around us at each and every bend in the trail." "I saw God in the faces of my fellow hikers who cared for me when I was struggling." "I felt God in the silence and heard Him on the wind."* Then Doug, one of our elder and wiser men chimed in. I paraphrase: *"I got a deep sense of God's faithfulness and longevity, and permanence through this landscape. Imagine the incredible forethought He put into providing us with oil beneath the surface so very, very long ago. He is a long-term God. He is into Creating and Creation for the long haul."*

Places like these ever so good Badlands, the bison skull and petrified trees all remind me that our God, Creator of the entire universe is in it for the long haul. This four-day time-out traversing the rugged topography of the Maah Daah Hey trail reminds me that God is so much bigger, longer, wider, and deeper than any of our current modern-day issues and hot buttons. He is *still* the *ruler* and *maker* of our world. Anxiety and unrest from recent political elections, global climate changes, terrorists and financial markets will all be outlived by a God who is in control and still moving and creating throughout our world and universe. These vast, wild spaces and panoramas have jarred my memory into remembering that God is God, and we are not.

Jesus reminds us: *"I have told you these things, so that in me you may have peace. In this world, you will have trouble. But take heart! I have overcome the world." John 16:33 NIV*

May you take heart and find peace in knowing that our God has been around a long, long time. May you trust that His grace is sufficient to endure and outlast any obstacle, issue or event in your life or in our world at large.

"I am the Alpha and the Omega," says the Lord God, "who is, and who was, and who is to come, the Almighty." Revelation 1:8 NIV

In the beginning, was the Word, and the Word was with God, and the Word was God. John 1:1 NIV

In the beginning God created the heavens and the earth. Now the earth was formless and empty, darkness was over the surface of the deep, and the Spirit of God was hovering over the waters. Genesis 1:1-2 NIV

The heavens are yours, and yours also the earth; you founded the world and all that is in it.
Psalm 89:11 NIV

Marcello and Concha

She meandered into the open space of the church wandering to and fro. She appeared curious about what lay within the corners of the church, and about these strange gringos who had invaded her small village and church. She couldn't have been much over four feet tall and was somewhere in her mid-forties or maybe fifty-something. So hard to tell with these villagers. Her classic Mayan white dress with colorful embroidery draped over her skeleton-like body, down to her knees. Not much meat on those bones I said to myself. I smiled and offered up my best Spanish version of "Welcome and how are you?" She stared back at me, silent and distant. I spoke the same words this time more clearly and louder. The same strange vacant stare was all that she returned. I shrugged it off to the fact that many of the older villagers only spoke native Mayan, so most likely she didn't understand any Spanish, and much more likely my particular Spanish.

This lady came to our Bible school activities every afternoon with regularity. I don't have a clue if she understood a thing that was taking place, but she seemed to enjoy the buzz of activities of songs, games, crafts, and shenanigans typical of our mission trips. Occasionally I would catch her laughing hysterically out loud, only it was never when something funny had happened or been said. She seemed to hear or see things in her own little world. I later learned her name was Concha, and another more astute villager quietly leaned over and whispered that she was not so right in the head. Ok, now it all made a little more sense.

Coming to and from our man cave or Casa Hombre, where the boys were housed, to the church we most often encountered another strange character. He stood on the corner just a block from our worksite. He wore the same tattered and stained white t-shirt the entire length of our stay. He would frequently stand for hours at a time, heels together, toes pointed out in a duck-V, back hunched staring blankly into space. Each time I passed him I offered up a friendly "Hola" or "Buenas Dias" and only silence was returned, along with a penetrating stare. The boys and I joked about him from the privacy of our hammocks and jested that he belonged in a creepy horror film. If he had appeared in our doorway some night, we would have died of heart failure.

Mid-week I learned his name was Marcello, and he was a brother to Concha. How fitting I thought to myself. Marcello too came to each day's festivities and wandered amongst the crowd never saying a word and never changing his facial expression. He just stared and maintained an odd little smile.

I privately inquired about the pair from a few of the other villagers and the local pastor and gained very little tangible information other than that they had another brother who was similar. Anyway, they seemed harmless and they seemed to be enjoying themselves.

As the week of our mission trip experience came to a close, our gang began handing out their donations. Normally we pick families or children that we have become attached to, or close to in some way. Often times, we try to repay a kindness or servanthood shown to us by giving away special items or clothing.

The most prized possessions we give away are the beautiful quilts that were made by the women of First Lutheran Church. We are each given one at our commissioning service, and we use it throughout the week to ward off the evening chill. Then on our final day, we bless a person or family by giving it to them. I gave mine to a family of ladies who had taught us how to make hand-made tortillas. They were beyond thrilled.

As I scurried about the village attending to last minute details, I witnessed a most beautiful sight; a Godly teaching, a movement of the Holy Spirit if you will. Walking away from the church were Concha and Marcello, each draped in a colorful, warm, new quilt. Most of us love to give to the loveable or cute, to payback a kindness or give to someone we love or are connected to. We will rarely give time or possession or money or love to the stranger, the misfit, the odd duck or the mentally ill. Yet two of our group members had seen with Christ's eyes and had followed the leading of their Lord Jesus. They had reached out to and loved the unlovable and simply given the warmth and affection of a cozy blanket to someone that neither understood our words, nor who we were.

Jesus mastered in the art of loving the unlovable; grotesque lepers, unloved prostitutes, despised tax collectors, prideful wealthy folk, powerless children, penniless widows, stray orphans and the crazy people of every town, school, village or church that everyone else teases and mocks.

It is easy to love and give and serve the loveable and lovely. Jesus teaches us to love and serve the unlovable and unlovely. Who are the unlovely and unlovable in your midst? (Photos compliments of Jon Forness)

Rollie Johnson

And Jesus took the children in his arms, placed his hands on them and blessed them. Mark 10:16 NIV

"If you love those who love you, what credit is that to you? Even sinners love those who love them. ³³ And if you do good to those who are good to you, what credit is that to you? Even sinners do that. ³⁴ And if you lend to those from whom you expect repayment, what credit is that to you? Even sinners lend to sinners, expecting to be repaid in full. ³⁵ But love your enemies, do good to them, and lend to them without expecting to get anything back. Then your reward will be great, and you will be children of the Most High, because he is kind to the ungrateful and wicked. ³⁶ Be merciful, just as your Father is merciful. Luke 6:33-36 NIV

A man with leprosy came to him and begged him on his knees, "If you are willing, you can make me clean." Jesus was indignant. He reached out his hand and touched the man. "I am willing," he said. "Be clean!" Immediately the leprosy left him and he was cleansed. Mark 1:40-42 NIV

Mess to Message

It's just a little weed. Just want to fit in and get a little buzz.

Party like a rock star this weekend. Everyone else is doing it. Let's get wasted.

Mom and dad are clueless anyway. I'm not hurting anyone but me and I'm actually having fun!

Marijuana led me to harder drugs as weed didn't just cut it anymore. Pretty soon I wasn't just doing drugs and alcohol for fun on weekends. Pretty soon I needed something to pick me up when I came down. And then I needed something to calm me down when I was too high. Before I knew it... I was full blow addicted. I was a mess.

At sixteen I moved out of my home. I thought I knew better than my parents, and all I did was fight with them anyway. I bounced from place to place. With no source of income to supply my addiction, I chose to sell. The money was good and that became addictive in itself. I found myself in a vicious circle of selling to use and using to sell.

I became ashamed of myself and who I had become. I so desperately wanted to reach out to my parents, but who could love who I had become. Besides, I had broken a hundred trusts already. I continued on a very downward and slippery spiral of paranoia, selling and using drugs. I lost friends to suicide, overdose, and prison. I was hopeless... truly without hope. I continued my descent into a very dark world. I could see no way out.

And then it happened. My friend, or so-called friend, the rat, wore a wire for the police during a drug deal. And before I knew it I was in handcuffs and soon wearing a humiliating orange jumpsuit. My shame washed over me like heavy mud. I was so disgusted and ashamed of who I had become.

I lucked out, the judge was lenient as it was my first offense and I cooperated fully. The gavel fell and I was sentenced to two years in the federal pen. My life was at rock bottom. I could not look at my mom and dad for shame and regret.

The normally loud, restless and often disrespectful confirmation class of 7th and 8th graders was silent. All eyes were aptly focused on my dear friend Isaac who was courageously sharing his life… **His** story with all of us gathered. I kept pushing back the large lump in my throat as I listened, often with damp eyes as my gratitude for and pride in Isaac bubbled up inside. He was sharing so freely, so honestly, so from the heart about his struggles and wrong choices with these kids. I could see his message was landing on open and needy hearts.

In my phone call the day before asking if he'd come and share, he immediately and softly responded; "Rollie I've been waiting for this. If I can help even one kid through this, I'd be so happy." Isaac told of the ugly and difficult truth of where he had gone, and he talked so honestly about the complete mess he had made of his life. But more importantly, he then began to 'round the corner and share how God had used his time in prison to restore and redeem his life. God had taken his gigantic ugly mess and over these past several years, now this evening… turned his mess into **His (Isaac's and God's)** message of redemption, restoration, and a fresh start.

The class applauded loudly as Isaac made his way to the back of the room. As I finished with some class details, I could see Isaac silently weeping in back. God was using the cathartic power of sharing **His** message to bring about mutual continued healing in Isaac and everyone in the room.

Isaac has courageously agreed to share the stage with me this Sunday, October 14th at 9 and 11 am in Celebration Worship. I will be interviewing him as he shares his amazing journey with all of us. I will not give away too many details but here are some teasers.

How Isaac forgave his betrayer. How Isaac thanked his betrayer for what he'd done.
Restored and forgiven and completely renewed relationships with his parents and family.
A strong woman who stood by his side through thick and thin.
The power of a mother's ongoing and continuous prayers for her son. Never, never quit praying.
Thank God for prison
Two beautiful daughters and a new one expected soon.
Five years plus of sobriety and clean living.
The loneliness of sobriety and starting over with no real friends.

Is your life a mess? Or is there a corner or pocket of your life that is sticky, messy and hurtful to you or others? Come hear about real life, the real power of prayer, the real way which God can take our self-made messes and turn them into a powerful message for you to share with others.

Here is a brand-new song I just came across that is not only beautiful to listen to but touches my heart with the truth of her words. Her words echo so well Isaac's message of restoration, renewal, and redemption. "Even When You're Broken" by Julie Yardley. https://www.youtube.com/watch?v=pmPNUvQmexo

If God loves you, forgives you, and accepts you completely… Why are you so hard on yourself?

Few Christians recognize how radical their posture in the world truly is. Their past is absolutely forgiven, and *their future is absolutely certain*, so that more than any other body of people on the face of the earth, they are free to live in the present! Tim Hansel

Being confident of this, that He who began a good work in you will carry it on to completion until the day of Christ Jesus. Philippians 1:6 NIV

If we have made peace with our flawed humanity and embraced our imperfect identity, *(by totally trusting in Gods good love and forgiveness)* we are able to tolerate in others what was previously unacceptable in ourselves. Living by grace inspires a growing consciousness that I am what I am in the sight of Jesus and nothing more. Assured of your salvation by the unique grace of our Lord Jesus Christ" is the heartbeat of the Gospel, joyful liberation from fear of the final outcome, a summons to self-acceptance, and freedom for a life of compassion towards others. Once again, gentleness towards ourselves constitutes the core of our gentleness with others. Brennan Manning, The Ragamuffin Gospel

Micro and Macro

Soft, fluffy, dispersed clouds floated silently beneath clear powder-blue skies pushed by an invisible cool breeze. The setting sun illuminated the multi-colored striations, canyons, and coulees of our beloved badlands.

Shane and I sat atop an unnamed ridgeline overlooking the Little Missouri River bottomlands. We mostly sat in silence soaking in the grandeur and majesty of all that lay before us. The late evening sun illuminated the pinks and purples, yellows and rusts and grays of horizontal striping. Each color had been assigned to their own parallel bands. The endless ridgelines faded to infinity on the distant horizon.

A great peace, contentment, and sense of awe settled over me. I sensed the same sentiments emanating from my son. How privileged I felt sharing the beauty of Creation alongside my son. I silently whispered prayers of thanks and gratitude; both for the magnificence that lay before me and for the joy of sharing this moment with Shane. I am indeed a very lucky man.

Day two of our four-day camping trip, found us three miles deep in the canyon hiking and exploring with no agenda but to follow the Spirit of adventure. Azure skies, moderate temps and invigorating sage-scented air made for ideal hiking conditions. Arriving near the floodplain we noticed a prairie dog town about a mile away and so we followed our instincts in that direction. We had soon gained a small grassy knoll overlooking Prairie Dog Central and the loud chirping and barking were loud and unceasing. Our dog Bruno had never witnessed such a sight, and he soon got caught up in a never-ending and pointless game of "Whack-a-Mole!" Final score: Prairie Dogs 107- Bruno 0.

As I removed lunch from our backpack, I noticed a bleached white, two-inch bone lying near my pack. Upon picking it up I realized it was a lower mandible from a deceased prairie dog. The tiny jaw bone still held a front incisor and one molar. The root holes for another three molars were clearly visible. How crazy to find such a minuscule bone in the midst of a wide-open prairie!

Questions began pouring into my psyche. How long ago had he or she died? Was it a coyote, an eagle or rattlesnake or natural causes that had caused the death? Although, I'd guess that all deaths in nature are of natural causes! How long had he lived? Was he born here? How many siblings? How many offspring?

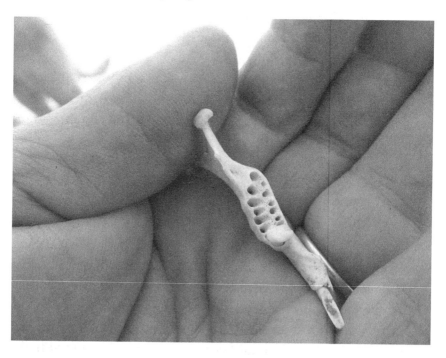

And then my thoughts took me deeper. This bone was magnificently crafted; so detailed, so function- specific, so exact in form and purpose.

Sperm from a male and an ovum from a female had formed together, and out of those two separate molecular miracles this mini jaw bone was birthed and formed. And this mandible is just one of several thousand little miracles that took places to form the lungs, and claws, and veins, and liver, and fur, and eyelashes, and brain, and molar, and incisor, and blood cells of one little unknown prairie dog in a forgotten corner of the vast and lonely badlands! OMG!

Oh My God... *You* were present in the *Micro;* the molecular and cellular and atomic levels of creation that are unseen to all of us. *You* were present in the formation of all the separate yet interdependent and interconnected parts and pieces of anatomy that formed this unknown furry rodent. And *You* were the one who breathed the unknown factor of life and existence into this creature.

And *You* were the one present and moving in the formation of the *Macro;* the magnificent sunset, the floating clouds, the cool wind, and the painted coulees and canyons that we witnessed from high atop the rim. You were present in the thousands of millennia and forces of earth, weather and geology that sculpted, carved and painted this holy and sacred badlands. You are the *God of the Macro and the Micro* and everything in between.

God is all around us. God is present and He reveals himself in both the large and small of our lives; from magnificent badlands panoramas to the microscopic of cells, atoms, and protons. And remember that part of God's presence here on earth right now is you. May you take some time to contemplate the miracle of God's creation in the Macro and the Micro, and even in your own life, your body, your mind, and your spirit.

For it was you who formed my inward parts; you knit me together in my mother's womb.
I praise you, for I am fearfully and wonderfully made. Wonderful are your works;
that I know very well. My frame was not hidden from you,
when I was being made in secret, intricately woven in the depths of the earth. Psalm 139:13-15 NIV

"Therefore I tell you, do not worry about your life, what you will eat or what you will drink, or about your body, what you will wear. Is not life more than food, and the body more than clothing? Look at the birds of the air; they neither sow nor reap nor gather into barns, and yet your heavenly Father feeds them. Are you not of more value than they? And can any of you by worrying add a single hour to your span of life?
Matthew 6:25-34 NIV

When I consider your heavens, the work of your fingers, the moon and the stars,
which you have set in place, what is mankind that you are mindful of them,
human beings that you care for them? You have made them a little lower than the angels
and crowned them with glory and honor. You made them rulers over the works of your hands;
you put everything under their feet: all flocks and herds, and the animals of the wild,
the birds in the sky, and the fish in the sea, all that swim the paths of the seas. Lord, our Lord,
how majestic is your name in all the earth! Psalm 8:3-9 NIV

Monarchs and Milkweeds

There Is No God! So sayeth the blind men and women of this generation. When frenetic hyperactivity, over-scheduling and constant dependence upon cell phones and computers rule our days. Our eyes and attention have been diverted from the mysteries and wonders of the sacred and holy all around us to the minutia of a thousand distractions found on the tiny screens of our techno world. We indeed are the new blind. We have become the most unaware and distracted generation in the entire history of humanity on planet earth.

The gentle, cool, autumn-like breeze taunted and teased the soft stems of the local popple trees causing them to wave and shimmer emitting their soothing, soft music that calmed my spirit. I smiled at the wonder all around me. Towering stately white and red pines stood stoically as guardians over the forest. The deep dark green-blue of abundant spruce was complimented by the contrast of the black and white birch. Sturdy and grounded oak and ash added a sense of strength and longevity to the surroundings. Deep cobalt blue skies enhanced a sense of peace and serenity.

I was walking through the wonder-filled terrain of Camp Wilderness, north of Park Rapids taking a break for some solitude and conversation with my maker. Leaving behind the nineteen something 4th through 6th graders and other adult leaders from our Go Wild Weekend, I was seeking some much needed quiet time. Entering a broad clearing I happened upon a very large patch of milkweed.

How ironic I thought to myself, as we had been working with milkweed stalks all weekend to teach kids how to make cordage from the fibers of the dried stalks. Milkweed stalks along with stinging nettles and dogbane have been used for millennia by primitive peoples to fashion ropes, bow-strings, nets, and harnesses. I had been teaching kids first how to extract the strong fibers from the stalks, and then how to craft robust cordage from these fibers to make a necklace or bracelet. For those who successfully completed a strand of cordage, I gave them a stone arrowhead to complete their necklace.

As I stood walking among the milkweed I noticed several flitting

Paying Attention II

and fluttering monarch butterflies. Their beautiful orange and black colors stood in contrast to the greenery of the milkweed patch.

The monarchs floated to and fro, landing here and there, always landing on another milkweed either on the purple flowers, or the broad leaves or on the budding seed pods. These remarkable monarchs danced and fluttered silently going about the business of being a butterfly, with only me, as their sole witness.

I knelt quietly to observe and sense the holy and sacred happening before me. I felt a strong reverence and connectivity having handled and played with milkweed all weekend, teaching others to notice and use what God has laid before us in the ordinary and often overlooked humble milkweed plant. I knew of the incredibly strong connection and symbiotic relationship between milkweeds and monarchs. Their lives and life cycles are intimately and divinely intertwined. Yet to the world at large, the beauty, and intricacy, and marvel of this relationship goes unnoticed. Most of us are blind and unseeing to the Godly in our midst. Imagine how many milkweed plants we walk or drive by each day. Imagine how little attention we pay to the unfathomable story of the common and ordinary monarch butterfly.

Pause if you will, to watch this remarkable story contained in the short little video:

Link to: National Geographic, Growing Up Butterfly Video
https://www.youtube.com/watch?v=kHby5DmmOUY

Every time I watch this amazing story, I cannot help but know there is a loving, intelligent, benevolent, and all-knowing God who created and oversees our incredible universe. Science and all of its various branches of chemistry, biology, physics, and math can only, in the end, point to and acknowledge that they bow to, and operate in the coordinated and connected universe of God.

There is no God? I beg to differ. Take off your blinders, set aside your phones, walk amongst the milkweeds, kneel and observe the monarchs. They have much to teach of God and his remarkable world.

We may ignore, but we can nowhere evade, the presence of God. The world is crowded with Him. He walks everywhere incognito. And the incognito is not always easy to penetrate. The real labor is to remember to attend. In fact to come awake. Still more to remain awake. C. S. Lewis

"The simplest and oldest way, then, in which God manifests Himself through and in the earth itself. And He still speaks to us through the earth and the sea, the birds of the air and the living creatures upon the earth, if we can but quiet ourselves to listen. Agnes Sanford

Psalm 8
When I look at your heavens, the work of your fingers, the moon and the stars that you have established;
what are human beings that you are mindful of them, mortals that you care for them?
Yet you have made them a little lower than God and crowned them with glory and honor.
You have given them dominion over the works of your hands; you have put all things under their feet,
all sheep and oxen, and also the beasts of the field,
the birds of the air, and the fish of the sea, whatever passes along the paths of the seas.
O LORD, our Sovereign, how majestic is your name in all the earth! Psalm 8: 1-9 ESV

More Than Enough

Entering my new temporary home, I felt relieved. Two other pilgrims and I had traveled together for the past four hours to arrive with a mix of anticipation and anxiety to finally arrive at the Catholic Retreat Center; Pacem In Terris near Isanti Minnesota. My host for the weekend, and cabin namesake; Saint Paul, would be praying over me for my two-night hermitage. 'Good to know' I thought to myself, thank you St. Paul!

The hermitage was surrounded by gorgeous oak dominant woods. For some reason, in this particular area, many of the oaks had held on to their rust-colored leaves adding a tinge of color to mostly black and white snow- covered landscape. The oak leaves seemed to mimic and mirror the color of my hermitage. A strong sense of peace and contentment settled over me, being wrapped in beauty outside and warmth and coziness inside. I nestled into the comfy rocking chair and began my silent retreat.

After a few hours of rocking, reading scripture, praying, journaling, and reflecting I began to grow hungry and reached for my basket of food for the weekend.

I was reminded by my first experience as I arrived at Pacem, and was given the basket. I remember thinking; *"Is that it? Are you kidding me? Where's the meat? Where's the butter? What no snacks? What about my daily cappuccino? What about my post meal chocolate? What about some cookies? I'm going to starve!"* I had a feeling of scarcity and lacking. I look back now and laugh, as this simple basket of food has become one of my favorite parts of the Pacem experience and one of its greatest teachers.

Paying Attention II

Reaching into the simple basket, I grabbed one of the two freshly baked, round loaves of bread. I removed its twist tie and plastic wrapper and held the bread up to my nose and breathed deeply of its sweet, earthy aroma. I broke it almost ceremoniously and gave a quiet thank you. Next, I cut several slices of fresh Wisconsin cheddar cheese and added a shiny apple to my plate. Pouring some wine into the blue-enameled tin cup I began my meal.

Tearing a small morsel of the bread and placing it in my mouth, the sweet flavor burst forth bringing pleasure of body, mind, and spirit. Occasionally partnered with a slab of cheese, new flavor combos invaded my taste buds. Often times I would dunk my bread into the deep purple of the wine and the two seemed to be perfect palette partners. This simple meal had become an event in and of itself. It had been given for both sustenance and pleasure. And I was the recipient of these marvelous gifts of the senses.

Finishing off my meal was the dessert of a crisp, healthy apple. I soon realized that I was full, but more importantly, content. I had been filled with this good, wholesome food and I was lacking nothing.

Normally, back home I would never have looked at this plate and thought of contentment or being full. But this simple meal had been provided giving me abundance beyond my needs.

This experience gives me ample food for thought as well. Normally we all eat distracted. We talk with coworkers over a hasty lunch, we watch TV as a family as we race through a meal. I most often read a magazine or newspaper and the food and eating is just background noise. Evening snacks while we watch a movie or the Vikings game. Road trips demand that we snarf down some convenience store something-or-another that has sat for hours under a heat lamp. Even a fancy dinner out with family and friends is focused more on the conversation than the pure gift of food.

Rarely do we quietly savor the gift of food. Rarely do we offer up gratitude for the gifts of sustenance, flavor and creative cookery. We're just too distracted and too busy to fully appreciate what has been placed before us. Slowing down in the quiet of a hermitage allowed me to realize what a gift, food is to our lives.

The other key concept that surfaced during my extended quiet time, is that I most often overconsume. Certainly, I over consume food at each meal, and even more so between meals in the form of snacks, lattes, chocolates, cookies, and cakes. This simple meal has reminded me of how little we need, and how far we have moved from God providing enough and sufficiency, into the realm of excess, surplus, extra and outright gluttony.

This Christmas season has the ring of excess and surplus to it. Do more, buy more, have more, get more. We are bombarded with Black Friday's and Cyber Monday's and Christmas songs on radios that start before Halloween. More Christmas office parties, more kid's concerts and programs, and the constant pressure to give or have the "next great thing," or the latest iPhone Max 19G!

I'm guessing that when Mary and Joseph arrived at the inn, they must have thought *"This will never do! It's not enough! What were they thinking?"* But the reality of a lowly barn, beds of straw, the simplicity of a roof overhead proved to be more than enough to birth the savior of the world.

Paying Attention II

Maybe God is calling you to simplicity this Christmas season. To know and embrace the "enough" that God has given to you. Maybe it is time to release, let go of, throw away or say goodbye to worldly expectations to do and have everything. Maybe God is calling you to slow down, to savor, to embrace and to realize that he has generously provided more than enough.

And my God will supply every need of yours according to his riches in glory in Christ Jesus. Phil. 4:19

But seek first the kingdom of God and his righteousness, and all these things will be added to you. Mt. 6:33

I am not saying this because I am in need, for I have learned to be content whatever the circumstances. I know what it is to be in need, and I know what it is to have plenty. I have learned the secret of being content in any and every situation, whether well fed or hungry, whether living in plenty or in want. I can do all this through him who gives me strength. Philippians 4:11-13 NIV

Good Morning _____ (your name),
I am the Lord your God. Today I will be handling all your problems. Please remember that I do not need your help. If the devil happens to deliver a situation to you that you cannot handle, DO NOT attempt to resolve it on your own. Kindly put it in the SFJTD (something for Jesus to do) box. It will be addressed in my time, not yours.

Once the matter is placed in the box, do not hold on to, or attempt to remove it. Holding on or removal will only delay the resolution of your problem. If it is a situation that you think you are capable of handling, please consult me in prayer to be sure that it is the proper resolution. Because I do not sleep nor do I slumber, there is no need for you to lose any sleep. Rest my child. If you need to contact me, I am only a prayer away.
Love eternally,
The Lord your God

Mr. Tambourine Man

It's 7:54 am and he works his way down the aisle and heads for the southwest corner. He leans forward and scoots along with a shuffling gait. Removing his coat, he gently lays it over a chair and takes his seat. He quietly leans over and from a crumpled bag, he removes his instrument and sets it upon his lap. A gentle smile continually permeates his face. Many Sundays he is sweating from the long walk from his apartment.

It is Sunday, and we are in Celebration Hall, and our friend Milton has arrived, and seated himself up front and right side, as he does week after week just in front of the baptismal font. At 8 am sharp our worship band begins a quick run through of songs for the upcoming worship services and as we rehearse, so does Milton. From his chair, he faithfully taps out a rhythm on his worn and well-used tambourine. Pa rum pum pum pum.

After practice, the band, preacher and sound crew all circle up for quick introductions, a question of the week and prayer time. Milton joins in the circle and has become one of our worship family. Laughter is the rule of the day each week, with lots of kidding and ribbing that flies back and forth between bandmates. Milton laughs easily and seems to enjoy being part of the gang. His constant upturned grin is contagious and loveable.

During our 9 am worship, Milton quietly plays along with each song. He refrains from playing his tambourine on the slower, more melodic songs. He seems to light up on the last song which is usually loud, fast and upbeat. After worship, he sets down his tambourine and heads for a cookie in the gathering place. A few minutes later, he can be found back in his chair where he quietly and patiently waits for the next service that begins at 11 am. And then we press the repeat button. Pa rum pum pum pum

Milton Little Owl is a Native American and proud member of the Spirit Lake Band *Mni Wakan Oyate, Santee Sioux*. He is generous, cheerful, gentle, quiet and a lover of life and Jesus. For years Milton has shared his talent on the tambourine often times with his attendant Chelsea at his side. Many times, he just comes faithfully on his own. In addition to playing his tambourine, Milton loves to sing. And he sings with great gusto and enthusiasm. Pa rum pum pum pum.

Week after week, year after year Milton has played and sang. He sings because he has a voice to sing praise and he plays because he loves to **add to** worship. Rarely have I ever witnessed anyone acknowledge him or thank him. He gives 100% of himself to worship and does so with a complete lack of ego or pride, and certainly has no conscious thought of recognition or accolades. He sings and plays from the heart to worship… because that is what worship is supposed to be! **Bringing** and **giving** the best of who you are! Pa rum pum pum pum.

Let's be honest… the great bulk of us worship to meet our own needs. For most folks worshiping these days, we bring the same mentality to worship as we do watching TV; we are worship *Consumers* and we carry our remote/clicker in our hand. We come with the expectation of *what will I take from this* worship! "Oh, I love *that* song… but not so much the new one. I'll sing… but just loud enough so no one hears me. I can't sing… so I don't. I'll sing but only the songs I know and like. Not this preacher! He/She is so…. Fill in the blank! We often sit like a Russian judge at an Olympic gymnastic meet… I'll give that song an 8.7! But the message… only a 4.5! It was way too… fill in your blank.

But true, real, Godly worship has to do with what *you bring*, not what *you take*. God can speak biblical truth to your heart through any given preacher that *He chooses*… But will your prejudice, bias, closed heart, or preconceived mindset allow Him to speak to you? Or will you have the hard and calloused heart of the rocky ground in the parable of the four soils of the sower and the seed?

And do you sing with gusto, with enthusiasm, with all your heart, soul and mind? A simple reminder that the first and most important commandment in all of the Bible simply declares: "Love the Lord your God with all your heart, soul and mind!" That is worship! Full body, heart, soul and mind worship!

Come they told me pa rum pum pum pum
A newborn King to see pa rum pum pum pum
Our finest gifts we bring pa rum pum pum pum
To lay before the King pa rum pum pum pum
rum pum pum pum rum pum pum pum
So to honour Him pa rum pum pum pum

The little drummer boy came to honor the newborn king. He came and *gave*, he did not take. He *brought* what he could do to the worship table… he played his drum. Maybe next time you come to worship in Celebration Hall, take a look up forward and right. Look for the baptismal font, and there seated just to the right will most likely be Milton. Pay attention, observe closely and watch… he may have a thing or two to teach us all about good, and right, and biblical, and Godly worship. Milton is our very own little drummer boy. Pa rum pum pum pum.

Let everything that has breath praise the Lord! Psalm 150:6 NIV

Therefore, I urge you, brothers and sisters, in view of God's mercy, to offer your bodies as a living sacrifice, holy and pleasing to God—this is your true and proper worship. Romans 12:1 NIV

The Lord says: "These people come near to me with their mouth and honor me with their lips, but their hearts are far from me. Their worship of me is based on merely human rules they have been taught, Isaiah 29: 13 NIV

Rollie Johnson

Shout for joy to the LORD, *all the earth. Worship the* LORD *with gladness; come before him with joyful songs.*
Know that the LORD *is God. It is he who made us, and we are his, we are his people, the sheep of his pasture. Enter his gates with thanksgiving and his courts with praise; give thanks to him and praise his name. For the* LORD *is good and his love endures forever; his faithfulness continues through all generations. Psalm 100:1-5 NIV*

Neglected

Stumbling through the shadows, I fumbled to flip several switches on the fuse box. Light flooded the warehouse pushing out the darkness, and the familiarity of space and being at home brought a smile to my face. We were back in our canoe shack where we had birthed four, twenty-six feet long Voyageur North Canoes in 2014. There before me rested three of our behemoth, whale-sized creations, each quietly resting on their own saw horses. The trio of vessels had arrived in our emergency care room in desperate need of some TLC.

I had recently been out to the farm to retrieve the trailer which held the trio stacked in a pyramid and brought them home ready for a ride down the Red River. Upon closer inspection, my heart sank as I could witness that they were in rough shape. Apparently, the farmer had removed the trailer each spring from the barn, and not returned them until after harvest, leaving the trinity exposed to the elements of rain and the damaging UV rays of the sun. The sun had done significant damage to the surfaces of the massive hulls, causing the varnish to peel, flake and become rough and scaly. Running my hand over the normally glassy smooth hulls, caused me to cringe and pull away.

The rain had wreaked its havoc as well. Mold and mildew had darkened the normally bright and glowing ash gunwales. I was saddened by their current state as they had fallen so far from their magnificent beginnings. They had become just a flickering glimmer of their former selves. I quietly took ownership and accepted the fact that they had too long sat exposed and neglected.

An email blitzkrieg blasted out to the hundred or so participants who had shared in the five-month-long process of creating these vessels from a simple pile of cedar, ash, fiberglass cloth and resin. Several of the faithful responded; "I'll be there. Count me in." Doug, Karen, Wesley, Diane, Big Jim, Chuck, and Paul arrived with elbow grease and willingness to serve. Wes even took a day off work to be with us. Upon arrival, Diane stated, "I have a lot of myself invested in these canoes. I journeyed with them to float the Upper Missouri in Montana, and then they carried me safely through the Boundary Waters. You bet I'm going to be here!" The pride showed strongly on her face.

Soon the hum and drone of noisy machines filled the room as masked worker bees sanded each hull down to the fiberglass. Within a couple of hours, the hulls were a dull-white smooth. The gunwales were next, as the mold, and darkened wood was ground away and old caulk pulled from the seam. They too were soon glowing softly with the bare cream- white wood of raw ash. The gunwales and hulls sat almost begging to be coated in new varnish that would bring out the beauty of their cedar strips and return a glowing, shiny reflection back to their smooth shapely surfaces.

We returned to the shack for several successive days. We repainted the white upturned stern and bow of each canoe and touched up each animal totem or emblem. Several coatings of varnish had restored a mirror-like luster and glossy finish to both the hull and gunwales of each boat. The three canoes stood proudly, appearing grateful to be restored and refurbished to the beautiful creations for which they were meant to be.

Returning to the shack alone, I quietly sat soaking up a thousand memories of faces and images from the original canoe build. Young and old, grandsons and granddads, women and girls, boys and men, rich men and paupers, Americans and immigrants had all gathered to build something bigger than ourselves. I had been privileged to stand alongside each person as we crafted these magnificent canoes into existence.

As I walked alongside the Assiniboin, letting my hand gently caress her smooth, glowing and shapely gunwales, I could not help but think of the word neglect. Neglect is most frequently not active, nor intentional. Neglect normally doesn't come with malice or harmful intent. It just comes with the busyness and hyperactivity of modern-day life and the slippery passage of time.

We neglect to do our home repairs which then become unnoticed blemishes on our life's landscape. We don't even see the disrepair anymore. We neglect deadlines, car maintenance, savings, yard work and more, often at a price. But most of all what we neglect are relationships. The busyness and hectic pace of life cause us to pass by and not pay attention to the normal maintenance and repairs that are necessary to keep relationships functioning, glowing and healthy.

Rollie Johnson

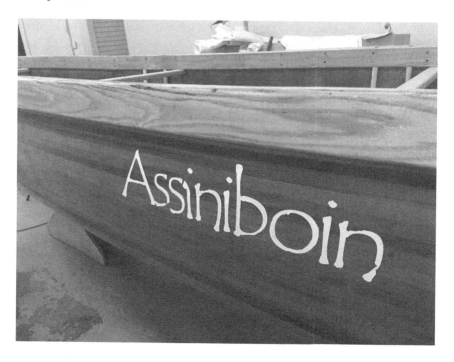

Usually, it's those that are closest to us that we fail to notice and pay attention to. Marriages tend to take the heaviest toll from neglect. It's usually not mal intent or purposeful hurt that rots a marriage, it's simple neglect; leaving it out exposed to the elements with a lack of protection and care that causes mold and mildew to darken what began as a healthy, lively, and glowing relationship. It is sooo easy to neglect. Especially when neglecting involves virtually no effort or work on our parts!

Aging parents sit neglected for distance or time, dear friends drift apart for lack of care and effort or a simple phone call. Children long gone from the nest lead their own busy lives and the cats in the cradle with the silver spoon. The beer belly grows and the double chin births a third as we neglect our one-and-only God-given body. Our church suffers as we neglect to involve ourselves when others can do it.

But most often the source of all neglect comes from the bottom-line neglect of our own souls. We are the one and only caretakers of our own souls. If our souls have long gone neglected, it is because we have allowed it. No one else is culpable. We are the guardians of our souls.

Paying Attention II

The great news is this: God is the Master restorer of souls! After all, he is the original craftsman and creator of our soul! He alone can restore, renew, refresh, refurbish, rebuild, recreate and reenergize *your* soul! And He eagerly awaits each of us to simply make the invitation; *"Jesus renew my spirit, refresh my soul!"* The work of soul restoration and renewal will be His, *not your* effort or strong will. You simply surrender and make yourself accessible and available!

I have a hunch. Prove me right or wrong. My guess is that the more you allow your own soul to be refreshed…the better you will be for restoring and reenergizing other aspects or relationships in your life. God makes beautifully restored creations from those who simply give Him access and availability.

He leads me beside still waters, He restores my soul. Psalm 23 ESV

He gives power to the weak and strength to the powerless. Even youths will become weak and tired,

and young men will fall in exhaustion. But those who trust in the Lord will find new strength.
They will soar high on wings like eagles. They will run and not grow weary. They will walk and not faint.
Isaiah 40:29-31 NLV

And the one sitting on the throne said, "Look, I am making everything new!" And then he said to me, "Write this down, for what I tell you is trustworthy and true." Revelations 21:5 NLV

And the God of Grace who called you to his eternal glory in Christ,
after you have suffered a little while, will himself restore you
and make you strong, firm and steadfast. 1 Peter 5:10 NIV

Then your light will break forth like the dawn,
and your healing will quickly appear;
then your righteousness will go before you,
and the glory of the Lord will be your rear guard.
Then you will call, and the Lord will answer;
you will cry for help and he will say:
Here am I.
The Lord will guide you always;
he will satisfy your needs in a sun-scorched land
and will strengthen your frame.
You will be like a well-watered garden, like
a spring whose waters never fail.
Isaiah 58:8-9,11 NIV

Not Knowing

The fog had enveloped the entire mountain. At times we could only see fifty to one hundred yards in front of us. The way was unclear, the path non-existent as we made our way cross-country up into the higher lakes basin. This was the second day of the Johnson family Griswold backpacking vacation to the Cloud Peak Wilderness, in the spectacular Bighorn Mountains of Wyoming. Day-one had been taxing for Shane and Marissa, who were newcomers to lengthy backpacking trips, and the initial five miles of uphill trail hiking had certainly worn them out. Karina, a veteran of many of our adventure trips, and her new dog Yukon seemed to have fared better and had energy to spare.

Day two found us in the fog and drizzle as we left the trail and began bushwhacking our way to our destination at a high lake. With no trail to hike, Shane seemed to be enjoying the game of searching for rock cairns, little piles of rock spaced occasionally to mark an intended route. We were connecting the dots of rock cairns and laughing all the way. After a couple of hours of hiking the fog grew thicker and thicker and our final rock cairn led us to the edge of a boulder field that appeared to be endless. We each gingerly and tentatively worked our way slowly through the boulder-field, hopping from boulder to boulder. As the visibility diminished, and sense of bearings ebbed, my sense of anxiety and tension grew.

I am one who likes/needs to see and know. I like knowing what I'll be doing tomorrow and next week. I want to know where my career and life are headed. When I can't see… I grow anxious, worried and fearful. I need to be reminded that it's ok to NOT KNOW. To instead trust and keep walking and enjoy the hike! Take a listen to these beautiful words from Sarah Young from the great devotional book Jesus Calling:

As you look at the day before you, you see a twisted, complicated path, with branches going off in all directions. You wonder how you can possibly find your way through that maze. Then you remember the One who is with you always, holding you by your right hand. You recall My promise to guide you with My counsel, and you begin to relax. As you look again at the path ahead, you notice that a peaceful fog has settled over it, obscuring your view. You can see only a few steps in front of you, so you turn your attention more fully to Me and begin to enjoy My Presence. The fog is a protection for you, calling you back into the present moment. Although I inhabit all of space and time, you can communicate with Me only here and now. Someday the fog will no longer be necessary, for you will have learned to keep your focus on Me and on the path just ahead of you.

I've never thought of fog as a protection, nor have I ever really felt peace when my vision is obscured by the fog. I usually instead, have a sense of anxiety or tension when the way is obscured or hidden. I like seeing where I'm going and knowing what's ahead. Yet, I like this new twist, this new take on fog. When I am actively following Christ, I don't have to see what's around the next bend, I don't have to know what I'll be doing tomorrow, or next week, or in one year, or in my retirement. I'm simply called to walk, in trust, in conversation, in companionship and enjoy God's presence along the journey. This is freeing, liberating and so full of grace! I don't have to know! It's ok to NOT KNOW!

If your pathway is uncertain, or life trail obscured by the fog, give thanks! Enjoy the protection and peace and lean into your relationship with God.

For we live by faith, not by sight. 2 Corinthians 5:7 NIV

…The righteous will live by faith." Galatians 3:11 NIV

For I know the plans I have for you declares the Lord, plans to prosper you and not to harm you, plans to give you hope and a future. Jeremiah 29:11 NIV

OLD TREE

The gigantic sequoia-like conifers towered high above the subtropical marshy landscape. Some reached skyward over 100' tall and had trunks whose bases exceeded twelve feet in diameter. It's hard to believe that these gargantuan trees grew so tall and so wide and in such abundance. Who would have thought that western North Dakota could support such a massive forest?

Along my hiking journey through the badlands, I encountered several dozen petrified tree stumps. Research shows that these trees most likely came from the Paleocene epoch, from 65-55 million years ago. These petrified stumps, trunks, and limbs dotted the landscape at various points along my journey. I would often stop to rest alongside these ancient monarchs. I liked to run my hands over these ancient trunks tracing the rough textured grain lines with my fingertips. I enjoyed sitting, observing, listening, wondering and pondering.

I can sort of comprehend a hundred years. Pondering a thousand years things start to get pretty fuzzy and blurry in my head. Jump to a million and my brain turns to Jello. Contemplating multiple millions of years…my cerebral connections just overload and short circuit!

What did these immense trees witness during their short stay on this earth? What roamed beneath their tall canopies? Dinosaurs? T-Rexes? Did long-necked brachiosaurid nibble at their limb-tips? Did sauropods browse beneath their shade? How can a living, then a dead tree, then change to solid rock? Where did all that water go? And how did this whole landscape turn to arid, dry badlands? Were some of these tree's relatives transformed into the Bakken oil that we so desperately extract out of the landscape to fill our SUV's and jet skis?

In a lonely, silent and forgotten valley, I sat beside this prehistoric witness of a time long past hoping for revelation, wanting this rock to speak and pass on wisdom and insight beyond myself. But alas only silence came, as my questions echoed down the parched coulee never to return.

The bible doesn't much speak about the Paleocene or Jurassic periods or fossils or dinosaurs. Not many sermons are preached on how our Christian faith lives intersect with petrified trees or old rocks or brontosaurus bones embedded in the baked backdrop of the Bakken. But on this day, I sat pondering how does all this ancient history fit in with school and church shootings, global climate change, ranting presidential candidates, raging out-of-control weather patterns of tornados, floods, earthquakes and tsunamis, the massive violence of terrorists driven by religious fanatics, racial upheaval in our land of freedom or my friend who is battling for his life fighting cancer? Like the questions asked of my primordial tree stump mentor… only silence echoed back.

I offer no answers, nor insight, nor wisdom. Just observation. Near the end of my journey, I notice a beautiful thing. There, growing out of one of these million-year-old petrified stumps, was a small juniper tree. The juniper tree had embedded its own roots in the nooks and crannies of the petrified tree roots. New, healthy life force was reaching heavenward from the ruins of long ago.

I make known the end from the beginning, from ancient times, what is still to come. I say, 'My purpose will stand, and I will do all that I please.' Isaiah 46:10 NIV

He said to me: "It is done. I am the Alpha and the Omega, the Beginning and the End. To the thirsty I will give water without cost from the spring of the water of life. Revelation 21:6 NIV
Then God said, "Let the land produce vegetation: seed-bearing plants and trees on the land that bear fruit with seed in it, according to their various kinds." And it was so. The land produced vegetation: plants bearing seed according to their kinds and trees bearing fruit with seed in it according to their kinds. And God saw that it was good. Genesis 1:11-12 NIV

He split the rocks in the wilderness and gave them water as abundant as the seas; Psalm 78:15 NIV

Go into the rock, hide in the ground from the fearful presence of the Lord and the splendor of his majesty! Isaiah 2:10 NIV

Paddling in the Dark

"Day 35 found us wind bound all day. We had already begun to ration meals and had just eaten a skimpy supper. Our guide, Jan, announced that we should break camp and at sunset we'd start off for a full night paddle to make up for lost time. So at 9:30 pm the 9 of us apprehensively loaded the 26' voyageur north canoe and shoved off in the growing darkness. My emotions were mixed. On the one hand excited and thrilled to be trying something new, yet nervous and anxious in the eerie gloom of the night. The night was clear but moonless and we kept a good mile of distance between us and the shore to avoid rocks.

The northern sky shone in all its glory of stars and the ghostly Milky way. Around 1:30 am the northern lights showed up and put on a phenomenal light show that was magnified by the huge reflecting pool of Lake Winnipeg. The whole evening took on a surreal atmosphere in the complete darkness, with nothing to gauge your bearings, speed or progress but the vague darkened silhouette of the shorelines treetops. Only the dipping of paddles, the gentle breeze, and splash of wave meeting canoe were heard throughout most of the night. At 4:30 am with a glowing sky to the east we landed our canoe. We were all quite chilled and quickly laid out our tarps and sleeping bags and immediately fell to sleep on the pebbled beach. We had made a good 35 miles."

The preceding words are taken from my journal and then later converted into a magazine article recounting the trip I made in the summer of 1977 between my junior and senior years of high school. It was a 70-day, 1,300-mile canoeing expedition made with 8 other young men into the wilds of the Canadian north. This particular segment recounts our journey up and across the 300- mile long, 80-mile wide Lake Winnipeg. Being several days wind-bound, drastically behind schedule, and running out of food, we committed to a full night paddle. Night paddling is dangerous any time, but especially on the large inland sea of Lake Winnipeg. We paddled all through the ink-black night in utter darkness, which was an unnerving feeling; to be paddling forward into the darkness of the unknown without ever being able to see any form of destination nor obstacles that may lurk above or below the surface of the water.

Each summer about this time of year, a scent on the breeze, or a specific songbird, or a certain sound of leaves rustling in the wind takes me back to that incredible, arduous, and memorable summer. I think back to that strange sensation of paddling without sight or perception and am reminded that much of our faith life we are called to do the same. So much of our lives, we are called to simply walk forward to where God is calling. Often times we may not even know the intended

Paying Attention II

destination or route, yet God calls us forward step by step, even in the midst of unnerving darkness.

Maybe you are walking or padding through a dark or difficult time where you cannot see the outcome, purpose, meaning or destination. That's ok. Keep walking. And hold on to the One who can see you through, and make sense of the darkness and confusion.

A sea captain only very rarely actually sees his destination. For weeks or months, he simply and faithfully follows the compass.

A ship is not built to stay in safe harbor. It is built to sail the high seas!

Man cannot discover new oceans unless he has the courage to lose sight of the shore.

> ... and Peter got down out of the boat, and walked on the water and came towards Jesus. Matt. 14:2 NIV

And I said to the man who stood at the gate of the year, "Give me a light that I may travel safely into the unknown." And he replied, "Go out into the darkness and put your hand into the hand of God. That shall be to you, better than light and safer than a known way."

Passion

The small intimate theatre was packed. Anticipation and excitement filled the cozy space. The lights slowly dimmed and silence replaced the din. From stage right, a man dressed all in black, walked in and sat, placing a guitar upon his left knee. His long, slicked-backed salt and pepper hair, held back in a tight ponytail. A soft light appeared from above shadowing his darkened outline. His foot began to tap and then his guitar literally exploded with sound as he strummed, stroked, plucked and slapped his way up and down the fretboard at a dizzying speed. He became his own orchestra adding rhythm and texture to the melody line. He appeared to be in his own world, almost oblivious to the crowded room. His face contorted with a wide range of emotions. Through his fingers and face came one loud and clear message; "Passion!" And his passion was infectious and contagious as his energy filled the entire room. I was completely drawn into his passion.

After finishing his first song, two men, also dressed in black, but with contrasting clean white dress shirts, descended the spiral staircase from stage left, and took their places alongside the guitarist. A stage light filtered down highlighting their faces. As a new song began, the two began tapping their high heeled dress shoes and clapping their hands loudly in syncopated, yet coordinated rhythms creating a whole new percussion section. Within seconds, they began to sing adding a new layer of stimulation and excitement. The room came alive with sound and movement as the singers wailed, clapped and stomped their feet to the driving beat of the guitar. Their faces contorted with emotion drawing each audience member into their web of zeal. It seemed as if the singers sang not notes, nor tangible words but they sang of "passion!" And their passion was infectious and contagious as their energy spread and filled the room. I was completely drawn into their passion.

And then she appeared. The true Spanish flamenco dancer of Sevilla, Spain. Dressed in red she commanded the stage and demanded all eyes follow her every move. Her lithe, slender and agile figure moved with grace, strength, and elegance, using every inch of floor space as she stomped and stamped and twirled her way to and fro all across the tiny stage. She owned the room and everyone's rapt attention. She clapped and snapped weaving in and out of the guitar music and singing like a matador controlling the bull. And her face… her face drove the storyline of emotion and fervor. The sweat beading from her brow and her grimaced face spoke of pure passion. And her passion was infectious and contagious as her energy filled the room. I was completely drawn into her passion.

Leaving the theatre that evening all I could think of was the word "Passion!" I wanted to go and immediately sign up to take guitar, singing, and dancing lessons! And that's what passion does! It's infectious and contagious. When you meet someone who is passionate, they rub off on you, and you want to do and be like them. Their passion moves you in positive directions.

Sadly, so is the opposite of passion, a little thing that I detest; apathy. Apathy is also contagious. It can spread like a bad infection from one person to another. It can bring down a business, deteriorate an office group, degrade a team, breakdown a family, or slowly rot a marriage. Whereas passion builds and grows energy, apathy drains energy and breeds cesspools of indifference, lethargy, and boredom. Apathy is the bane of teachers, professors, speakers or worship leaders and bosses.

What are you passionate about? It is good and right to be passionate. I have many such passions; the outdoors and nature, bow-hunting, climbing, creating, crafting with wood and flint, and even our beloved and often times frustrating Vikings! But in the end, we will all stand before our Maker and Creator and be judged; were we passionate or apathetic towards this one called Jesus?

I've always been drawn to the word "enthusiasm." It's so similar to passionate. It comes from the Greek word enthousiasmos, which consists of the root words "theos" (god) and "en" (in). Thus, enthusiasm literally means "God within," or filled with God. Therefore, when you encounter an enthusiastic person, often times you will also find a man or woman of faith!

Would anyone who meets you know what you're passionate about? Would they say you are passionate about anything? Is what you're passionate about something significant that points to God? Or does all of your passion get squandered in the trivial and benign? Would anyone who knows you say you are passionate about your faith? Could they tell that you are passionate about your relationship with Jesus? Or would they most likely get a lukewarm faith reading? If they dipped their finger in your faith cup would it be tepid, apathetically cool or passionately warm?

Do you worship with enthusiasm? Are you a passionate worshiper? Do you bring it all to the table? Sing for all your worth? Pray with honesty and transparency? Listen with an open hungry heart? Embrace others in your midst who are broken-sinful-wonder-filled-Godly creatures? Or do you just bring apathy, indifference, lethargy, and boredom?

Our world needs men and women who are passionate about God and about God's work to be done here on earth. God's not looking for perfect, but I believe he does care about passion. Would you be one of them?

Your calling/mission is where _your passions_ meet with the _needs of the world_!

I came that they may have life and have it abundantly! John 10:10 ESV

So, whether you eat or drink, or whatever you do, do all to the glory of God. I Corinthians 10:31 NIV

For where your treasure is, there your heart will be also. Matthew 6:21 NIV

Don't you realize that in a race everyone runs, but only one person gets the prize? So run to win! All athletes are disciplined in their training. They do it to win a prize that will fade away, but we do it for an eternal prize. So I run with purpose in every step. 1 Corinthians 9:24-26 NLV

Perspective

Gently knocking on the heavy door, I quietly waited for a response. "Come on in," was the answer I was hoping for. As I pushed open the door an enthusiastic "Hey Rollie" greeted me accompanied by a warm smile from my good friend David. He appeared genuinely excited to see me. Stretching out my hand I shook his with gusto. I pulled up a chair alongside his bed and began conversing to catch up.

David's newly balding head betrayed his predicament. Being careful not to mess with the wires and tubes I handed him a water glass. David launched into a litany of procedures he was undergoing in his fight to overcome his recent diagnosis of leukemia. I was quite impressed by his newly acquired vocabulary of drugs and medications as he pointed to a plethora of clear bags hanging from his IV stand. This brave husband and father to two beautiful young girls spoke openly of his physical and mental battle of recent weeks and the roller coaster of emotions with which he has had to wrestle. I prodded with questions of "How's your marriage holding up?" "How about finances David?" "What about the girls?" He spoke clearly and honestly of the struggle and the strain but always smiled with hope and optimism that seemed to permeate the room. On his rolling bed table sat a copy of "Jesus Calling," and I smiled knowing from where David's strength and hope had come.

As I looked out the window, through the wooden blinds, I could see my workplace, First Lutheran Church. It looked so different from seven floors up in the Sanford Oncology unit. The giant smokestacks

Paying Attention II

and fans of the hospital and distant water tower added a new perspective to the mundane of my normal weekly routine. As I finished praying for David and his family I walked to the elevator in silence. Entering the elevator, I took a huge bite of humble pie and pondered.

Just the day before I had fallen into an ugly funk after having met with my tax lady. Apparently, Uncle Sam needed more of my money. And Lots of it. I had quickly created my own little Pity Party and spent the day feeling sorry for myself, depressed and worried about the large amount of money I owed, the bad timing of a big upcoming vacation and launching of my second book, and the proverbial; "How can I ever pay for this?!!!" That ugly funk and black cloud had accompanied me all the way to the 7th floor. From my time spent on 7th-floor oncology, my Pity Party was immediately dissolved and evaporated in the presence of David. Perspective. Perspective had changed my view, changed my attitude and changed my gratitude.

Recent weeks have found me waking long before dawn to chase and try to outwit our local Thomas Turkey. My hopes of sending a very pointed dinner invitation directly to Tom via my longbow have been thwarted time and time again. The Local 405 Turkey Union has been totally uncooperative. To say I've been frustrated is putting it mildly. After a few of these hunts, I've come home grumpy, tired, frustrated and sulking.

After yesterday's hunt, I came home to check my emails. One email smacked me up hard to the side of my brain. The part that has to do with perspective and attitude. The email was from my good friend Rory. Several years ago, Rory suffered a severe brain aneurysm that completely changed his life. He no longer can walk nor talk. He now communicates from his wheelchair, via a computer that reads his eye movements. As he focuses on a letter on the screen, he blinks his eyes to click on letters. He had emailed me to invite me to an upcoming event.

My self-created frump and pity party was immediately challenged by a swift kick to my psychological derriere. I instantly realized the folly and frivolous nature of my whiny and selfish pity party. Having been challenged from the perspective of Rory's wheelchair, I once again came to a new outlook. I had to change my language: I get to brush my teeth. I get to mow the lawn. I get to tie my own shoes. I get to clean the dishes. I get to hug my wife and children. I get to drive Shane to practice. I get to vacuum the carpet. I get to cook supper. I get to take out the garbage. I get to go to a good and rewarding job. I get to walk my dog, Bruno. I get to play catch with Shane. I get to go and work out. I get to go for a run tonight. I get to repair the bathroom sink. I get to do laundry. I get to get up early and go hunting. I get to succeed or fail at hunting. Perspective had changed my view, changed my attitude and changed my gratitude.

Each week my son Shane practices soccer several times at Lincoln Elementary on the south side of town. I usually go for a run while he practices. Often times I'll run through the lovely Lindenwood Park. Sometimes I purposely choose to run through Riverside Cemetery. I strongly believe It's good for the living to run amongst the dead. As I run past hundreds of dreary and cold monuments and gravestones, I am reminded that today I have been given the gift of life. I have health. I have vitality. I can run. I can breathe. I can smell the birth of new life on the plants and trees. I can listen to and hear the vibrant music of the songbirds. I have eyes that can see the rebirth of spring all around me. These are simple, yet magnificent Godly gifts to be treasured, cherished and celebrated.

When I step back and see life from new perspectives, there is no room for self-pity. God has showered His multitude of blessings and treasures on all of us. Often times the greatest blessings are also some of the most taken for granted, overlooked and simplest of gifts. May you also take a look at your own life from the perspective of 7th floor Sanford, or Rory's wheelchair or from the grave. Perspective can change your view, change your attitude and change your gratitude.

The greatest of human freedoms is the ability to choose one's own attitude. Victor Frankl

Rejoice always, pray continually, give thanks in all circumstances; for this is God's will for you in Christ Jesus.. *1Thes 5:16-18 NIV*

The Constitution only gives people the right to pursue happiness. You have to catch it yourself. ~ Ben Franklin

When we enjoy what God has done for us, and when we express that enjoyment to God, *it brings him joy- but it also increases our joy.* God said "it's time to get on with your life! Do the things I designed humans to do. Make love to your spouse. Have babies. Raise families. Plant crops and eat meals. Be humans. This is what I made you to be. *Every human activity, except sin, can be done for God's pleasure if you do it with an attitude of praise.* You can wash dishes, repair a machine, sell a product, write a computer program, grow a crop, and raise a family for the glory of God. *Every act of enjoyment becomes an act of worship when you thank and praise God for it.* Rick Warren Purpose Driven Life

Rollie Johnson

Pictographs

The cobalt blue skies and frigid air had banished all clouds to the barrens beyond my perception. The arctic air was invigorating, and each labored breath filled my lungs with clean, pure, life-giving oxygen. The silent spruce, balsam, and pines were my only companions. These stoic evergreens stood impassive and unresponsive, offering neither encouragement nor disapproval as I toiled over the difficult portage and passed quietly through their silent north-woods domain.

The 180 rod (half-mile) portage was testing my stamina and resolve in the deep snow. I had entered the proverbial wilderness exchange program where I had bartered heavy work and toil in exchange for warmth and sweat. Fortunately, this time, I was traveling my back trail and the path was clear and partially compacted by my previous entry with snowshoes and heavy sled. Three days earlier I had traversed this same portage, following the narrow trough of moose tracks that had meandered along this trail to find his way to the next lake. Thank you, Bullwinkle!

With great relief and silent gratitude, I could make out the vast expanse of flat white of North Hegman Lake. I quickly descended the final curves of the portage and arrived back in the brilliant sunshine of the wide-open lake, grateful to be finished with my longest portage. I shuffled across a small bay to gain the lee and protection of the opposing shoreline out of the slight breeze. Grabbing a comfortable seat on top of my sled I guzzled some much need icy water, devoured several handfuls of GORP and soaked up the incredible wilderness that surrounded me. Prayers of gratitude wafted upward following the clouds of steam off my back.

My three days of solitude and silence on my winter-camping solo would soon end tomorrow when my guests were due to arrive. I was giddy with anticipation. Rest breaks never last long when winter camping, so within minutes I was traversing northward into the narrows of Hegman Lake.

I soon merged into the heavy ski and snowshoe tracks that cluttered the lake coming from the entry- point portage. I knew from previous adventures that I would soon arrive at the famous pictographs. I quickly arrived on site and stood below these incredible rock paintings. Part of my solitude was relieved, as I was welcomed back into the human fold by these signs of man.

Paying Attention II

I stood in awe for quite some time pondering and contemplating these magnificent works of primitive art. A man with outstretched arms, a wolf chasing a moose, and what appeared to be three canoes with people in them. Researchers believe these were painted with ocher, by Algonquin speaking natives most likely of the Ojibwa or Annishanabe peoples. Age? No one knows for certain... speculated guesses place them between 500 and 9,000 years old.

Any way you look at it, 500 or 9,000, it matters not, for the fact remains that these primitive pigments, painted by a long-ago Native American, have stood the test of time and endured. Imagine how many thunderstorms, droughts, forest fires, floods, sun-baked summer days, bitter cold below-zero blizzards, and tornadoes these paintings have witnessed and endured? It boggles my mind to even imagine what these pictographs have witnessed.

I think not, that anything of my own handiwork will endure much beyond my short lifetime here on earth. Maybe a piece of my woodworking furniture or one of my canoes or possibly one of my knapped flint knife blades if well cared for by one of my children, but most likely no more than few years beyond my lifespan. In our fast-paced, technology-driven, rapidly changing world, I believe we each are searching for something that is constant, unchanging and that will endure the test of time.

What is it that you cling to that will endure? Your popularity, status or fame? Your financial security or portfolio? Your health or beauty? Your children? Your career? Your awards and accomplishments? Your Facebook Likes? Your grades? Your athletic prowess? Your toys or possessions? Your political party? Your spouse? Your friends?

In her beautiful song, The Love of the Lord Endures, Joy Williams sings these Godly truths:

In all that I have found, Your evidence abounds. I've always sensed your fingerprints If I just look around. And yet this grand display, will all soon pass away, So I hold on to, the mighty truth, that your love is here to stay.

May you truly enjoy and marvel at the many magnificent works of man; from pyramids, to pictographs, to a magnificent music composition, to the marvels of flight, to miracles of modern medicine, to placing a man on the moon, or standing beneath a shimmering skyscraper; whether made by a Native American so very long ago, or tomorrow in a science lab. All marvels to behold, ponder and appreciate. But never forget that only One is worthy and will endure forever. Do you know Him?

Jesus declares: Heaven and earth will pass away, but my words will never pass away.
Matthew 24:35 NIV

For the Lord is good and his love endures forever;
his faithfulness continues through all generations Psalm 100:5 NIV

Highlights from Psalm 118 NIV
1) Give thanks to the Lord, for he is good; his love endures forever
8) It is better to take refuge in the Lord than to trust in humans.
9) It is better to take refuge in the than to trust in princes.
14) The Lord is my strength and my defense he has become my salvation.
29) Give thanks to the Lord, for he is good; his love endures forever

Poison Ivy

The great wilderness that surrounded our campsite on our recent SOLO week was lush with greenery. My lifelong favorite friends; the lofty and majestic red and white pines dominated the macro of the upper story. These stoic monarchs intermixed with the ever-dominant spruce, balsam, and scraggly jack-pines to remind us we were indeed in the "north." Adding life, motion and sound from their dancing leaves were the flourishing white birch, popples, basswoods, along with the enduring oak and ash. On these days of warm sunshine and cool breezes, the forest virtually danced with life.

Lower in the canopy grew the thick tangles of alder, and hazelnut bushes heavy with nuts. The bear and deer will eat well this fall. And surrounding our campsite grew the understory heavy and dense with brush and bushes of all sizes and shapes. It was here near to the ground I found an old and familiar adversary, my life-long nemesis; poison ivy.

Now I've known poison ivy intimately since my youth. Having had its nasty, itchy rashes more times than I can count, I know its face and shape like the back of my hand. I can pick it out in a sea of green and point out each individual plant like he was my own black-sheep brother.

During this week I must have tried to teach, show and point out over 20 times which plant was poison ivy to our curious team members. Folks were slow to catch on, as they would point to a three-leafed plant and ask; "Is that it?" I'd quickly respond, "No, sorry that is a wild strawberry." "Is that it?" "Nope. Sorry, that's a Hogs Peanut plant." "Is this one him?" No, sorry that's a baby wild raspberry plant"

But I **KNOW** poison ivy. And I know the negative influence he can have in life. I've felt it first-hand. The crazy thing is he gets mixed in along with many other look-alike plants that are wholesome, good and even healthy like the aforementioned berry plants. But poison ivy almost always grows in and amongst the good stuff. And to this day, I cannot tell you why God created and allows poison ivy plants to flourish. But they do.

Now in a week's time wandering and playing throughout the north woods, most of us came into physical contact with poison ivy. Just no way to avoid it. This was clearly demonstrated by the many, both large and small rashes that began appearing at the end of the week on most of our bodies. The last day people began showing off their many places of growing scabs, bumps and rashes. But it was funny… for as they showed off these ugly and sometimes painful inconveniences, they were all smiling and laughing. The poison ivy could not, and would not erase the positive outcome, influence, and faith growing experiences that we each had had throughout the week. There was just *sooo* much good and Godly in the week! The negative influence of poison ivy could not win, and the ongoing smiles and laughter proved it!

This completely reminded me of life in the church. The church, or our church, or any church for that matter is filled with lots of good and Godly, healthy and life-affirming people. And to my dismay, there are also plenty of Poison Ivy plants that grow and sadly flourish right in and amongst the good; The Negative Nellies, The Debbie Downers, The Grumpy Gus's, and the Frumpy Freddy's. These are the ones who sit in tight circles filled with gossip, complaining, grumbling, whining, nitpicking and criticizing.

Jesus himself tells the simple parable of the weeds. Most often people interpret the weeds as being evil in our world. For me, I think Jesus simply understood human beings all too well and was prophetically wise in knowing the pitfalls of what His church would be like.

"The kingdom of heaven is like a man who sowed good seed in his field. But while everyone was sleeping, his enemy came and sowed weeds among the wheat, and went away. When the wheat sprouted and formed heads, then the weeds also appeared. "The owner's servants came to him and said, 'Sir, didn't you sow good seed in your field? Where then did the weeds come from?' "An enemy did this,' he replied. "The servants asked him, 'Do you want us to go and pull them up?' "'No,' he answered, 'because while you are pulling the weeds, you may uproot the wheat with them. Let both grow together until the harvest. At that time, I will tell the harvesters: First collect the weeds and tie them in bundles to be burned; then gather the wheat and bring it into my barn. Matthew 13:1-23 NET

In the end, poison ivy never wins. To be sure, they will infect others with their contagious irritations. But the good and Godly who bless, affirm, appreciate, and cherish life and all that God provides with an attitude of gratitude will prevail. I still have no clue why God created or allows poison ivy to flourish. But that will never stop me from immersing myself in His wondrous creation!

> The devil succeeds in laying his cuckoo eggs in a pious nest… The sulfurous stench of hell is as nothing compared with the evil odor emitted by divine grace gone putrid. Helmut Thielicke

And we know that in all things God works for the good of those who love him, who have been called according to his purpose. For those God foreknew he also predestined to be conformed to the image of his Son, that he might be the firstborn among many brothers and sisters. And those he predestined, he also called; those he called, he also justified; those he justified, he also glorified. Romans 8:28 NIV

I had a dream that death came the other night, and heaven's gate swung wide open.
With kindly grace an angel ushered me inside, and there to my astonishment stood folks

Rollie Johnson

I had known on earth, and some I had judged and labeled unfit and of little worth.
Indignant words rose to my lips, But were never set free;
For every face showed stunned surprise, Not one expected me.
Anonymous

Rappelling

The fear was palpable. Anxiety hovered overhead like an unwanted bee. Yet there was also great excitement, anticipation, and positive expectation. Warm, gorgeous sunlight flooded our faces from the west. Beads of sweat balanced on my brow.

Forty-some kids, ages six-67, had assembled on the third-floor roof of our church for an evening of rappelling. Most all were rookies to the skill of rappelling but had come for the thrill of adventure or more importantly to face and overcome their fears. And face them they did!

After a little orientation and actual rappelling demonstration, we assembled all into harnesses and helmets in preparation. There were first graders, and 5th graders, and middle schoolers, and high schoolers, and moms, and dads and even a couple of exemplary role model **grandfathers!** *(WE ARE NEVER TOO OLD TO LEARN, GROW, FACE OUR FEARS AND TRUST GOD EVEN MORE!)*

There were three stations, each with a doubled rope that was secured to a bomb proof, immovable, rock-solid anchor. This anchor is the key to any rappelling situation… after all, your whole life is literally and figuratively tied into, and dependent upon this anchor to support and hold you. It had better be bombproof, immovable, and rock solid!

For added fail-proof security and safety, we also had one of our veteran climbers backing up each person with a belay. Each belayer was tied securely to an anchor as well. So, if you happen to freak, fail, flail or fall... absolutely nothing would happen! You would simply be held firmly by your secure anchor and loving belayer! No harm done!

Each participant upon their turn would be properly tied in by their belayer, double checked, and then triple checked by me. And next is where the rubber meets the road... or more importantly where faith and trust meet real-life fear, worry, and anxiety.

As each rappeller stepped up onto the edge of the church wall with 35' of gaping empty space behind and below them, they were required to recite out loud from our laminated tag-board sign; *"Life is Hard, Challenging and Scary, but I will trust God to see me through it."*

And then began the sometimes excruciating battle of getting your body to back over the edge, placing all of your weight, your entire being onto the rope/anchor when your mind and senses are screaming *"Go back to the safety of where you came from!"*

Let us remember for a moment that *all* fear, anxiety, and worry is future based, it's anticipatory, it is a negative expectation that something ...forth coming will be hurtful or negative. Whether it's fearing our dentist appointment next week, a speech you must make tomorrow, a weighted exam you must take, getting on an airplane, a review you must face with your boss, the results you're waiting for on a medical test, starting the "what will I do now" of retirement, wondering whether my kid will survive middle school or the ultimate fear of all; facing our own mortality.

And so, in life, the question becomes; *"Is God big enough, strong enough, and reliable enough to hold me fast and securely through what I'm fearing or anticipating?"* Most of us in real life fall back on our learned behaviors of worry, fear, and anxiety, rather than choosing faith and trust. We prefer to stay in the safety of our known, familiar and secure lives, even if that is a pain-filled, miserable, shrinking, and fearful life!

Each participant took the edge with a variety of behaviors or stances. Some shaking with nervousness, some teary-eyed for the fear, some with nervous laughter, some with the silence of absolute focus and concentration, and some with faces riddled with doubt and trepidation. Yet for those who persevered in and through the fear, doubt, nervousness, and anxiety... a most amazing thing happened. As they leaned back and fully trusted in the anchor and got over the actual edge, they began to see that the anchor was indeed reliable and trustworthy and soon a sense of being held safely led to a feeling of exhilaration, joy, and fun! By the time each landed on good ol' mother earth, most were back up to the roof within a minute for another ride!

The great thing about rappelling is that it takes very little strength or ability of your own. It's not a muscle or athletic issue. Any strength or reliability comes from your anchor. It is the strength and power of the anchor that upholds and saves. Not your own effort, ability, skill or strength. Your job is to simply trust. Very simple in concept, but often times incredibly difficult to do!

What do you fear tomorrow? What makes you anxious about next week? What is causing the anxiety that hovers over your life like an annoying bee? Is God big enough, strong enough, wise enough to see you through it?

I don't believe God is asking you to muscle through it, power down, and add more effort. Nor do I believe He wishes for you shrink into worry, fear, and anxiety. What He does desire, is for each of us to have courage, step up to the edge and put our complete trust in him, surrendering our body, mind, and spirit. After all, *Life is Hard, Challenging and Scary, but I will trust God to see me through it.*

> The Holy Spirit releases his power the
> moment you take a step of faith.
> *Obedience unlocks God's power.*
> God waits for you to act first. Don't wait to feel powerful
> or confident. Move ahead in your weakness,
> doing the right thing *in spite of* your fears and feelings.
> This is how you cooperate with the Holy Spirit,
> and it is how your character develops.
> "God waits for you to act first." What step can
> you take today that will move you forward
> *in spite of your fears and feelings?*
> Rick Warren, Purpose Driven Life

Fear knocked at the door, Faith answered.
And lo… no one was there.

> *Be strong and brave. Don't be afraid or terrified of them, because the Lord your God will go with you. He will not leave you or forget you… Don't be afraid and don't worry! Deuteronomy 31: 6-8 NIV*

> *When I am afraid, I put my trust in you.
> In God, whose word I praise—
> in God I trust and am not afraid.
> What can mere mortals do to me? Psalm 56:3-4 NIV*

Rest

The fire crackled and spat. The amber and auburn flames danced through the window of the wood-stove making us feel welcomed and at home. The oaken and ash logs released their energy, lending their warmth and light to the circle of men gathered 'round the hearth. We felt relaxed and at peace, here in the heart of the shack. No electricity, no cell phones, no radios, no TVs. Just propane gas lights, and the warmth of wood burning in the stoves.

Ten men had said "yes" to the invitation. Of the hundreds invited and informed, just this small eclectic group of guys has responded affirmatively by moving from good intentions to actual movement and commitment. The whys and hows of who God had called were unknown to me. Or maybe, God had called on many others who had simply tuned Him out or turned away from His quiet gentle invitation. I knew not which, but was simply grateful and pleased by the good faces who shared this small circle with me.

This unique experience was our annual men's winter cabin retreat. We had snow-shoed a half-mile into this remote back-woods cabin in the dark of night passing through timbered woods and crossing over a marshy river. I had asked the men to turn off their headlamps at the start of the trail, to better experience the cold north woods at night. A spectacular star-filled sky dome surrounded our overhead view and a brilliant half-moon illuminated our path like a giant streetlamp. The freshly fallen powdered snow was thick and deep and twinkled under the light of the taunting moon. Cold, fresh, clean Northern Minnesota air filled out lungs and invigorated our bodies.

Our days had been filled with hiking and exploring the surrounding woods, lots of laughter, spontaneous conversations, quiet times of reflection, reading scriptures, cribbage, card games, and fantastic and filling foods, and an occasional barley pop. There had been a healthy and holistic balance of alone time and together time. A balance of planned activities and plenty of free time to make one's own agenda.

We had gathered 'round the wood stove for our second evening's group time. I began with a simple and easy question by asking the fellas who had taken a nap this afternoon. All ten men raised their hands. I then asked the guys; which of you normally takes a nap in your everyday normal life back home? All hands dropped except for mine. (I'm a lover of daily naps!) Not a one. And yet everyman to the last one of us had taken a deep, relaxing and for many of the guys, a full 2-hour comatose nap that afternoon!

I believe that one of the primary reasons that God had called each of these diverse men out of their ordinary lives was to *give to each of us a gift*. A much lacking, neglected and forgotten element to a healthy and balanced life, a thing called…REST!

In our go-go, hyper-scheduled, hyperactive, over-achieving, over-programmed world we do so much, but end up having empty, tired, anxious, weary and worn souls. And what good is it my friend to gain the whole world, yet lose your soul? And rarely, so very rarely can we achieve rest on our own by staying in our normal, daily routine, and rutted lifestyle. For we tend to fill any empty spaces with more and more activity, or endless thumbing through our cell phones or entering the twilight zone of TV to drown out the anxieties and issues that lurk in our head and our world.

That is why God often calls us *to retreat*. Retreats call us out of our daily patterns and routines. Retreats shake us out of the ordinary and draw us into the extra-ordinary. Retreats strip away our defenses of schedules and cell phones and allow space and time for God to speak to us, to engage with others in real and honest and meaningful conversations that we rarely have in our day-to-day. Retreats call us into the gentle and natural rhythms that Jesus so beautifully demonstrated by going off to be alone to pray, in order that He could be filled to come back and engage and minister to those around him in community.

Retreats cause us to pause, to reflect, to ponder, to listen and to look at our lives, our thinking patterns, our behaviors, our relationships and our daily practices in a new light. Retreats often call us to discard, or to lessen, or to let go, or to close.

During and after our retreat weekend at the cabin, I heard many similar comments from our diverse group of masculine souls. *"Man, I really needed this weekend." "I feel so refreshed, so renewed." "My soul was starving, God fed me to the brim." "I hadn't realized how empty I was, how tired my life had become." "I got some perspective. I needed this to take a good honest look at my life." "My life has been racing. I couldn't see that or how to stop it." "I'm going home rested. I'm ready to make some changes."*

God calls each of us to rest. He calls us to do that **daily**, by spending time with him alone in the quiet of conversational prayer. He calls us to rest each **week** by modeling for us the practice of Sabbath. And occasionally God whispers our name and invites us to retreat with Him away from our family, our spouses, our children, our jobs or our friends to breathe new life and vitality into our weary and worn souls. It is only good, right, and Godly that we should say "yes" to His invitation. May you have the courage to say "Yes!" to God's calling to rest and retreat.

He Leads me beside still waters, He renews my soul. Psalm 23 ESV

Does God indeed need to rest? Of course not! But did God choose to rest? Yes. Why? Because God subjected creation to a rhythm of rest and work that He revealed by observing the rhythm Himself, as a precedent for everyone else. In this way, He showed us a key to order in our private worlds. Gordon McDonald

Come to me all you who are weary and burdened, and I will give you rest. Take my yoke upon you and learn from me, for I am gentle and humble in heart, and you will find rest for your souls. For my yoke is easy and my burden is light. Matthew 11: 28-30 NIV

Be Still And Know that I am God. Psalm 46:10 NIV
   Be still before the Lord and wait patiently for him. Psalm37: 7 NIV

I wonder if the snow loves the trees and fields, that it kisses them so gently? And then it covers them up snug, you know, with a white quilt; and perhaps it says "Go to sleep, darlings, till the summer comes again."
   — Lewis Carroll, Alice's Adventures in Wonderland & Through the Looking-Glass

Ronaldo

We recently took a two and a half week Griswold Family Vacation through Spain and Portugal. Planes, trains, automobiles, buses, subways, taxies, boats, bicycles, and miles and miles of walking and gawking gave us the hands-on experience of these two amazing countries. It was incredible!

Massive and majestic cathedrals that brought awe and wonder that reached for the skies. We witnessed paintings and sculptures that have survived for hundreds of years crafted by the world's most famous artists. We walked through fortresses and castles that date back hundreds and sometimes thousands of years and crossed bridges built by the early Romans. We tasted food from all over the planet and walked narrow streets of cobblestone so narrow you could touch each wall. We drank more than enough delicious sangria, and my two-cup daily cappuccino limit was exceeded on several occasions due to the overabundance of quaint outdoor street cafes that were everywhere. We heard about kings and queens, knights in shining armor, and the melding and intertwining of Jews, Muslims, and Christians in the history that has shaped our world. The layers of history in these countries are mind-boggling.

Our final day in the bustling city of Madrid took us on an amazing tour of the Santiago Bernabéu Stadium, home of the Real Madrid soccer team. Real Madrid is one of the most dominant club teams in the history of soccer, and where Portuguese soccer star Cristiano Ronaldo plays during the regular season. We toured the seats way up in the nose-bleed sections, walked through their unbelievable trophy room and watched video after video of champions, mind-boggling goals and the rich traditions and history of this amazing team. We even got the locker room journey and then ambled onto the field and sit in the seats of the team. Our thirteen-year-old soccer-head Shane was in his glory!

According to ESPN, Cristiano Ronaldo is the **# one** most famous and well-known athlete in the world. Besides being at the top of the list of the elite all-time greatest soccer players, he is rock-star famous with his chiseled good lucks and supermodel face. The ladies go wild! He endorses or models for hundreds of products and his name appears on the back of millions of soccer fan jerseys. He is at the forefront of the current World Cup Tournament playing for his home country Portugal, and his name alone brings in billions of dollars.

Please take a moment to watch this fun and intriguing video of Ronaldo in Disguise in Madrid.
Video: https://www.youtube.com/watch?v=8H_DSErYUZk

I find this video delightful. Nary a single person pays attention to him for almost the first full hour.

He playfully begs several people to engage with him, but most walk by, shrug him off as just another street performer, ignore him and move past. Some watch mildly interested from a distance, but they refuse to interact personally. They play it distant and safe. Finally, it takes a child, who doesn't have social walls built up, who just takes things at face value, and who isn't afraid to look foolish. Man, does he get the surprise of his life for daring to simply engage and play with the bearded man!

It's a classic case of; *"Out of Context."* You just don't find the most famous athlete in the world simply playing soccer in an everyday mundane plaza of Madrid. After all, famous super-star soccer players are to be found in gigantic, magnificent soccer stadiums. Right, that's where they're supposed to be. Not in our everyday, ordinary, and often times mundane world.

Where do you look for God? Church right… that's where he's supposed to be! In the big, magnificent, beautiful building, the house of God, the sanctuary, right? God does play there on occasion. But I believe he spends the bulk of His time out there in our everyday, ordinary lives. The question of the day is… Would you recognize Jesus if He actually walked by you? What if he was mischievously inviting you to play with Him, to engage with Him on a deeper level? What if He has been circling around you continually, longing to be with you, to converse with you, to walk alongside you, and to grow in relationship with Him. Could you… would you dare to be like the little boy and actually play with Jesus?

Might it be that God is wearing the mask of your coworker today? Might Jesus be sitting quietly in the old house next door? Might He be sitting downtown on a sidewalk? Maybe God is sporting a different skin color beyond your own? Might His voice be whispering on this evening's breeze? Maybe you'll encounter Him hidden in a sunset at your lake? Might He be wearing the face of someone you despise?

God is so completely unlimited. He can appear anywhere, anytime, in any shape or person He chooses.

Maybe this week you and I can pray for eyes to see and perceive God's presence in our world. And then may we have the courage to drop our adultness, and simply play with and engage with Jesus.

At that time Jesus said, "I praise you, Father, Lord of heaven and earth, because you have hidden these things from the wise and learned, and revealed them to little children. Matthew 11:25 NIV

Jesus said, "Let the little children come to me, and do not hinder them, for the kingdom of heaven belongs to such as these." Matthew 19:14 NIV

And he said: "Truly I tell you, unless you change and become like little children, you will never enter the kingdom of heaven. Matthew 18:3 NIV

"The whole earth is a living icon of the face of God. ... I do not worship matter. I worship the Creator of matter who became matter for my sake, who willed to take His abode in matter, who worked out my salvation through matter. Never will I cease honoring the matter which wrought my salvation! I honor it, but not as God. Because of this, I salute all remaining matter with reverence because God has filled it with his grace and power. Through it, my salvation has come to me."— St. John of Damascus (675-749)

> "Now if I believe in God's Son and remember that He became man, all creatures will appear a hundred times more beautiful to me than before. Then I will properly appreciate the sun, the moon, the stars, trees, apples, as I reflect that he is Lord over all things. ...God writes the Gospel, not in the Bible alone, but also on trees, and in the flowers and clouds and stars."— Martin Luther (1483-1546),

> I believe in God like I believe in the sunrise, not because I can see it, but because I can see everything it touches. C.S. Lewis

Rory's Farewell: Closing A Chapter

Returning from a recent vacation to Spain and Portugal, I arrived home to catch up on emails. An email from my dear friend Rory Eidsness caught me off guard. I read the following:

"I wanted to tell you this in person, but I was told that you were not getting back from your vacation until July and I'm already in Colorado. Thanks for all you did for me over the years, and especially your friendship. If you are ever in the Denver area make sure that you email me and stop by. Thanks again, don't be a stranger. Love, Rory"

The finality of this short and to the point letter tugged at my heart. I was deeply touched. A chapter of my life had just ended. The book had been closed and now placed upon the memory shelf. I felt a wide mix of emotions, some tough to name out loud, but misty eyes betrayed the heart of what I felt.

Rory and his wife Kari had built a house outside of Denver a few years back. Upon Kari's retirement from teaching this spring, they put their Fargo home up for sale and moved west while I was gone. I had missed the big farewell party. I admired his courage to uproot, move away and start a brand-new life in a new land. His ability to take risks and act courageously from the silence of his wheelchair is beyond compare.

To be truthful this note was rather verbose and lengthy. Especially from Rory who is usually short and to the point. He wastes no verbiage on excess words, drawn-out grammar or emotional fluff. With his computer mounted to a long arm on his wheelchair, he uses his eyes to blink, to click on letters on his screen. The computer reads his eye movements and responds to each blink of his eye. The process is slow, arduous and tedious. I felt honored to receive such a lengthy, heartfelt, and gracious note from him knowing the effort involved.

Our friendship had grown over the years especially since his devastating stroke in 2006 that left him speechless and confined to a wheelchair with little or no use of his limbs. What did remain though was his keen wit, eagle-like observations, and courageous heart to persevere, adapt and overcome all that life has thrown at him.

We had partnered together on many challenging endeavors. Two half-marathons, a full-marathon, several 5ks, hunting deer with his crossbow and numerous speaking engagements to schools and businesses. Each challenge brought innumerable obstacles, trials and often failures. Laughter was our normal antidote to these challenges, and persistence and hard-headedness carried us through to eventual successes. Being the same age, and ironically having had the same college degrees in

Park & Recreation, (Our wives kidded us to no end about our high achieving, high paying degrees!) we were well-suited partners on the running road, or in the hunting blind. Ding and Dong, Dumb and Dumber, Tweedledee and Tweedledum, either way, we had become strong friends over many adventures shared together.

And so, with a bit of melancholy, I close that chapter. A stage of my life has ended. All good things come to an end as the cliché goes, and with that closing comes a wide mix of emotions.

We will all close innumerable chapters in our lives. Often these closings pass without proper acknowledgment on our parts. Our first-born heads off to kindergarten, no longer needing us all day. A high schooler leaves home to begin college in a far-off land. The last child moves out leaving us an empty, quiet nest. A football or volleyball season ends. A job loss or leaving one job for another new one. A move to a new house or city. A girlfriend leaves, a relationship falls apart, a divorce splits a marriage or family. Age or declining health take away former abilities. A beloved boss changes jobs, a close coworker resigns. Retirement is both a thrilling and terrifying closing for so many.

Paying Attention II

And for all of us, often the most difficult of all closings is losing a loved one to death. This chapter closing is often the most final, most devasting and difficult to accept and work through. To lose your one and only mother or father, your beloved spouse, or a sibling, a dear friend or worse yet a child can be brutally hard and devastating to face the finality of that closing chapter.

My heart breaks for those who face these closing chapters on their own, who do not know and love the Lord. I cannot imagine how empty, alone, hopeless and bleak these endings must be. We must all, no matter who we are, face and walk through many chapters closing in our lives. Many of these closings will come with devasting shock, heavy grief, sadness, confusion, anger or emptiness. Yet the truth is we need not go through these closings alone. For those who know, call on, and walk with Jesus there is so much more.

*For I know the plans I have for you," declares the L*ORD*, "plans to prosper you and not to harm you, plans to give you hope and a future. Jeremiah 29:11* NIV

Be strong and courageous. Do not be afraid or terrified because of them, for the Lord your God goes with you; he will never leave you or forsake you. The Lord himself goes before you and will be with you; he will never leave you nor forsake you. Do not be afraid; do not be discouraged. Deuteronomy 31: 6-8 NIV

Be strong and courageous, because you will lead these people to inherit the land I swore to their ancestors to give them.! Remember that I have commanded you to be strong and courageous. Don't be afraid. Because I the Lord your God will be with you everywhere you go. Joshua 1: 6-9 NIV

Fear not, for I have redeemed you; I have called you by name, and you are mine!
When you pass through the waters, I will be with you; and when you pass through the rivers,
they will not sweep over you. When you walk through the fire, you will not be burned.
For I am the Lord your God. Isaiah 43:1-2 ESV

I am fortunate, although this chapter or partnering together on various endeavors with Rory has ended, our friendship remains and God willing, that will continue for many years to come. And we must remember that with each closing chapter, a new one begins. New opportunities, new endeavors, new possibilities for those who know and trust in the Lord.

I pray that God would bless Rory and Kari in their new home and that they will experience many wonderful new beginnings in Colorado.

May your close your chapters well, and then move forward in positive expectations of where God may lead you! You do not go alone!

Paying Attention II

If you knew Who walks beside you on the way that you have chosen, worry and fear would be impossible.

You'll get through this. It won't be painless. It won't be quick. But God will use this mess for good.
Don't be foolish or naïve. But don't despair either. With God's help, you'll get through this. Max Lucado

Sanctuary

Stepping through the threshold, I entered the sanctuary. I was the only person present. It felt good to be alone in the quiet surroundings. I slowly moved left and chose a comfortable spot. I grinned for the peace of this holy and sacred space. Though being the only human present, I was definitely not alone.

All around me was a choir of a several dozen birds all of a different species each singing songs of praise in their own unique God-given voices. Beethoven or Mozart would have had difficulty composing such beautiful compositions. And there was no holding back, no shyness, no false humility of; *"Oh I can't sing."* They simply sang because God had given them a voice and a song to sing.

Surrounding me were also a hundred plus trees who had also come to give their best praise to our common Creator. The warming robust breeze of the Holy Spirit was invisibly passing through the sanctuary causing each tree to wave its palms to and fro in a more Evangelical than Lutheran, full- body worship. Even the dull gray-green underbellies of each leaf were exposed by the fervent movements.

Geese and ducks could be heard sounding off from the orchestra over the dike and several squirrels added their own enthusiastic chitter-chatter to the sacred music. Brilliant life-giving sunshine poured in from the east adding life and color and depth to all that surrounded me. I smiled and took a long, delicious swig of aromatic coffee. I could not help but join in and celebrate with all the others. Worship from the divine space of my back deck was in full service.

Where do you worship? When do you worship? If you're only place and form of worship is on Sunday morning for one hour at a church, I'd have to say ... you're missing the boat with God. The saying goes; "Just because you stand in a garage, doesn't make you a car." Similarly, just because you stand in a church, doesn't mean that you are a Christian with an active and ongoing relationship with Jesus. The life of real faith goes so much farther and deeper than one hour on a Sunday!

Barbara Brown Taylor, in her insightful book; An Altar in the World, writes these poignant words: *Do we build God a house so that we can choose when to go see God? Do we build God a house in lieu of having God stay at ours? Plus, what happens to the rest of the world when we build four walls-even four gorgeous walls-cap them with a steepled roof and designate that the house of God? What happens to the riverbanks, the mountaintops, the deserts, and the trees? What happens to the people who never show up in our houses of God?*

If you are a fisherman, do you pause throughout your day offering praise, thanks, and worship for the magnificent beauty of the lake and the unseen universe that lies beneath the surface of the water?

You that golf, do you take a few quiet moments during your 18 holes to ponder the beautiful partnership of man's maneuvering of the landscape and God's phenomenal creation that surrounds you? Do you give thanks for the gift of free time, and ability to walk and share with friends, for sunlight and green grass?

You that enjoy the garden or farm, do you pause to give thanks for the earth and the miracle of seeds that birth into food like vegetables or scented flowers that beautify the landscape? Do you give thanks that you get to partner with God in tending the soil to bring life and food into the world?

You that enjoy the privilege of a lake home, do you quietly sit upon the deck or dock and give thanks and praise for all that has been given to fill your cup to overflowing? Do you share that overflow with others?

Do you genuflect at the simple gift of a glowing sunset or the pitter-patter of rain on your roof?

You that quietly sit in excited anticipation in the deer stand or duck blind, do you quietly offer up words of gratitude, thanks and praise for the interconnected creation that surrounds you, the countless creatures of the forest, for the bounty of a successful hunt and food that is untarnished by chemicals, additives and antibiotics?

You that run or bike, can you throughout your run or ride worship, giving thanks for health, life, vitality, a strong beating heart and the beauty of both nature and mankind that you witness on your journey? Can you send off prayers of intercession for those you pass by?

Churches are good. I'm glad we have them. But there are so many more places, spaces and times to give thanks and worship God. May you know that wherever you are… is a great place to start.

Can it be that grace takes us by surprise in the midst of the ordinary and the repeated? Why shouldn't this be so, because grace is from outside us, not within? It is God's interruption, his wonderful invitation. For most of us, God's command doesn't take us away from what we are presently doing. It fills our lives with new significance by reordering our priorities and requiring us to submit our activities and plans to the test of Christian concern and love. Gerhard Frost

> *Be joyful always; pray continually; give thanks in all circumstances, for this is God's will for you in Christ Jesus.*
> *1Thes 5:16-18 GNT*

"Now if I believe in God's Son and remember that He became man, all creatures will appear a hundred times more beautiful to me than before. Then I will properly appreciate the sun, the moon, the stars, trees, apples, as I reflect that he is Lord over all things. …God writes the Gospel, not in the Bible alone, but also on trees, and in the flowers and clouds and stars."— Martin Luther (1483-1546),

"We have seen that the Son of God created the world for this very end, to communicate Himself in an image of His own excellency. ... When we behold the light and brightness of the sun, the golden edges of an evening cloud, or the beauteous (rain)bow, we behold the adumbrations of His glory and goodness; and in the blue sky, of his mildness and gentleness."—Jonathan Edwards (1703-1758), preacher and Pastor

SAVORING

Driving north on Broadway, I had just come from Hornbacher's with a load of groceries. In my lap was a slotted, clear plastic container of plump, ripe blueberries. Like I often do, I was shoveling handfuls into my mouth and devouring them by the bunches. The stoplight caused me to pause, and I glanced at the container. These blueberries were huge, as big as my thumbnail and beautiful shades of deep, dark lavender and blue. I grabbed a single one rolling it between my fingers and then popped it into my mouth. I bit down as the juicy flavors burst forth into my mouth. Ahhh, now that was delicious! What a gift that one berry was!

As the stoplight gave me permission to go, I pondered how I approached these blueberries. Why was I gulping these by the handful when I could actually spread out the enjoyment by savoring the individual gift of each berry? Why did I consume at such a voracious speed and volume? I began to realize that my approach to much of life is that of devouring and consuming, and not always savoring or appreciating.

In the days since I've pondered this thought of savoring; relishing, cherishing, treasuring or delighting in some object or experience. I know I don't do very much of it, and I'm guessing much of our world does far less than I.

Paying Attention II

Coffee seems to make most of our world go 'round these days. But most of the folks I witness, whether watching their kid's soccer game, driving down the freeway, prepping for their day at breakfast, reading the paper or hitting the hissing Keurig machine at work use coffee as background noise. We are barely conscious that we are drinking it because we are doing some other activity as we consume it by habit. Yet coffee, when properly appreciated is a gift: an earthy, rich scent that permeates the room long before it hits our taste buds. Maybe, we should pause more often, to simply sit and savor the gift itself. And give thanks for the gift and the Giver of gifts.

Music is such a rich treasure. It permeates so many aspects of our lives. Most of us travel to and from work with some kind of music, many of our workplaces and offices play music in the background. High school and college students can rarely be found without earbuds or headphones privately blasting their favorite tunes as they walk to and from classes. I love working on some sewing or woodworking project while music plays in the background of my man-cave or garage. Music is the dominant feature in our worship services, yet for most, it's simply white noise, a necessary part of the experience.

But rarely do we take time to savor music and the miracle that it is. How crazy it seems to me that horsehair sliding across a taut string can produce the gorgeous heart piercing melody of a solo violin. And equally mind-boggling is that deep within the electronic mysteries of my iPod is some element that sends invisible signals to my remote speaker and somehow that speaker sends unseen waves through the air that my ear picks up and through the even greater mysteries of biochemistry of my brain I can hear incredible music that brings a smile to my face and pleasure to my soul. Maybe, we should pause more often, to simply sit and savor the gift itself. And give thanks for the gift and the Giver of gifts.

What about the incredibly creative, intricate and miraculous gift of sex? Do you ever savor this extraordinary gift? Do you ever pause to give thanks for this wonder-filled gift? Finding it uncomfortable chatting about sex in a Christian/church devo? I would simply ask this; Who is the author, inventor, and creator of such an astonishing gift? For many people, sex is just another activity to check off the "to do" list. Yet for those who pause and slow down to appreciate this remarkable experience one can only give thanks. Maybe, we should pause more often, to simply sit and savor the gift itself. And give thanks for the gift and the Giver of gifts.

We live in a fast-paced, hard-driving, go-go-go, get it done world. We constantly consume products, food, drink, vacations, activities, and experiences. We race from one experience to the next, barely pausing to truly appreciate or savor the moment that we are in. Most often we are thinking about the next activity or agenda item, or meal while we consume another that we do not even appreciate or cherish in the current moment of now.

Gifts, blessings, and treasures lie all around us. God has been more than generous in the placing blessings in our world. The pace and speed of our lives often prevent us from seeing or fully appreciating these gifts. Often times we in this "First World" of America have been given so many gifts and treasures that we are often blinded by the piles that lie stacked all around us. We are seeking and searching for the "next" treasure when all about us lay mountains of blessings. We have become blinded by our own abundance.

This Easter week is called Holy Week. I pray that for you and me it would become Holy. Holy in the sense that we would slow down, pause, breath-deeply and savor some of the many gifts that God has placed in our world. May you savor the time spent with family or friends. May you savor the scent of Easter Lily's at church. May you savor the fresh, clean spring air. May you savor the sight and sound of your first robin returning from the Southlands. May you savor the rich and delicious food at your table. May you savor a good friend and conversation. May you savor in the gift of forgiveness and freedom promised to you this Easter Sunday.

"The kingdom of heaven is like a treasure hidden in the field, which a man found and hid again; and from joy over it he goes and sells all that he has and buys that field. Matthew 13:44 NIV

I will give you hidden treasures, riches stored in secret places, so that you may know that I am the LORD. Isaiah 45:3 NIV

Let everything that has breath praise the Lord! Psalm 150 NIV

Whatever is true, whatever is noble, whatever is right, whatever is pure, whatever is lovely, whatever is admirable- if anything is excellent or praiseworthy- Think about such things! Philippians 4:8 NIV

"I am leaving you with a gift—peace of mind and heart. And the peace I give is a gift the world cannot give. So don't be troubled or afraid." – John 14:27 NLT

"I pray that God, the source of hope, will fill you completely with joy and peace because you trust in him. Then you will overflow with confident hope through the power of the Holy Spirit." – Romans 15:13 NLT

Sea Turtle

The blazing hot Caribbean sun beat down upon our shoulders and backs, and the warm, humid ocean breeze cleansed us from the inside out with each breath. Tepid, salt water splashed at our knees and thighs healing up scrapes and scratches from a week's worth of concrete work on our village work site. Having just spent a week working in the tiny, isolated village called San Simón, in the Yucatan peninsula of Mexico, building four block homes, our tired and sore bodies were relishing the rest time under the refreshing warmth of the Mayan sun and surf.

Shane, my eleven-year-old son, was along for his first mission trip experience, and he had been begging to try snorkeling. I reluctantly agreed to rent two sets of equipment, as I figured he would half-heartedly attempt it for a few brief moments, then out of fear or anxiety, want to move on to something easier. He's normally risk-aversive when it comes to new activities, but I certainly wanted him to give it a try, and I knew from previous visits what possible treasures lay hidden beneath these soothing turquoise waters.

We stood waist deep in the surf awkwardly walking backward with ungainly flippers attached to our feet. Gaining chest-deep waters, I began having him practice breathing through the snorkel. At first, standing fully erect in the open air, then slowly lowering his face to the water, then finally moving towards submersing his full face and head. He successfully achieved all of this with surprisingly little hesitation. The salty taste and wide mouthpiece felt ungainly and claustrophobic, to begin with, but soon we settled into the loud and rhythmic raspy breathing of underwater snorkeling. With images of an all-black Darth Vader, I quietly mimicked; "Kqueeeeck…Kqueeeeck… Shane …. I am your father!"

We slowly flipper kicked our way further out into the bay seeing our first fish along the way. Shane tightly gripped either my hand or the edge of my swimsuit for most of the way, and within minutes, magic happened. There just eight feet below us was a massive four-foot long sea turtle quietly feeding on the ocean grass at the bottom of the sea floor. He was magnificent! We hovered above him giving each other wide-eyed expressions of joy and enthusiastic thumbs up hand signals and knuckle bumps.

The turtle's rounded head extended out well past his shell as he nibbled the green sea grass. I was amazed by the beautiful interlocking, puzzle-like configuration of his spectacular green, grey, and amber shell that created a stunning camouflage. His appendages were perfectly formed flippers that fanned out from his large rounded frame, which also continued the interlocking camouflage theme. What an exquisite and odd creature this was. For us flatlander Norsemen from the hinterland, this tortoise was right out of Jurassic Park!

A tap on my shoulder had me look to my right, where a saucer-eyed Shane was motioning down and to our right, where another even bigger turtle was swimming by. We soon flew into formation above and slightly behind this behemoth and followed in pursuit. I was amazed by the smoothness and grace by which this large creature moved through the water. He appeared to be quietly flying and gliding rather than swimming through the water. He emanated a sense of perfect peace and tranquility in his movements and presence. I was in awe. A better man was I, for having been in his presence, and I could only whisper a hundred thank yous to our common Creator for allowing me, and especially my son to experience these memorable moments. Before leaving the sea, we had swum face to face with eight different tortoises and one stingray and I believe that Shane will cherish these moments for a long, long time.

Imagine if Shane had never taken the risk of getting his feet wet.

What if he had given in to fear and anxiety and stayed on the comfort and security of dry ground, or never said "yes" to the mission trip or snorkeling? The beautiful and marvelous blessings of the undersea world demand a price, and that is *to risk*.

Our faith in Christ is much the same. God can only bless those who take steps in His direction, to move from where they are to where He calls. One of my biggest frustrations in church work is; getting people who claim they want to grow, to take the *"next step"* in their faith life. They rarely do. The beach or the pew is always so much safer and more comfortable.

Listen to these wise and insightful words from Leonard Sweet from his book Aqua Church.

"Boarding" was one of Martin Luther's favorite definitions of faith. The person who doesn't have faith, he said, "is like someone who has to cross the sea, but is so frightened that he does not trust the ship. And so he stays where he is and is never saved because he will not get on board and cross over." The test of faith is "getting on board." Our pews are occupied by people who want to be moved, but who don't want to move. It is not just a few people who are bedridden all of their lives- we are becoming a church of, for and by the bedridden and beached. This unholy predicament that the church finds itself in today- fear-ridden, safety-fixated, immunity-seeking, risk-averse in a high-risk post-modern culture- can be reversed only if the church abandons it risk-free approach to ministry and mission and rediscovers the gangplank. The good news is that our cultural phobia is both treatable and preventable. The danger for the church today lies with armor and brakes. The benefits lie with risk and speed.

God has a plethora of blessings, marvels, and wonders to shower upon you. You will not be able to experience these from the beach, the pew or the sideline. They lie just below the surface of your everyday world, yet remain invisible from where you are. You must dive in!

Then Peter got down out of the boat, walked on the water and came toward Jesus. But when he saw the wind, he was afraid and, beginning to sink, cried out, "Lord, save me!" Immediately Jesus reached out his hand and caught him. "You of little faith," he said, "why did you doubt?" Matthew 14:29-31 NIV

Even though I am nervous, anxious and afraid, I acknowledge and own my fears, and choose to allow God to see me through this.

> Fear knocked at the door, Faith answered.
> And lo… no one was there.

Every tomorrow has two handles. We can take hold of it by the handle of *anxiety*,
or by the handle of *faith*.
Feed your faith and your fears will starve to death.

Shadows in the Woods

The winter woods were dark and silent. From my perch 20' high in a sturdy oak, the landscape was nothing but 50 shades of gray. The crisp air was somewhere in the single digits, but the walk in had pumped my internal furnace with life-giving heat and forced warmth into my many layers of clothing. I sat quiet and attentive, looking like the proverbial Stay Puff Marshmallow Man, yet warm and comfortable from my lofty roost.

With only a few days remaining in our Minnesota deer season I was determined to fill my tag, even if it meant arising in the darkness and braving the severe cold. These pre-dawn sits are filled with what feels like eternal waiting. And waiting, for a hyperactive, impatient person like myself, is never very stimulating, especially in darkness.

And darkness has a way of amplifying fears, worries, doubts, and struggles. For me, in the pre-dawn blackness when there are no visual stimuli to distract and entertain, my thoughts turn inward. Most days this positively nudges me to prayer. I give thanks and gratitude for that which was yesterday, the blessings and Godsends, and starting with thankfulness then leads me to surrender the day ahead and asking for Godly wisdom, insight, and priorities. Other days when I allow the temporary darkness to dominate my psyche, I see difficulties, problems, and boogiemen in both the shadows of the woods and in the life ahead of me that day.

After some time of sitting and waiting, I became aware of a darkened, oval-shaped shadow laying a mere 12 yards in front of me. It seemed unfamiliar, out of place and in stark contrast the snowy background of the forest floor, but the shape and outline matched nothing of the surrounding stumps, downed trees or broken branches. As with all shadows, when you stare at it for any amount of time, you can't make out any details and our imaginations run wild. Our human eyes were not meant to make details out of shadowy figures in the dark.

My gut hunch told me it was a dead deer. Focusing on the shadow did no good, so I would look away scanning the rest of the forest for a moment, but I was continually drawn back to interpreting the oval-shaped shadow.

With each slow tick of the silent dawn clock, a minuscule, imperceptible addition of light was added to the forest and after looking away for a minute or three, and then back to the shadow, a piece of detail or small shade of color was added. Soon my vision clarified bit by bit and I could then make out an eye, then an ear and then confirming my suspicion was the whole shape of a small yearling deer. Had she been hit by another nearby bow-hunter last evening? Had she been hit by a car on the road to the north and limped here to die of internal wounds? Had she eaten too much corn from a neighbor's well-meaning food pile?

Apparently, this was the only deer in the woods, for after a couple of hours of no further sightings, my toes and fingers were begging for movement, so I descended the tree to check out and attempt to solve the mystery.

I instantly noticed gray hair everywhere, and upon arriving could see a rear haunch had been devoured. In the light dusting of snow from the previous night, the telltale tracks of our local coyote could be clearly seen in and around the deer. Had Wiley E. been the perpetrator of the murder scene? Or merely a free-loading scavenger after the fact? The sign and tracks did not readily reveal cause, motive, sequence or wrongdoer.

The death of this fawn will remain a mystery. No one will stand over it to grieve or mourn. No one will lament her passing. But in her passing, she will pass on energy and life to many others. Spore revealed that in addition to the coyote, a large fisher had joined in the feast.

Crows had partaken as well. Soon with the melting of winter's snow, a variety of mice, meadow voles and squirrels will feast upon the calcium-rich bones, and a plethora of insects and larvae will break-down all remaining skin and flesh. There is no waste in the natural world order.

The death of this deer reminds me that much of the difficulty and struggle that happens to us in this world will remain a mystery. I have learned with age that we do not get the answers to all of our questions. The big; *"Why did this happen?"* of our lives often goes unanswered. Why did my fiancé leave me two months before the wedding? Why did my mother die at so young an age? Why did my dear friends Rich and John who were both two of the kindest and most godly men I know, die of cancer? Why have I had to wrestle with anxiety for so many years? Why so many failures with my bow? Why Sandy Hook? Why ISIS? Why war? Why 9/11? And the list goes on both personally and for our world at large.

I'm reminded that God has not promised answers or explanations. He has simply promised *His presence*. Answers and explanations may come in the afterlife, but for now, I believe God simply asks us to follow with faith and trust. We don't always get all the pieces to the puzzle, and rarely do we get to see the complete big picture. All the cards aren't laid upon the table. If you could see how everything is supposed to be and how it all fits together, there would be no need for faith, no need to trust in God to provide. God calls us to trust and obey, to follow, keeping our eyes fixed on Him, not the chaos, the unknown, and the uncertainty that lay all around us.

Today whether you face triumph or tragedy, joy or sorrow, victory or defeat… hold tightly to the hand of God with your trust and faith.

And we know that in <u>ALL</u> things God works for the good of those who love him, who have been called according to his purpose! Romans 8:28 NIV

I will lead the blind by ways they have not known, Along unfamiliar paths I will guide them; I will turn the darkness into light before them and make the rough places smooth. Isaiah 42:16 NIV

... God has said, "Never will I leave you; never will I forsake you." The Lord is my helper; I will not be afraid. What can man do to me? Hebrews 13:5-6 NIV

And the God of Grace who called you to his eternal glory in Christ, after you have suffered a little while, will himself restore you and make you strong, firm and steadfast. 1 Peter 5:10 NIV

Praise God in his sanctuary; praise him in his mighty heavens.
Praise him for his acts of power; praise him for his surpassing greatness.
Praise him with the sounding of the trumpet, praise him with the harp and lyre,
praise him with timbrel and dancing, praise him with the strings and pipe,
Praise him with the clash of cymbals, praise him with resounding cymbals.
Let everything that has breath praise the Lord. *Praise the* Lord. *Psalm 150 NIV*

Shane in the Boundary Waters

After filling out our permit, we jostle our sleds up and over the large snow berm and slide onto the 2 ½ mile portage single file. Having left Fargo, ND in a snowless winter, passing brown dirt fields and a snowless northern Minnesota on our long bus ride, we were thrilled by the 18" of fresh powder snow all around us. Ahhh! The almost always magical Boundary Waters Canoe Area Wilderness snow pocket delivers again! Fluffy white snow has covered the pines like a recently frosted cake, and we truly feel like we are traveling through the mysterious seven levels of the candy-cane forest! The crisp, fresh air fills our lungs and the strong exercise begins to warm our bodies from the inside out, and I began to hear a flurry of; *"This is so Awesome!" "Man is this gorgeous!" "We're in a winter wonderland!"* I smile knowing the captivating powers of the BWCAW winter are already beginning to permeate the soul of each group member.

Rounding out our gang of nine goofballs, is my 10-year old son, Shane, on this his first foray to the winter Boundary Waters. I can sense his excitement, anxiousness, fear, wonder, and continued non-verbal questioning of whether he has what it takes to complete this little winter expedition.

For 35 plus years, I have been bringing kids and adults of all shapes, sizes, and ages on various wilderness adventures as a full-time youth minister. There is something about wilderness travel i.e.; canoeing, backpacking, winter camping that demands a high toll of body, mind, and spirit that most comfort-seeking, pain-avoiding, certainty-craving, risk-aversive, technology-addicted modern folk refuse to pay. And thus, they will never reap the deep rewards that wilderness pours out on those who say "yes" to the challenge and adventure of the BWCAW.

Most parents think that what their kids really want and need is a trip to "Wally World," or a warm beach somewhere down south. All good and fine, and I've been to and enjoyed both, but when push comes to shove, I believe that where real character growth and development takes place is in the wilderness, traveling under your own power. It is here, immersed in creation that one discovers one's true self in both strengths and weakness, and living in and traversing through creation, that one builds a stronger and deeper connection to the Creator and fellow wilderness sojourners. All of this and more are my prayers for Shane.

I am proud to have him in our group, but also a bit apprehensive as a parent wondering if I have pushed too hard or asked too much of his little fourth grade legs on this rigorous adventure. I know of my own struggle and strain with each uphill climb and the tug on my waist belt with the weight of the heavy sled as I huff and puff my way forward leaning on my poles... and I continually watch and wonder how he is doing. I also worry about how he will handle the cold and the massive workload of camping in the winter.

As we struggle over the lengthy portage, I can see that Shane is having difficulty keeping up with the rest of our adult legs, so I place him up in the front of the line to give him a psychological boost. I do my best to distract his attention though affirming him, and asking lots of questions about his soccer heroes and his current thoughts on next year's chances for the Vikes. None of my trail leader tricks nor parenting psychology work and he sees right through my all my ploys and retreats into his own silence. I'm feeling like "Jerk Dad of the Year" for underestimating the length of our trek. I send off a few silent prayers for his strength, and wisdom and patience for me.

Retreating into my own silence, I soon realize that we are experiencing one of the great truths and gifts of wilderness travel. We have arrived at the great teaching lesson and moment of self-realization for Shane. The trail has grown very difficult, wearisome, and arduous and no one can make those steps for him. He must persevere, endure and carry on in spite of the pain, tiredness, and hardships of the trail. He must find new depths of strength and perseverance from within.

Whether it is a long day of paddling into a raging wind, a week of continuous wet rainy weather, climbing a mountain pass, enduring a hatch of black flies or hoard of never-ending mosquitos, or groaning beneath the weight of a canoe or food pack on a never-ending portage, these difficulties shape and refine our character. These struggles of trail life both reveal our character, i.e. bring out the best and worst in people, and more importantly build our character and inner strength to endure and persevere in spite of difficult circumstances. And after all, isn't wilderness trail life just simply a metaphor for real, everyday life?

As a parent, I want nothing more than to remove the pain and difficulty for Shane. But wisdom and the reality of the circumstances win out, and we continue on step by step. Right, then left, over and over again. I must allow Shane to experience it all on his own terms.

Jesus is a straight shooter. He pulls no punches.

*"I have told you these things, so that in me you may have peace. **In this world, you will have trouble**. But take heart! I have overcome the world."* John 16:33

Therefore, do not worry about tomorrow, for tomorrow will worry about itself. Each day has enough trouble of its own. Matthew 6:34.

These are simple truths that most of us try to avoid, run away from, or push under the rug. Yet our daily lives speak these truths so loudly. So, the question then becomes not if or when troubles, difficulties, or struggles will come, but rather how we will deal with and face them. Whether the problems are on-trail in the wilderness, or in the ordinary grind of daily life, we that follow Jesus, can call on a strength, power, and wisdom far greater than our own.

When you pass through the waters, I will be with you; and when you pass through the rivers, they will not sweep over you. When you walk through the fire, you will not be burned; the flames will not set you ablaze. Isaiah 43:2 NIV

Consider it pure joy, my bothers, whenever you face trials of many kinds, because you know that the testing of your faith develops perseverance. Perseverance must finish its work so that you may be mature and complete, not lacking anything. James 1:1-2

Not that I have already obtained all this, or have already been made perfect, but I press on to take hold of that for which Christ Jesus took hold of me… one thing I do, forgetting what is behind and straining for what is ahead, I press on toward the goal. Philippians 3:12-14

…but we also rejoice in our sufferings, because we know that suffering produces perseverance; perseverance, character, and character hope. Romans 5: 3-4 ESV

I CAN DO all things in Christ who gives me strength. Philippians 4:13 NIV

Shane's First Buck

The sun had already set. Light was leaking out over the horizon to the west, as shadows and darkness crawled in from the east. We were right in the middle of "magic time," that crepuscular period when animals are most active and moving. Although this late October afternoon had been a beautiful and warm day, deer sightings had been sparse at best. My eleven-year-old son Shane sat in his 15' ladder-stand, and I was strapped in another six feet above him in my perch. The afternoon although gorgeous and pleasant, and been quite uneventful other than the constant racing of squirrels to and fro. At times, their footfalls and rustling of leaves distracted us into looking their way in hopes of seeing a big buck

Shane had sat for the better part of 2 hours, impatiently kicking his feet, picking at the bark on the tree, poking this, prodding that, and occasionally looking up and whispering, "Dad... how much longer?" Pre-adolescent males are not particularly gifted for sitting still and quiet, upon a 2' x 2' platform high in a tree! He, the semi-reluctant hunter, was most likely tolerating this time as a way to please dad. With only minutes of shooting light remaining, his wait was almost over.

The subtle sounds of hooves on dry leaves were soon heard coming our way. I leaned over and whispered to Shane, "Deer coming... stand up and get your bow ready!" He immediately came to attention and readied himself and his bow. The rustling of leaves grew louder as the "clickety, clickety, clickety" rhythm of steady deer steps came closer and closer. Within seconds the audible sounds morphed into a deer's body that materialized from the gray shadows moving our way.

Shane in his amped-up adrenaline rush immediately drew back his bow, so I whispered, "Let down, he's too far away!" Shane obediently complied as the deer began a slow walk around the back side of our trees. As the young buck gained the 20-yard mark, I whispered: "Draw back now and shoot when ready!"

The buck slowed to a stop, and then came a brief pause. Next came a "shoosh," as Shane released his arrow, and it immediately buried itself somewhere in the darkness of grass and leaves missing its intended mark. I smiled knowing intuitively, that Shane had most likely not even aimed but rather just shot in the excitement of the moment. I leaned over again and whispered, "Reload!" Shane's nerves had grabbed hold of his hands as he fumbled to place another arrow unto his bow, which he successfully achieved after a few seconds and again drew back. The deer stood stoically alert, yet unsure of what had caused the disturbance in the force. Silence... then another "shoosh" as Shane's second arrow again missed its target.

The young buck, now nervous, switched directions and began to take a few stiff steps away. I reached for my grunt call and issued a couple quiet "grunts" just to keep him interested, and it worked. The buck turned again and proceeded forward crossing broadside to us, and another grunt brought him to a stop. A brief silence ensued followed by the "shoosh" of Shane's third shot, and an instantaneous "thwack," as arrowhead met deer flesh. The deer took four or five hops, and then, all we could hear was the rustling of grass.

"Shane! I think you nailed him!" I hissed loudly. "Dad, I can't stop shaking! I think I'm having seizures... I can't stop shaking! My heart is pounding a million miles an hour!" Shane muttered back. In the darkness, I raised my hands toward heaven, grinned from ear to ear and silently shouted a gigantic "THANK YOU!!!!"

After a brief wait and great vertical conversation, we descended, retrieved his missed arrows, and quietly proceeded to where we had heard the rustling of leaves and grass. And there, to our great delight, lay the beautiful young buck. High fives and hugs ensued, and then came "thank you" prayers as we knelt before the fine gift of meat and memories. Anatomy lessons followed as we gutted the deer and placed Shane's tag upon his first bow killed deer. Shane then softly confessed, "Dad, I'm a little sad right now." I place my arm around his shoulder and replied back, "I know, that's part of the hunt. I would be worried if you didn't feel any of that. What you're feeling is normal, ok, and part of the process when you take an animals life." He nodded as if he understood, at least in part.

In the darkness of night, we carted out the deer under the prominent presence of the Big Dipper and North Star. I smiled the whole way, giving silent thanks and praise for what had taken place as gentle and quiet conversation ebbed and flowed from father to son, back and forth.

I don't claim in any way shape or form, to know how God feels, I'm just not that smart, but it has to, in some small way, feel like I did during these moments of the hunt with my son Shane. I just smiled throughout the whole experience. Being together, conversing, coaching, listening, advising, sharing thoughts, feelings, failures, triumphs, successes, highs and lows, life and death, and we did it all together.

Isn't this what our heavenly Father seeks and invites us to do with him? It's not about rules, and regulations, should and shouldn'ts, do's and don'ts, theology or knowledge, or how naughty or nice you have been. It's about relationship... doing the whole nine-yards of life together in ever ebbing and flowing conversation, honesty and intimacy of presence and enjoying one another's company through the good, the bad and the ugly of life!

If you are one who has been a drone for God, obediently and grudgingly following the rules and regulations of church life... I urge you to STOP! And instead invite God into your daily walk, your work life, your hobbies, your passions and your dreams, your relationships, your success, and your failures to experience the God of Jesus in a more real and personal way. What Jesus desires of you and me, is simply relationship.

May you go out and enjoy God's presence and favor in your favorite pastime or hobby!

But seek first his kingdom and his righteousness, and all these things will be given to you as well.
Matthew 6:33 NIV

I have come that they may have life and have it to the abundantly! John 10:10 ESV

Jesus answered, "I am the way and the truth and the life. No one comes to the Father except through me. If you really know me, you will know my Father as well. From now on, you do know him and have seen him." John 14:6-7 NIV

But these are written that you may believe that Jesus is the Messiah, the Son of God, and that by believing you may have life in his name. John 20:31 NIV

Showing Up Owl

Out of the corner of my eye, a flash of white and gray, just inches from my face caused my heart to skip a couple of beats! The startle practically caused me to fall out of my tree stand from fright. It was early morning just at first light, long before sunrise as the woods was just awakening. My camouflage and rare stillness must have been working because the creature seemed completely oblivious to my presence. And there perched on a branch just a few away, stood a magnificent great horned owl. For a couple of minutes, he careened his neck all around scanning the ground around us most likely in search of easy prey; an unsuspecting mouse, or unwary rabbit.

Once my heart quit pounding, I said to myself, "This is Awwwwesome!" Now I've seen plenty of owls in my day, and had some fairly up close and personal encounters, but this guy was almost sitting in my lap! And he was incredible! His fantastically camouflaged grey, brown and white plumage made him blend into the surrounding trees and I simply sat in awe and wonder of this marvelous avian predator.

He stood stoically, perched and unaware of the close proximity of an even larger fellow predator sitting just a few feet away. After briefly scanning the hunting grounds below, he did the classic "owly" thing, and slowly twisted his head around and up at me as I stared directly into his huge golden eyes. We locked on in a mutual stare-down, each of us sizing up the other. I felt as if he was looking directly into and through the inner thoughts of my soul. It didn't take him long to access sizes, and he wisely (owly pun intended) figured out that I was waaaay bigger... and off he flew, without so much as a whisper of sound, into parts unknown.

Wow, was I one lucky guy or what! What a unique and wonder-filled encounter. I hadn't planned on it. In fact, if you'd given me the assignment to go and get close to a big owl, it would probably have had odds of a million to one. My real goal and purpose of the day was to shoot a monster buck. That didn't happen. Seeing the owl was purely a beautiful and Godly coincidence... a bonus if you will, for being there, and just showing up.

An hour later, I had the privilege of watching two little bucks spar and fight, push and shove for about 15 minutes right in front of me. A rare and unique scene played out all fall but rarely witnessed by most folks. Again, it was not the movie I'd paid to see, but what a wonderful blessing to behold and witness. Truly a bonus if you will, for being there, and just showing up. I would never have seen it, had I chosen to sleep in.

There is something so simple and profound in just showing up. It's not a huge thing, just more of a consistent thing. The more you show up, the more you see, experience and learn. And often what we show up for is not what we receive. But when you're open and seeking and searching... great things can be revealed.

So... How 'bout you? Are you showing up? How's your showing up time when it comes to daily quiet- times with your Maker and Creator? How about showing up times for worship? What's your attitude these days when you enter worship? Are you filled with expectancy and anticipation for the wonder of what might land in front of you? Or are you dreading who's preaching or leading worship, or bemoaning the song selection, grudgingly chewing over the latest church politics, or simply wondering if the Vikings will actually make it to the playoffs?

Even in your daily routines, or everyday repetitive, humdrum, mundane work habits God can show up in surprising ways! Sometimes all it takes is inviting God to show and reveal himself to you as he is hidden in the ordinary of your normal life.

I certainly don't have spectacular owl encounters every time I go into the woods. That's what made this one so special. But, when I show up time after time consistently, I have the great privilege to be filled with awe and wonder at the surprises God places in my path.

I pray that today you will show up and be present with God. You never know what surprises and wonders he will place in your path!

Trust in the Lord and do good; dwell in the land and enjoy safe pasture. Delight yourself in the Lord and he will give you the desires of your heart. Commit your way to the Lord; trust in him and he will do this. He will make your righteousness shine like the dawn, the justice of your cause like the noonday sun. Be still before the Lord, and wait patiently for him. Psalm 37: 3-7 NIV

Be joyful always; pray continually; give thanks in all circumstances. 1 Thessalonians 5:16-17 ESV

Signs of God in the Desert

The sky was pure azure and not a cloud could be seen. The 40-degree temps were unseasonably cool for this region, but after 20 below-zero back home, this was refreshing. I felt relieved and relaxed having spent the past three, 12-hour days driving my dad through rainstorms, blizzards and the monotony of the southern great plains. We had arrived safely the evening before to the desert oasis of Mesa, Arizona. An early morning run and a hearty breakfast at the local café with dad, had me relaxed, smiling, and taking in all the new scenery of this place I'd heard so much about.

Dad's car was having some issues, so we drove into a nearby repair garage, and the kindly gentleman consented to take a look at it for us. "It'll take about an hour to run the diagnostics, so go ahead and have a seat." Not one to sit idle too long, and not having been properly amped up yet from my usual morning latte, I punched in coffee shops to my cell phone. Immediately pins popped up on my map and lo and behold, there, conveniently located just 10 blocks away was Mecca; a Starbucks Cafe! "Dad, I'll be back in one hour!" And off I went.

Bathed in brilliant sunshine I sauntered down the amply wide sidewalk of a busy avenue. The broad parkway and open blue sky gave a wonderful feeling of spaciousness, light, and positivity. Passing the entryways to a couple of trailer parks for "Active Mature Adults," I briefly pondered my eligibility for access. I definitely had the active part down, but not sure if I qualified for the "mature" part.

Tall, skinny palm trees whose palms and foliage exploded like fireworks at the top, dotted the avenue and trailer parks much to my delight. Fine, neatly groomed gravel beds replaced lawns in all of the places I'd normally expect to see green grass. I smiled, "We're not in Kansas anymore Dorothy!"

Ambling on, I soon came to a magnificent Saguaro cactus in front of a rental store. I was fascinated and left the sidewalk to get up close and personal with this strange and fascinating creation. From afar, the saguaro was so intriguing and inviting, and yet as I drew closer, I realized the reason it's called a cactus. A gazillion tiny thorns protected every millimeter of surface area on this huge cactus. I don't think I could have touched any part of this cactus, without harm. It was a literal self-defense masterpiece, a citadel of self-protection. Spikey thorns protruded in all directions, making its exterior impenetrable to all outsiders.

I pondered for a time, the genius behind this natural feat of engineering. This self-preservation marvel reminded me of many people I've met through years of ministry. Attractive and luring from afar, yet upon attempting to draw close and get beyond the surface level, they exhibit a magnificent emotional defense of spiny, prickly psychological thorns that scream: "Off limits! Stay away! Do Not Enter!"

Continuing on my coffee sojourn, I soon came upon a large bed of roses at the entrance to a retirement park. Having not seen a rose in months, I sauntered over, bent down, and inhaled deeply of the sweet raspberry-like scent of the largest one. I sampled a full lung full of each colored variety. Yellows, pinks, reds, and whites. They bobbed and weaved in the strong wind and seemed to have opened up their petals to the full exposure of the life-giving sun. These roses were a godly gift in the dryness of the desert southwest.

One rose, in particular, seemed to almost glow with accents of yellow and gold emanating into the deep scarlet of classic rose. The windy movement and play of sunlight and shade made the rose to appear to throb with color. God had done marvelous wonders here in the desert with both the roses and saguaros.

I continued on my trek and could soon see the sign to Mecca attached to a local supermarket. As I turned right moving through the parking lot, I could see a homeless woman seated on the curb. Arrayed around her, were bags and belongings and she held the standard issue cardboard sign in her hands. Having to pass by her on my way to Starbucks, from ten meters away she shouted out, "Nice Sweater!"

I said "Thank You!" as I passed directly by her side, and offered a; "You up for a coffee?" She quickly responded with an enthusiastic "Yes, thank you!" I responded; "What'll you have?" She bellowed back; "Black please." "You got it, one black coffee coming up!"

I returned sipping from my own savory black-vigor-in-a- cup, carrying another for her. She had stood in my absence and as I handed her the cup, I took a seat on the dusty concrete and invited her to do the same. I introduce myself with a handshake which she reciprocated with a, "Hi I'm Margie."

Margie had long unkempt blond hair that glowed brightly in the sunshine. Her face was tan and leathered most likely from living full-time outdoors. I guessed her to be in her forties maybe, fifty possibly. Hard to tell in cases like this where life had worn her down and out. She immediately proved chatty and friendly and seemed eager for the company. At her side lay another empty Starbucks cup, indicating this to be a well-chosen location.

It became more than obvious from her first few sentences, that the primary reason for her being here on the street, like so many others, was due to mental illness. Her rapid-fire string of thoughts and stories

Paying Attention II

were like a box of ping pong balls poured onto the street bouncing in all sorts of random directions.

I had hoped to sit and chat with Margie for a time having no agenda of my own, but it became apparent that meaningful dialogue would be futile. I quietly said "Goodbye and God Bless you" which she returned back to me.

As I stood to leave, she shyly inquired if I'd be interested in having one of her colored drawings as a thank you. "Yes, I would, thank you." She fumbled through a stack of papers from her marker coloring book and handed me this one. Her full name was signed on the back side. Proof positive that gratitude and gratefulness can happen even in a parking lot from a homeless woman.

My walk back to the repair garage was slow and contemplative.

Foremost in my thoughts were Ms. Margie. How does she fit into God's plan? What series of life situations and tragedies had befallen her to cause her to live life on the streets? If I could walk back through the movie of her life, would her current status make more sense? Would she ever be healed of her emotional turmoil and many psychological issues here on this side of death? What would Jesus do… If he were here and met her face to face? Would he lay his hands upon her and heal her, or just bless her and tell her He loved her? What does Jesus expect of me?

My slow walk down the boulevard in Mesa reminded me that being in relationship with God is a full-time endeavor. Following Jesus is not a switch that you turn on and off. We don't get to open our "God Box" on Sunday morning at 9 am close it at noon, and then go about our everyday life. God is embedded in our everyday life; in all spaces, all places, all activities, all encounters, and all relationships and all experiences if we but only have eyes to see and ears to hear. I had been on vacation of sorts or maybe more like a vacation with purpose. Yet God still invites us to seek Him, observe Him, be with Him, pay attention to Him, and serve Him.

Wherever you are this day, invite the Holy Spirit to reveal God's presence to you.

Enjoy this fabulous and short video: **Eating Twinkies with God**
https:// www.youtube.com/watch?v=y9N8OXkN0Rk

> I shall but pass this way but once; any good, therefore, that I can do or any kindness that I can show to any human being, let me do it now. Let me not defer nor neglect it, for I shall not pass this way again.
> William Penn

Too often we underestimate the power of a touch, a smile, a kind word, a listening ear, an honest compliment, or the smallest act of caring, all of which have the potential to turn a life around. Leo Buscaglia

And whatever you do, whether in word or deed, do it all in the name of the Lord Jesus, giving thanks to God the Father through him. Colossians 3:17 NIV

Sinner Saint

The call came on my cell phone asking for me to meet the family in the family waiting room. Sandra had been found unconscious on her apartment floor, and she now lay in a coma in the ICU of the hospital. At forty plus years of age, Sandra was a mother of three, a daughter to a loving mom and dad, a beloved sister, and deeply cherished friend.

It appeared that all these important relationships had been packed into the tiny waiting room. Worried faces, tears, and silence filled what little space remained.

I knew most of the names that went with each face, as I hugged my way around the room, but one man stood out as a stranger to me. He was dressed in black from head to toe. A large skull adorned the back of his ragged vest which draped over his torn and soiled sweat-hood. A dingy, dark stocking cap covered his long, curly, unkempt, shoulder-length hair that appeared to have been unwashed for some time.

His forearms that protruded from rolled up sleeves, and his neck and face were covered in a jumble of blue-black tattoos. It appeared to me that there were more tattoos than unpainted skin. The left corner of his upper lip curled upward in a permanent snarl, possibly the result of a previous brawl, or an accident. A polite family member introduced him to me as Donny, the boyfriend of Sandra. I shook his hand, but my judgments had already been made. In my head, I had instantly assigned not-so-nice labels to the man and did so with extreme prejudice.

As the next several days of agonizing waiting unfolded, we moved the base camp of loving supporters and family members to the basement of our church to provide a more roomy and comfortable space. Pizzas and subs were ordered, little kids burned off nervous energy in the gym, and the crack of billiard balls hitting could be heard above the din of conversation, laughter and crying. A constant movement of people coming and going, hugging, loving, and caring for one another; good grieving to be sure.

Over these days my heart was slowly transformed from contempt and judgment to deep compassion and empathy for Donny. I frequently followed him out to the parking lot where his nervousness and anxiety demanded a smoke. He sat hunched over on the curb outside the entryway where I secretly feared the small, but highly vocal group of church Pharisees would condemn, protest and cry out for his ousting.

As I sat with Donny several times over these days, I began to see and know the man behind the tattoos. My heart broke as I heard of his stories. His was mostly a life of rejection and being unloved. Addictions and demons lurked as a shadowy wolf-pack forever nipping at his heels. Two stints in prison, a tragic car accident that almost took his life, and a never-ending string of dead-end jobs and failures added up to a life of mostly survival. In his two-year relationship with Sandra, he stated, "She was the only one who just loved me for who I am, with no judgments."

I finally gathered up the courage and asked him to tell me about the meaning behind the many tattoos that were visible from just his forearms alone. There were skulls, faces, knives, creatures, flags, fangs, and each blended in with the next. Two tattoos fairly jumped off his arms and screamed at me in blatant juxtaposition of one another.

On one hand was a large swastika, a symbol of hate, prejudice, evil and everything foul. On his other hand, neatly spelled out on each knuckle were the letters; W.W.J.D. or for those who missed this craze: What Would Jesus Do? My head was dizzy with thoughts and questions as I tapped his knuckles and quietly queried, "Tell me about this one."

His snarled lip and accompanying lisp softly spoke; "That was when I accepted Jesus in my life during my last prison time." The ginormous lump of guilt and shame in my throat made swallowing hard at best. All of my judgments and prejudice had lodged themselves in my gullet as a reminder of my own false piety and sinful nature.

And then and there, in this humble, broken, beaten man's tattoos showed a perfect picture of each of us: a swastika and W.W. J. D. Poignant symbolism for our true nature; sinner and saint, broken and beautiful, rejected yet redeemed, lost but loved, wounded and now healed, all, by the grace of a loving, forgiving God.

I grew to love Donny over these days in the hospital, the church, and the funeral home. His honesty was refreshing. He stood in contrast to the many masks, polished postures, forced smiles, lovely clothes, posing, cover make-up, pretense, and pomposity that many of us interact with day to day in the life of the church. I need to embrace and remember Donny.

May you and realize and remember that we are not so different. We are each a beautiful mix of sinner and saint loved by a grace-filled God.

On hearing this, Jesus said to them, "It is not the healthy who need a doctor, but the sick. I have not come to call the righteous, but sinners." Mark 2:17 NIV

"Do not judge, or you too will be judged. Matthew 7: 1 NIV

They also will answer, 'Lord, when did we see you hungry or thirsty or a stranger or needing clothes or sick or in prison, and did not help you?' "He will reply, 'Truly I tell you, whatever you did not do for one of the least of these, you did not do for me.' Matthew 25: 44-45 NIV

Religion that God our Father accepts as pure and faultless is this: to look after orphans and widows in their distress and to keep oneself from being polluted by the world. James 1:27 NIV

Jesus said to him, "Today salvation has come to this house, because this man, too, is a son of Abraham. 10 For the Son of Man came to seek and to save the lost." Luke 19:9-10 NIV

Squirrels in the Attic

I returned home late Sunday from a great week out west hiking and camping with my kids. Upon entering the house my wife, Ady, quickly ushered me upstairs with a sour look upon her face. She pointed to our bedroom and said: "walk in there." I proceeded down the hall and was immediately blasted by a foul odor as I entered our bedroom. "It's been that way for three days!", she pleaded. It was truly an affront to my sense of smell. The bedroom was neat and tidy by all appearances, yet this overwhelming stench hovered in the air. My clean-up and unpacking chores immediately took second fiddle to the task of locating the source of this olfactory affront to our sacred living space.

Living where we do, in Oakport Township, with our home surrounded by huge oak and ash trees, number one suspect on my list was: "squirrel." We'd heard scratching and scuffing noises over recent weeks and I'd combed every nook and cranny trying to find and block any entry holes. Maybe my work had paid off, but one had gotten trapped inside. Out came the step ladder, face mask, gloves and up into the cramped, hot and never pleasant "ichullation" filled attic. It was overwhelming seeing the sea of foot thick fiberglass insulation, wondering where to start, and wondering how to move my body through these tight spaces without falling through the ceiling. My first attempts were half-hearted and fruitless. Then I simply followed my nose and began digging through the thick blown-in insulation and bingo… there it was... a dead young squirrel. Yuk! But happy to have found it, only to find two others nearby! Triple yuk!

I'd finally gotten to the source of the stench and it wasn't a pleasant experience in any way shape or form. The only good was that now the air could clear, and we could all return to breathing good ol' clean fresh Minnesota air. Three dead squirrels in the attic create quite an ugly stench! Trust me. And even though they were way up in the attic, that stench affected much of the rest of our home!

This whole experience made me think of our lives, mental health-wise, that is. We can appear neat, tidy, organized, together, clean and upbeat on the outside, yet the stench of dead squirrels in our mental attic can really affect all parts of our being. We may put on our Sunday morning church smile, but that can only be masked for so long. Eventually, the stink from past hurts, pain, rejection, loneliness, neglect, grief, anger abuse, alcoholism, etc., shows through in subtle and sometimes pretty obvious ways.

I spent some time with a gifted and wise Christian therapist long ago, who bluntly stated one day; "Rollie, you just need to spend some time getting more comfortable with the furniture in your attic." I.e. you need to recognize, acknowledge, face, confront, accept and learn to live with some of those dark corners of your life.

Sometimes, good solid, continued quiet time/prayer times can help. Sometimes long-term daily journaling can be a superb Godly tool in self-discovery. Sometimes it's stepping out of our normal comfortable life and going on a mission trip or adventure that can stimulate growth, self-knowledge, and understanding. Sometimes a good and trusted friend, pastor, therapist, counselor or spiritual director can be a Godly gift in helping us find and root out some of those "dead squirrels" that have crept their way into our mental and spiritual attics. I think the main thing is... *to have the courage*... to crawl up in there and do the work of finding those stinky buggers!

I'm a huge believer in holistic living and good mental, spiritual, physical and social health. I believe God meant for them all to be interconnected. More importantly, I believe that Jesus modeled, lived out, and spoke continually about living in ways that promote holistic living. Jesus was Godly in that he created us for who we are, yet human enough to have felt all of the good and difficult emotions we go through. His words ring with the truth and strength of having lived them out in the real world where hurt, pain, rejection, and suffering are par for the course.

My prayer for you this week would be that you would not have any squirrels in your attic! But if you do… have the courage to go find them, and put them in a more appropriate space!

Love one another as I first Loved you! John 13:34 NIV

You will grieve, but your grief will turn to joy. John 16:20 NIV

I came that they might have life and have it to the abundantly. John 10:10 ESV

The spirit of the Lord is upon me, because He has anointed me to preach good news to the poor. He has sent me to proclaim freedom for the prisoners, and recovery of sight for the blind, to release the oppressed, to proclaim the year of the Lords favor. Luke 4:18 NIV

It is not the healthy who need a doctor, but the sick. I have not come to call the righteous, but sinners.
Mark 2:17 NIV

Love your enemies, do good to those who hate you, bless those who curse you, pray for those who mistreat you… be merciful, just as your Father is merciful. Luke 6:27 NIV

Come with me to a quiet place and get some rest. Mark 6:31 NIV

Love the Lord God with all your heart soul and mind and with all your strength. Second is this, love your neighbor <u>as</u> yourself. Mark 12:30-31 NIV

Strange Track

Walking north towards Sanford hospital to visit a friend, I synched my hood tight to guard against the stinging and biting bitter-cold wind. I looked both ways crossing 7th Avenue, spinning my whole body due to poor peripheral vision from my hood, and proceeded into the Sanford wind tunnel. Immediately upon gaining the sidewalk, I came across a set of tracks most strange and peculiar, that caused me to stop and ponder.

I side-stepped to the right so as not to disturb the tracks and followed alongside. There before me were the clean, clear, crisp and distinct tracks of a single walking pedestrian and a lone bicyclist. These tracks stood out because they were not the normal white compressed tracks within a white snow-covered sidewalk, but something so much stranger. These were distinct, precise, clear-cut white tracks, laid out upon the dark background of a mostly snowless sidewalk. These particular tracks stood out as extraordinary, abnormal and bizarre. It was almost as if someone had purposely sculpted or molded these tracks upon a clean sidewalk. I pondered and ambled along racking my brain as to the *"how did this happen?"* I was determined to solve the mystery.

Weighing all the evidence and surveying the surrounding scenery for clues I finally realized that I was witnessing a set of ***paradoxical*** tracks; tracks that behaved ***opposite of the norm***. The most likely explanation is that the walker and the biker had journeyed the sidewalk early in the morning while it had a light fresh coating of snow. The weight of the biker and walker had compressed the snow beneath boots and tires and that compression had hardened and solidified the snow of the tracks. A strong breeze or possibly even the broom sweeper had then cleared the sidewalk of the rest of the snow leaving only the hardened tracks on the now barren sidewalk. Case closed.

Paying Attention II

These tracks have journeyed through my thoughts frequently of late as I've tried to ponder their meaning and significance. They have led me to realize that much of our life of faith and the life of Jesus is pure **paradox.** The ways of God and the way of our daily walk with Jesus are often times held in **paradox** or opposition to the way of the world.

Our world values paper certificates hanging on office walls, Master's degrees, Doctorates, intelligence, logic, and in-depth theological explanations. The more you know, the smarter you are, the higher your standing in the world. But Jesus walked in the opposite direction. *At that time Jesus said, "I praise you, Father, Lord of heaven and earth, because you have hidden these things from the wise and learned, and revealed them to little children. Matthew 11:25.* What Jesus desires is faith, not intellect. You cannot think your way to God.

The world values winners, people who make it to the top, people who achieve, who excel, who can dunk a basketball, or catch a football, or sing a song, or are skinny and look beautiful. Jesus walks in the opposite direction and declares a new world order for those who wish to follow Him. *The greatest among you will be your servant. For those who exalt themselves will be humbled, and those who humble themselves will be exalted. Matthew 23: 11-12 "So the last will be first, and the first will be last." Matthew 20:16*

The world values the self-promoter, the self-made individual, the self-sufficient, and the self-confident, the self-reliant, the self-righteous. In the world it's all about me; the self. But Jesus' teaching travels the road of life in opposition to this way of the world. *Then Jesus said to his disciples, "Whoever wants to be my disciple must deny themselves and take up their cross and follow me. For whoever wants to save their life will lose it, but whoever loses their life for me will find it. What good will it be for someone to gain the whole world, yet forfeit their soul? Matthew 16:24-26 For those who exalt themselves will be humbled, and those who humble themselves will be exalted. Matthew 23:12*

The world values strength, power, and might. The world wanted a mighty king, an invincible warrior, a power-filled president, or a musclebound superhero. God chose instead to move in the opposite direction by sending a helpless baby. *An angel of the Lord appeared to them, and the glory of the Lord shone around them, and they were terrified. But the angel said to them, "Do not be afraid. I bring you good news that will cause great joy for all the people. Today in the town of David a Savior has been born to you; he is the Messiah, the Lord. This will be a sign to you: You will find a baby wrapped in cloths and lying in a manger."* Luke 2: 9-12 NIV

The world tells us to always be strong, to always be at the top of our game, to show no weakness, to show no faults. Jesus moves us in the opposite direction. He knows and allows for our own human weaknesses and frailties. In relationship with Jesus, we have the freedom to accept and embrace the entirety of our humanity. *"My grace is sufficient for you, for power is perfected in weakness." Most gladly, therefore, I will rather boast about my weaknesses, so that the power of Christ may dwell in me. 2 Corinthians 12:9-11 NIV*

The world says to find go and find yourself, be all you can be, get all you can get, and live for the moment. Jesus teaches the opposite. He declares that the only way to truly find yourself, and become who you were meant to be, is by surrendering to God and being in relationship with him. *"Whoever finds his life will lose it, and whoever loses His life for My sake will find it." Matthew 10:39 NIV*

May you remember that God's ways are not always in sync with the ways of our modern world. We are the guardians and keepers of our own souls and therefore we must guard, protect and screen out that which enters our hearts and minds. We must remember that God's ways are often paradoxical.

> *For my thoughts are not your thoughts, neither are your ways my ways, declares the Lord.*
> Isaiah 55:8 NIV

STEVE

The view from this high up was refreshing, new and different. A shift in perspective can very much alter your viewpoint. Just a stone's throw from my habitual daily routine I was seeing my humdrum surroundings from a novel viewpoint. Smokestacks, water towers, steeples and rooftops, circular fan vents, quadrangular buildings of all shapes and sizes lay below me. The early morning bright sunshine that was low to the horizon cast deep contrasts of light and shadow. Humanity scurried below on the sidewalks and street corners with the buzz of daily activity. People and cars moved in a never-ending random pattern of places to go, things to do, and people to see. A change in perspective is always good.

And then I turned from looking out the window and remembered where I was; 7th floor, Sanford Hospital, oncology. I returned my focus to my friend Steve, lying on the bed fighting his way through a life-threatening battle with leukemia. Bald now from the chemo, and once again receiving chemical concoctions of who knows what via a string of IV's. His room stood in strong contrast to the tedium of busyness, activity, and movement I had just witnessed outside below. No, here on the 7th floor, was stillness, quiet, contemplation and the eternal weight of… waiting. Unlike the rest of the world that was racing about below us with all the tedium, repetitiveness and hustle and bustle… here in this room, we were dealing with the heart of the matter… matters of the heart.

Though fighting for life, Steve remained strong. A firm grip held my hand with a strong life force beating from within. His blue eyes were clear and focused. When I asked, "How goes the battle?" He quickly responded with a smile and the words; "Well, my life has pretty well boiled down to these four words;

'*I trust you Jesus.*'" I too smiled back, our eyes locked on one another's.

I glanced at his small table and noticed the familiar face of one of my latest life's companions, the devo book "Jesus Calling", by Sarah Young. I smiled again and noted that he must have read today's devo. I opened the book to March 30th and read aloud; "*I AM TAKING CARE OF YOU. Trust me at all times. Trust Me in all circumstances. Trust me with all your heart. When you are weary and everything seems to be going wrong, you can still utter these four words; 'I trust You, Jesus.' By doing so you release matters into My control, and you fall back into the security of My everlasting arms.*"

I couldn't help but notice how appropriate these words had seemed to me earlier in the morning during my quiet time. And now sitting here on the 7th floor, I was powerfully moved by the strength and depth of Steve's faith and how even more appropriate these words must be for a man fighting for life. Steve's witness and testimony were from the heart, from someone walking right up to the very edge of life and death.

The gospel of his life and faith spoke more loudly and clearly than any manufactured or well thought through sermon. I left the room humbled, moved, inspired, and refocused. Sometimes a slight change of perspective can very much alter your attitude and perception of this life.

Today the sun is shining in all its magnificence upon the entire landscape. It is warm, inviting and freeing, and will feel so good on face and body alike especially for us here in the Northland. It is free and generous, and benevolent and unrestricted. It will pour out its blessing upon all; the poor and the wealthy, the healthy and the sick, the construction worker and the white collared banker, the crack addict and the sports hero, the homeless and the housewife, the popular and the invisible, the newborn baby and the aged dying in a home. The sun will not select, or hand-pick or prejudice upon whom it will pour out its blessings. No, it will shine down upon us all.

Will you have the perspective and vision and gratitude to know that you are indeed blessed?

Now on his way to Jerusalem, Jesus traveled along the border between Samaria and Galilee. As he was going into a village, ten men who had leprosy met him. They stood at a distance and called out in a loud voice, "Jesus, Master, have pity on us!" When he saw them, he said, "Go, show yourselves to the priests." And as they went, they were cleansed. One of them, when he saw he was healed, came back, praising God in a loud voice. He threw himself at Jesus' feet and thanked him—and he was a Samaritan. Jesus asked, "Were not all ten cleansed? Where are the other nine? Has no one returned to give praise to God except this foreigner?" Then he said to him, "Rise and go; your faith has made you well." Luke 17: 11-19 NIV

> The greatest of human freedoms is the ability to choose one's own attitude. Victor Frankl

Whatever is true, whatever is noble, whatever is right, whatever is pure, whatever is lovely, whatever is admirable- if anything is excellent or praiseworthy- Think about such things! Philippians 4:8 NIV

Taking Inventory

Sometimes we need to stop and take inventory. Sometimes we need to slow down enough to take stock. Sometimes we need to put on the brakes of our crazy busy life to count our blessings. Sometimes our cup is so full, that we cannot see all that it contains.

As my life pushes rapidly towards the 60 mark, I'm learning more and more to recognize what is important and what's not. I'm wanting to see with eyes of gratitude and appreciation the blessings both large and small that overflow my life's cup. I also want to give gratitude where it's due and bless those who have blessed me.

Paying Attention II

For the past 15 years or so, each September has found me roaming the high country of Colorado's Mount Zirkel Wilderness Area soaring along the continental divide. The mountain Wapiti or elk is my reason for entering the wilderness. With my backpack full, and longbow in hand, the mountains demand from me toil, sweat, aching thighs, and burning lungs just to enter her domain with no guarantee of success nor that I will even see any elk.

Several times I have gone alone to this vast wilderness, to seek out and experience true solitude, to be alone with my Maker and Creator and to divest myself from the electronic addictions of this age. I've enjoyed the freedom that comes with going solo. All decisions and consequences are mine and mine alone. I have treasured these times of aloneness and sacred seclusion.

Yet for the great bulk of these years of wilderness elk hunting, I have gone with my old friends Duncan Puffer and John Flaherty. My friendship with these two characters goes all the way back to jr. high where we were band buddies and played football together. Through all the years of high school, college, dating, marriages, divorces, kids, jobs, and all that life throws at us, we continue to rendezvous in the high country to chase elk. It has become a sacred time of brotherhood and friendship.

Mind you, every year we chase elk, but most years we have been very successful at not being successful. That's a very euphemistic way of saying we've not had much of a fatal impact on the elk herd! Lately, we have been telling the truth to each other: we love to take our **bows out** for a camping trip! Our bows seem to love the experience!

As I look over my life and take inventory, I have grown to appreciate and give thanks for these two friends more and more. They have walked with me through the difficult mountains and valleys of both the wilderness and my life. Loyalty, integrity, honesty, openness, character, humor, love of creation and laughter represent my two friends.

I couldn't let these friendships go unnoticed, unacknowledged or unappreciated. It was time to do something about it. And so, it came to pass that a few weeks before Christmas I approached my favorite jeweler Steve Hahn. I brought him two elk ivories (each elk has two actual ivory teeth in the upper roof of their mouth.) that I'd been saving. I asked him to create rings using the ivories. They had to be masculine and stylish.

A week ago, the package arrived with the rings and as I opened the container I was thrilled with the craftsmanship, elegance, and beauty. We could now enjoy the **Fellowship of the Ring**, or maybe the **Brotherhood of the Elk.** I carefully crafted a heartfelt letter to each man, shipped off the ring and letter to John and Dunc and awaited their surprise and response.

Again, and again I'm reminded that is far better to give than receive. I was giddy with anticipation knowing they would be both surprised and thrilled by both the gift and the thoughts behind the gift. They did not disappoint, and my smile grew with each response via texts and phone calls. Ahhh the satisfaction of giving well! The Fraternal Order of the Silver Elk Ring had been sealed!

Do you have a good friend? Do you treasure a good coworker? Do you have an excellent boss? Do you have a loyal employee? Do you have a faithful teammate? Do you share a special bond with a sister or brother or uncle or cousin? Do they know or realize it?

Most of us live with over-flowing cups. Most of us live with over-abundance and yet we take so much in our lives for granted. Most of us barely even recognize that we are blessed. We live in a world of selfish entitlement. Many of us live with over-abundance and yet still crave and seek the ever evasive **"more."**

Maybe it's time to stop and take stock of your many blessings. Maybe pause the hectic button of your life, and take a look around you... not just at the "stuff", but the "who" of your life. The gift of gratitude, of saying thanks, of offering words of appreciation and affirmation is an art that is slipping from our world.

In Luke 17:11-19, we hear how Jesus healed ten desperate and broken lepers. Only one returned to him and lay prostrate on the ground to give thanks and praise for the blessing of his healing. Jesus replied; *"Were not ten made clean? Where are the other nine?"*

Would you be counted as the **"one"** who returned with gratitude and praise? Or would you simply be one of the crowd, one of the entitled, **one of the nine** who never uttered a single word of thanks or gratitude?

Rejoice always, [17]pray continually, [18]give thanks in all circumstances; for this is God's will for you in Christ Jesus. 1 Thessalonians 5:16-18 NIV

Let everything that has breath praise the Lord! Psalm 150 NIUV

As iron sharpens iron, so one person sharpens another. Proverbs 27:17 NIV

TEARS

The lump in my throat grew larger. The wetness in my eyes came not from sweat or rain, but from reservoirs of emotions lurking way beneath the surface. And this... well, this was about the 5th or 6th wave of such intense emotions. And try as I might, I could not hold back... and the tears and lump just kept growing.

My tears were not from sadness, nor sorrow. Those twins very rarely release my external waterworks, but these came from something far stronger; from the pools of inspiration, witnessing triumph, achievement, and someone prevailing against all odds. I frequently glanced to my side to see if Shane might be feeling something similar. I was hoping he was. How could he not?

The touching and powerful scenes that were tugging at my heartstrings were running across the screen in front of us from the movie McFarland USA. An absolutely inspiring and touching film about a cross-country team made up of unknown heroes who climb out of the poverty, prejudice, bigotry and endless exhausting work in the migrant fields of California. At the heart of the film is their coach, played by Kevin Costner, who has to move his family to the dirty, dusty town of McFarland after being fired as an over-zealous and hard disciplining football coach. In a last-ditch effort to provide for his family, he has to take the only job left in this forgotten and neglected town made up of mostly Hispanic farm workers. He and his family feel like the proverbial fish out of water and he begins both his teaching and coaching with less than enthusiastic anticipation. He and his family feel out of place and long for another life and location.

As the story progresses, the family begins to become accepted and love on and cared for by this Hispanic community that is rich in culture, deep in tradition, strong in love and commitment to family and a hard work ethic rarely seen by suburbanites. The family falls in love with both the people and the community. The coach begins to observe "potential" for both running and scholastics in his students who have nothing, who are given no opportunities nor vision and work endless hours under the hot California sun helping to provide for their families. He agrees to form a new cross-country team and coach these seven kids who have neither heard of cross-country nor own a pair of running shoes.

The coach loves on these kids, believes in them, hangs with them, and lifts up their expectations of themselves and their future. Most importantly he stays put. He blooms where he is planted. He blossoms where he is. He immerses himself in the community where he landed. He is given a small group of kids in front of him and these become his focus, his work, his ministry if you will. And because he stays put, and blossoms where he is planted… lives are changed and from those changed lives, generations are impacted.

This movie was a great reminder to me of the impact and positive difference we are all called to make… *right where we are.* On our immediate families, in the mundane workplace where we spend so many countless hours, and through the all-to-familiar neighborhood of our day to day lives. Maybe on our given sports team or even in the church where we often forget that here too is the neighbor we are called to love as we love ourselves, or forgive their trespasses as God first forgives us ours.

I, in my restlessness and impatience, am often looking over the horizon to "the next big thing," the great event or project or ministry or opportunity where I can make a "Big" difference. Sometimes I need to be reminded that my ministry today is the people right in front of me. To do the small things, the unpopular things of servanthood, and love on those who are already placed at my feet.

Jesus specialized in ministering to and serving anyone and everyone who crossed his path. He had that gift of being in the here and now. Lepers, blind folks, hookers, rich young rulers, impoverished widows, soldiers, greedy tax collectors, fisherman, and children. Simple acts of being present, caring, and lending a listening ear and a compassionate focused gaze.

When we are responsive to Gods quiet calling and gentle nudging's, we can make a difference in the lives of those who cross our paths in day to day life. May you have eyes to see and hands to serve those whom God places before you.

For I was hungry and you gave me something to eat, I was thirsty and you gave me something to drink, I was a stranger and you invited me in, I needed clothes and you clothed me, I was sick and you looked after me, I was in prison and you came to visit me. Matthew 25: 35-36 NIV

The Burn

We weren't lost. We knew exactly where we were both in real life and on the map. We were camped along the eastern shore of Alpine Lake, across from the island. Knowing where we were was good, yet we both felt a great sense of anxiety, fear, and worry. Tears welled up in Karina's eyes (my eldest daughter) on several occasions and I withdrew into my own silence. I tried a couple of times to remind us that we were healthy, had good gear; i.e. tent, sleeping bags, etc. and plenty of food. That helped us both intellectually, but not viscerally, in the gut where it counts.

Karina and I were on day six of a ten-day backpacking trip in the Wind River Mountains of Western Wyoming. We were attempting a very difficult 100-mile high-traverse of the entire mountain range, from south to north weaving in and out along the continental divide. More than 80% of the route is cross-country, off-trail, using map and compass for route finding. We'd already crossed the divide five times and had traversed too many boulder and snowfields to count.

Earlier in the morning, we had summited our fifth pass over the divide, and looking back westward had noticed what appeared to be a major storm system moving quickly onto the Winds. We had to make a decision to stay on route in the high alpine country, along the divide to stay on route and finish what we'd started, or head to lower country and avoid the possible dangerous exposure in the alpine terrain. We bantered back and forth for several minutes and then resolutely agreed to end out quest, surrender our goal, and head for the lower terrain of the Wind River Indian Reservation where I had led several youth trips in years previous.

Our chosen decision would carry with it a heavy toll of six miles of cross country, bush-whacking, brush-busting, steeply descending terrain to arrive at Alpine Lake, where I knew we could pick up some outfitter trails that led back to an exit and trail-head on the eastern flank of the mountains where we could hitch a ride back to our truck.

We began our descent which was difficult, but uneventful working our way first down snowfields, then slowing picking our way down steep rocky slabs, downed timber, boulder fields and stream crossings for the first few miles. Progress was slow but steady. Then we entered a massive burn area that had been scorched within the past few years. Dead, charred, barren trees were everywhere, and along with the burn came the blowdown that blocked progress in all directions. Progress slowed to a snail's pace, and every inch gained was a cause for celebration.

For several hours we crawled and clawed our way over and under broken trees, roots and charred earth, our arms and faces now camouflaged by the black soot and ash. I kept commenting to Karina; *"If we can just make Alpine Lake, we should be able to find trails to lead us out."*

To our relief, Alpine Lake finally lay before us, and to our dismay and dread, so did the burn that completely surrounded the entire basin of the lake. We gained the far shore and our moods sank further as any and all signs of trails had been obliterated by the fire and following years of erosion. Adding to our dismay was the fact that we had no maps for any of the terrain beyond Alpine Lake to the trailhead. We would have to rely on only my memory.

We set up camp, and made a good supper and began talking through options. Our biggest fear was not- knowing how far the burn extended. Maybe the entire forest had been burned the whole way out! Maybe those last 20 plus miles would be just like today and with no trails, no map, and filled with blowdowns.

As we conversed, I asked Karina how she was doing. Through tears, she shared that she was ok but nervous and scared. I quietly admitted the same. I shared that throughout our difficult day though, I had said a hundred silent prayers, giving thanks for God's guiding each and every footstep, and offering my trust to Him. These are two guiding themes; trust and gratitude, from Jesus Calling devotional book by Sarah Young, that I read most every day. After all, we had come safely through some incredibly rough terrain, with barely a scratch, and no twisted ankles or bad falls. God had proved incredibly faithful so far.

Karina smiled and nodded, "Yes, I know. I kept saying the verse from our Devil's Tower climbing trip over and over and over; *'Have I not commanded you? Be strong and courageous. Do not be afraid; do not be discouraged, for the Lord your God will be with you wherever you go. Joshua 1:9'" NIV* As both a dad and youth leader I smiled. It was pretty cool to hear, my daughter using scripture in a practical, hands-on, real-life situation.

Sleep was evasive for me that night. Darkness and slow-moving time seemed to amplify worry, discouraging imaginings, fear and negativity. I did my best to counter that natural downward slide of my thought process by continually reciting some favorite scripture verses:

Paying Attention II

"I am with you and will watch over you wherever you go, I will not leave you. Genesis 28:15" NIV

God has said, "Never will I leave you; never will I forsake you." The Lord is my helper; I will not be afraid. What can man do to me? Hebrews 13:5-6 NIV

Do not be anxious about anything, but in every situation, by prayer and petition, with thanksgiving, present your requests to God. And the peace of God, which transcends all understanding, will guard your hearts and your minds in Christ Jesus. Philippians 4:6-7 NIV

    Morning finally arrived, and we readied ourselves for the day ahead. We'd made a plan with several options depending upon what we found along the way. We said a prayer and set out trusting in our compass bearing based on my memory of the next lake two miles away over the ridge. Slow and steady, slow and steady. We spread out keeping our eyes peeled for any old tree blazes, rock cairns, and/or remnants of a trail.

    Filtered sunlight graced our morning. Slow and steady, slow and steady sure enough, after a couple of hours the next lake appeared before us. **Trust** and **gratitude**, **Trust** and **gratitude**.

As we had feared, arriving at this next lake found the entire valley scorched and burned as well. Our original exit plan looked doomed. Yet, I had to remember that God had led us very safely and carefully so far, step by step, slow and steady. Why would he not continue to do so now when we had surrendered to the guidance of His Holy Spirit?

We made several more decisions throughout our day, evaluating what lay before us, and doing our best to live and move through what had been laid before us. A funny thing happened throughout our day. We began to laugh more at our situation, we talked and shared more deeply about our lives beyond the surface, and asked each other thought-provoking questions. I couldn't help but whisper prayers of gratitude for getting closer to my own daughter through the trials and struggles of this insane journey. Hardship and difficulty were drawing us closer together.

The final route we chose would take us up a long, trail-less valley to another 11,000' pass that would send us back west away from our vehicle. As the day wore on, we soon left the burn and found ourselves once again in the land of the living with lush greenery of pine and spruce. The way forward revealed itself more freely, and by day's end, we'd left the tangle of blowdowns and difficult cross-country travel and camped in a spectacular and beautiful alpine cirque. Peace settled over our landscape and within our hearts. God had once again proven Himself trustworthy and reliable. I could not help myself, giving thanks over and over again. **Gratitude** and **trust**.

How about you? Is there a difficulty in your way? Are you going through a dry, burn, impossible situation?

Can you hunker down in **gratitude** and **trust**? He has proven Himself to be trustworthy and reliable!

The Death of Stewart

Only one brave soul dared show up for Sunday's snowshoeing. The impending blizzard had most seeking refuge in a warm blanket and steaming hot coffee in front of a TV. Several texts by others said; "No way am coming out in this stuff!" Mary Ann had proved game and appeared in the driveway full of anticipation, enthusiasm and bundled up to the max. She cautiously asked if we were still on, and I replied; "Let's go for it. It's a beautiful day!" And off we went scurrying over the dike getting blasted by the biting and bitter north wind and blowing snow.

Within a minute or three we'd gained the refuge of the woods and within seconds, the wind became a moot point as the magic of the winter wonderland unveiled her beauty to us. Several inches of soft powdered snow lay atop the foot of previous crusted snow. Each lifting of our snowshoes created a quiet "poof" of fluffy white powder. The windward sides of all the trees were frosted with snow, and the winter woods had become a monochromatic world of black and white. Snowflakes silently descended all around us as if we were standing inside of our own personal snow globe.

We made our way silently through the woods occasionally stopping for gentle conversation. Tracks of deer, mice, rabbits, and coyote intermingled with our own larger big-foot like impressions. All in all, it was a good day to be alive. A good day to have health and vitality.

A good day to fill our lungs with crisp, clean, fresh air. A good day to walk and exercise in the peaceful winter woods.

Snowshoeing is always a slow-paced process. Slow and steady wins the non-race. Slow and quiet and stillness allows one to observe, to become aware and to notice. Slow helps us to lift up our eyes and pay attention to all that is around us. And if one is lucky, nature will provide interesting and unique observations.

This day proved no different, as we descended imperceptibly into the cattail-choked coulee. In the center of the winding coulee, was an open pathway of snow-covered ice. A perfect travel corridor for man and beast alike. The slight depression of the coulee and the thick 6-8' high cattails kept us protected from the biting wind.

As we rounded a bend I happened to glance upward and caught the tell-tale shadowy outline of two snow-covered bedded deer not 20 yards from us on the coulee's edge. They had spotted me first as their radar like ears were on full alert. The heavy falling snow and fading light made them appear like grey ghosts. Quietly turning to Mary Ann, I "shushed" with my index finger to my mouth and pointed in their direction and whispered "deer!"

Speaking softly, I told Mary Ann to scoot up onto a small mound of snow to see better. As we did, I noticed three more sets of phantom ears hidden behind falling logs. We stood silently staring at the deer and them, us. I was shocked that they had not spooked earlier as they were directly downwind of us. They seemed to be silently communicating that this situation could, if we agreed, be a truce, a détente if you will. They appeared cozy and comfy, huddled in their snowy beds, wanting only to be left alone. We mentally signed the accord and continued our journey with heavy snow falling all around us.

We soon came to a pinch in the brush-choked coulee. As I maneuvered my long snowshoes and ducked my body through the narrow opening, I happened to notice below me just inches above the surface of the snow a sight most strange.

There, hanging perfectly from a small branch was a frozen mouse. He was hanging by his front hands as if he had been performing pull-ups and simply ran out of gas. An odd sight to be sure, as I wracked my

Paying Attention II

brain trying to deduce the cause of death and prior events leading up to his passing. I gently picked up the frozen mouse, pursed my lips and blew off the snow from his head and back. I quietly declared; "Stewart is dead."

How peculiar this was as I looked over his body looking for signs of injury, or distress. Finding none, the mystery of this perfectly preserved frozen corpse remained unsolved. The "why" of Stewart's death would remain unanswered.

Our lives will have many such unanswered "whys," and for many of us who walk this journey of faith, unanswered "whys" can become a major stumbling block for growth and forward movement. Many of us will get stuck at "why?" Some people when stuck at "why," will simply walk away from God rather than live with the unanswered questions. It's often easier to blame God than to live with the unknown answers.

Why did my mother die so young? Why did my folks have to divorce? Why do I suffer from depression and anxiety? Why did my father never show or speak love to me? Why did my boy/ girl-friend walk out on me? Why did the tornado/flood/fire destroy my home? Why did I lose my job? Why can't I beat this addiction? Why did my son/daughter make so many wrong decisions? Why can't I find Mr. or Mrs. Right? Why does my child have cancer? Why 911? Why school shootings? Why would a good God allow so much suffering and tragedy to happen to the world and me? Why would I want to believe and follow that kind of God?

I learned long ago, that if you "have to know" the answer to the question "why," you will most likely never know peace or contentment. You have just two choices really: Remain in a state of agitation, dis-ease, dis-content, anger, and anxiousness by demanding and waiting for an answer from God, or surrender your "why." Surrendering your "Why" is simple, but most often not easy. Surrendering your "why" reaffirms that God has the ultimate view from 60,000'. **He** has the bigger picture. **He** has the overall view. **He** can see our past, our present and our future.

Surrendering our "why" is a tangible and practical step of real faith. It's saying that; "Jesus, in spite of this tragedy/setback/failure/struggle/loss/pain I **will** trust you. I will trust that you can see me through this, and you can take this tragedy/setback/failure/struggle/loss/pain and weave it into the fabric of my life to bring about growth, deepened trust and progress for me and possibly others."

It's always your choice as to which path you take. God has given you this immense freedom. You can stay stuck in the yuck of why, or move forward by trusting in God's promise:

*And we know that in **ALL** things God works for the good of those who love him, who have been called according to his purpose!* Romans 8:28 NIV

This is absolutely God's promise. May you have the courage to trust Him and surrender your "whys."

*I will lead the blind by ways they have not known,
Along unfamiliar paths I will guide them; I will turn the darkness into light before them and make the rough places smooth. Isaiah 42:16 NIV*

We live by faith, not by sight! 2 Corinthians 5:7 NIV

And the God of Grace who called you to his eternal glory in Christ, after you have suffered a little while, will himself restore you and make you strong, firm and steadfast. 1 Peter 5:10 NIV

God's purpose in testing is to build stronger faith.
The devil's purpose in tempting is to destroy faith;
to take you away from God. Rick Warren

God can bring good out of the worst evil. Rick Warren

The Devil

The magnificent sunrise began peaking over the eastern horizon just upon our arrival into the crow's nest. We carefully picked our way and dropped down 10 feet with a sigh of relief having finished the initial 150' scramble to begin our actual route. Even though it was still only 5:30 am, the heat and exertion had us sweating and breathing hard. It was now "go time," where reality met with our anticipations, and for me, I faced an old and familiar "frenemy;" anxiety. We were now about to begin the actual roped-up climbing of Devil's Tower in eastern Wyoming.

Our chosen route and daunting challenge of the day stood looming high above us; El Cracko Diablo or Devil's Crack, with an intermediate rating of 5.8. El Cracko is an intimidating vertical crack that shoots upwards for 300' and seems to disappear into the blue of the Wyoming sky. The top of the 800' tower stood hidden beyond our threshold of perception somewhere high above. Whether or not we would stand on its summit, remained to be seen.

My good friend and climbing partner, Rob Zachariason, was here for his first attempt at Devil's Tower. I felt confident in Rob's climbing abilities and had full and complete trust in him to hold my life in his hands. Over many years of ministry, I have led several church groups to the tower and climbed it a dozen times or so, but this was the first time I had come with just a friend. It felt freeing to simply be responsible for only myself and my partner.

For months Rob and I had trained faithfully at our local YMCA climbing wall, and although it was a great practice ground and helped us get our bodies in shape, and some of our techniques dialed in, there is no way to replicate the length, height, and intensity of a real rock climb. The 25' walls of the Y, pale in comparison to the lengthy 160' pitches (one length of rope or climbing sequence) that we would encounter on the Tower. So, although we both felt prepared as best we could, there remained many unanswered questions, fears, doubts, and worries.

For Rob, as a first timer, there had to be the questions of "Can I do this?" "Do I have what it takes?" "Have I learned the proper techniques and skill sets to make it up?" For me who had climbed it several times, I did have the benefit of prior successes, but also carried the fears and worries of knowing what this vertical world can do to your "head." I knew all to intimately well of the gut level fear, and visceral anxieties provoked by the Tower. For months I had both looked forward to and yet at the same time dreaded the upcoming climb, knowing full well I would have to face myself and my anxiety.

A great deal of my prayer time in the past months had been devoted to surrendering my fears, worries, and anxieties. Somedays I had secretly hoped for a reason to cancel the trip. But, in the end, I would always come back to this little-known fact; If we walk away from our fears/anxieties, they win and they shrink our world. When we run from that which we fear, our world shrinks. When we bravely ask for God's help and courage to face both our fears and ourselves, we grow, we expand, and we become more for the world. Facing our fears creates freedom! It doesn't matter if its fear of flying, standing up to our boss, confronting a friend, signing up for a new class and becoming a beginner again, saying yes to rehab and treatment for your addiction, standing up to a bully in school, or saying goodbye to a dead-end job to start anew. When we face ourselves truthfully with God by our side, and walk towards our anxieties instead of running away, we are rewarded with growth, strength, and a renewed sense of self-worth that then makes us more useful to the world and serving God.

Paying Attention II

As Rob and I began our preparations for the climb, in the relative safety of the crow's nest, a strange sense of calm began to sweep over me. It was not a denial of the arduous task ahead of us nor a pushing away of the scariness or fears we were about to face, but it was a true sense of God's answered prayers. He had answered my prayers, and I was free to climb, free to enjoy the adventure, free to soak up the incredible unique surroundings and beauty of the day, free to rise to the challenge, free to succeed or fail, free to engage my body and brain in the skills and mastery of the climb itself.

We climbed beautifully as a team and surprisingly I enjoyed every minute of it. The journey was not easy. We both grew exhausted with the heat and the intensity of the difficult climb. Nearing the top of the most difficult 160' pitch, worn and weary, soaking in sweat, I slipped and fell. But the fall was a moot point. I was held safely by a good friend, a strong rope that connected us, and a rock-solid anchor. When you are connected to the rock-solid anchor of God, failure is not fatal. It is simply a chance to rethink, retry, rest, refocus and get back at it.

After several hours of climbing, and then four 150' rappels we made it back to mother earth safe, sound, completely exhausted, bone-dry thirsty, and the better men for what we had experienced. God had answered our prayers a thousand times over. Relief and gratitude poured over our bodies and spirits.

One of my favorite songs of late that we sing at worship is "Fear is a Liar" by Zach Williams:

Video Link: https://www.youtube.com/watch?v=sQTnREEtuNk

Fear, he is a liar, He will take your breath, Stop you in your steps
Fear he is a liar, He will rob your rest, Steal your happiness
Cast your fear in the fire 'Cause fear he is a liar

These lyrics nail it. Fear is a liar, and fear is of the devil. And the devil is the father of all lies. Don't believe what the devil tries to sell you through your worries, doubts, fears, and anxieties. Those are not of God. When you listen to God's word, your world gets wider, deeper, stronger and better. When you listen to fear and anxiety, your world will shrink and you will be lesser for listening to them.

How ironic, that while climbing El Cracko Diablo (the Devil's Crack) on Devil's Tower, that God's will and word won out over the lies of anxiety, fear, doubt and worry of the devil himself!
May you have the courage to trust in and lean into God. Trust what he says about you and what you are capable of in this world.

For a visceral look at the climbing experience, click on these two-video links!

https://www.youtube.com/watch?v=zUOCFa6u0eQ&t=3s
https://www.youtube.com/watch?v=bvTryG1RT64

Paying Attention II

I can do all things in Christ who gives me strength. Philippians 4:13 NIV

Nothing will be impossible for you! Matthew 17:20-21 NIV

If God is for us, Who can be against us? Romans 8:31 NIV

For the Spirit God gave us does not make us timid, but gives us power, love and self-discipline.
2 Timothy 1:7 NIV

Don't measure the size of the mountain. Talk to
the one who can move it. Max Lucado

Fear knocked at the door, Faith answered.
And lo… no one was there.

When I am afraid, I put my trust in you. In God, whose word I praise—in God I trust and am not afraid. What can mere mortals do to me? Psalm 56:3-4 NIV

The Hands of a Murderer

Sliding my driver's license into the trough below the glass barrier, I smiled at the deputy who greeted me with a friendly smile and asked about my agenda. I leaned into the circular voice holes and stated my business. "I'm here to visit Donny _____. I'm from First Lutheran Church." She took my license and grabbed a three-ring binder and rapidly thumbed through it to find my page. Verifying who I was, she slid a visitor's badge into the trough and pointed to the elevator; "Second floor, follow the lines to the purple visitor's nook." I nodded with understanding knowing the drill from dozens of other visits and thanked her.

Entering the barren stainless-steel elevator my sense of confinement, dis-ease, and claustrophobia began to grow. A loud ding and the door opened into the hallway I've dubbed the "thousand-yard walk." Turning right, I began walking down the seemingly endless, featureless, barren corridor of concrete block and immaculate shiny floor tile. It is a walk I dread, as I have always done this walk alone adding to my sense of isolation, oppression, and heaviness. The quarter-mile tunnel seemed to take forever to pass through, and finally, I took a left through the purple door of the Cass County Jail.

Several windows lined the one wall, each with a basic black, old-school telephone, stainless-steel privacy dividers and matching steel counter. My invited guest had not arrived yet, so I paced, fidgeted and rocked in my chair. With no cell-phone or diversion, my nervous energy had nowhere to relieve itself.

After many minutes, I heard doors being opened from the other side and Donny was ushered in to take a seat across from me behind the thick glass divider. He was dressed in the dull-orange standard issue prison jumpsuit. His hair was long and disheveled like he'd recently awoken. He sported a matching dirty-blond, scraggly and scruffy beard. Upon seeing me he flashed a smile of recognition that held very few teeth. Most likely from years of meth and lack of self-care. He reached for the phone as did I, and then folded his remaining hand on the counter. I stared at his hands, knowing that he had recently used those same hands to take the life of his friend in a drunken argument gone awry.

Donny had grown up at our church. He had been active in confirmation, Sunday worship, and many trips and outings. A good kid, for the most part, a bit odd in some ways, but what teenager isn't a bit odd. Over the years he'd occasionally drifted in and out of church life, and the last time I'd seen him was at the hospital when I'd visited him after an overdose. As with then, he seemed grateful to see a familiar face, as he quietly shared, "It's good to see you, Rollie." "Good to see you too Donny."

Our conversation coughed and sputtered gaining little traction. It was awkward and tough to break through with the obvious large elephant in the tiny room; the heinous crime that he'd committed. I did my best to reassure him that he was loved by God, that his family loved him and grieved for him. I promised him that I'd call his grandparents to tell them I'd visited. He seemed grateful for the gesture and asked me to tell them how sorry he was and that he loved them. I asked him to put his hand on the plate glass as I did the same and prayed for him. Hand to hand we prayed and my heart broke for Donny, for what his life had become, and for all the brokenness, hurt, and pain that rippled outwards to so many others from his poor choices.

I left Donny and returned to the endless hallway heavy with a thousand tangled thoughts and a quagmire of somber feelings. Reaching the outside of the jail I breathed deeply of the openness and clean fresh air, relieved to experience real freedom. I said a few thank you prayers.

Thank God there are jails and thank God that I don't have to stay in one! I quietly muttered "there but for the grace of God go I."

Jails and prisons, thank God that we have them and thank God for the many fine and good men and women who work so diligently in these facilities. We need these secure, firm and impenetrable fortresses.

And thank God for the many fine folks who persevere in jail ministries, bringing hope, a second chance, redemption, and forgiveness to those who have known so little.

For many of the men I've visited over the years, jail time has been the turning point, a chance to reflect and assess how they got there. Many of these men have turned back to God seeking a new beginning, a fresh start and a chance to move in more positive directions. For many men and women, jail was an answered prayer to turn their lives around.

In Luke 4:18 Jesus declares; *"The Spirit of the LORD is upon me, for he has anointed me to bring Good News to the poor. He has sent me to proclaim that captives will be released, that the blind will see, that the oppressed will be set free,"* This was quintessential Jesus speaking out his personal Mission Statement. It is also the mission statement we inherit by being a follower of Jesus.

Concrete and steel prisons are ominous and obvious. We are certainly called to visit and minister to those who are incarcerated. But there are a plethora of more-subtle, hidden, veiled prisons that bind most of us and inhibit our true freedom as followers of Jesus.

Many of us are bound by the shackles of addictions to food, shopping, work, alcohol, praise, people-pleasing, social media, cell phones, pornography, or constant activity.

What about the prison of poor mental health that is epidemic in depression or anxieties that limit who we are and what we are capable of?

What about the walls of loneliness and isolation that keep us from experiencing real community and connectivity? The shut-in elderly, the young adult who just can't find a space or place to belong? The single mom slugging it out to provide for and care for her young? Or the teenager who struggles to wade through the muck and mire of adolescence?

Many wrestle against the bars of a lifeless and hollow marriage, making us feel entrapped and walled in with no way out.

Some of us are trapped by an aging and failing body or mind.

Maybe you are in your own invisible prison right now and you are bound by unseen chains that inhibit or impede being who you were created to be. Seek first the source of freedom, Jesus and His Holy Spirit. Surrender to the One who can make you free. And if you are mostly free of the shackles that bind, reach out to another and help to release the prisoner, help the blind to see, and set the oppressed free. This is your calling.

It is for Freedom that Christ has set us free! Stand firm then, and do not let yourselves be burdened again by a yoke of slavery. Galatians 5:1 NIV

Now the Lord is the Spirit, and where the Spirit of the Lord is, there is freedom! 2 Corinthians 3:17 NIV

My friends, you were chosen to be free. So don't use your freedom as an excuse to do anything you want. Use it as an opportunity to serve each other with love. All the Law says can be summed up in the command to love others as much as you love yourself. Galatians 5:13-14 CEV

> *He upholds the cause of the oppressed and gives food*
> *to the hungry. The Lord sets prisoners free,*
> *Psalm 146:7 NIV*

Then you will know the truth, and the truth will set you Free! John 8:32 NIV

> *So if the Son sets you Free, you will be free indeed! John 8:36 NIV*

"You have heard that it was said to our people long ago, 'You must not murder anyone. Anyone who murders another will be judged.' [22] *But I tell you, if you are angry with a brother or sister, you will be judged. Matthew 5: 21-22 NIV*

But I tell you that anyone who looks at a woman lustfully has already committed adultery with her in his heart. Matthew 5:28 NIV

The Man with the White Car

For most of the weeks of our now gone summer, I have driven to and from work each day passing a sight most benign and mundane, quite ordinary if you will, and yet so very strange and noteworthy. On the north side of Wall Street as I make the turn by the gas station, sits a massive mound or long hill of clay. This clay had been piled up a few years back, alongside the massive retaining pond from which it had been extracted, to aid in flood control in our humble little Oakport Township.

Each gorgeous morning of our summer and early fall, I would drive by the 200-yard-long pile of clay. Each day, there parked along-side of the road was a little white sedan. Depending on when I passed by, there were usually 1-3 bulky dump trucks stirring up dust as they lined up to receive a load of clay to be delivered to some project off in parts unknown to me.

No matter when I passed by, morning, noon, or late afternoon the same white car was parked there, and the owner of that car was operating alternately a large faded yellow bull-dozer and a massive front-end loader. The times I passed by when no dump trucks were present, he was in the big dozer pushing earth into large piles. I noticed he was methodical and calculating as to how he approached and tore apart the mountain of clay. Each day the mountain grew smaller.

Paying Attention II

When a dump truck showed up, he could be seen scooping huge amounts of clay with his giant front-end loader, maneuvering it with incredible skill and agility, forward and backward to scoop up, then dump the load with precision and neatness. His finesse with such heavy equipment showed incredible skill and mastery of machine. All the while an enormous American flag fluttered proudly in the wind above his yellow and black Clydesdale.

All of this is nothing noteworthy. But what caught my eye each evening, was that no matter how torn-up or chaotic, or messy, or destroyed the job site had been during the day, it was ALWAYS returned to a smooth, gently sloped, pleasing to the eye, symmetrically shaped hill. No matter if I drove by early in the morning before work hours, or late in the evening running errands, there was always a pleasing, well groomed, safely sloped hillside!

I began to pay attention! I mean if it were me, and if I'm going to start over tomorrow doing the same thing, tearing apart a mountain, and load it on to trucks, why would I bother to clean up and neatly groom the hill? I'm just going to make the same mess tomorrow? Why waste all that time grooming and tidying up. As the days turned into weeks, and weeks into months I came to greatly admire the man with the white car. He was so good at what he did. He must care deeply about what he does. He must take great pride in his work. He must stand for quality, dedication and hard work. He must have believed in excellence over mediocrity. He certainly went beyond the average and, chose the extra mile. Each day I found myself affirming the man, blessing him, and appreciating him in my thoughts.

But there was one huge problem… the affirmations, the blessings, and the appreciating never made it outside my head. The words of appreciation remained in my private thoughts. And as much as I might wish that just by simply thinking good words and blessings for this man, I could affect him, the reality is… those thoughts would never reach that man if I did not speak those affirmations with my mouth directly to him, face to face, man to man. Oh, believe me, I thought about it, dozens of times. But that would be so awkward, right? I mean who drives into a constructions site and tells a dozer guy that he's doing a terrific job? That's crazy stuff, right? Why does a macho, blue-collar, heavy-equipment operator need an "Atta Boy" anyway?

Finally, my conscience screamed loud enough to make me put my money and words where my beliefs are. So, last week I gathered up my courage, shifted my FJ Cruiser into 4x4, and drove into the bumpy and muddy job site. I could mentally just hear him saying *"What in the heck is this little guy doing in here where the big boys play?"*

I shut off my vehicle, stepped out and self-consciously walked over to where he was perched high above me in the front-end loader. He shut it off as I climbed the ladder to the cab. Swallowing hard, as he opened the cab window, I awkwardly blurted out; *"Hey I just wanted you to know that you do a fantastic job out here. I've been watching you each day for months all summer and I can tell you really care about what you do, and I appreciate how you make this hill so neat and tidy each day. You do a great job. Just wanted you to know that."* Phew!!!

A beaming smile grew across his face and his shoulders drew back and he appeared to sit a little taller in the saddle. I paraphrase his response: *"Well you know, a man's gotta take pride in what he does! Got to do the best he possibly can. If you don't take pride in your work it's a reflection of your character. Ya know I just love what I do."* He pointed upward towards his giant American Flag. *"Did you notice the flag? I'm pretty damn proud of that too!"*

Yes, I did, and so much more. Roman, was his name, and he appeared more than grateful that I would stop, pay attention to, and point out the quality and character of his work. He appeared blessed by both my visit and my words. Funny thing is, as I drove off through the job site, I rode a little taller in my saddle knowing that I had made someone else's day.

You and I have been blessed, to be a blessing. We can do that with our time, our money, and our possessions, but one of the most practical, simple and most effective ways that we can bless others is through our words both written and spoken. You may think the world of someone, you may believe they stand for excellence, you may have strong admiration for one of their qualities or positive attributes, you may have witnessed them perform a superb act, or seen them do incredible work, you may have seen them perform heroically under pressure, you may have felt a positive mark and impact on your life from them ... but if those words remain silently stored in your head...

then you have wasted an opportunity to be a blessing. And they have missed out on an incredible blessing that maybe only you can bestow upon them. Thinking an affirmation, a kind word or a blessing does NOT COUNT! Thinking it does no one any good. You must act with courage to speak out loud or on paper your truth!

Have you blessed your kid's soccer or hockey coach with a kind note of appreciation for their passion, expertise, or investing in your child? Have you told the Starbucks window lady that her bright smile has bettered your day? Have you shaken hands with and looked into the eyes of your child's Sunday school or confirmation teacher and thanked them for loving on your son or daughter? Bosses, have you noticed the excellence and success of your employees and made a big deal of it with them? Employees, have you paused to stop in your boss's office to offer a kind word of thanks or appreciation for their leadership, their compassion or expertise? (Often, it's a lonely and unappreciated life at the top.) Can you notice and point out to your next supermarket check-out clerk when they are kind, friendly and helpful to you? Have you thanked an influential teacher or coach for investing in you? Can you offer up a kind word or handshake to the Walmart greeter that most people walk by? Would you dare to buy a homeless man a McDonalds meal and fellowship with him? Have you heard a sermon that blessed you… did you seek out to the preacher or text them a thank you? Or simply walk out the door like most of us? Have you noticed, paid attention to and commented on a kind or well-done act by your husband or wife? Did he cook a delicious meal? Did she clean the laundry room to high standards? Did his latest yard or house project go unnoticed or worse yet un-thanked in sincere ways?

You and I have tremendous power to use both our tongue and our brain to impact the world in positive ways for Jesus. We **CAN** make a difference in people's lives in simple, easy ways by just paying attention to and then acting with a blessing or kind word. And the greatest benefit of living your life with affirmations and blessings is that you get blessed by doing it!

Here's a challenge for you; Ever notice who some of the most content, full of life, charismatic, energetic, and beloved people are?

They are the ones that have mastered the art of affirmation; noticing, paying attention to and acting on blessing others with their words! They have learned to do it continually as an everyday habit!

May you have the courage to speak the words that have been given to you in your heart and head. Go out and bless someone in Jesus name! In the immortal words of Dirty Harry; "Go ahead Punk… make someone's Day!"

Praise only works with three types of people:
men, women, and children.

Whatever is true, whatever is noble, whatever is right, whatever is pure, whatever is lovely, whatever is admirable- if anything is excellent or praiseworthy- Think about such things! Philippians 4
Therefore encourage one another and build each other up, just as in fact you are doing. 1 Thessalonians 5:11
Let no corrupting talk come out of your mouths, but only such as is good for building up, as fits the occasion, that it may give grace to those who hear. Ephesians 4:9 NIV

Too often we underestimate the power of a touch, a smile, a kind word, a listening ear, an honest compliment, or the smallest act of caring, all of which have the potential to turn a life around. Leo Buscaglia

The biggest secret of dealing with people:
Give honest and sincere appreciation. Dale Carnegie

Let us spur on one another towards love and good deeds.
Let us encourage one another.
Hebrews 1-:24-25 NIV

THE MOST IMPORTANT MAN IN THE WORLD

Approaching the field, I searched the crowd and diamond for my friend. The infield was a bustle with excited players. Upon gaining the third base side, I spotted Zach warming up with his attendant Shelby. I shouted loudly; "Hey Zach!" He lifted his head, searched through the bright afternoon blinding sunshine, and then upon recognizing me, he began to run in random excited circles. After settling down he walked over, gave me a big smile, and hug, and a high five. I could sense Zach's true delight knowing I was here to watch him. I had arrived at the weekly Monday night adaptive baseball program. It was game time!

One-half of the players took to the specially designed field in Moorhead that had a soft rubbery floor. They spread out at various positions, some alone, some with a parent, some with an attendant nearby coaching and cheering them on. Most carried a glove. A designated pitcher threw up some gentle pitches, the opposing team stood one at a time for their turn at bat. There were no strikeouts, and after several pitches, if the batter didn't hit the ball, they could opt for a tee. Every hit got cheers and accolades until each player had batted. Then they switched sides.

Every time Zach chased down a ball or got a hit I cheered as loud as I could. Well, actually, we all did, and we did it for everyone! It was fun and fascinating to watch. No one kept score and there was none of the usually loud or obnoxious parents on the sideline who questioned the refs call, or their kids playing time, or the decisions of the coach that we normally see in today's overly- aggressive, and hyper-critical parenting for success. This was refreshing. This was about the love of the game, participation and encouraging these special young athletes. Joy, laughter, and love flowed freely both on and off the field. I smiled, sensing more than a bit of the divine and holy in our midst.

Paying Attention II

Upon arriving in my office in the morning, I had two phone messages, both from a very excited and fast-talking Milton. Milton is our forty-something man who faithfully shows up each Sunday morning and plays his tambourine for each contemporary worship services. Milton has a pronounced speech impediment that causes him to slur and eat his own words, which makes him very difficult to understand. Between the two messages, I thought I had interpreted his invitation to a picnic later in the morning that he had spoken of earlier on Sunday.

Upon finding the correct location, I wandered through the blocked off street in front of the Vocational Training Center, and there waiting for me with his ever-present grin was my friend Milton. Today was VTC's annual picnic. I asked Milton to give me a tour of the VTC, and he enthusiastically agreed. As we moved throughout the large center, I was introduced to virtually everyone, both his coworkers and staff. Everyone seemed to know and love Milton!

I was so impressed by the incredible work and ministry being done here at the VTC for these very special people. Several clients sat at tables stapling and labeling mailings. Next Milton took me into the massive shop, and the hum of saws and machinery made it difficult to hear, yet the familiar pleasing scent of freshly cut pine and cedar made me feel at home. The shop builds gorgeous cedar Adirondack chairs and cuts various sized wooden survey stakes that they sell to contractors.

Each person had a specific task and machine that they worked on. As I toured each station, I loudly shouted a compliment or high-fived each worker. The genuine pride each person took in their work was obvious and their beaming smiles of appreciation lit up the shop. These beautiful and special folks had found meaningful and purposeful work. It was obvious that the staff supervisors showered love and affection on their workers.

Milton finished our tour by showing me the several bathrooms that he is responsible for cleaning each day. He proudly showed me each one, and what he has to do to keep it clean. His smile grew wider for pride in a job well done, and being able to show that off to someone else.

Leaving the shop, we sat a table on the street. The smell of burgers and hotdogs filled the air. There were plenty of wheelchairs and walkers, but most wandered through the tables freely. A fun and festive atmosphere surrounded us as friends, family, clients, and staff greeted one another, hugged and high-fived. I felt honored to have been invited by Milton to such a beautiful celebration. There was so much genuine love, affection, caring and acceptance going around. It was palpable.

Ironically the most powerful man on earth, The Donald, was standing before thousands just a few short miles away. People had stood in line for hours just to get a glimpse of him even if just in the motorcade. Scheels arena was packed to capacity, with standing room only outside. People, in general, are drawn to and seek out people of power, wealth, importance and fame. What is it that drives us or draws us to move higher and higher?

The most powerful man in the world would never have shown up at this picnic. His power, wealth and fame were too great to allow time spent with the humble, the lonely, the simple and the meek. Yet there is One greater than this most powerful man on earth. **He** is the most powerful man in the **universe**, and I know that He, Jesus, was present and weaving in and among these beautiful, loving people during out picnic and baseball game.

Jesus specialized in moving downward, like water flowing at a baptism, Jesus always moved to place Himself lower and lower to where the need was greatest. Jesus gave up all power, comfort, and prestige as the creator of the universe, to humbly lower himself and enter into a broken and flawed world as a helpless, powerless baby. Jesus purposely chose a downward path to walk and be present amongst the poor and oppressed. He never sought out kings, or princes or presidents, or the famous.

In all reality, Jesus trumps Trump any second of any day.

Jesus never sought fame or fortune, nor did he ever clamor for attention. He never sought wealth or worldly honors or accolades. He simply wandered and mingled with simple, hurting, people who were downtrodden, sinful and broken. He specialized in being with and present with the lepers, the lame, the lost and the lowly.

I don't believe Jesus would have attended the Trump rally. I have no doubt whatsoever though, that Jesus did, in fact, join us at the VTC picnic, and the adaptive baseball game.

May you and I follow Jesus' example. May we put aside our natural desires to connect with fame, wealth, power and the upward climb of material wealth and recognition. May we instead move downward to seek out those who are in greatest need of a Jesus touch or presence. You are the face, words and hands of Jesus in our world.

Blessed are the meek, for they will inherit the earth. Matthew 5:5

just as the Son of Man did not come to be served, but to serve, and to give his life as a ransom for many." Matthew 20:28

Sitting down, Jesus called the Twelve and said, "Anyone who wants to be first must be the very last, and the servant of all." Mark 9:35

Whoever serves me must follow me; and where I am, my servant also will be. My Father will honor the one who serves me. John 12:26

And whoever would be first among you must be slave of all. For even the Son of Man came not to be served but to serve, and to give his life as a ransom for many." Mark 10: 44-45

In all things I have shown you that by working hard in this way we must help the weak and remember the words of the Lord Jesus, how he himself said, 'It is more blessed to give than to receive.'" Acts 20:35

The Path

The sun blazed brightly and beat down upon us with a rare October heatwave. Sweat trickled down our brows from both the heat and the exertion of the trail. Pure, deep, cobalt blue skies met precisely with the jagged tan and grey horizons of badlands hills and coulees. Dark green juniper trees laced the landscape and hillsides along with the occasional brightly yellowed cottonwoods and aspen which added color and contrast to the dry desert landscape. Perfectly parallel layers of pinks and purples, coffees, grey, and rusts splayed out across both hill and valley forming a horizontal stratum to the entire panorama.

We were here hiking a twenty-mile portion of the 140-mile Maah Daah Hey hiking trail in western North Dakota. The rugged beauty, magnificence, and grandeur of this terrain are difficult to capture in words. Literally, every twist, turn or bend in the trail revealed some new magical vista, breathtaking outlook or unique rock formation. The combined long- term effects of rain, wind, erosion and time had created some of the most creative and intriguing natural sculptures. I at times felt as if we were embedded in a Star Wars movie and had been planted into another world light years away.

This Maah Daah Hey trail is pure eye candy for the soul. The expansive vistas, wide open plateau crossings, and endless snaking valleys seemed to open my mind, settle my spirit and give me a perspective beyond my normal self. The profound silences devoid of man's machines and technologies that ring and beep, allowed my spirit to soar and rise above the perceived problems, daily issues and petty situations that so often drag down my attitude and demeanor. The gentle sounds of nature; the quiet breeze tickling the leaves of a cottonwood, birds chirping, the overhead flight of honking of sand-hill cranes, and the chorus of coyotes were all soothing melodies that calmed the restlessness and noise of my normally agitated body, mind and soul.

The combination of vigorous physical exercise, disconnecting from man-made electronics, quiet, solitude, immersion in nature and man to man honest conversations on the hiking trail or 'round a warm fire was renewing each of us. God was in the process of restoring, re-creating, refreshing, recharging and revitalizing each person down to their core. The Bad Lands were working as God's own repair and revive clinic.

The principal of the Maah Daah Hey is really quite simple; just follow the path. And yet the MDH is unique in that it uses 6"x6" posts that are placed throughout the entire length of the trail. The premise is that you should be able to see the next post from the post you are at. You simply connect the dots so to speak, by following the trail, post to post. The posts are branded with a sign of a turtle. The turtle is the symbol of the MDH, and is a perfect metaphor; go slow and steady, enjoy the journey, don't race or rush. Just walk faithfully, slow and steady. Keep your eyes up and enjoy and relish all that has been placed before you.

In hiking the MDH, one rarely gets to see more than one post in front of you. Occasionally you'll get a glimpse of a second or third post way out there on a high plateau, but most of the time you simply follow along one post a time. One step at a time, one post at a time moves you steadily forward towards your goal. You never get to see the entire route as it twists and snakes and turns and dives and climbs continually through hill and dale, coulee and ridge top. Imagine how overwhelming it would be to actually see all those posts laid out... before you. Your spirit would be crushed and exhausted seeing the volume, distance, effort and workload ahead of you. NO! On the MDH... one step at a time, one post at a time, slow and steady helps you both enjoy the journey and the beauty that surrounds you and eventually in good time, arrive safely at your destination. Simply follow the way of the turtle, the path that is laid out before you.

Jesus said quite bluntly and clearly; *"I am the way and the truth and the life. No one comes to the Father except through me." John 14:6. NIV*

Today can you follow the way, the path one step at a time, one post at a time, can you live in this one day that God has set before you. If your eyes and hopes and dreams or worries or fears or anxieties are set on a time or place out there in the future somewhere, you will completely miss all that God has placed before you today as His blessings, teachings and learning opportunities. Today may have difficulties, struggles and gut-busting, thigh burning, uphill climbs that zap your energy, challenge your sanity and test your faith to be sure. But, there will also be hidden blessings and treasures strewn all about your path if you but have eyes to see them. Jesus lays it out very concisely;

> *"I have told you these things, so that in me you may have peace. In this world you will have trouble. But take heart! I have overcome the world." John 16: 33 NIV*

Whether you turn to the right or to the left, your ears will hear a voice behind you, saying, "This is the way; walk in it." Isaiah 30:21 NIV

This is what the Lord says: "Stand at the crossroads and look; ask for the ancient paths, ask where the good way is, and walk in it, and you will find rest for your souls. But you said, 'We will not walk in it.'
Jeremiah 6:16 NIV

The Road Less Traveled

The rolling plains lay before us like a vast never-ending sea of green grass and blue-grey sage. Billowed clouds floated across the deep blue sky like battleships in formation heading eastwards. Late afternoon sunshine bathed the landscape in warmth and amber glow elevating both my mood and outlook. Distant hills and landmarks that appeared to be within easy reach, took far longer to gain as we were lost in the time and space warp of the western Dakota prairies.

As our vehicle rose with the gentle ascent of the high way to the high point in the gap of the butte, I decelerated and signaled right. Turning on to a little known and almost hidden forest road, I shifted the FJ Cruiser into 4-wheel drive. Let the fun begin!

We slowly ascended the rough and rugged, poorly maintained road weaving left and right to maintain the higher ground, bumping and bobbing upwards through the sweet-smelling ponderosa pines we continued upward. Gaining the top of the mesa the road leveled out. Crossing through a gated fence we proceeded to follow a grassy trail virtually untouched or unused for months. The un-trampled knee-high grass gave testimony that we were the lone and sole visitors this summer. Proceeding southward we quietly gained elevation until we reached the edge. Shutting off the truck, I could almost hear the gasp in Rob's voice as he witnessed the incredible beauty and vista before us. *"Welcome to camp, my friend! This is our home for the evening! Welcome to Slim Buttes."*

We literally made camp right where we camped, parked hanging our hammocks near the edge of the 150' cliffs for a magnificent penthouse view. Peace, serenity and beauty surrounded us filling our senses of sight, sound and smell and adding a quiet stillness to the end of our day.

As we roasted brats and beans over a crackling fire our sore and aching bodies craved the nutrition. Ice-cold water and barely pop soothed our parched palettes. Our early morning climb of Devil's Tower in eastern Wyoming had zapped our energies. In exchange for the euphoria of a successful climb, we had paid a costly price of exhaustion and painful muscles, most of which had heretofore gone unrecognized. This peaceful and picturesque campsite was bringing healing to body and spirit alike.

Paying Attention II

Finishing off a brat, Rob inquisitively asked; *"How did you ever find this place? It's gorgeous!"* I laughed and had to hesitate before answering. *"I guess it's just from years and years of exploring, pouring over maps and poking and prodding here and there. I just go."*

You'll never find these hidden unique places in a travel brochure, or guide book. It's not Wally World or Jellystone Park where all the masses congregate. These are places that you must find on your own.

We live in the most unique country in the world. As citizens of the U.S., we have access to enormous amounts of public land in National and State Forests and Grasslands. Millions and millions of acres of land free to any of us who choose to adventure and explore in both vehicles and on foot. And the great benefit for people like me is that most people don't! Most people stick to the common path, the paved highway, the known road, the travel brochure, and the tourist attractions. We have such an immense gift in the form of freedom, that few of us embrace or use.

I believe our faith lives are so very similar. God gives us such immense freedom. We receive the freedom to explore and cherish life in all its facets of love, relationships, family, work, and play. I believe one of the greatest freedoms he bestows upon us is the freedom to become the unique and wonder-filled person that he created us to be. Yet, most of us, out of conformity, simply chose the path that everyone else is on, and go where everyone else is going, and get what everyone else has, and act like everyone else to fit in and be accepted. And yet the irony is that the closer we are in our walk with Jesus, the more freedom we will experience. And this complete Godly freedom will develop in us the unique personality and life's path for which he created us.

C.S. Lewis writes: The more we let God take us over, the more truly ourselves we become- because he made us. It is when I turn to Christ, when I give up myself to His personality, that I first begin to have a real personality of my own.

Out of the park C.S.! Well said!

Do not be conformed to this world, but be transformed by the renewal of your mind, that by testing you may discern what is the will of God, what is good and acceptable and perfect will. Romans 12:2 NIV

We are all called to the same life of faith; to love God with our heart, soul, and mind, and to love our neighbor as ourselves. And we are all called to serve others through our gifts, time and talents. But we are not called to be Christian Drones who look, act and sound alike. Choose freedom! Choose the road less traveled! Explore and follow the unique path that God is calling you to experience.

The Road Not Taken- Robert Frost

Two roads diverged in a yellow wood, And sorry I could not travel both
And be one traveler, long I stood, And looked down one as far as I could
To where it bent in the undergrowth; Then took the other, as just as fair,
And having perhaps the better claim, Because it was grassy and wanted wear;
Though as for that the passing there, Had worn them really about the same,
And both that morning equally lay, In leaves no step had trodden black.
Oh, I kept the first for another day! Yet knowing how way leads on to way,
I doubted if I should ever come back.
I shall be telling this with a sigh, Somewhere ages and ages hence:
Two roads diverged in a wood, and I—
I took the one less traveled by,
And that has made all the difference.

Then you will know the truth, and the truth will set you Free!
John 8:32 NIV

So if the Son sets you Free, you will be free indeed! John 8:36 NIV

Now the Lord is the Spirit,
and where the Spirit of the Lord is, there is freedom!
2 Corinthians 3:17 NIV

It is for Freedom that Christ has set us free! Stand firm then, and do not let yourselves be burdened again by a yoke of slavery. Galatians 5:1 NIV

The life of faith is a life of freedom within the boundaries of love and in the context of responsibility. It is to let the Spirit make us more truly what God knows we can be. Gerhard Frost- Journey of the Heart

The Things We've Handed Down

It was a big day. A cause for great celebration! Joseph Natwick, one of First Lutheran's own son's, was being ordained as a pastor. A long and faith-filled journey had led him in a twisting, turning, and circuitous route that ended up back at the altar in First Lutheran Church. I've had the unique privilege of a ringside seat to watch Joe's life evolve and develop over twenty plus years. I watched as he grew and evolved as a musician and for many years, he joined us on the Celebration stage to help lead worship playing guitar, bass, singing and often playing his trumpet. He and his brother Jake often did duets. He became a familiar and friendly face to anyone who joined us for worship.

As he grew through adolescence, he started jumping in on many of our outdoor adventure trips. Winter camping in the Boundary Waters, the original canoe building project, canoe trips, backpacking in Wyoming and the ultimate adventure of climbing Devil's tower in Wyoming. Joe was finding his true self and his Creator in the midst of Creation. Exactly, what I've hoped for, for each participant over all these years, but not all seeds fall on receptive soil. The strong seeds of faith had definitely found fertile ground in the heart and life of Joe. So I smiled, wholeheartedly, as I shared in the celebration of Joe's ordination.

The Forum newspaper carried a very nice article of Joe the week before, where he stated that one of his key moments of faith awakening, was on one of our youth retreats at Camp Wilderness. He mentioned how impactful the Blindfold Faith Walk was for him, in which we lead participants who cling to a common rope, in the darkness of the night, blindfolded through the forest. Joe speaks of it as one of his "Ah ha" God moments, so to speak.

Though very proud to have been the leader of that retreat and activity, I can hardly claim any credit for its origination. For I remember, clear as day, a long time ago, when I was a 9th grader attending a youth retreat at Camp Wapogasset bible camp in Amery, Wisconsin, when my then youth pastor, Craig Hanson, had us partner up and do a similar blindfolded trust walk. I too remember having an "ah ha" faith moment where something clicked inside me, and I came home telling mom and dad that; "I get it," just a little bit more about this God thing. The visceral experience of blindness, and walking in the dark, trusting in someone that I could not see, just made sense in my gut. The activity was experiential, not just the empty words and rhetoric of one more talking head sermon or confirmation lesson, but a hands-on, full-body, life-faith experience. What had worked for me, via this experiential faith walk, was given to me by Craig. I had simply handed it down several dozen times, to others, and woven it into the fabric of my own ministry.

On my bookshelf are two special bibles. One has the gilded, golden words; Beverly Ann Miller stamped on the cover, my mother's maiden name. Within the well-worn pages, are many notations written in her lively cursive. Reading her notes, and catching what she'd underlined, allows me renewed insight into the depth of faith that she so passionately handed down. The other bible is that of Louise Johnson, my father's mother, my grandmother. She too loved her Bible and wore it out with notations, underlines, and endless use. Her undying faith passed down through my father, landed in a receptive heart. I pray, with all my soul, that this passionate faith, will also be handed down to my three children.

My eldest daughter Karina, and her husband Taylor, just returned from a week of backpacking in the Sawtooth Wilderness of Idaho. My middle daughter Marissa just re-upped her membership at the NDSU rock climbing wall and climbs there twice a week with gusto and enthusiasm. I smile with pride and gratitude that my young ladies have continued to pursue interests and passions that have simply been, handed down.

Faith, passions, and interests are most often caught, not taught. I couldn't agree more. And one never knows what will get caught, or handed down. I often worry over what negative traits my own children will have picked up from me. Sometimes the bad stuff, if not checked, will also get handed down. Anger, anxiety, fear, prejudice, hatred, negative attitude, abuse, addiction, cursing, a critical spirit, disrespect, workaholism, or laziness can all be modeled and handed down just as easily as the good stuff.

May you and I pay careful attention to what we model, say and do. There are real-life, and eternal consequences for who we are, and what we hand down in this world.

Train up a child in the way he should go, Even when he is old he will not depart from it. Proverbs 22:6 ESV

Fathers, do not provoke your children to anger but bring them up in the discipline and instruction of the Lord. Ephesians 6:4 ESV

Discipline your son, and he will give you rest; he will give delight to your heart. Proverbs 29:17 ESV

I have no greater joy than to hear that my children are walking in the truth. 3 John 1: NIV

Jesus replied: "'Love the Lord your God with all your heart and with all your soul and with all your mind.' This is the first and greatest commandment. And the second is like it: 'Love your neighbor as yourself.' All the Law and the Prophets hang on these two commandments." Matthew 22:37-39 NIV

My son, keep your father's command and do not forsake your mother's teaching.

Bind them always on your heart; fasten them around your neck. When you walk, they will guide you;
when you sleep, they will watch over you; when you awake, they will speak to you.
For this command is a lamp, this teaching is a light. Proverbs 6:20 NIV

Timberwolf

He glided effortlessly over the landscape. His purposeful stride appeared as if he floated over the surrounding topography. He followed a trail carved in the dirty snow that would soon lead him directly in front of me. I marveled at his rich, thick coat of hair and fur that tussled in the slight breeze as the warm afternoon sun illuminated a hundred variations of colors of which I could barely name a few. Along his back and shoulders were lengthy, luxuriant black guard hairs, silver and gray, mixed with light highlights of tan and coffee that subtly merged into the white of underbelly. A long, profuse bushy tail followed his fit, powerful body. His weight held forward of center in the chest, and four long legs carried a purposeful gait.

As he neared my vantage point, he paused, standing stoically to face me, a mere four feet away, he on a slight rise in the terrain which put him at eye level. His dished facial mask was centered by his golden eyes that appeared to have been outlined with thick dark mascara giving him an intense, focused, and haunting gaze. His penetrating stare seemed to pierce into my soul searching and probing for answers that I did not possess. I shifted uneasily under the intense scrutiny.

I felt a fervent sense of awe and privilege to be in such intimate proximity with this apex predator of the northern woods, this, the mystical and mysterious Timber Wolf, a.k.a; *Canis Lupus*.

He stood tolerant and ascetic as he averted his resolute stare from me, raising his regal head to sniff the southerly breeze. Was he scenting the herd of elk bedded a mere 150 yards away? Had those intoxicating scents aroused in him a hunger? A yearning for the chase? Was he reminiscing freedom long lost, or lamenting what could not be?

Soon his haunting gaze returned to me... and then a thing most strange happened. He began to quietly whimper. I felt as if I was in my living room listening to my dog Bruno, beg to be let outside. Was he too, begging, pleading, imploring, to be released, to be set free? My heart broke. I did not possess the power or authority to release him. The chain-link fence of Bismarck's Dakota Zoo stood between us and held this majestic creature prisoner to the boredom, monotony and endless repetitive routine of a life lived on one-half acre.

In recent days since my encounter with the yellow-eyed wolf, I have been troubled by convoluted thoughts and feelings. On the one hand, without the cage and prison of the zoo, I would not be writing these words. I could never have had that up-close, personalized face to face encounter with a live wolf, nor my children, nor the thousands who visit this zoo and zoos like this across the planet. And yet my dominant and pervasive thought that rips at my gut, is that a magnificent predator like this wolf was not meant to spend his life pacing back and forth in circles behind a chain link fence! He was created for so much more! Our Creator fashioned and purposed him with highly specialized talents, abilities, and traits. None of which involve pacing in the same-old, same-old, enclosure day after day.

I wonder... for many Christians, if it is not the same. We were purposely built, created and fashioned with a highly specialized set of talents, abilities, traits, and personalities. Yet in our daily life routine and ritual habits of faith life, we simply pace back and forth in our tiny little, familiar, known, and comfortable cages wearing deep ruts into the topography of life's terrain. We yearn and whimper for something more, something different, something that we know is missing and we can scent and sense is just out of bounds.

Maybe the fence that hems us in is *the world* with its expectations of get more, buy more, make more, have more, so we slave away at our routine jobs to earn the pay that will seemingly provide the funding to catch up with the Jones's who live just outside the fence.

For many of us the churchy rules, traditions, regulations, rituals, habits, religiosity and expectations of who, what and how a "good" Christian *should be,* fence us in on all sides. The Jesus we claim to follow and believe in; the *"Lion of Judah,"* has been castrated, declawed, defanged and stuck inside the fence often called *"the church."* So we plow into another lifeless worship service giving nothing of ourselves, endure a monotonous string of religious words called a sermon, throw in the leftover scraps of our God-given income to the offering plate, and walk out the door asking, *"Is this all there is?"*

A life lived behind the fence is hardly what we were created for! We are created, purposed and gifted for so much more. Listen to these fantastic, life-giving words; *"It is for freedom that Christ has set us free. "Stand firm, then, and do not let yourselves be burdened again by a yoke of slavery." Galatians 5:1*

For many of us, we pray to "God," and some of us take it one more step of intimacy by praying to Jesus. But rarely do we tap into and engage the power of the Holy Spirit that has been gifted and planted inside of each of us. It is a *fact*, not wishful thinking. The *Spirit* of God indwells within each of us. And this spirit is no wimpy, benign, passive, weak or routine spirit! You and I have the privilege to live with and be led by the power and freedom of the Holy Spirit!

So maybe this week, it's time to switch it up a bit, let go of the rote, normal prayer routine, step outside the boundaries and pray to the Holy Spirit. One word of caution though... Watch out! For where the winds of The Spirit blow... great, wonderful and unexpected events and encounters will shake you out of those ruts!

Now the Lord is the Spirit, and where the Spirit of the Lord is, there is freedom. 2 Corinthians 3:17 NIV

For the Spirit God gave us does not make us timid, but gives us power, love, and self-discipline.
2 Timothy 1:7 NIV

But you will receive power when the Holy Spirit comes on you; and you will be my witnesses in Jerusalem, and in all Judea and Samaria, and to the ends of the earth." Acts 1:8 NIV

In him and through faith in him we may approach God with freedom and confidence. Ephesians 3:12 NIV

The wind blows wherever it pleases. You hear it sound, but you cannot tell where it comes from
or where it is going. So it is with everyone born of the Spirit! John 3:8 NIV

In the same way, the Spirit helps us in our weakness.
We do not know what we ought to pray for,
but the Spirit himself intercedes for us
with groans that words cannot express. Romans 8:26 NIV

Topes

The deep, rich greenery of the surrounding rainforest was nurturing my chilled soul, long frozen from a long North Dakota winter and frazzled church work. The warm sun dappling through openings in the canopy added highlights and bright spots to both the thick flora and my mood. The clean, thick, humid air was cleansing me from the inside out. The winding two-lane snaked relentlessly over and through and around the thickly foliated mountains of southern Chiapas as we dove deeper into the Lacandona jungle headed for the Guatemalan border.

As our road passed through numerous small hamlets and villages, we continually encountered the ever-present Mexican speed reducer called "topes", their version of speedbumps. Each little settlement had several topes, spread across their length of highway to slow down passing vehicles. To say that these topes worked is to also say that they readily added to the carsickness factor as we would speed up, brake to a slow halt, and repeat hundreds of times throughout our journey. I came to curse the dreaded topes!

Not only did topes serve as a safety device for both pedestrians and vehicles alike, but they also served to further capitalism. At virtually every tope, men, women and most frequently young children would rush out alongside our van hawking their wares loudly, hoisting in the air with both arms their merchandise of freshly peeled oranges, bananas, tortillas, sugar cane, and a variety of other fresh produce. Their beautifully tanned faces and pearly white teeth showed brightly in the warm light of the Mexican sun just inches from my open-air passenger window.

At each passing topes, I simply smiled, waved and issued a polite; "No Gracias!" For the few brief seconds of each roadside encounter, their eyes would lock on mine, and it appeared as though they were most likely intrigued by this blue-eyed, graying gringo.

As our journey continued, I continually pondered; what is my role here? As someone who has been given so much, how do I connect to or react to or help out these who have been given so much less? How is it that I have so much, and they so little, simply due to the location of our birthplaces? The tension in my soul would not abate.

Our winding roadway dove deeper into the green abyss as we pushed onward to the south. And then, after several hours, the highway simply terminated at a large river. We'd made it; the Usumacinta River. Across the river lay the country of Guatemala. Along the shore were dozens of 30-40' long, narrow boats, and we made our way to the water's edge as several boat captains schmoozed and haggled for our business. Choosing the friendliest one, ironically named "Rolando", we boarded his long boat and headed downstream for the 15-mile journey to the riverside ruins of Yachitlán. Along the fabulous journey, crocodiles slid from the muddy shores, and when the captain cut the motor a band of howler monkeys could be heard growling across the river. To the uninitiated, they sounded more like full-size African Lions roaring at close range.

On our return journey, I sat in the bow of the boat, with warm sunshine and thick wind blowing on my face, pondering this unique place on the planet, again contemplating my connection to this land and its peoples. Mentally I traced the origins of this scenic river from the highlands of Chiapas down the border and out through the coastal plains of Tabasco. I followed the western coast of the Gulf of Mexico past Vera Cruz, on up past Matamoros and the border to Corpus Christi, and moving east I find the outlet of the mighty Mississippi and turn north to New Orleans. I trace the Big Muddy northward past St. Louis, and onto St. Paul. Taking a left at Fort Snelling, I head upstream on the Minnesota River past Mankato and New Ulm and head northwest to pass through Lac Qui Parle, Big Stone Lake, and Lake Traverse and onto the Bois de Sioux Rivers that then form the Red River of the North. I float this downstream eventually passing through Fargo Moorhead, and on the northern limits of Moorhead, I turn right onto the Oakport Coulee which snakes its way northward a mile or so, and then I park my canoe along the edge of the dike, climb over and arrive in my yard.

So maybe, I have a greater connection to these border people than I originally thought. We share at the very least a common geographic connection via waterways. What I do with my water resources could eventually affect them and vice versa. In these times of global warming, this connection becomes more real. We share a common backyard; planet earth.

So today I continue to ponder, how I may become a better steward of the resources that God has given me, in ways that honor Him, the earth that He has provided, and my fellow neighbors near and far.

"Treat the earth well: it was not given to you by your parents, it was loaned to you by your children. We do not inherit the Earth from our Ancestors, we borrow it from our Children." Ancient Indian Proverb

God blessed them and said to them, "Be fruitful and increase in number; fill the earth and subdue it. Rule over the fish in the sea and the birds in the sky and over every living creature that moves on the ground." Then God said, "I give you every seed-bearing plant on the face of the whole earth and every tree that has fruit with seed in it. They will be yours for food. And to all the beasts of the earth and all the birds in the sky and all the creatures that move along the ground—everything that has the breath of life in it—I give every green plant for food." And it was so. God saw all that he had made, and it was very good. And there was evening, and there was morning—the sixth day. Genesis 1:22-28 NIV

Each of you should use whatever gift you have received to serve others, as faithful stewards of God's grace in its various forms. 1 Peter 4:10 NIV

Tourist or Pilgrim

The massive cathedral was packed. Several hundred sat in the pews, and several hundred more of us stood wall to wall using every nook and cranny of the ancient church. I leaned with my back against a massive pillar that rose a hundred feet towards towering arches high in the ceiling. A sense of the holy was present and tangible. I could feel it deep inside.

People of every shape, size, and color were present and there was a unique sense of both anticipation and closure in the air. People had come from all corners of the earth. Dozens of languages could be heard quietly mumbling before the service began. But with all the variety of people gathered in the massive cathedral, one could boil down the crowd into two basic groups; tourists and pilgrims.

Unfortunately for me, I fell into the tourist category, a role I care not to play. Tourists visit very temporarily, take lots of pictures which are now-a-days mostly the "selfie" type of this generation. Being a tourist has very little investment. Very little skin in the game. Very little is demanded of a tourist. Simply show up, snap few photos, and move on to the next attraction or distraction you might say.

The great bulk of the crowd though were "pilgrims" who carried backpacks, walking sticks or trekking poles. Many wore headbands and nylon hiking shorts or walking pants. Many sported duct-taped toes, many had knees wrapped in athletic tape. Some were twelve years old, some were eighty-seven. Some walked with a distinctive limp.

Many had the look of joy and satisfaction for completing a long and arduous journey. Some you could observe were saddened and nostalgic for having finished a significant chapter in their lives by completing this journey. Many hugged friends they had met along the way. Most of these pilgrims had walked for four to six weeks and over 500 miles hiking the world-famous Camino de Santiago, or Way of St. James. Gathered here in the Iglesia de Santiago de Compostela marked the end of their pilgrimage.

The Camino de Santiago has been around for a wee bit of time; starting in the 8th century and has grown ever since. People from all walks of life come to make this famous pilgrimage.

Starting on the French side of the border, this historic journey traverses much of northern Spain from the snow-covered mountains through the wheat-filled plains of the "Meseta" and dozens of small towns and villages along the way. Aged castles and churches fill the route with history and intrigue. Each day pilgrims travel at their own pace, carrying a light backpack of clothes on their backs for 10-15 miles.

Following the clamshell signs that mark "The Way" on cobblestone streets and road signs, they stop each afternoon at a Hostel where they can find a clean bed, lodging, and meals for a reasonable price and tend to their blisters, sores and body aches.

Of late the Camino de Santiago has become quite popular: a chic, hip – "cross it off your bucket list" type thing to do. You can meet people from all over the world, party like a rock star each night, eat exotic foods, drink fabulous wine and challenge yourself to say; "I did it." But the true intention of the pilgrimage and many still hold to the original purpose, is to simply walk "the way" with God. That is, walk for an extended time, remove yourself from the ordinary distractions of daily life and talk with Jesus as you walk. You put your trust in God to provide for you through the kindness and hospitality of the Hospitallers, those who run the hostels. You are to learn from their grace, compassion and servant's heart. And then you just walk… and you talk with your Maker and Creator.

And with this long and tiring journey, God goes to work on you. With this huge investment of yourself and your time, you wrestle with Him. You share what's causing you anxiety and fear and worry. You surrender your idols and things that you cling to so tightly like your identity, your job, or your toys. You ask difficult questions and walk through the answers many of which are never given on your journey. You listen and you reflect. You shout in anger, exhaustion, and frustration, and at times you lift your arms in praise for a magnificent sunrise, or one more day to walk the trail of life, or humbly give thanks for the kindness shown by a stranger. Sometimes you are just silent, knowing that God is present and walking by your side.

Tourists never go that deep. Tourists take the easy way. Tourists show up and snap a couple of photos and move on to the next distraction. Tourists show up on Sunday mornings at church then leave never having been affected internally. Tourists let others teach Sunday school, lead VBS, cook for a funeral, give sacrificially to the church, or go on a mission trip. Tourists are about the destination and the selfie, pilgrims are about the journey with God each and every day. Tourists run to the next big thing, pilgrims ask how can I see and experience

God today on my daily walk. Tourists love noise, crowds, activity, and distraction. Pilgrims love silence and the sound, sights, and scents of creation that bring life and healing. Tourists come to church and just sit. Pilgrims sing with all their heart soul and mind even if they can't sing because that's what worship is all about! Tourists take. Pilgrims give and experience and live life to the fullest knowing that God is with them at every bend in life's trail. They know that God is in the difficult, arduous and painful challenge of an endless uphill climb, and that God is in the easy, celebratory coasting downhill, and that God is also in the mundane, endless plodding of the boring flats of everyday life.

I have taken many such pilgrimages over the years. My pilgrimages were never about going to a holy or sacred shrine or church but mostly solos into and through wilderness areas of the north and west. I have found each of these solo experiences to be incredible journeys into understanding myself and strengthening and deepening my relationship with God. When you walk alone for extended periods of time without the distractions of computers and phones, it is only natural to turn your heart, your eyes, your ears and your voice to the One Who Made you.

To hike or walk for exercise is good and healthy for the body and mind. It's an excellent daily habit or discipline. But let it not stop there… just raw exercise. To walk humbly while talking to God your Creator and Maker moves to the realm of Holy and Sacred. There is something wholesome, right, Godly and healing about walking. One need not travel to Spain. You can simply go out in nature and walk humbly with your God. You can do it today. May God be with you and bless your journey. *Buen Camino!*

*To act justly and to love mercy
and to walk humbly with your God. Micah 6:8 NIV*

*Thus says the LORD,
Stand at the Crossroads, and see, and ask for the ancient paths,
Where the good way is, and walk in it;
And you will find rest for your souls. Jeremiah 6:16 NIV*

Trust in the Lord with all your heart and lean not on your own understanding; in all your ways acknowledge Him, and He will make your paths straight. Proverbs 3:5 NIV

If you knew Who walks beside you on the way that you have chosen,
worry and fear would be impossible.

When you walk in beauty outside,
You walk in beauty on the inside.

Everybody needs beauty as well as bread.
Places to play in and pray in, where nature
may heal, and give strength to the
body and soul alike. John Muir

Tracks in the Coulee

The morning had passed most uneventfully. Having logged a couple of hours seated in my tree stand since long before dawn, the single digit temps had stiffened my body. Wrapped from head to toe in down and wool, like the proverbial poofy Micheline Man, I had been quite comfortable. With only my eyes and cheeks exposed to the elements of cold and wind, I was determined that the severe cold would not rob me of the opportunity at a big buck. Having only seen a couple does at a distance too far for my longbow, I had reached my patience quota and opted for packing up and descending to mother earth.

I always enjoy the morning hike out as it's a chance to stretch my legs and explore the woods for sign and spoor. With the recent dusting of snow, it would be easy to discern who else was sharing this small copse of woods north of town, either man or beast.

As I approached the southern end of the woodlot, I chose to scoot down into the coulee proper. Pushing my way through the dense cattails and swamp grass I quickly gained the flat opening of the creek bed. With the recent light snow-fall, the creek had become a virtual reverse chalkboard, or whiteboard if you will. A perfect tracking medium. The black of tracks meeting ice contrasted perfectly with white of the snow. Of course, a couple of our local whitetails had used this easy pathway as a highway of sorts. Their easily discernable heart-shaped tracks were easy to follow as they meandered down the coulee.

Our local Wiley E. Coyote had also been frequenting this freeway as he ambled back and forth leaving his mark on occasional tufts of cattail or grass. Wiley E. had left the classic 4x4 pad marks of the canine family and easily identifiable oval-shaped track shape. His gate showed a moderate hunting gate as he sniffed and poked his way towards parts unknown.

To my delight, running alongside the edges of the cattails were the tell-tale 5x5 toe pattern and rounded track of an otter. The otter had scampered along the creek checking out every grassy tunnel or opening most likely seeking out an unwary rabbit or muskrat. His much smaller cousin and fellow mustelid, *(family of animals that secret a potent scent from anal glands)* a buck mink had also rambled down the creek in the opposite direction, behaving much like his larger cousin, exploring, poking and peeking into any available nook or cranny.

What a busy night it had been on the Oakport Coulee! And what a great diversity of travelers! One species of prey and three distinct predators! I was thrilled to be reading this recently published book now spread out before me on the white pages of the creek ice.

We **all** leave tracks. Everywhere we go, every time, every animal, and every human. And one of the great truths of tracking is that a line of tracks will always lead to either a living being… or a dead one. No exception. There is no in between.

So, if a gifted tracker were to follow the recent tracks of your life as they meander through the world… would they find a person alive, living life to the fullest, living on purpose with meaning and significance? Living in relationship and in cooperation with the God of the Universe to make a positive difference in our world for the short period of time we are here on planet earth? Or would they find a dead being? Or worse yet… a zombie, who goes through the motions and actions of life… imitating life so to speak, but not really living? Would the trail of your life, be a worthy path for someone else to follow? As we read the sign of your life, what would we see? What would be the landmarks? Would your tracks point to self-service or service towards others? Jesus boldly declares: *I have come that they may have life, and have it abundantly. John 10:10 ESV*

"I am the way and the truth and the life. No one comes to the Father except through me. John 14:6 NIV

God gives us such immense freedom to choose our path, our way, our career, our mate, our pass-times and so much more. And yet if we travel the path of life without getting *"Jesus"* right. We will lead a mostly empty, fruitless and unfulfilling life.

But seek first his kingdom and his righteousness, and all these things will be given to you as well. Matthew 6:33

May you live a life filled with purpose, joy (choosing an attitude of gratitude), contentment and positive impact. I believe the only way to do this is to be in a relationship with Jesus!

But because of his great love for us, God, who is rich in mercy, made us alive with Christ even when we were dead in transgressions—it is by grace you have been saved. And God raised us up with Christ and seated us with him in the heavenly realms in Christ Jesus, Ephesians 2: 4-6 **NIV**

The Dash *Author: Linda Ellis*

I read of a man who stood to speak at the funeral of a friend

He referred to the dates on her tombstone, from the beginning to the end

He noted that first came her date of her birth, and spoke the following date with tears,

But he said what mattered most of all was the dash between those years

For that dash represents all the time, that she spent alive on earth.

And now only those who loved her Know what that little line is worth.

For it matters not how much we own; the cars, the house, the cash...

So, when your eulogy is being read with your life's actions to rehash

would you be proud of the things they say about how you spent your dash?

Treasure

We drove the winding highway with windows open, wind blowing warm air through our hair savoring a spectacular summer's day. The inviting country scenery opened up all around us with rolling hills, farmlands and mountains in the distance. At our back lay the ever-bustling, always crowded, hyper-congested and often, claustrophobic mega-city of Guadalajara, Mexico. It felt freeing to leave behind the seven million others who share that tight space, and breathe deeply of open space, greenery, fresh air and a true sense of liberation.

At the wheel, was my brother-in-law, compadre, and dear friend, Guy, a bloody English chap who makes me laugh at myself and the world with his hilarious and witty British banter. We hit it off from day one long ago marrying into the same Mexican family and each year we bugger off for an adventure or two to process life and marriage, explore and laugh until we can't breathe anymore.

As we headed westward, the looming figure of the Volcan de Tequila dominated the horizon, and as far as the eye could see were beautiful rolling fields of the blue-green agave plant. After growing for seven years, the underground pineapples are harvested and processed to become the world-famous Tequila.

After a delicious lunch of rotisserie chicken from a local street-side vendor, we headed further west with a very soft agenda. On most of our little adventures, I have done my homework and research for locating various famous sources of obsidian, the volcanic glass that had spewed forth from the Tequila volcano hundreds of thousands of years ago. The ancient Aztecs and their predecessors were masters at harvesting these lithic resources for knives, spear points, arrowheads, and surgical blades. This year I hadn't logged any new research from the internet or scientific journals to find new sources. So, we were just off to see if we could find La Joya, a place rumored to hold the rare arco iris or rainbow-colored obsidian.

I hadn't brought a map and thought I knew from memory where to go. Soon we realized my memory had failed and we were not on target. After stopping to ask several locals we got back on track but ran into a construction project in a small town that completely blocked our progress with no marked detours we'd have to backtrack. It was no real set back with our soft agenda, as we were mostly just enjoying the day, the drive, the fantastic scenery, good banter, and laughter. Rainbow obsidian would have to wait.

Nearing another small town, we pulled over to inquire of a couple of young guys seated along a dirt road about where we could find any colored obsidian. A twenty-something type character seated on his motorbike, smoking a cigarette, quipped back in Spanish that he could show us some blue stuff. "Fill my gas tank and I'll show you the way!" We nodded enthusiastically and shouted; "Vamanos!" Off we went, trying to keep up with him as he raced down dusty back roads on his whiny motorized steed.

When we stopped to fill his gas tank in a tiny unknown village, I asked his name. "Rey" or "King" was his response. Perfect I thought to myself, for this cocky, young, bronzed, muscle-shirted dude. Off we went on narrower and narrower back roads and farm lanes until we came to a large iron gate, where Rey had dismounted to open and hold the gate.

Rey leaned into our window and stated that he had to get to work, but all we had to do was follow this trail up the mountain and we could find what we were looking for. Guy and I looked at each other and laughed out loud! We might have just been totally scammed and that is one happy Rey, leaving with a full tank of gas! But with nothing to lose and time on our hands we headed up the winding dirt mountain road smiling all the way. Was the "King" telling us the truth? Would we find treasure? Or had we just fallen for a classic; sleight of hand, shell game, or "Scam the Gringos?"

We spend the better part of the afternoon wandering via truck and foot over a beautiful mountainside. Stoic oak trees with giant wide leaves covered the hillside that left easy open walking under their canopies. With a warm dry Mexican sun beating down, freedom to roam and wonder, and possible treasures to discover… it was a good day to be alive.

Sure enough, our brief friendship with Rey, had taken us in a new direction, and true to his word we began stumbling into a wide variety of various colored obsidian; grey, and dull green, and even a silver luster. And to my absolute delight, we found some gorgeous aqua green with beautiful blue streaks running through the rock!

We left that mountain late in the day, with the sun falling softly over our backside. We were sweaty tired and deeply fulfilled. We had immersed ourselves in new terrain and topography and encountered several kind and friendly locals who guided us along the way. Guy and I had chatted deeply about life, kids, work and marriage as men rarely get a chance to do. We had laughed deeply at ourselves and the crazy world around us. And as an added bonus we had a couple of small buckets of absolutely gorgeous rocks to bring home and create works of art and function. All because our road, our route, our intention, our destination, our goal had been blocked.

So often when our goal, or life path or intention gets blocked, we view it as God stopping our progress. We crinkle our forehead, a frown covers our face, we shake our fist at God and shout at least from the inside; "Hey God! I know what I want/ need! Why are you shutting this door in front of me!!?? I know what I'm doing!" This is a totally normal and human response to a roadblock.

But to the person who walks by faith, who leans on and is guided by the Holy Spirit, a roadblock, or detour, or closed door can simply be a beautiful invitation to something completely new and unexpected; a beautiful Godly surprise and positive spiritual blessing. Looking back, I thank God for the wonderful roadblock that stopped us from reaching our intended destination of La Joya. There were so many beautiful blessings, surprises and discovers waiting for us in the detour.

Oftentimes God blesses and encourages our goals, dreams, and intentions. But sometimes, He asks us to trust him in the detour, the roadblock, the delay or the closed door. Maybe instead of fighting Him, you can relax, soften your agenda and trust him on the wonderful and exciting journey the Holy Spirit will guide you upon on the road less traveled.

Thus says the LORD: Stand at the crossroads, and look, and ask for the ancient paths, where the good way lies; and walk in it, and find rest for your souls. Jeremiah 6:16 NIV

I will lead the blind by ways they have not known, Along unfamiliar paths I will guide them; I will turn the darkness into light before them and make the rough places smooth. Isaiah 42:16 NIV

Prayer of St. Francis DeSales

Do not look forward to the trials and crosses of this life with dread and fear. Rather look to them with full confidence that, as they arise, God to whom you belong, will deliver you from them. He has guided and guarded you thus far in life.

Do you but hold fast to his dear hand, and he will lead you safely through all trials. Whenever you cannot stand, he will carry you lovingly in his arms. Do not look forward to what may happen tomorrow.
The same eternal Father who cares for you today will take good care of you tomorrow and every day of your life. Either he will shield you from suffering or he will give you the unfailing strength to bear it. Be at peace, then, and put aside all useless thoughts, vain deeds, and anxious imaginations.

Trust in the LORD with all your heart, and do not rely on your own insight. In all your ways acknowledge him, and he will make straight your paths. Do not be wise in your own eyes; fear the LORD, and turn away from evil It will be a healing for your flesh and a refreshment for your body. Proverbs 3:5-8 NIV

Treasures from Trials

Sixty miles deep into a ten-day backpacking trip, my eldest daughter Karina and I were struggling through the toughest and most demanding part of our trip. We had been bushwhacking and brush busting our way down a steep valley for the better part of our day six in the heart of the Wind River Mountains of western Wyoming. Adding to our frustration and exhaustion of thick forest cross-country travel, was the fact that we had entered an area that had been burned sometime in the past 4-6 years. The burn and following wind storms, winters and snowfall had wreaked havoc on the forest leaving blowdowns as far as we could see. Covered in soot, and weary from crawling over and under the endless maze of trees and brush we stopped to catch our breath and get out bearings. The rush of the nearby stream brought white noise to my already dulled senses.

For a brief moment I glanced down and left, and through my thickened and slowed brain I perceived an object that grabbed my attention. "Yes" sure enough... it was an elk antler and upon further observation, I was thrilled to discover its matching mate was also present and attached to the original skull! I was ecstatic with my new discovery and I shouted at Karina as I smiled from ear to ear! How cool! A beautiful 6 x 6 perfectly symmetrical elk-rack! What a rare and gorgeous find! Karina came running and was also quite impressed by my find, but certainly not nearly as enthusiastic as me.

I soon realized I couldn't take such a large treasure with me especially given the current tangled terrain, the difficulty of our situation, and long distance we must still travel. But this great treasure-find had brightened our spirits in the midst of a trying day.

I immediately dug out my multi-tool and extended the pliers. I flipped over the skull and proceeded to extract the two ivories from the upper pallet that are so prized by hunters and our Native American predecessors. Most non-hunters are unaware that elk have actual ivories. It is thought that ivories are possibly a left-over remnant of prehistoric elk that had tusks.

Karina appeared a bit grossed out by this process and thought me a bit crazy and the task unnecessary. I simply nodded and said that "These were treasures and how ironic that we've found them on the most difficult and challenging day of our trip." I mumbled something along the lines of "I'll make something out of them." Anyway, our day had been brightened by this wonderful surprise gift in the midst of our hardship and ordeal.

A few days before Christmas I meandered down to our local Jewelers and asked my friend Steve what he could create with these two elk ivories. He showed great excitement and scratched out a simple design with a pencil and scratch paper. I was thrilled with his concept. A week later I received a message from Steve saying my project was finished and I grew giddy with anticipation to see his final creation.

As he lifted the lid on the box, a huge smile grew over my entire being! The earrings were absolutely gorgeous! They would be a perfect tribute to the memorable journey we had shared in the mountains of Wyoming. A fitting token to honor what we had shared together as father and daughter in the wilderness. This unique gift is on its way to once again surprise and hopefully delight Karina and remind her of both our struggle and triumphs in the mountains.

These earrings would also serve to remind us that out of difficulty, struggle, anxiety, pain and confusion God can surprise us with wonderful and unexpected gifts and treasures if only we have eyes to see and a sense of wonder to appreciate that God is present in both the ups and the downs of our life's journey.

Paying Attention II

Imagine the chances of us finding this little treasure in the midst of the vast, rugged and isolated wilderness of the Wind River Mountains? One in a million… or more most likely? I think this discovery of the antlers and the ivories were nothing more than a specific, packaged surprise gift to a specific pair of weary and worn life's travelers. And I know the Giver… personally.

It is most often easy to see and experience God in the highs, on the mountain tops when beauty is all around, and you can see with your eyes all that surrounds you and you know where you are and where you are going. When success and triumph are yours for the taking. It is another thing altogether, to understand that God is real, is present and is watching over you in the midst of being lost, lonely, afraid, anxious, worried, exhausted and confused.

Jesus states quite simply and bluntly: *"I have told you these things, so that in me you may have peace. In this world you will have trouble. But take heart! I have overcome the world." John 16:33 NIV*

He also promises; *"... surely I am with you always, to the very end of the age."* Matthew 28:18-20 NIV

So if you are weary and worn, struggling and lost in the forest of endless struggles, or straining to overcome the mountain of debt, grief, and pain, or heavily burdened by a failed or broken relationship, know that God is present, God is at your side, God is working on your behalf and that God is working on your character to build stronger muscles of trust. And if you are open to the leading and guiding and mentoring of the Holy Spirit, you will even find beautiful and wonder-filled treasures, right at your feet… Even in the midst of your confusion, lostness, and suffering. Keep your eyes open!

> *but we also glory in our sufferings, because we know that suffering produces perseverance; perseverance, character; and character, hope. And hope does not put us to shame, because God's love has been poured out into our hearts through the Holy Spirit, who has been given to us. Romans 5:3-5 NIV*

And we know that in all things God works for the good of those who love him, who have been called according to his purpose. Romans 8:28 NIV

> *"When you pass through the waters, I will be with you; And through the rivers, they will not overflow you. When you walk through the fire, you will not be scorched, Nor will the flame burn you. "Do not fear, for I am with you Isaiah 43: 2 & 5 NIV*

Trumpeter Swans

We snaked our way across the frozen marsh weaving between tan cattails and wispy rushes that waved in rhythm to the wind. Weathered gray tamarack trunks stood stoically as guardians over the swamp. We wandered past several large earthen domes whose north sides still held a cap of snow while the southern exposed faces were dark with sticks and mud. The beavers hidden beneath must be counting the days until the warmth of spring would bring their first open water swim.

As we crossed over the marsh, we gained a small island in the middle that fairly begged to be summited. It promised a 360-degree panorama and held a single naked birch tree and a feisty red oak that had still retained the great bulk of its rust-colored leaves. One can only image, why some of these hearty trees retain their clothing, while the majority of others prefer to strip down for the winter.

As we crested the small hummock my eyes instantly caught the out-of-place darkened periscopes. Three hundred yards away to the west in the center of the frozen ice, stood a pair of trumpeter swans. Their white bodies virtually invisible against the matching background of snow, yet their upside down, "L" shaped necks gave them away. I was shocked to see them here in the middle of winter. Had they arrived early from a mild winter somewhere down south? Were they in a great hurry to get to the great north of Canada to visit relatives? Had global warming thrown off their migration schedule? They seemed as curious about us as we for them, and they stood their ground fully aware of the nine large predators that had gained the small rise on their staked-out marsh. The long distance between us must have been a comfortable buffer as each group stood their ground.

Our eclectic group of nine was our mid-winter men's retreat group out for one of several snowshoe exploration hikes. Men ages 26 to sixty-something had said "yes" to the call and were now enjoying the pleasure of the many benefits to this experience; fresh clean air, full body exercise, adventure, exploration, camaraderie, laughter, scenic vistas, and self-growth. Smiles of enjoyment and discovery were the expression du jour.

We stood upon the crest of the small knoll admiring the swans to our west when suddenly the unmistakable sound of trumpets sounded from the eastern edge of the swamp. And there passing over the tree line, where the blue of sky meets the dark green of pine and spruce, flew another pair of trumpeter swans. We turned out necks as the graceful pair flew side by side in an elegant arc that to our surprise and delight brought them directly overhead at low altitude. Their massive wing spans seemed to beat in sync and it was as if the flight was perfectly timed and choreographed for a Super-Bowl Star Spangled Banner grand finale.

The flying duo was announcing their presence to both us and more importantly the standing pair. The latter duet was vigorously proclaiming quite loudly to all guessing on our part; "This is our pond!" The flying couple gently arched and feigned a landing near them, then thought otherwise, gaining altitude and flew off to the west. How could we have been so lucky to have witnessed this 30-seconds of interaction in this exact space and time?

Back in the rustic yet cozy shack, the magic continued. Each evening the crackle and spit of the fire were all that could be heard as we gathered in an arc around the wood stove. No radios, no televisions, no cell phones, no thumb talking, no screens of any kind, just man to man real conversation and honesty about life and faith. Several men commented that we rarely get to converse on this level with other men. Certainly not on Sundays at church, rarely at our work sites and most men are not good at creating this level of intimacy and conversation in normal friendship groups. But in the sacred space of the shack, the Holy Spirit had descended and seeped into every corner of the small living room. The Holy Spirit acted like a can opener, allowing men to risk vulnerability, express a failure, grieve a loss, celebrate a triumph, and share genuine confusion and not knowing. One could honestly and openly declare, "I don't have all the answers, and I certainly don't have it all together." And all were met with acceptance and support.

That is one of many reasons why we "retreat." Listen to Mr. Webster: *retreat; a period away from normal activities, devoted to prayer and meditation, often spent in a religious community, a quiet secluded place where people go for rest and privacy, a period of quiet rest and contemplation in a secluded place.*

I would wager to guess that each man who dared to take the risk of saying "yes" to this retreat, went home with a plethora of benefits; fresh insights, newly found friendships, peace, restoration, rejuvenation of spirit, positive memories, and a deepened sense of trust and faith in God. May you also recognize your need for retreat and have the courage to say *"yes"* to the Holy Spirit's nudging and calling you into deeper intimacy and trust with your Maker.

After feeding the 5000, Jesus said to them, "Come with me by yourselves to a quiet place and get some rest." So they went away by themselves in a boat to a solitary place. Mark 6:30-32 NIV

At once the Spirit sent him out into the wilderness, and he was in the wilderness forty days Mark 1:12 NIV

Very early in the morning, while it was still dark, Jesus got up, left the house and went off to a solitary place, where he prayed. Mark 1:35 NIV

Violin

My fingers wrapped clumsily around the neck. The bow I held ineptly in my right hand. The body, I placed upon my shoulder and tucked beneath my chin. The awkwardness I felt was palpable, yet I felt no shame, for all others in the room were struggling as much as I. And then upon command, I placed bow upon string and eeked out a few squeaky notes. My mental picture flashed fingernails upon chalkboards.

This was my first attempt on my son Shane's violin for parent's night at Horizon Middle School, a chance for parents to learn about and try out our kid's orchestra instrument. Mr. Cole provided passion, humor, and excellent teaching to all of us novices for our half-hour lesson. I smiled throughout the whole lesson just to experience something new and invigorating. I could barely get my bow and violin to cooperate in producing the most rudimentary and crude of sounds, let alone music. How crazy; this beautifully shaped wooden instrument of which I've grown so fond of over the years was now just a hollow, lifeless object in my hands.

This past Sunday, I shared the sanctuary stage with the First Lutheran Orchestra. Our little skeleton worship band was crammed into a tiny corner by the expansive strings. During the choir anthem, I stood hovering directly over the two lead violinists Jane and Alex. I became entranced by the mastery that each of these virtuoso's held over their instruments. I became lost in the beautiful dance that flowed as their parts each played off one another, sometimes in harmony, sometimes one floating above the other. Other times their notes pirouetting around one another in a teasing, flirtatious manner that only pulled me deeper into their melodious composition. It was as if the violin had become a part of each of them; eyes, ears, arms, fingers, elbows, bow, and violin all flowing together from a genius center. I was witnessing pure virtuosity in its finest, purest form.

I have pondered since that day, how a violin in one person's hands like mine, can barely make a legible sound, and a very displeasing one at that! Yet in the hand of a virtuoso like Jane or Alex, the music made, seems to reverberate directly from heaven. And, I contemplate the long and arduous journey that must have taken place for each of these maestros in the process of achieving such mastery of their instruments. Had they been given Godly gifts or aptitudes planted in them at birth, or were their achievements simply the result of years of hard-won practice, dedication, and perseverance? Or is it both? I wonder what Shane's journey will look like ten years from now if he continues to travel down the road of life alongside his violin.

In my own life, I seem to have become a jack of many trades, certainly master of none. As my wife Ady, put it one contemplative and humorous day, "Honey... you are the most talented guy I know.... at worthless things!" I can chip a crude knife or arrowhead from a piece of flint, I can sew my own jacket, I can climb rocks, paddle a canoe, find my way through the mountains, fashion a bow from a chunk of wood, sing a song with my seven-note range and lead worship on my guitar with the six chords I know. On all such skills or talents, I am a yeoman at best, and I fall miles short of the monikers; master, maestro or virtuoso.

Praise God for those who have achieved maestro and virtuoso status! I honor and respect them and like this past Sunday, I take pure delight in listening and watching and experiencing their finely-honed craft.

Praise God for the yeoman, the pluggers, the novices, the beginners and the rank and file of all talents, trades and crafts. For I think it matters not so much what level of ability you achieve, but rather to whom you realize your talent, gift or abilities come from. Have you figured out a way to bless the world through the gifts, talents, and abilities that God gave you? And do you give thanks and gratitude to the great giver of these gifts?

The world is filled with egotistical, self-centered maestros and masters in all fields; from football stars to farmers, from preachers to porn stars, musicians to mommies, presidents to postal carriers, CEO's to childcare workers, attorneys to auto assemblers. May you and I be ones that recognize and acknowledge the true giver of all gifts. And then use these gifts to bless the work around us with passion and purpose.

And whatever you do, whether in word or deed, do it all in the name of the Lord Jesus, giving thanks to God the Father through him. Colossians 3:17 NIV

Whatever you do, work at it with all your heart, as working for the Lord, not for human masters. Colossians 3:23 NIV

There are different kinds of gifts, but the same Spirit distributes them. There are different kinds of service, but the same Lord. 1Corinthians 12:4-5 NIV

Waiting to Die

We entered the almost new retired living complex. It felt more like a five-star hotel than a retirement home. Having just opened a few months before, everything was new; new carpets, fresh paint, elegant stonework and even a lovely wall fountain that trickled a welcome to each person entering. We were greeted by a warm and smiling receptionist as we inquired where we might find Herb. The receptionist didn't miss a beat giving us the room number and hand signaling directions as to how we might find him through the maze of corridors and lounges.

My friend John had agreed to come and visit Herb with me. Herb had apparently taken several turns downhill in recent months both physically and mentally. We were here to check in on him, converse and also bring him communion. We continued our journey onward to the memory care unit.

We followed the labyrinth of hallways and street names and finally arrived at a large opening of a warm and welcoming lounge. We inquired of one of the workers where we might find Herb. Her big smile and friendliness put us at ease as she led us left to a cozy fireside area and pointed to Herb.

What lay before us caused my heart to skip a few beats. My upbeat mood dropped ten notches. There before us was a large semi-circle of 10-12 elderly people. The bulk of them sat stooped over staring at their laps. The remainder stared blankly ahead into empty space. All were neatly dressed and tidy, we could tell they were well cared for by the many friendly and smiling attendants that shuffled all about. As I scanned the circle only depressing thoughts raced through my mind. It was more than obvious… these folks had already checked out. They were here gathered in the circle… ***waiting to die.***

Gathering my wits, I pushed down all the negative thoughts and did my best to smile as I knelt on one knee to greet Herb. As I introduced myself and John, Herb lifted his head and seemed to be grateful for the interruption. Remnants of his former keen wit, humor, and vitality showed through off and on clicking in and out like a poor McDonalds drive through connection. I could tell he was thankful for our visit but pretty sure he had no clue who we were. After some brief conversation engaging him on his favorite love of sports, we gave him communion and prayed for him as we held his hand. A glimmer and spark of recognition showed in his face knowing what was happening was good and holy.

As we left the building my brain couldn't let go of the sadness we had witnessed and how so many of our loved ones these days are going through similar situations. It almost seems epidemic. Maybe it's just that we live longer, or maybe we're all eating chemically laced foods… who knows. It just points to the fact that life is unfair, life is hard, life is extremely difficult and we never know how our lives will end. I tire of seeing good, intelligent, hardworking, successful people who were once vibrant, witty, movers and shakers and Godfearing folk, deteriorate and decline into oblivion.

I've thought about that visit many times in recent weeks. That circle of 12… waiting to die. Then I think of so many people I encounter both at church and in ordinary life who struggle on the opposite end… ***they are waiting to live.*** People who are waiting for something, some situation, some change of circumstance, some event, someone, some resolution, something over the horizon to really engage, to be content, to take risks or to experience joy and embrace life. The sad truth is that those somethings or someones rarely come to pass.

"I'll be happy/content/at peace when… I have more money, when I'm out of school, when I have kids, when my kids are gone, when I get a better boss, when I finally get a job, when I get a better job, when

I'm out of debt, when I have a girlfriend, when I get married, when I get a different house, when I buy a newer car, when I get a different husband, when I'm not depressed or anxious, when I lose some weight, when I figure out who I am, when my back quits hurting, when my son quits using drugs, when we find a better church... and the list goes on and on.

One of the painful hard truths of this world is that life is difficult. And just because we are lovers and followers of Jesus does not make us immune from the tragedies and struggles of life. Illnesses, cancers, debt, health concerns, natural disasters, poor economies, job loss, broken relationships, accidents, children who go astray, friends that betray us, divorce, wars, ISIS, school shootings and the list goes on and on. We live in a turbulent, problematic and arduous world.

All of this, and especially my recent visit with Herb, remind me that we must choose life and lean forward with faith, trust, gratitude, risk, and perseverance. In the exceptional movie Shawshank Redemption, Andy Dufresne, played by Tim Robbins, speaks eloquently to his friend, *"Red"*, played by Morgan Freeman. *"You better get busy living or get busy dying."* For so many of us, we are stuck in a bland purgatory between neither really living, and just waiting to die.

For many Christians, their whole belief system revolves around making sure that they are "saved" that they've "made it" onto the last train to heaven. That they're guaranteed a ticket on the escalator bound for the pearly gates. But Jesus says in John 10:10, *"I have come that you might have life, and have it abundantly!"* He is saying that he is for us, He is here with us, he has given us life abundantly in the here and now! It's not just about our future. It's about living abundantly now!

What are you waiting for? Jesus promises us His strength, His wisdom, His resources, His guidance, His forgiveness, His joy, His abundance, His hope for the here and now, and for our future!

May you lean into and chose to live the life you have been given to the fullest. Hold God's hand as you move through both the triumphs and trials of this life. Give thanks and trust God in all you do. Chose life!

Rejoice always, pray continually, give thanks in all circumstances; for this is God's will for you in Christ Jesus. 1Thes 5:16-18 NIV

Come to me all you who are weary and burdened, and I will give you rest. Take my yoke upon you and learn from me, for I am gentle and humble in heart, and you will find rest for your souls. For my yoke is easy and my burden is light. Matthew 11: 28-30 NIV

*We rejoice in our sufferings,
we know that suffering produces perseverance;
perseverance character; and character hope.
Romans 5:3-4 NIV*

When the Bottom Drops Out

The sunshine was brilliant and blinding. The white wilderness was expansive and awaiting, ready to swallow us whole into the jaws of endless pines and snow. We piled out of the warm vehicles and nervously packed our sleds with duffle bags loaded with gear, clothing, food, and equipment. The frigid below zero temps outside the vehicles began immediately sucking heat from our beings. Fingers and faces were the first to feel the effects of these extreme temps.

With snowshoes donned and ski poles at the ready we were off and cruising down the trail of what I assumed was the correct beginning to the Blandin Dog sled trail northwest of Ely, Mn. After ten minutes of huffing and puffing, the warmth of body exertion began to restore a right feeling in my body. With the core temperatures restored, warmth and feeling soon returned to my fingers. Looking back on our pack train of human sled-dogs, beards were frosting over and steam breathed from each man's mouth making us look like a snaking dragon.

Our group of eight men was in high spirits, now that we were finally moving and on-trail. Half our crew were winter camping veterans and half were anxious rookies ready to test their mettle. Our destination of Ramshead Lake in the Boundary Waters Canoe Area Wilderness should lay 3-4 miles down the trail. Our pace was brisk due to both the cold and pre-trip jitters. Personally, I was excited to be trying out a new entry point, and anticipating new terrain. All and all, it was a good day to be alive.

Rollie Johnson

Our trail snaked its way through pine and spruce past several private cabins. I had been advised that this was the case and so we continued on our way. After an hour of hiking, all were warm and sweating on the inside from the strong exercise, but I grew uneasy as the reality of our route was not matching up with that of my map or my preconceived expectations of anticipated landmarks and crossings. Several times I left the group alone to scout ahead and verify we were on the correct trail. Nothing matched up. My sense of irritation and frustration grew with each step and I feared the group's confidence in my leadership may be falling along with the temperatures.

After coming to an expansive beaver pond and marsh area, we spread out sending small teams in each direction hoping to find the sled dog trail that would lead us into the Boundary Waters proper. All groups returned with a "Nope." Fortunately, our group of eight men maintained high spirits, positive attitudes and a strong sense of humor, taking all set-backs, wrong turns and retracing of our route in stride.

It became obvious to me that I had messed up and got us started on the wrong trail somehow. It was now time to adapt and overcome and make due to the best of our abilities given my mega-mistake. We were obviously not in the actual Boundary Waters Wilderness Area, but we were certainly in a gorgeous and scenic location that provided all we would need. Flat heavily snow-covered lake space for snow caves, good water, and a thickly spruce/pine covered protected area for our campfire and kitchen. An instantaneous group conclave was convened and a unanimous vote for making this our new home was approved 8-0.

We quickly set about the hard work of setting up our new village. Three fellas set about the task of carving out a firepit and kitchen on shore in a tightly packed spruce grove. We would need the protection of the pines from the wind. They would also find a few large logs for sitting.

I proceeded to stomp out two side by side 10-12' circles on the edge of the pond where the drifted snow was deepest. All remaining hands began shoveling copious quantities of snow into the center of each ring.

In time, with lots of great banter, generous amounts of laughter and ribbing, and glorious brilliant sunshine all around us, the two mounds grew and grew. When they reached the seven-foot-high mark, I called a halt to the piling. The ginormous snow mounds would now sit for a few hours in preparation for the excavations.

All hands now went about the never-ending task of gathering enormous amounts of firewood. The huge stacks would need to last us through the evening hours and still have enough for a good, long breakfast. I grabbed Jon and the ax and we headed 100 yards out on the pond to create our water hole. We chopped and chopped creating a three-foot wide circle that extended down through the deep ice. After 20 inches of good solid ice, a final whack and good clean and clear water began bubbling up to fill our water basin.

As the sun set over the saw-toothed horizon of pines, we gathered around a large and roaring fire to warm both bodies and spirits. We gently tossed our tin-foil dinners into the blazing orange coals and soon the sizzling sounds and smells of hamburger, onions, potatoes, green peppers, and carrots filled the air. Having expended enormous amounts of calories in work all day, we tore into our steaming hot dinners like a pack of ravenous wolves bringing warmth, and sustenance to our tired bodies. Good food bringing fuel for both warmth and work. Ahh... how satisfying to be alive and healthy in the great north woods.

A couple of hours later in the deeper dark of night, like 8 dwarves singing "Hi Ho, Hi Ho it's off to work we go," we donned our headlamps and headed to the snow caves to begin mining. Working in three-man teams we began the cautious task of carving out the snow caves. "Slow, steady and gentle fellas!" was my mantra.

After an hour of carving and removing snow, we had two spacious domed sleeping chambers and connecting tunnel all lit by the soft, gentle, yellow glow of candles embedded in the walls. I whispered a quiet prayer of gratitude knowing that now our crew would be safe and warm in the well below zero temps.

By now a gorgeous full moon had risen over the horizon to light up the entire pond and surrounding woods casting long shadows everywhere. The moon created an eerie and mystical luminosity that was amplified by a light haze that hung over the landscape most likely due to the severe cold. How cold was it? Hard to tell.

After warming and drying by the fireside, and some good conversation and prayer time we headed off for some much-deserved sleep. Seven men slowly filed into the snow cave condo and I headed to my awaiting cozy hammock in the trees. Sleep came fast and easy. At least at first.

Nights are long while winter camping. With an early sunset and early bedtime, the nights go on forever. Somewhere deep in the night answering nature's call, I awoke to exit and found my steaming breath had frozen both zippers to my two sleeping bags, as well as the two zippers on the hammock. A brief moment of claustrophobic panic ensued before finally freeing all four zippers.

With such a long night, most of us rose before true sunrise to scramble up and gain the warmth of the restarted campfire which was slow to give off its life-giving heat. It was as if the fire was preserving its own warmth, and reluctant to share it with us. It had been a rough night for all, and most had struggled to get good sleep. Tired faces and gallows humor prevailed as smiles and laughter were shared across the fire pit. "Gee Rollie, that was fun! Sure glad I signed up for this!"

As the fire gained its strength and roared to life defying the cold, we partook of a hearty breakfast of sausage, egg and cheese McMuffins accompanied by copious amounts of steaming hot coffee. Life and vitality crept back into our beings from the inside out. The brilliant sunshine rose over the pines and a beautiful blue sky, crisp day lay before us to enjoy. Spirits were high now, knowing the day would bring a warming trend.

Around noonish, my daughter Karina and her husband Taylor came skiing onto our pond and shouts of a joyous reunion could be heard. Hugs, handshakes went around the horn and we invited them up to our fireside café for coffee and tea. Taylor began to reiterate their days beginning; "Well, we got up late at the cabin. Then we looked at our phones to see the weather. We had planned to come and ski in to visit you, but when we saw the actual temps, we said; 'Why bother, they're all dead now anyway!" The group roared with laughter!

We had anticipated twenty below temps based on watching the forecasts all week. No problem whatsoever. We've had worse many times before. But Taylor showed us the screenshot and our raw temp was somewhere between -38 and -42 below zero! No wonder we hadn't slept well! All the men in the circle laughed, shrugged it off, and stood a little taller knowing we had made it through some pretty severe cold. The bottom had definitely dropped out.

The bottom had definitely dropped out. Our well-made plans, agenda, and destinations had completed dropped out due to some fairly large mistakes and wrong decisions on my part. It's difficult to arrive at the proper endpoint when you begin your journey from the wrong starting point. I had committed some rather significant errors in judgment. The temperatures of which we had no control of, bottomed out off-the-charts proving that man and his sophisticated technologies of weather predicting proved futile and ridiculous in light of nature's fickle inclinations.

But God in his mercies had taken my human shortcomings and the random movements of the natural world and woven the good, the bad and the ugly into something meaningful, significant and positive for our group. God had taken a wrong path, a misdirection, a mis-take, and difficult natural conditions to bring about growth, learning, and meaning for eight men in the frozen north. He had used cold, and humility, and difficulty to build character and faith and comradery through adversity. God has a wonderful habit of taking our blunders, missteps, and errors and weaving those into our lives for good, for learning, for growth and deepened faith. He most often uses adversity to bring about character development for those who know and trust him.

God had proven himself once again to be most faithful and trustworthy. When the bottom dropped out on our winter camping adventure… God was there and used the difficulties for our good. God can and will do the same thing in our everyday lives when we follow and trust him. If you've made a big mistake, committed a moral blunder, taken a wrong turn, or if the world has just thrown you a curveball or the bottom has dropped out on an area of your life, bring it to God.

Surrender it to Jesus. He can make something beautiful come of all situations. Trust him.

...but we also rejoice in our sufferings, because we know that suffering produces perseverance; perseverance, character, and character hope. Romans 5: 3-4 NIV

Consider it pure joy, my bothers, whenever you face trials of many kinds, because you know that the testing of your faith develops perseverance. Perseverance must finish its work so that you may be mature and complete, not lacking anything. James 1:1-2 NIV

And we know that in ALL things God works for the good of those who love him, who have been called according to his purpose! Romans 8:28 NIV

... God has said, "Never will I leave you; never will I forsake you." The Lord is my helper; I will not be afraid.
What can man do to me? Hebrews 13:5-6 ESV

When Was the Last Time... You Did Something for the First Time?

When was the last time you were a rookie, a beginner, a neophyte or learner and felt the awkward sense of not really knowing what you were doing?

When was the last time you took on the role of student, learner or seeker, rather than the role of expert, master, or teacher in your given field, area of expertise?

When was the last time you felt out of your comfort zone, pushed yourself out of the box of your normal routine, or stepped outside your everyday routine?

When was the last time you experienced stumbling, failure, and mistakes because you were actually learning something new?

When was the last time you actually stepped through the threshold and signed up for a new church offering; a study group, a mission trip, a retreat, a marriage seminar, a service project, an adventure to experience growth, faith-learning or immerse yourself in a new format or environment of serving God by serving someone else?

Kevin is a fifty-something dad. He's a middle school teacher and coach. He recently joined our *"In Search of Faith and Footholds"* rock-climbing and bible study class for confirmation with his 9th-grade son. Kevin had never tried rock climbing before. He showed up with an open mind and enthusiastic attitude and was eager to learn and test himself.

As he approached the wall for the first time, I could see in his demeanor the same anxiety, worry, and fear and doubt that each of the other much younger students carried. The same questions though not spoken out loud, were being broadcast by his body and mannerisms; "Can I actually do this?" "Will I look like a fool?" "What if I fail?" "What if I freak out in front of everyone?" "What if I can't do it?" "What if I embarrass myself?" "What if I'm not any good at climbing?"

To Kevin's credit, he persevered and acted in-spite-of his fears, doubts and worries. He brought his "A" game of attitude and effort and did superbly throughout our four weeks of class. He was a huge asset and inspiration to others to give the whole experience 100 %.

Most of us, especially men, are poor at trying something new. We like to be in control, in charge, and look like we know what we're doing. To trip, to fall, to be vulnerable, to fail, to make mistakes, to look awkward, to look like you don't have it all together, to not have mastery of the technique, to not be the best, or look the fool are not what we enjoy!

Yet if we are to be continually learning and growing as human beings, we had better be stepping out into the new; new habits, new thought processes, new ideas, new ways of experiencing life, new ways of growing in our faith in Jesus. It has long been a personal mantra of mine, that if your only source of spiritual nourishment is Sunday morning… you will most likely be a starving, shriveled, and malnourished soul.

Listen to these wise and insightful words from Leonard Sweet from his book <u>Aqua Church</u>.

"Boarding" was one of Martin Luther's favorite definitions of faith. The person who doesn't have faith, he said, "is like someone who has to cross the sea, but is so frightened that he does not trust the ship. And so he stays where he is, and is never saved because he will not get on board and cross over." The test of faith is "getting on board." <u>***Our pews are occupied by people who want to be moved, but who don't want to move.***</u> *It is not just a few people who are bedridden all of their lives- we are becoming a church of, for and by the bedridden and beached. This unholy predicament that the church finds itself in today-fear-ridden, safety-fixated, immunity-seeking,*

risk-averse in a high-risk post-modern culture- can be reversed only if the church abandons it risk-free approach to ministry and mission and rediscovers the gangplank. The good news is that our cultural phobia is both treatable and preventable. The danger for the church today lies with armor and brakes. The benefits lie with risk and speed.

So, get out there! Take a risk! Try something new! Know that it's "ok" to not be great at something! Learn a new skill, try a new hobby, sign up for a new class at church, step through the threshold from; "I've always wanted to do a mission trip," to actually going on one! Your time is limited! Someday… your "somedays" will actually end.

"No one puts new wine into old wineskins: otherwise, the wine will burst the skins, and the wine is lost, and so are the skins: but one puts new wine into fresh wineskins" Markk. 2:22 NIV

Anyone who stops learning is old, whether at twenty or eighty. Anyone who keeps learning stays young. The greatest thing in life is to keep your mind young. *Henry Ford*

*Therefore, if anyone is in Christ, they are a new
Creation; the old has gone, the new has come!
2 Corinthians 5:17 NIV*

Therefore, we do not lose heart. Though outwardly we are wasting away, yet inwardly we are being renewed day by day. 2 Corinthians 4:16 NIV

What, then, shall we say in response to these things? If God is for us, who can be against us? Romans 8:31 NIV

*Jesus looked at them and said, "With man this is impossible, but with God all things are possible."
Matthew 19:26 NIV*

Woman Running

The clean fresh air of the early summer's day felt good moving in and out of my lungs as I pounded-out a steady beat with my feet for the days run. Something, a plant, a tree or a crop had flavored the air with a distinctly sweet aroma that caused me to breathe more deeply through my nose. I smiled, savoring both the fragrance and the warm gentle sunshine as I continued on my run.

As I descended from the bridge down the winding bike path I could see before me a fellow runner working her way down the same pathway. I was moving more quickly than she, so I soon overtook her and almost laughed out loud as I passed her. In her one hand was a dog leash and at the other end of the leash was a hyperactive large dog that was doing its best to explore every bush, scent, and detour possible. It tugged and dragged and pulled her in multiple directions and rarely in the direction of her intended run.

In her other hand, she held a smartphone that was blasting out a song on speaker phone, and as I passed by, she was attempting to manipulate her phone to look up something on the internet or scan her Facebook or check her messages all while still running. It was purely comical to watch the three-ring circus of this woman's life for the 15-20 seconds I spent running by her.

I thought to myself… Wow, this the perfect picture of most of our lives! Multi-tasking four or five different things, with noise blaring, while moving at a rapid pace to some destination that we're not quite sure of and all the while being tugged by a beast that pulls us in random directions!

Now I'm the last guy on the planet that should ever critique someone else for being hyperactive and in constant motion! But I know from experience that the reason so many of us run and race through a plethora of endless activities is we don't want to slow down long enough to stare at the emptiness of our own souls. In addition, some of us try to drown out the noise of our own thoughts, feelings, problems, issues, anger, disappointments, hurts, and broken dreams by donning ear-buds or headphones to keep us from having to face and listen to a neglected soul that longs to be heard.

Robert Wicks in his book, <u>Touching the Holy</u> writes; "One of the reasons for this is that quiet, honest prayer is often unnerving. So, unconsciously knowing this leads many of us to develop a schedule in which we become too active to slow down and too full to make room for God. In an effort to run from our sense of emptiness and utter dependence on God, our minds become filled with anxieties and worries, our hearts heavy with actual or imagined losses in our lives, and our spirits weighed down with anger, hurts, and a sense that no one really understands… So when we enter prayer the first commitment must be to just stay put, not run away, and be disciplined and regular in our attention to our time with God."

Jesus knew well the busy, chaotic and frenetic life of busyness. After feeding 5,000 plus people, healing, teaching and preaching where every person wanted a piece of him, he wisely offers a beautiful invitation to his exhausted and spent disciples. *"Come with me by yourselves to a quiet place and get some rest."* Mark 6:31 NIV. He again invites you and me to do the same; *"Come to me, all you who are weary and burdened, and I will give you rest. Take my yoke upon you and learn from me, for I am gentle and humble in heart, and you will find rest for your souls"* Matthew 11:28-29 NIV

Activities, motion, and purpose-filled movement are all good. But they need to be in balance with the quiet, peace and rest that only God can provide.

May you today, take Jesus up on his invitation to *"Come and be with me."* And may you find rest for your weary souls!

If the devil can't make you bad…
He'll just encourage you to stay too busy.

Trust Me enough to spend ample time with Me, pushing back the demands of the day. Refuse to feel guilty about something that is so pleasing to Me, the King of the universe. Because I am omnipotent, I am able to bend time and event s in your favor. You will find that you can accomplish more in less time after you have given yourself to Me in rich communion. Also, as you align yourself with My perspective, you can sort out what is important and what is not. Don't fall into the trap of being constantly on the go. Many, many things people do in My name have **no** value in My Kingdom. To avoid doing meaningless works, stay in continual communication with Me. I will instruct you and teach you in the way you should go, I will counsel you with My eye upon you. Luke 10:41-42, Psalm 32:8 Sarah Young, Jesus Calling

Who Let The Dogs Out?

Winter.
Have you had enough?

Streets grow narrower. The snow- banks grow higher and higher. Drifted snow creates difficult driving. Stop signs and intersections are ice rinks making it impossible to stop, and then take forever to accelerate through as tires spin and spin. Our driveways have shrunk, and the high embankments make it impossible to see who is coming around the corner. Snow blowers are logging overtime or breaking down, and shovels have a direct linkage to our back pain. Schools close every other day giving our already bored kids another 15-hour day to do nothing but play video games, snap chat on their phones, and sink deeper into cabin fever, causing us to take another day off from work to watch them.

Each evening we watch the nightly local news, expectant, hoping above all hopes to hear our temperatures will rise above the zero mark. But they don't. The weatherman simply hits the repeat button on his auto-forecaster, and we hear again for the umpteenth time… *"Well folks, we've got another significant snow event coming this week!"* Followed by; *"Our temperature will plummet again with twenty-below zero temps and life-threatening wind chills."* Wow…. Deja Vue! And we're still in February!

I have a theory. It's called the Rollie Johnson Theory of Relativity. My theory goes like this; as the snow levels increase and snow banks rise, so too does the public's crabbiness, discontent, grumpiness, apathy, sleepiness, lethargy, melancholy, and general sense of malaise. Conversely, as temperatures dive for extended periods of time, so too does the energy level, politeness, kindness, patience, and sense of common courtesy in those around us. We witness it in the supermarket, in the parking lot and on the ever-narrowing streets. Teachers feel it in the schools. We certainly see it in our church and I'll bet most of us know it all too well in our homes. The ever-deepening snows and seemingly endless cold spells have many of us feeling trapped, irritable, overwhelmed, and cranky.

Paying Attention II

Well, if you've read this far, you're probably looking for some great insight or nifty little mental trick to help you feel better or adjust your attitude. So sorry to disappoint!

I don't have any! In fact, I'll admit I'm one who loves winter. I love the beauty of deep snow all across the landscapes. I especially love blizzards. They shut down schools, highways, malls and even God forbid; churches! They crush manmade egos and tell us who is in charge and who is not! They humble us. They slow us down. They make us pause. They put us back in our place. (I know, go ahead… send me hate-mail.)

Most of all, I have appreciated this: **The Season of the Dogs.** Sun Dogs that is, and we have had plenty of them! When the temperatures drop and invisible ice crystals fill the air, they magically appear almost always at or near the horizon at sunrise and sunset. Two, often rainbowed, orbs appear equidistant as independent yet perfect imitations of the one true sun. If you were visiting for the first time from another planet, you might assume that earth has three suns!

The reason I love sun dogs beyond their obvious physical beauty is that they always point me to God; the Trinity. We hear about this Trinity all the time but rarely do we flesh it out. We hear it in creeds, in liturgies and worship songs all the time, but rarely does anyone really connect the dots of the three, the Trinity; the Father, the Son, and the Holy Spirit. Yet creation does this so beautifully as demonstrated in the mysterious sun dog. Three separate yet equal and indivisible oneness! God, Jesus, and the Holy Spirit.

And the greatest take away from this is that the Holy Spirit actually dwells inside of each of us. We carry God inside of us! He, the great counselor is just a heartbeat away! We have access to **His** enormous strength and power. We can tap into **His** tremendous and unlimited resources of wisdom, creativity, and insight. And we can draw from **His** constant and steady source of peace. These are available to each of us 24/7/365. We are not limited by our own feeble strength or waning energy reserves. Our sense of peace or contentment is not limited nor dictated by circumstance good or bad.

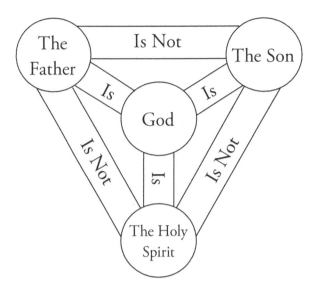

All of these benefits are your birthright, yet only available to those who take the time to be still in the presence of our Creator and Maker; God. If you want more peace, if you want more strength, if you want more joy, if you want more peace, if you want more contentment, then multiply the time you spend alone with God.

I'd love to promise you that winter will end soon. It will most likely not, and I have no magical powers to change that. But with what winter remains, the next time you encounter the holy and sacred sun dog, let it remind you of who you are, and that your worth and power come not from external circumstances but from Who dwells within you.

For this reason, I remind you to fan into flame the gift of God, which is in you, through the laying on of my hands. For God did not give us a Spirit of timidity/fear/anxiety, but a Spirit of power, love, and self-discipline.
2 Timothy 1:6-7 NIV

But you will receive power when the Holy Spirit comes on you; Acts 1:8 NIV

In the same way, the Spirit helps us in our weakness. We do not know what we ought to pray for, but the Spirit himself intercedes for us with groans that words cannot express. Romans 8:26 NIV

Do you not know that your bodies are a temple of the Holy Spirit, who is in you, whom you have received from God? You are not your own; you were bought at a price. Therefore honor God with your body. 1 Corinthians 6:19-20 NIV

As you make yourself more and more available for God's purposes, you will be asked to accomplish more and more. But, at every step, the true purpose of eternity is accomplished by His Spirit, not yours. All you offer is the vessel. You must be filled up for service. When you're ready to enlarge your territory, the Spirit of God will increase the power flow within you. You'll know you're working in the realm of a power greater than yourself. And though you'll be changed by that kind of experience, you'll need to stay connected to the source of power to keep getting results. Bruce Wilkerson, The Prayer of Jabez

Sometimes as Christians you and I find ourselves wanting to watch our circumstances, don't we? We focus our eyes on the storm. We get worried about the clouds and the rain and darkness. And when that happens, what we have to do is home in on the ministry of the Holy Spirit and let Him be our guide. Sometimes you have to put the blinders on." Lord help me not to look at the circumstances. Help me to hear and listen to what You are saying to me?" And then walk by the Spirit of God, and He will direct our paths. The Holy Spirit is like a lighthouse keeper who just loves to send that powerful beam out across the fog and the darkness. And when the Holy Spirit comes to live within you, He opens the Word of God so you can begin to understand it. He directs His light on its pages. He whispers meanings and insights into your mind. Sometimes those insights come as a quiet word of assurance in the night-like the soft glow of a nightlight. Other times they come like thunderbolts, suddenly lighting up the sky. <u>God in You</u>, David Jeremiah

Worship

The warm breeze tickled the leaves of palms and plant leaves causing them to dance and swing to and fro under the blazing Mayan sun. I slowly walked my way down the street soaking in the sweet scents of flowers and ever-present savory smoke from several homes where villagers prepared their evening meals over wood fires. It felt good to be alive and so peaceful walking through such beautiful terrain in this small village of Mexil, miles from nowhere, deep in the Yucatan Peninsula of Mexico.

I spied my destination just a block away, a bright purple, small block building. I'd heard the deep pounding of the bass since starting my walk. The sign outside said it was a Pentecostal church and I was heading to their 6 pm worship service.

I quietly stood in the entryway to take it all in, but with such a small room, I was the immediate elephant in the room. This pale-skinned, grey-haired gringo stood out like the preverbal sore thumb. Bright warm smiles from the children we'd played with all week greeted me with big open eyes as I silently took a seat in the last row. Throughout the service they would look back and smile, helping me to know that I was welcomed here.

Two large fans hung from the ceiling wobbling and spinning loosely hung by wire, beneath the tin roof. Thirty-some souls had crammed in this small space to worship as the electric piano, guitar, bass, and drums pumped out tune after tune over a very vibrant wall of speakers. We

Paying Attention II

alternately stood and sat with each new song. There were no worship hymnals, nor projector, nor screen. People just seemed to know the songs and they sang for all they were worth. I knew not the tunes nor the words, but I soon realized I did have something to contribute... I could clap. And clap I did with gusto and enthusiasm. And I gave it my all. After all, worship is what you bring to God, not what you take away from the sermon or how much you liked the songs. Upon my departure, my hands were sore from clapping so hard. It had felt good to come from worship and know that I'd given my all.

Later in the week, our crew of eleven was invited to an evening worship with our hosts for the week, a Presbyterian church. Ironically, it sat directly across the tiny street from the Pentecostals. Our gang filed in and took up most of the wooden benches filling the small church to the brim. The regular members, maybe eight to ten of them, were now all familiar friends from our worksite and afternoon VBS. It felt good to come and sit with them in worship.

This time there were no musical instruments, no guitars, or drums or piano. No P.A. system nor microphones. The worship elder simply stood up front and began each song as others joined in. No hymnals, no songbooks, no nothing. There were no words to read and more importantly no notes to read. And yet their voices were strong and mighty. They sang and worshiped with their whole body, mind, and soul. No one gave the pathetic excuse; *"Well I can't sing... there are no notes for me to read!"* Most of us did our best to hum along to our best ability as the tune became more familiar. We were simply called to worship with our Mayan brothers and sisters. We didn't have to know the words nor the tune. We were simply called to worship!

The gentle and humble pastor gave a beautiful short message in his best broken and rough English, and the message came through loud and clear for those who were willing to listen, to those who would allow God to speak through this man. There was no choosing who to listen to or tuning out due to prejudice or preference. God spoke through who HE chose... not us the worshipers.

These two contrasting worship services have stuck in my head all week as I mull over what it means to worship. We in most of our modern churches are spoiled, rotten brats. We want our favorite tunes, in our preferred worship style and only care to tune in to our preferred or favorite preacher. We balk and complain when things don't go our way. Some refuse to participate if there are no notes, some refuse to sing if it's a song they don't like or know. Some refuse to participate when the song or worship order is out of a blue book or a purple hymnal or placed on a screen. Some won't participate in worship unless it's connected to their cell phone and there is a laser light show and a slick rockstar on lead guitar. The list of excuses goes on ad-nauseum. Believe me, I've heard and seen them all.

So, it makes me wonder, if Jesus himself, showed up in the flesh at **our** worship service… what would he have to say? Would he be pleased? Would he prefer the Pentecostals or Presbyterians tiny, simple worship in Mexil? Or would He be more pleased with the great productions of modern contemporary worship centers or the traditional liturgical settings of hymnals and organs?

Maybe that can't be answered in broad sweeping generalized terms. Maybe it can. But I think the more important question is this; If Jesus sat next to **you** this week at worship… what would He have to say about how **you** worship?

Let the word of Christ dwell in you richly, teaching and admonishing one another in all wisdom, singing psalms and hymns and spiritual songs, with thankfulness in your hearts to God. Colossians 3:16

"Teacher, which is the greatest commandment in the Law?" Jesus replied: "'Love the Lord your God with all your heart and with all your soul and with all your mind.' This is the first and greatest commandment. And the second is like it: 'Love your neighbor as yourself.' All the Law and the Prophets hang on these two commandments." Matthew 22: 34-37

Praise the LORD *Praise God in his sanctuary; praise him in his mighty heavens.*
Praise him for his acts of power; praise him for his surpassing greatness.

Praise him with the sounding of the trumpet, praise him with the harp and lyre,
praise him with timbrel and dancing, praise him with the strings and pipe,
praise him with the clash of cymbals,
praise him with resounding cymbals. Let everything that has breath praise the L ORD *. Psalm 150 NIV*

The entire law is summed up in a single command: "love your neighbor as yourself." If you keep on biting and devouring each other, watch out! or you will be destroyed by each other. Galatians 5:13-15 NLV

The Lord says: "These people come near to me with their mouth and honor me with their lips, but their hearts are far from me. Their worship of me is based on merely human rules they have been taught. Isaiah 29:13 NIV

The cause of Christian unity at the present time, and indeed all through history, has been injured and hindered, because men loved their own ecclesiastical organizations, their own creeds, their own ritual, more than they loved each other. If we really loved each other and really loved Christ, no Church would exclude any man who was Christ's disciple. Only love implanted in men's hearts by God can tear down the barriers which they have erected between each other and between their churches. William Barclay-<u>The Gospel of John</u>

Zach

He shuffles his way towards the front of the church each Sunday Morning before and after the service to greet me. His excitement grows as the pace of his rocking back and forth from right leg to left leg accelerates. He wears a big infectious smile, yet rarely do his eyes meet with mine as he stares off to the side, and only occasionally does he chance direct eye contact with me. Within recent years, we have moved from a high-five to an awkward yet heartfelt hug. I smile with a genuine appreciation for the gift and the friendship, and then ask a couple of questions: "Did you play softball this weekend?" "Do you start basketball soon?" "Did you go to school this week?"

The inquiries are met with a quickened rocking back and forth, an even bigger smile, and sometimes a squeaky mumbled response. His gaze darts from left to right and I often place my hand on his shoulder, or gently rub his back. In his presence, I sense a genuine love and affection from him and certainly for him. There is no pretext, no posturing, no hidden agenda, no trying to impress nor manipulate nor maneuver. When he comes to me each week, I get a sense of the most basic kind of acceptance and love. It is what I believe must be, a window into pure Christ-like love. Though the difficulties he experienced during the birth process robbed him of a great many abilities and functions, he was given the incredible gifts of Godly joy, enthusiasm, and unconditional love in great abundance. Let me introduce; my friend Zach.

Paying Attention II

Most folks walk past Zach in day to day life. He might very well be invisible to most that walk past him in school, church, or the mall. He does not draw attention to himself, nor seek to be the center of anyone else's world. And yet, what most folks have missed is that Zach and others like him, may very well be a divine portal into an understanding of God and how he loves and accepts each of us.

Our world loves the self-promotor: the movers and the shakers, the go-getters and the climbers, the achievers and the champions. We love the young, the slender, the sexy and the beautiful. We admire the ones who have made fortunes and empires. We worship the ones who can throw a baseball or football or dunk a basketball. We stand in awe of those who can solve great puzzles of science or discover the mysteries of the universe. Yet, most all of us, run past or ignore the hidden windows of God's divine reflection in people placed in our midst, like Zach.

God is all around us. May you have eyes to perceive Him and experience His presence in a hidden vessel like my friend Zach!

And he said: "Truly I tell you, unless you change and become like little children, you will never enter the kingdom of heaven. Matthew 18:3 NIV

At that time Jesus, full of joy through the Holy Spirit, said, "I praise you, Father, Lord of heaven and earth because you have hidden these things from the wise and learned and revealed them to little children.
Luke 10:21 NIV

About the Author

Rollie Johnson is a unique voice calling from the wilderness to seek God in the quiet and stillness of nature and creation. Rollie has used creative outdoor adventures ministries over the past 38 years as metaphors for growing in life and faith. He is currently a Lay Pastor and Worship Leader at First Lutheran Church in Fargo, ND. Rollie is an avid outdoorsman, hard-core adventurer, craftsman, gifted speaker and has a keen eye for observing God's presence in the ordinary and everyday that will help you to grow in your faith journey. Rollie's unique writing style will entice and engage you in observing God in hidden places.